THE WORLD'S MOST BEAUTIFUL CG CHARACTERS

EXOTIQUE

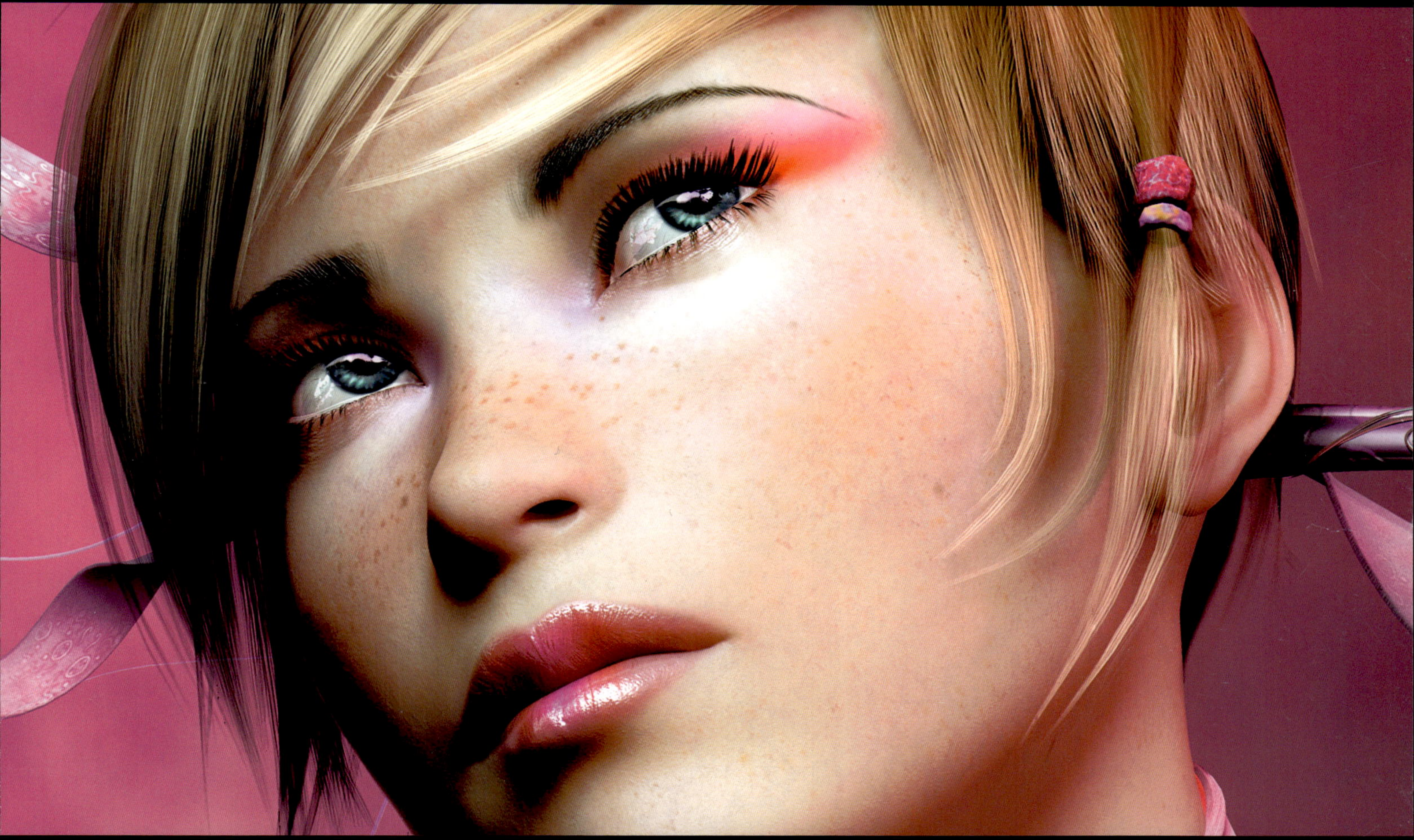

Edited by

Daniel Wade & Paul Hellard

Publishers

Mark Snoswell & Leonard Teo

EXOTIQUE

Published
by
Ballistic Publishing
Publishers of digital works for the digital world
Aldgate Valley Rd
Mylor SA 5153
Australia

www.BallisticPublishing.com

Correspondence:
info@BallisticPublishing.com

First Edition published in Australia 2005 by Ballistic Publishing

Softcover Edition ISBN 1-921002-26-3
Special Edition ISBN 1-921002-27-1

Managing Editor
Daniel Wade

Assistant Editor
Paul Hellard

Art Director
Mark Snoswell

Design & Image Processing
Lauren Stevens, Stuart Colafella

Printing and binding
Everbest Printing (China)
www.everbest.com

Partners
The CG Society (Computer Graphics Society)
www.CGSociety.org

Also available from Ballistic Publishing
EXPOSÉ 1 Softcover/Hardcover ISBN 0-97050965-2-4/0-9750965-1-6
EXPOSÉ 2 Softcover/Hardcover ISBN 0-9750965-9-1/0-9750965-8-3
EXPOSÉ 3 Softcover/Hardcover ISBN 1-921002-14-X/1-921002-13-1

Visit www.BallisticPublishing.com
for our complete range of titles.

Cover image credits

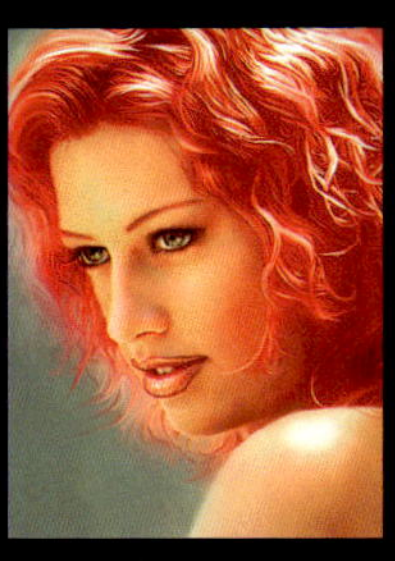

I was made to love you
Photoshop
Raffaele Marinetti, ITALY
[Front cover: EXOTIQUE Softcover edition]

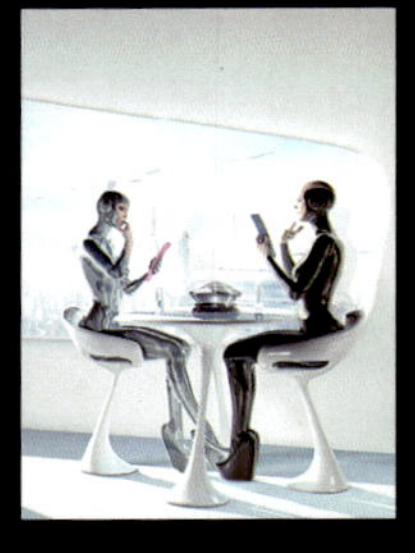

Lunch
CINEMA 4D, Poser, Photoshop
Benedict Campbell, GREAT BRITA
[Back cover: EXOTIQUE Softcover edition]

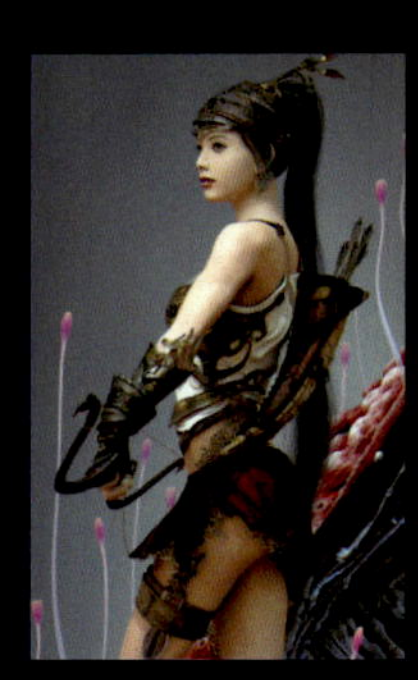

Divine Protection
3ds Max, Photoshop

CONTENTS

FEATURED ARTISTS

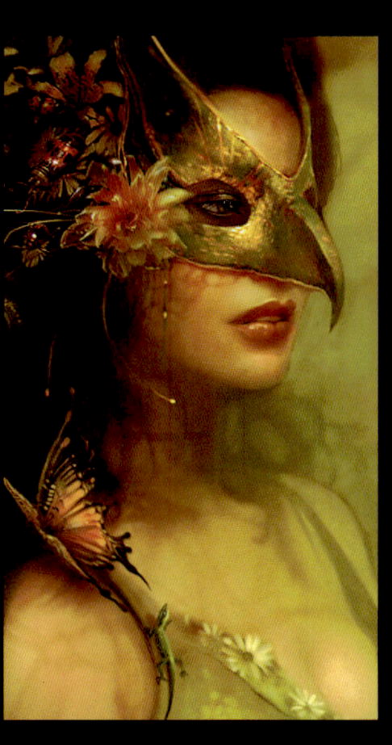
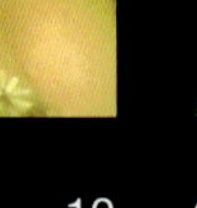
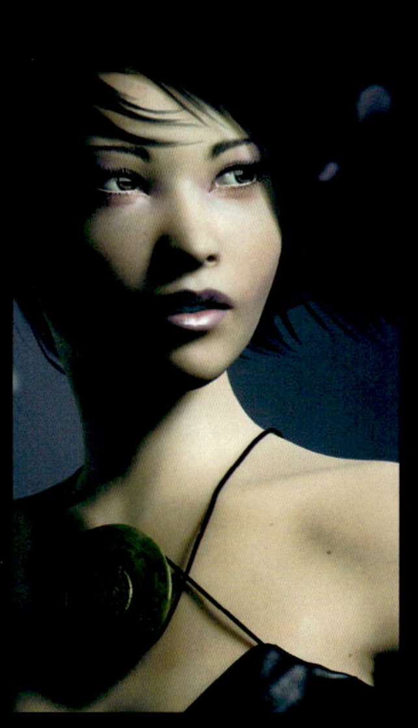
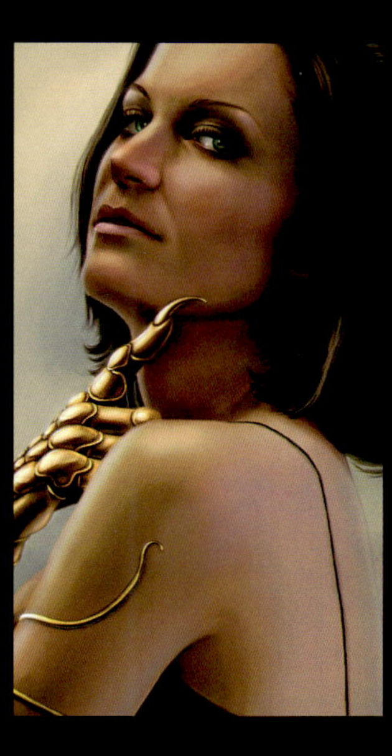
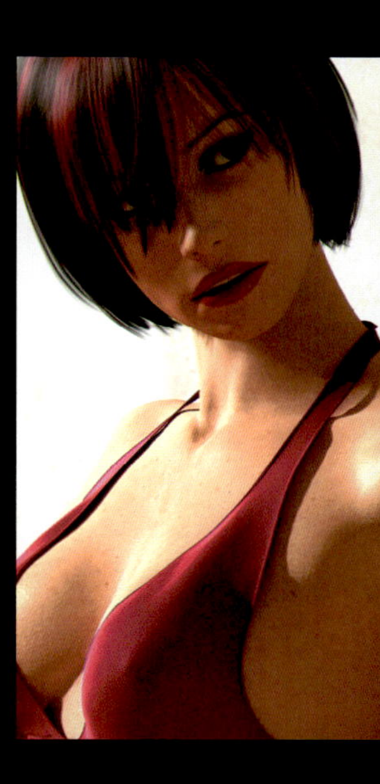

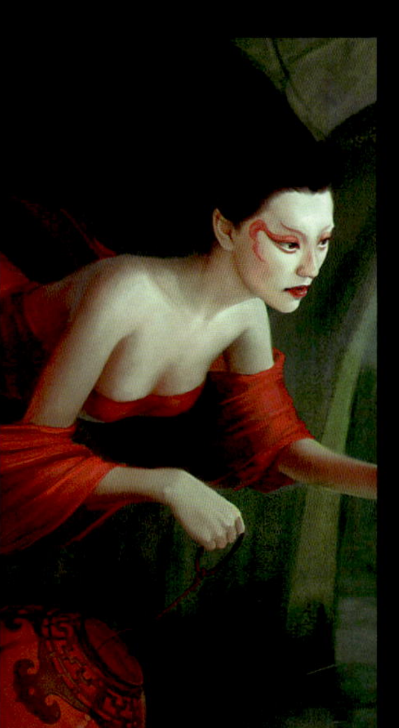
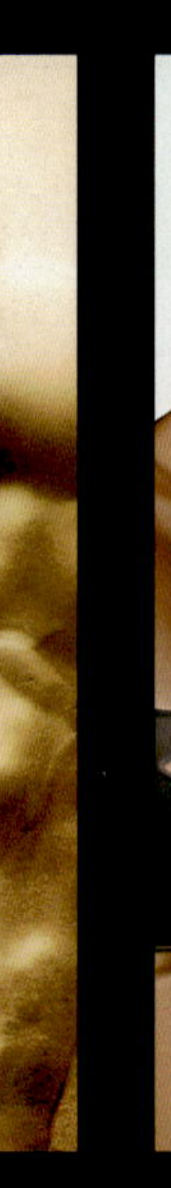
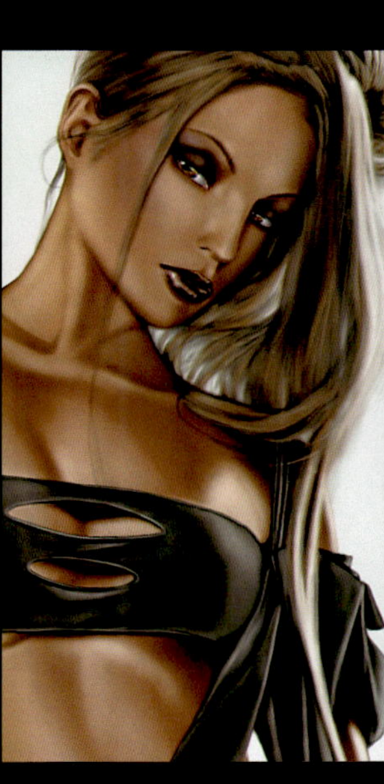

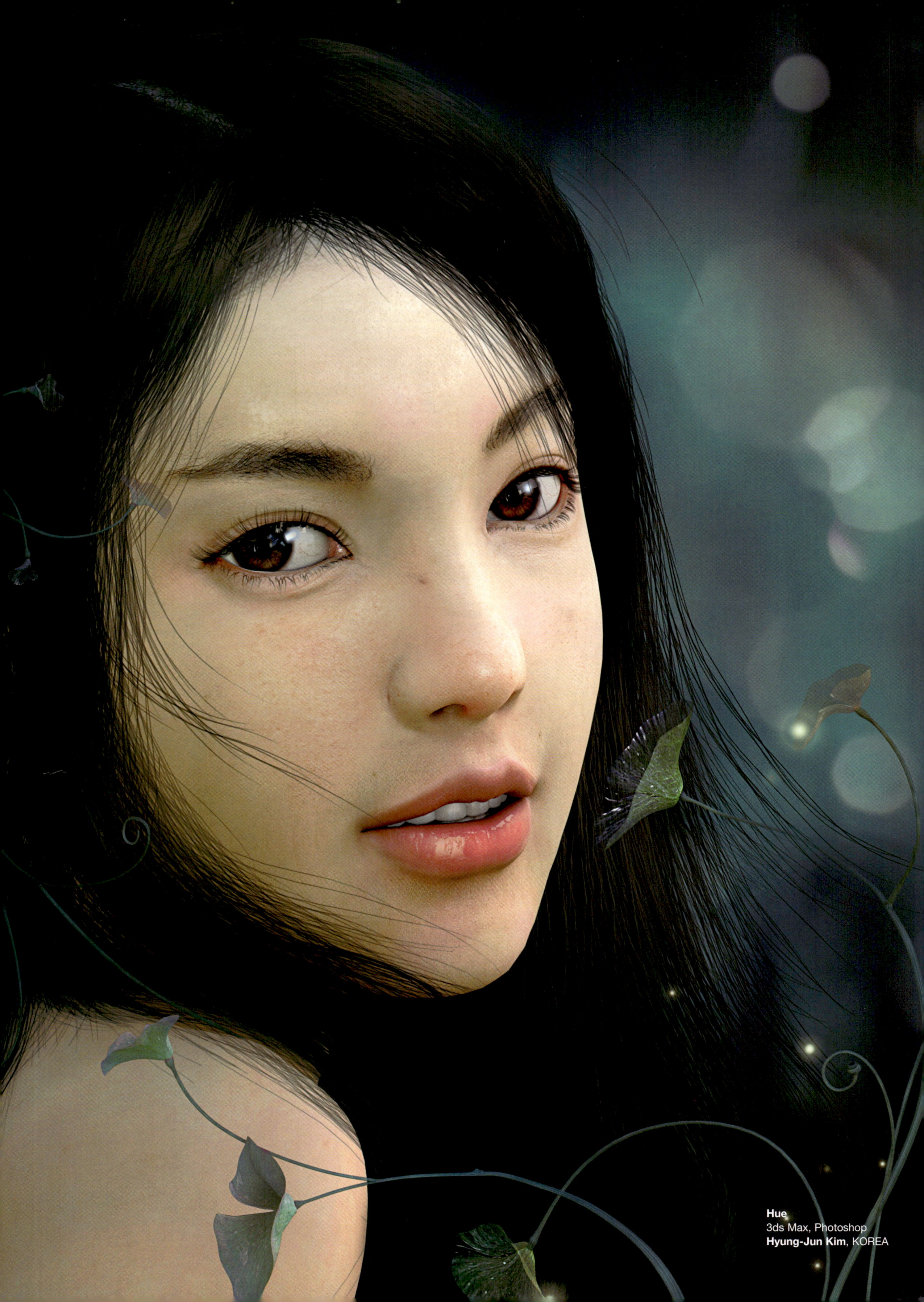

Hue
3ds Max, Photoshop
Hyung-Jun Kim, KOREA

In addition to being technophiles, digital artists are dreamers. They spend a lot of time dreaming up exotic characters—predominantly female characters. At least that's what we can deduce from the huge quantity of characters that get submitted for just about any call for entries we run. EXOTIQUE pays homage to the imagination and seemingly limitless creative talents of digital artists and the dream characters they bring to life. Just a few years ago this caliber of book would not have been possible—well at least not with the breadth and quality of work you see reproduced here. It's probably been six years or more since the 2D painting software has been good enough for any traditional artist to express themselves without hindrance. However, it's only been in the past four years or so that the 3D software has reached a point where it has been possible to reproduce the human form at any level of realism, and artistic interpretation ... and it's only in the past year or two that widely available 3D rendering tools have been capable of truly realistic skin rendering. As of this year (2005) nearly all 3D renderers have support for global illumination (bounced light illumination), diffuse specular lighting and sub surface scattering. All of these are required to realistically reproduce the subtlety of light interacting with skin. Finally, the technical limits have been removed, and artists are free to express themselves in both 2D and 3D realms without limitation.

All this technology is great, but it still requires a fertile imagination and keen artistic eye to conceive and execute an outstanding work of art. Owning sophisticated 3D software does not make it easy for anyone to create stunning and emotive images. The artist needs to design, model, compose, texture, light and render their work. Everything must be executed well and work in harmony to achieve the best result possible. Now, more than ever before, the digital artist must be aware of all the elements that combine to make an appealing and inspiring image. Natural talent and a good eye need to be augmented by a deep understanding of the subject, medium, light interactions and techniques.

By our interpretation art is all about telling a visual story and evoking an emotional response in the viewer. All great stories need characters. EXOTIQUE brings together the world's most beautiful CG characters in one book in genres from science fiction, fantasy, and anime, to photorealism and stylized realism. We hope that in years to come EXOTIQUE will document the development of the art and the world's best examples of digital character art.

The Call for Entries for EXOTIQUE invited artists to submit all types of characters. A total of 1,300 entries were submitted across all of the genres providing a truly wide cross-section of styles and subject matter to choose from. In addition to the gallery of artists, we were lucky to have eight high profile artists provide additional information on how they created specific characters. Featured artists include: Linda Bergkvist, Liam Kemp, Pascal Blanché, Jason Chan, Fred Bastide, Olivier Ponsonnet, Jean-Yves Lelcercq and Henning Ludvigsen.

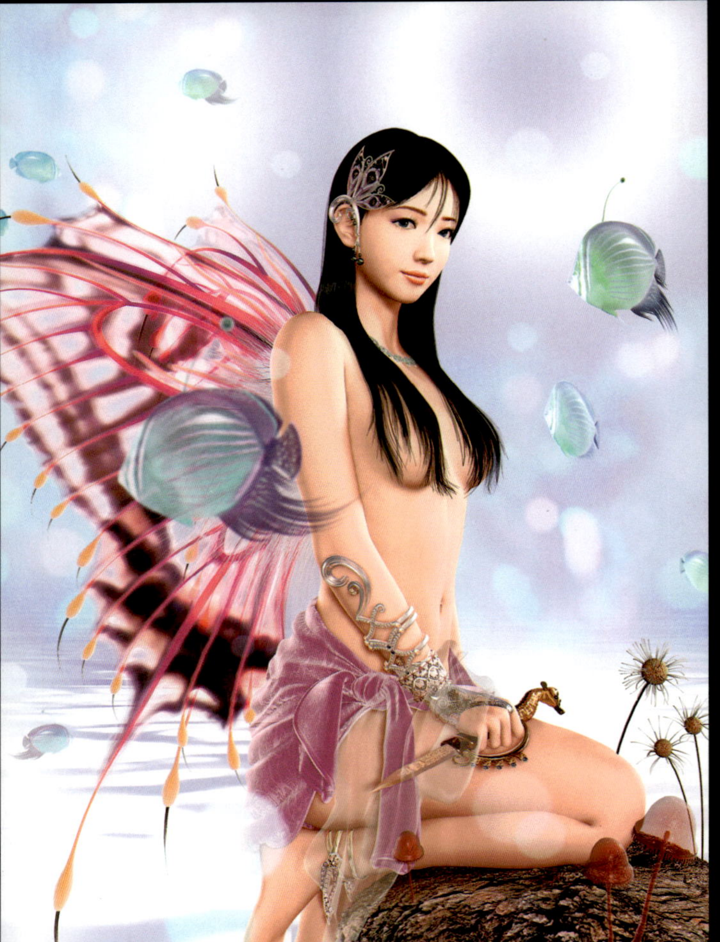

Butterfly
3ds Max, Photoshop
Hyung-Jun Kim, KOREA
[left]

Pink Sugar
3ds Max
Olivier Ponsonnet, FRANCE
[right]

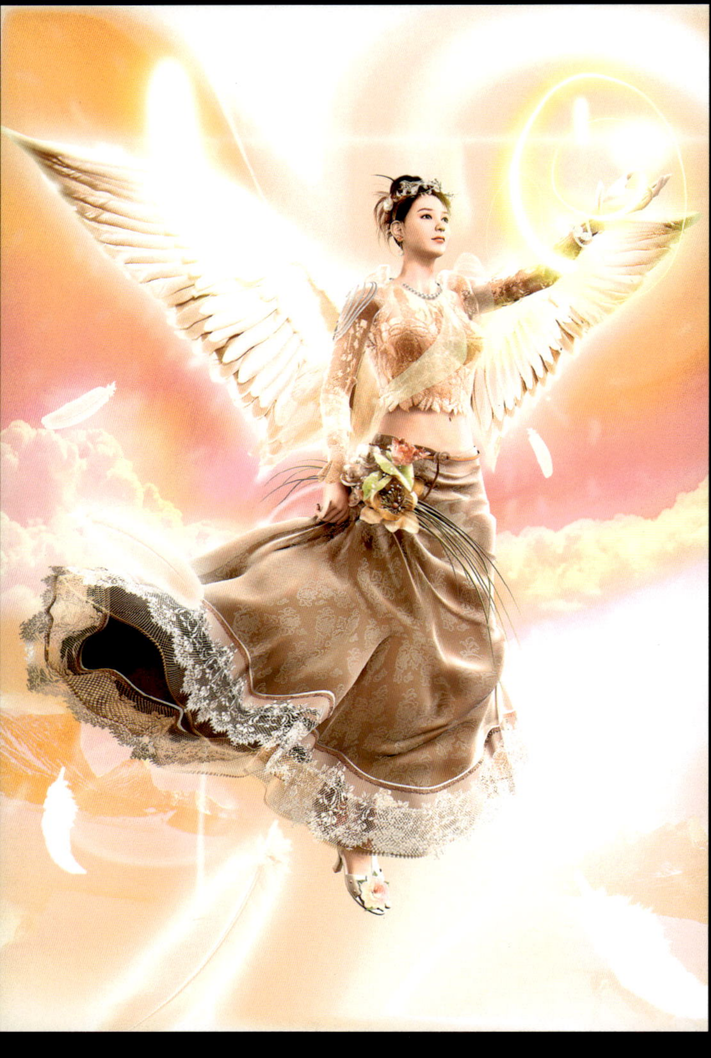

Fly
3ds Max, Photoshop
Hyung-Jun Kim, KOREA
[left]

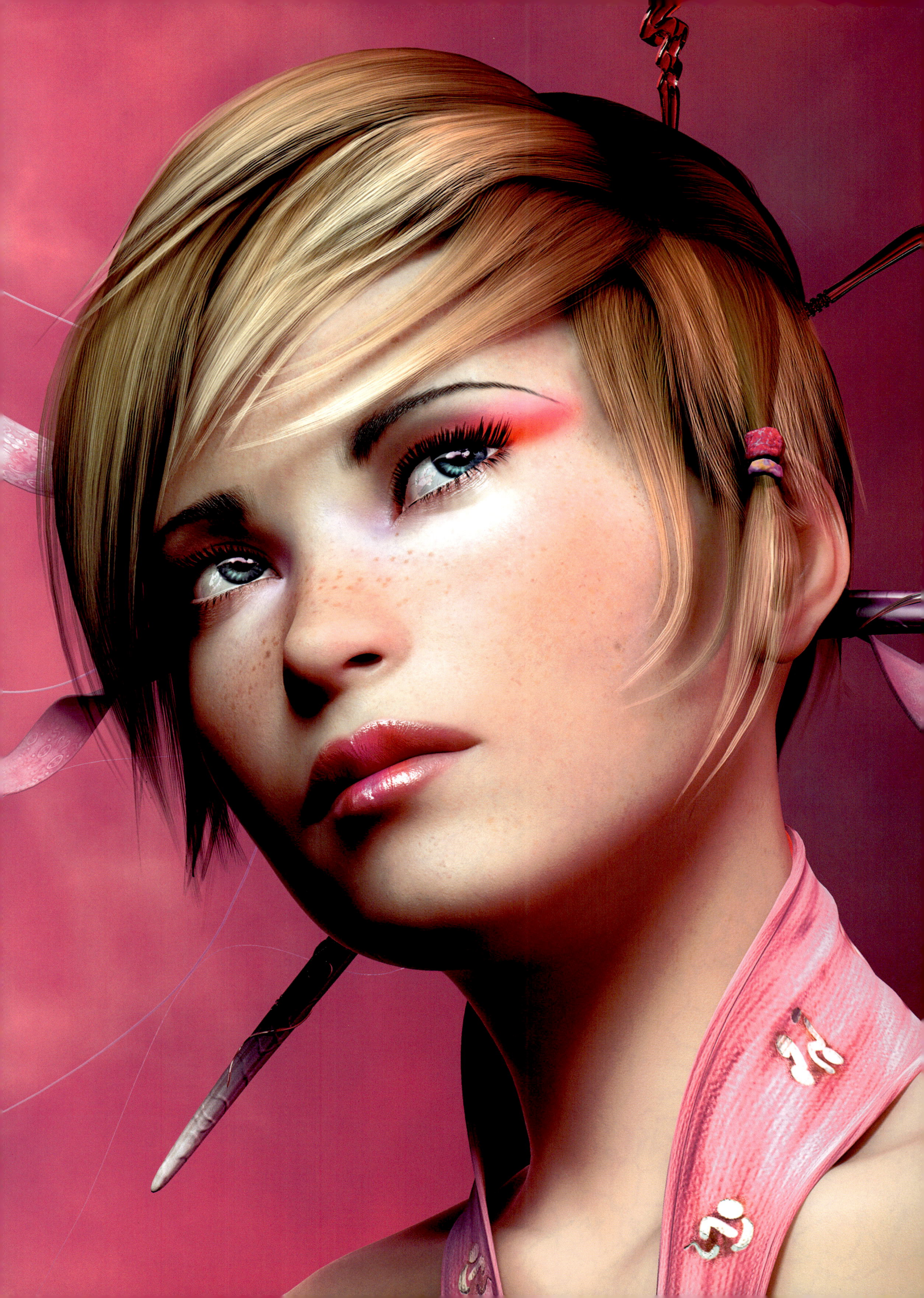

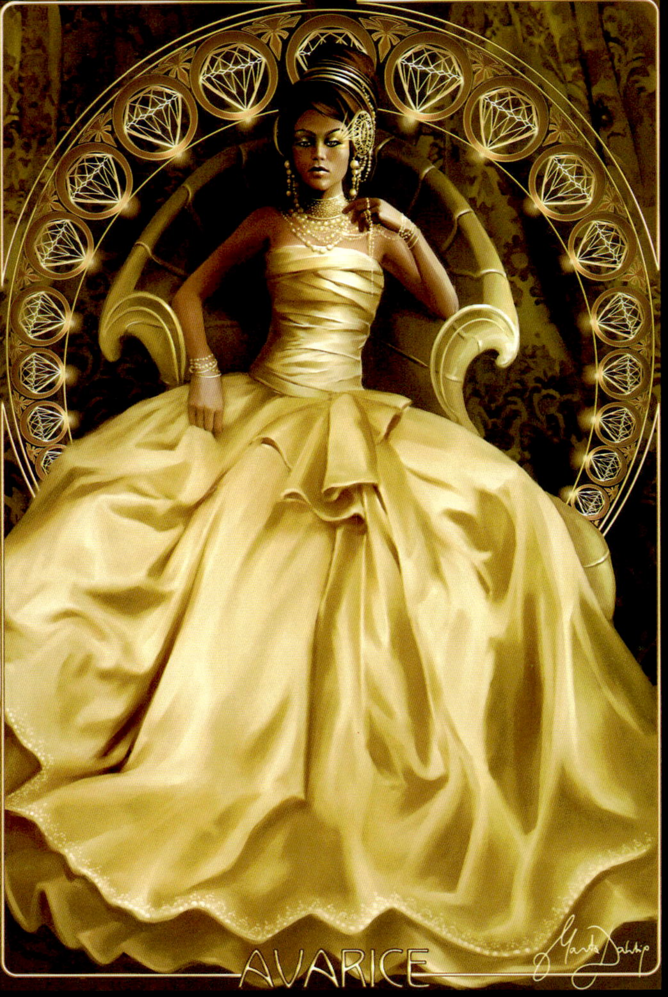

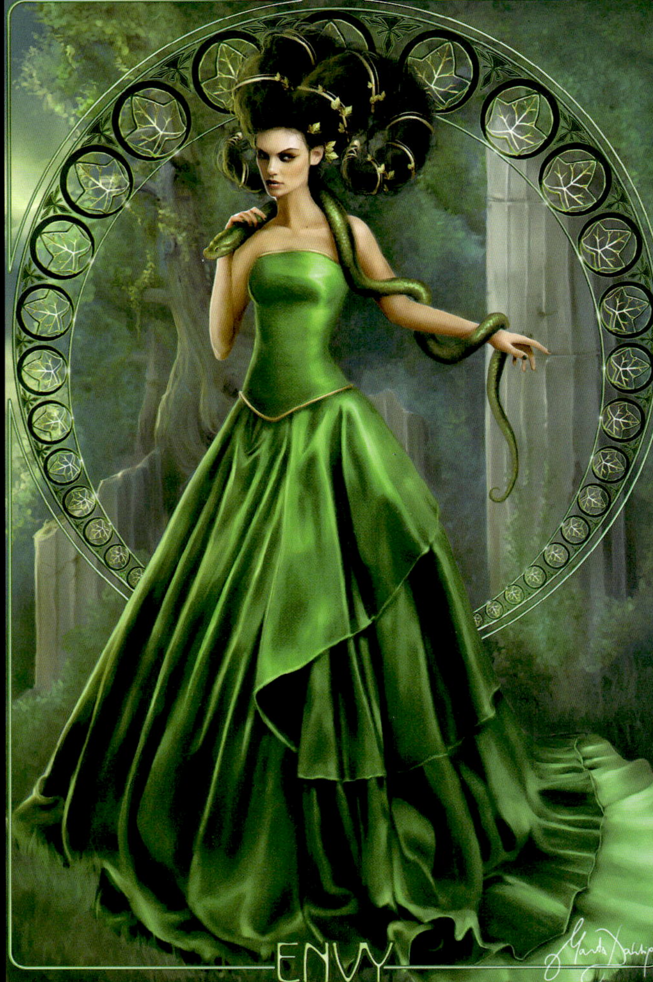

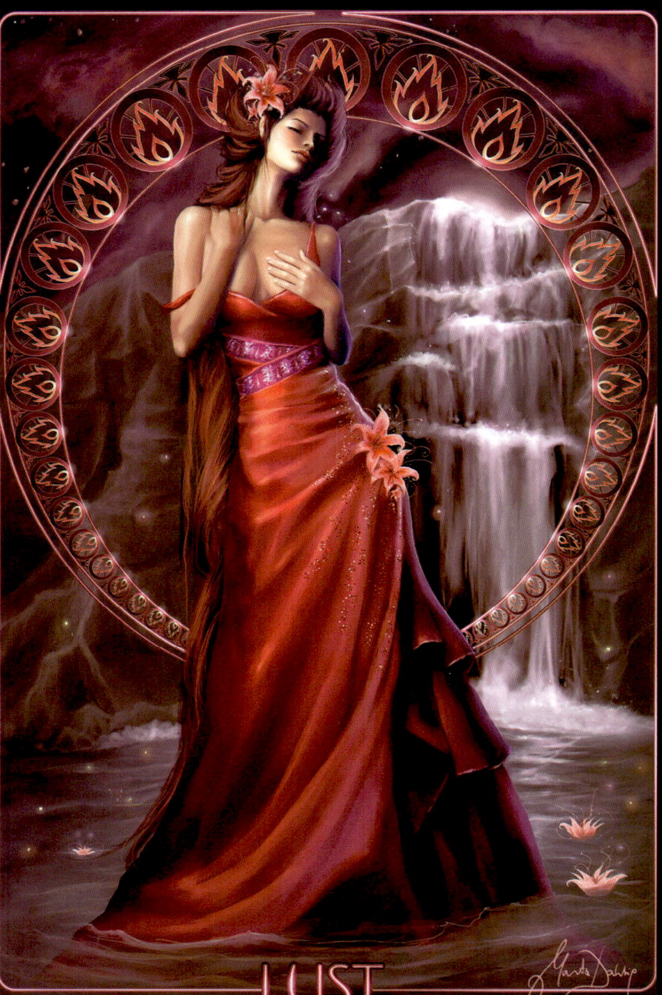

The Seven Deadly Sins: AVARICE
Painter
Marta Dahlig, POLAND
[above left]

The Seven Deadly Sins: ENVY
Painter
Marta Dahlig, POLAND
[above]

The Seven Deadly Sins: LUST
Painter
Marta Dahlig, POLAND
[left]

Restrictions
Photoshop, Painter
Jiansong Chen, CHINA
[right]

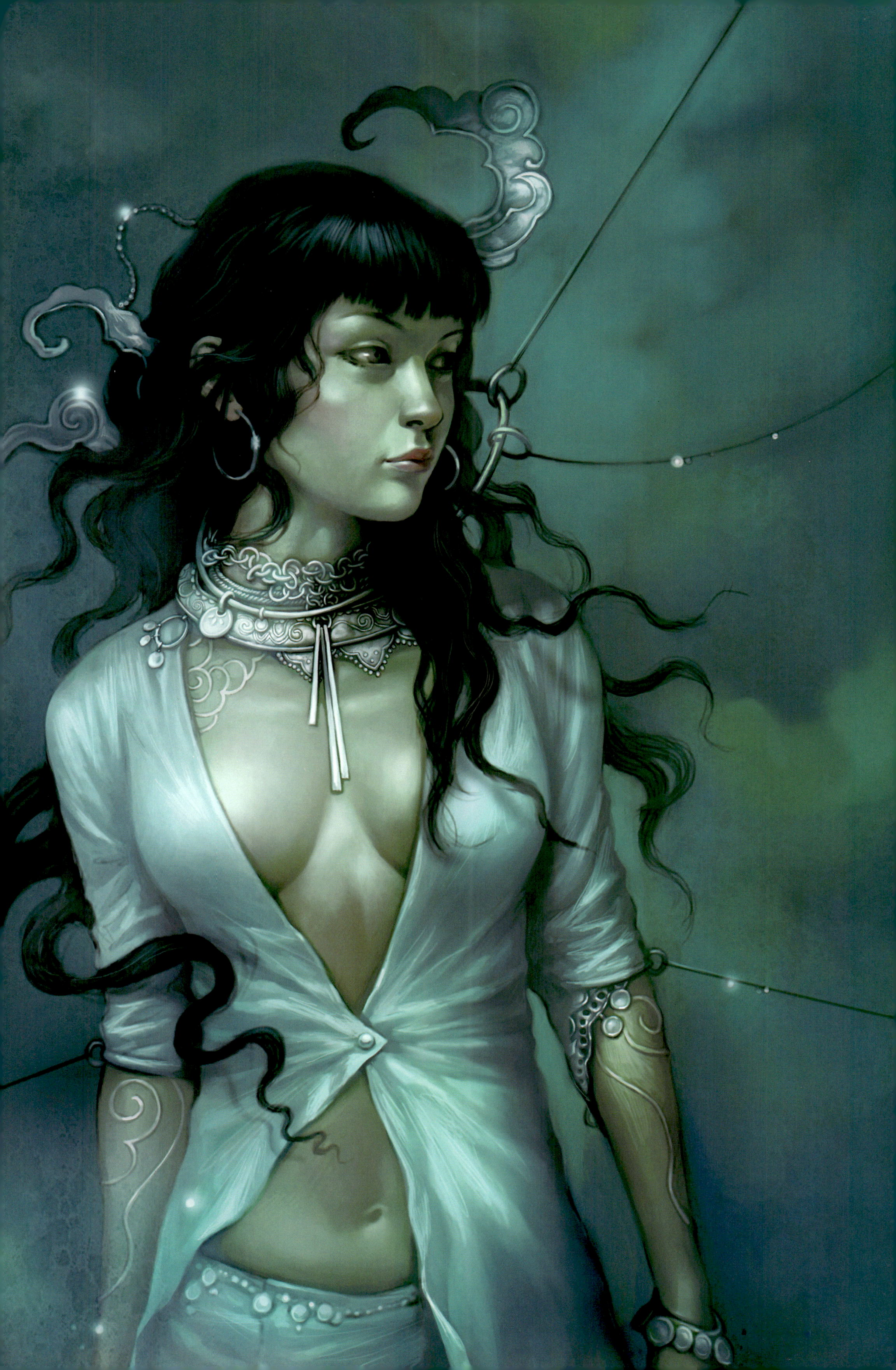

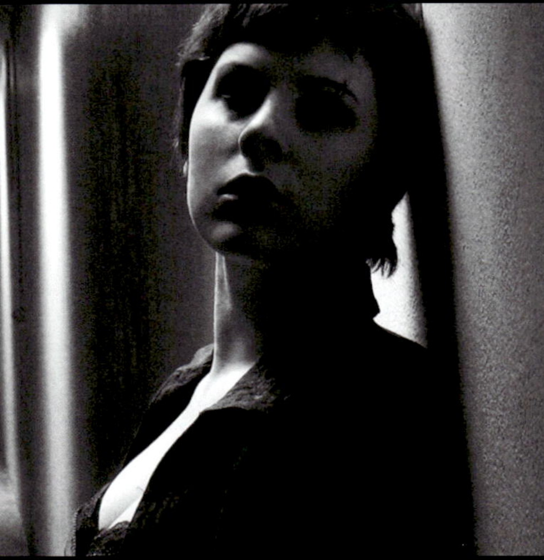

LINDA BERGKVIST

www.furiae.com
enayla@furiae.com

"What advanced me the most with my digital work was when I figured out that I could try all of the things that I was far too shy to do on traditional canvas."

Linda Bergkvist is an award-winning artist from Sweden whose digital paintings have been featured widely including Master and Excellence awards in the EXPOSÉ series. Linda is also co-author of d'artiste Digital Painting where along with three other artists she delves into her own style and techniques in the way she approaches her art. Linda is as much a storyteller as an artist with an evocative illustration style featuring mystical settings and stunning characters. Though she studied English with the intention of becoming a teacher, Linda cut her studies short to work as an illustrator. Linda now spends her time as a comic book colorist, a part-time teacher of Photoshop at a local university, and as a freelancer.

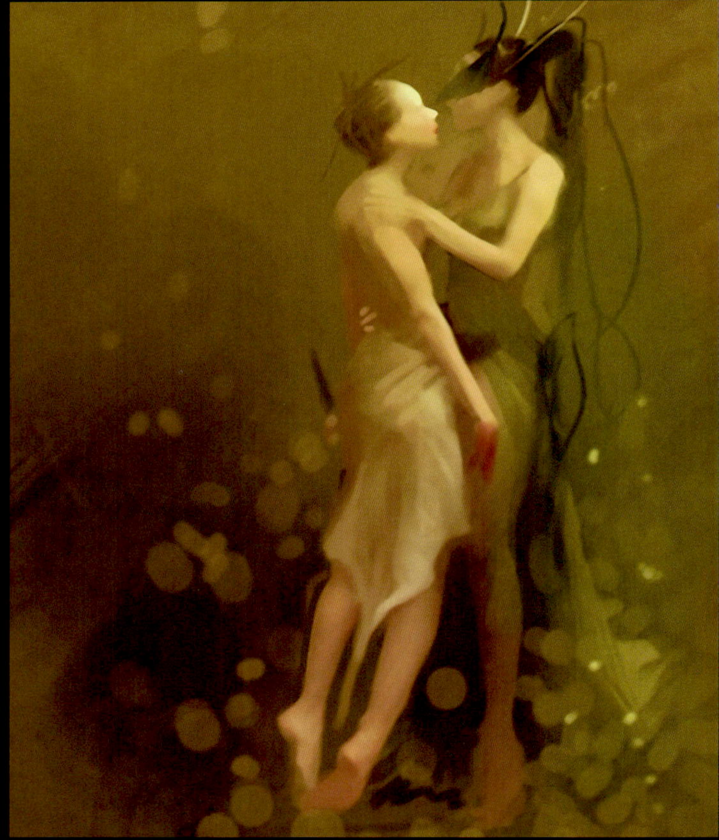

SKETCHING

I knew from the beginning that I wanted to make a picture that was laden with symbolism. It would have a theme of nature and human destruction, but in the guise of beauty. I wanted warm, rich colors of green, red and gold. One of the first things I did was to do a very quick color test. I sketched together the colors I had in mind to try them out before I used them in the initial sketch. Here, the funny thing was that the sketch ended up much murkier than I had imagined it, but by the time I reached the 'end' of the painting, I was back to using the colors I had in mind to begin with. The big mistake of the first sketch was that I had no idea of what I wanted to do with the legs of the character who represented Nature. I had no clue of their position, the shape of the feet or how she would balance. This caused me issues throughout the rest of the painting—you can see here, in the first sketch, how I 'skimmed over' painting the legs, not wanting to think about how I was going to do them. Not a good thing.

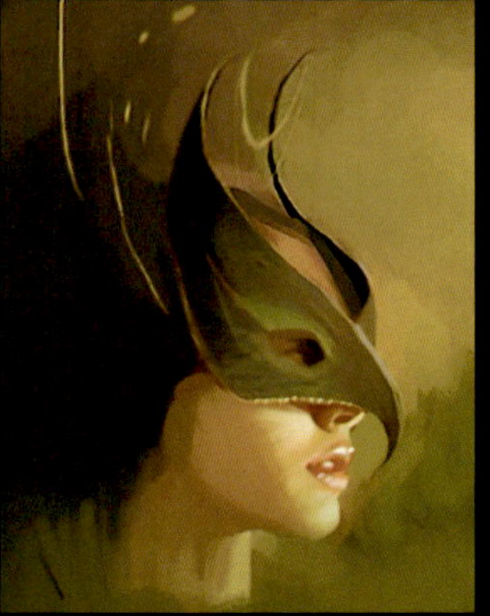
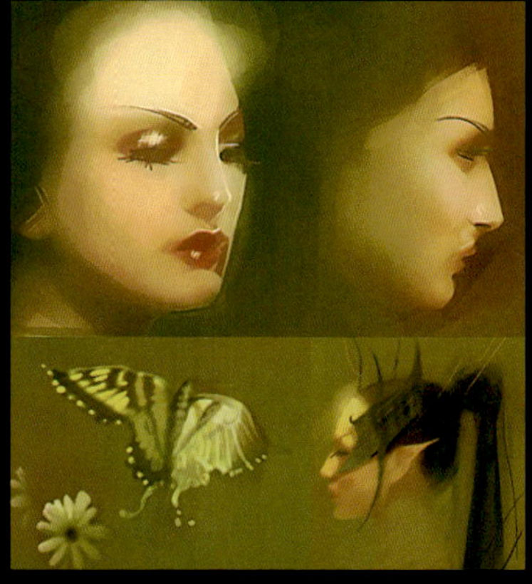
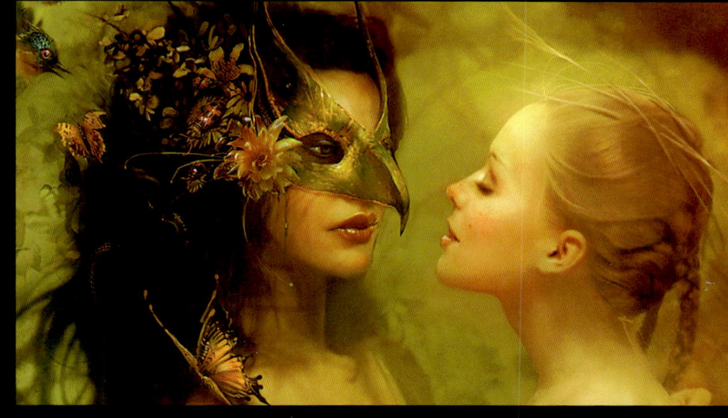
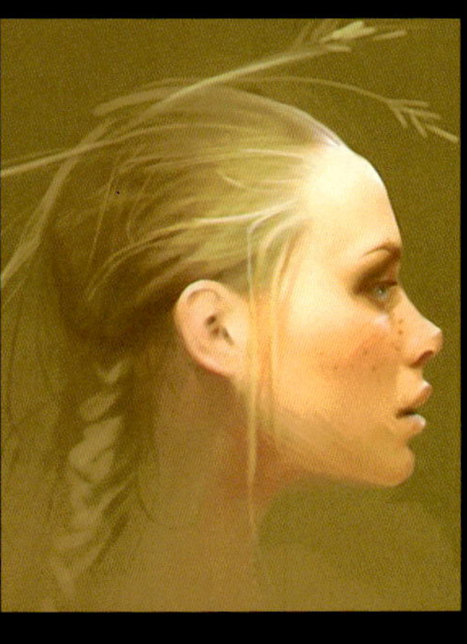

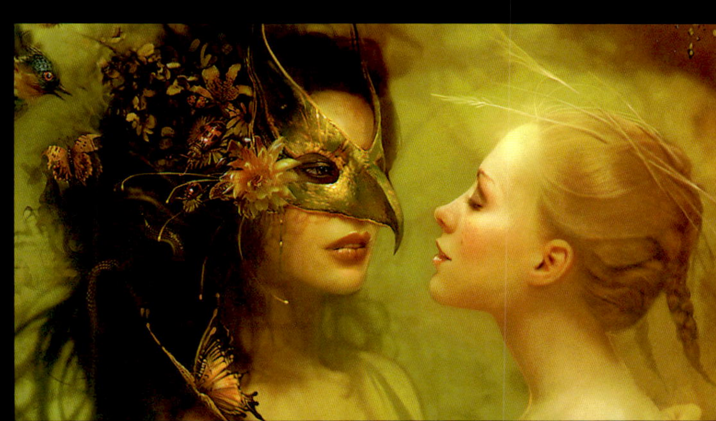

CHARACTER DESIGNS

When painting a character-driven piece, the designs and expressions of the people are essential. For this reason, before doing more than vague sketches of the faces in the painting, I sat down and played around with different versions of what they might look like. I tried to find features that would adequately represent what I was looking for, and ways to express emotions through small means. This way, I was able to find a design and look for both characters that was strong enough to sustain me throughout the entire painting. I never felt a need to change their appearance in any major way—so while other things, such as their feet (I hate painting feet) gave me insane amounts of trouble, their faces and outfits didn't. The steps in between the simple faces of the sketches and the ones in the finished painting were all in my head. I knew from the very beginning that there would be flowers in her hair, butterflies and snakes and leaves, but these 'smaller' details had no place in what were essentially just quick sketches to nail down the general look.

REFINING EXPRESSIONS

Getting the actual designs and the looks for a character right is one thing. Getting the minute, precise expressions to fit the exact feeling you want to convey, is a different thing altogether. Throughout most of the painting, I thought I had nailed the features of the character's faces, but close to the end I realised that there was room for a lot of improvement: discrete improvement. Having left the faces untouched for so long, I was now able to go back and rework many of the details. I parted Nature's lips, I repainted her eyes to add more life to them and felt that she now showed a lot more emotion. The repainting of the human's face followed closely, carefully rearranging her features to give her a more relaxed, tender expression. There was also the issue of her freckles. I don't have freckles myself so I don't have a lot of understanding of how they 'work' visually, so I sat down and looked up a lot of pictures of freckled people, to figure them out. These changes are tiny—some might not even notice them, but for me they made all the difference. Subtle is the key, here. Details in faces and costumes that some might never notice are there, but they still matter. I think a lot of these tiny things that we put lots of love and effort into, though not visible at first glance, still affect the image in a great way.

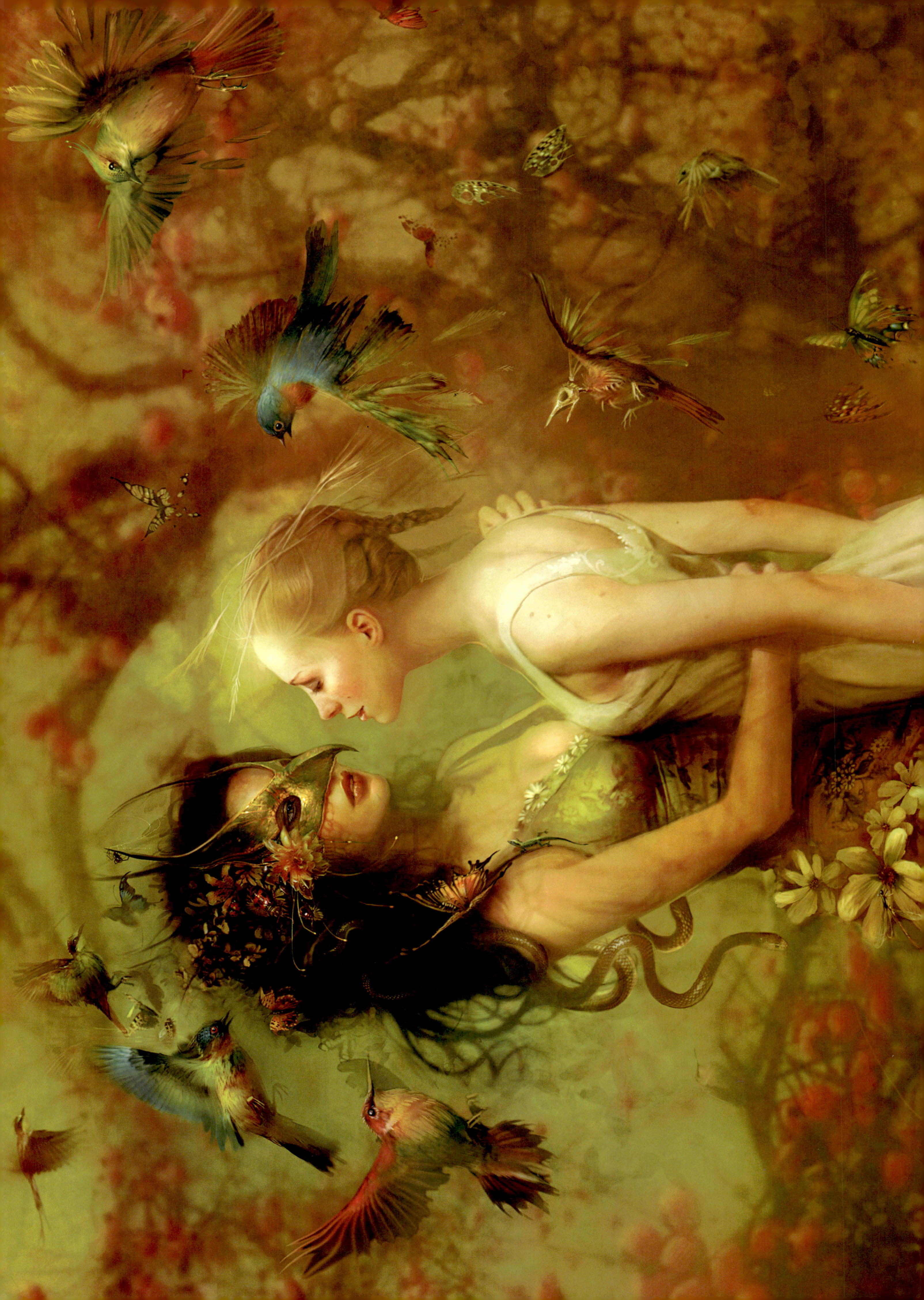

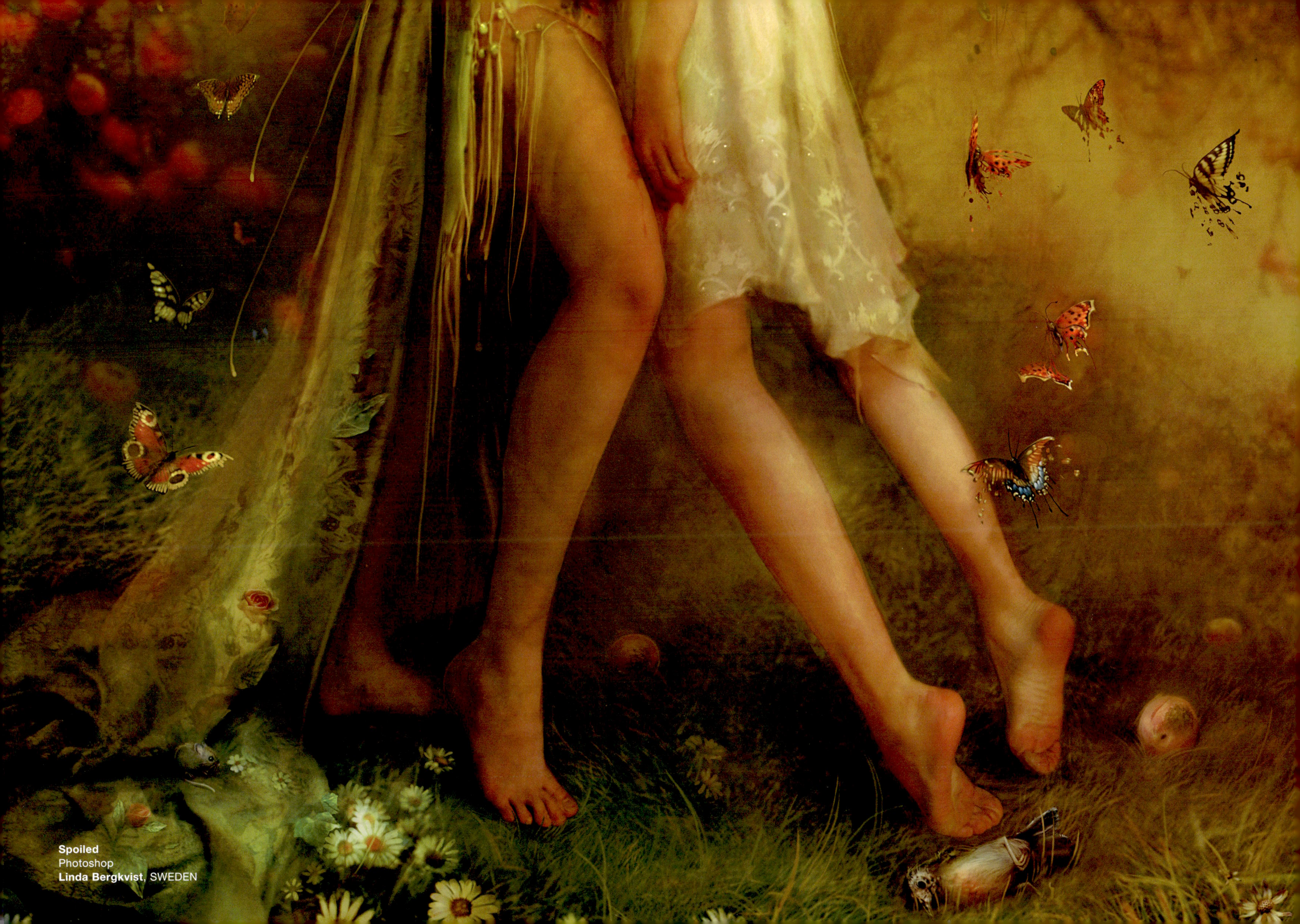

Spoiled
Photoshop
Linda Bergkvist, SWEDEN

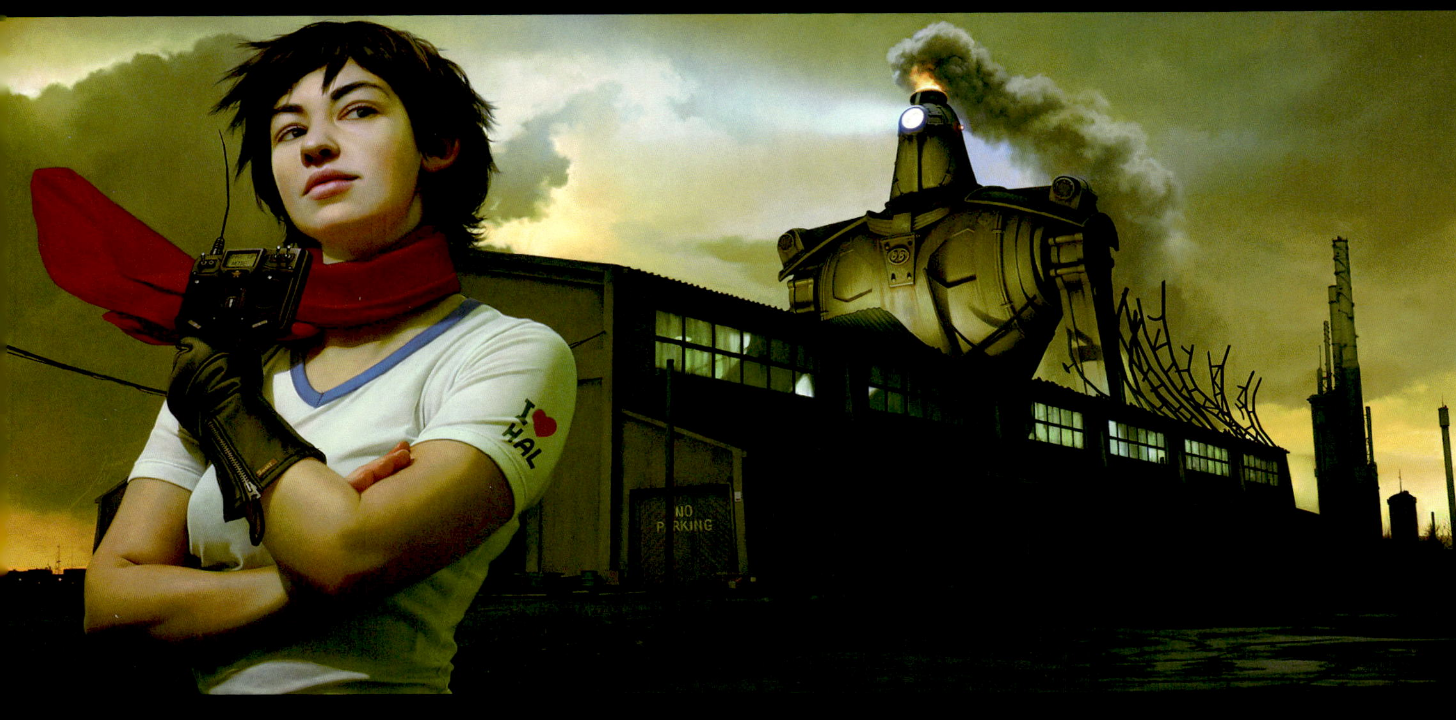

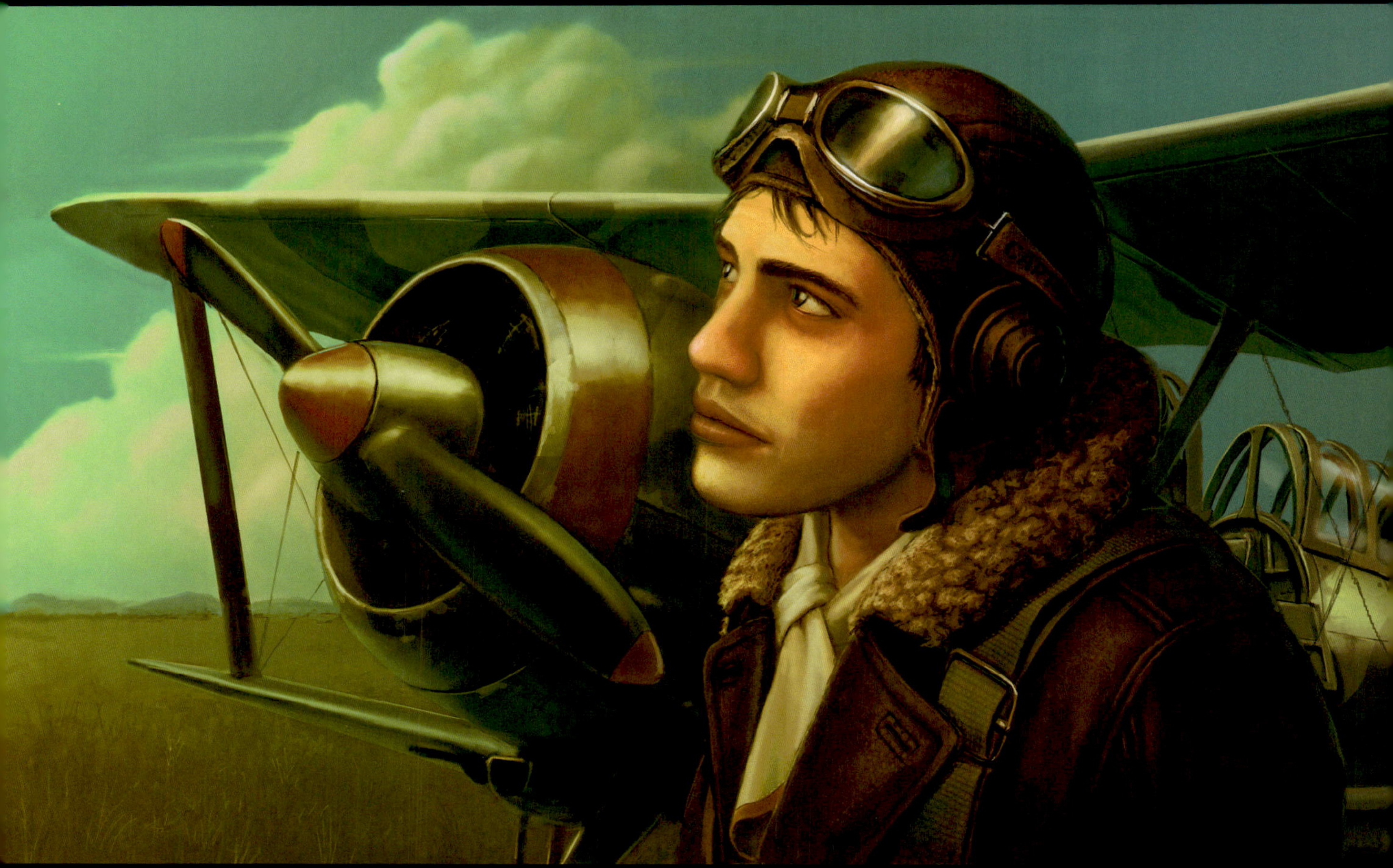

Wake up baby!!
Photoshop
Jose Manuel Fernandez Oli, SPAIN
[top]

John
Photoshop
Armin Stocker, AUSTRIA
[above]

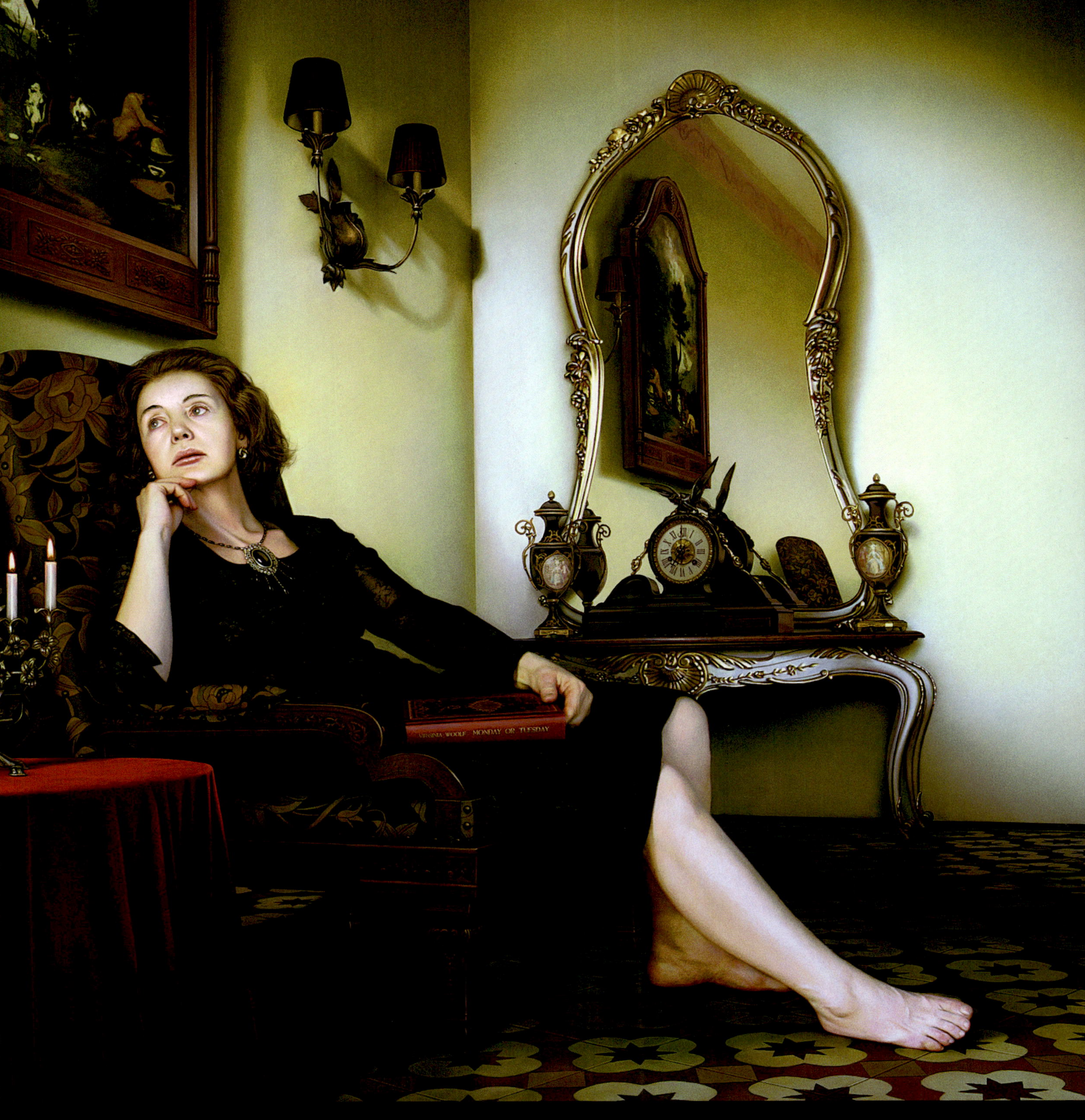

Existence

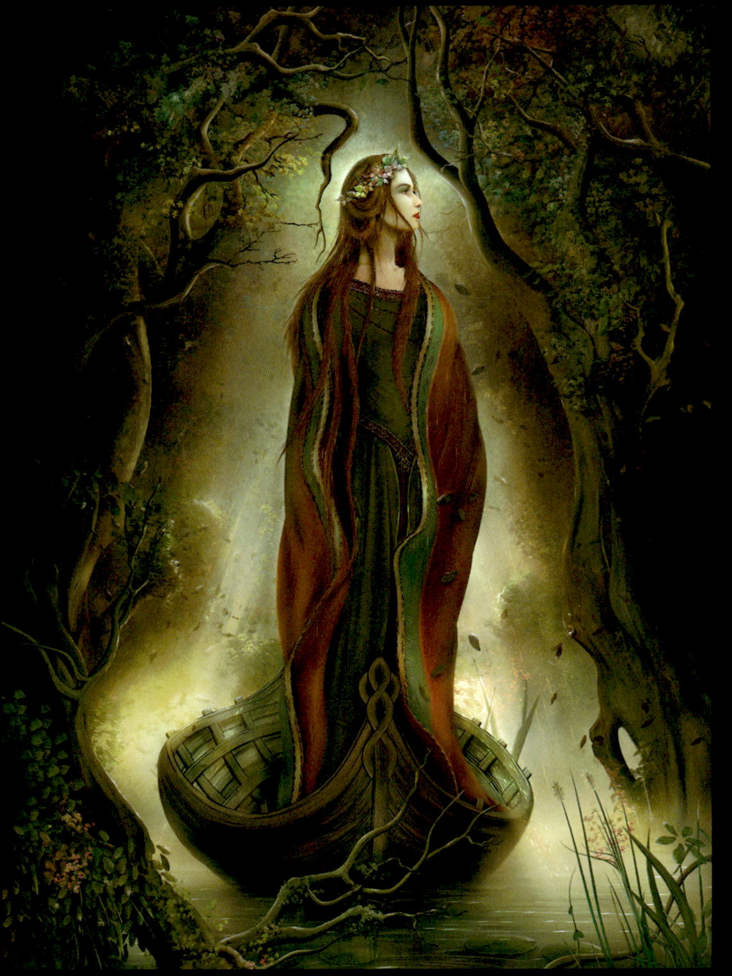

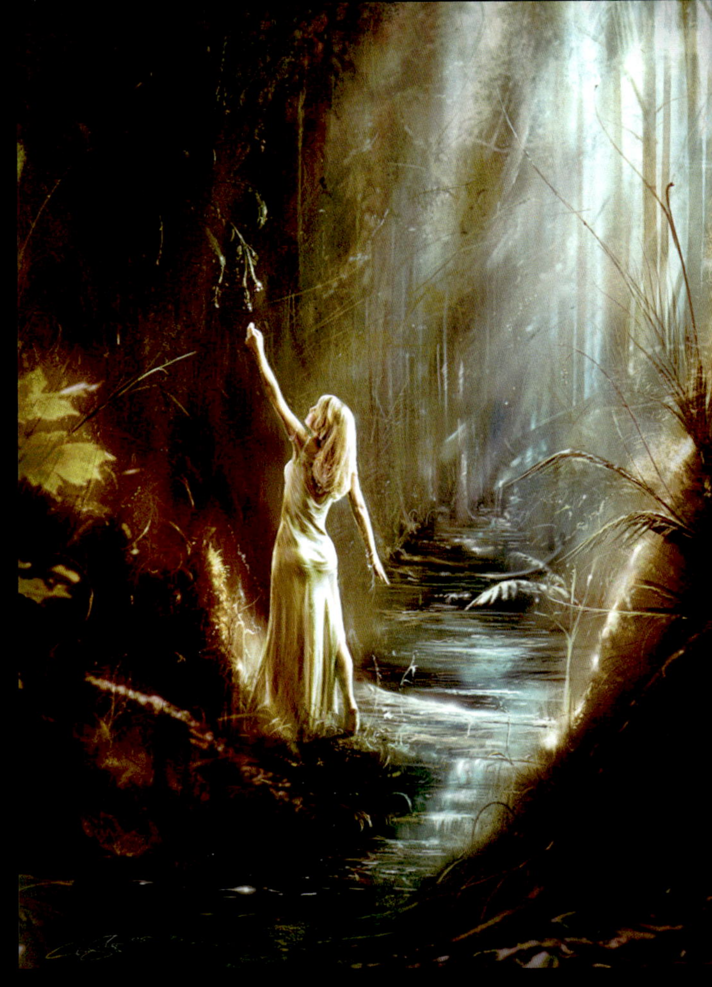

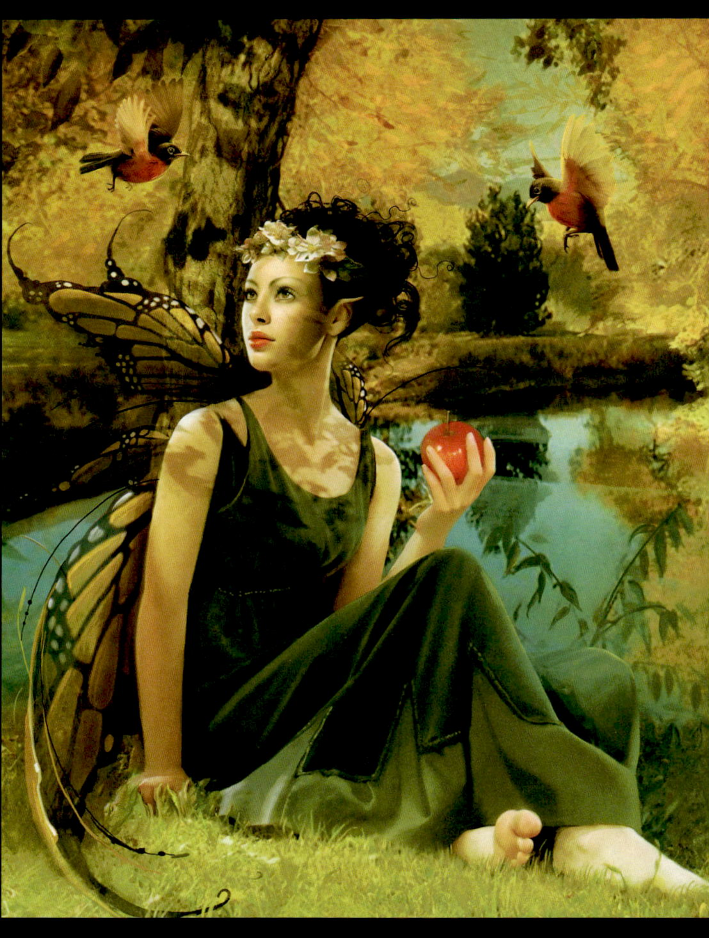

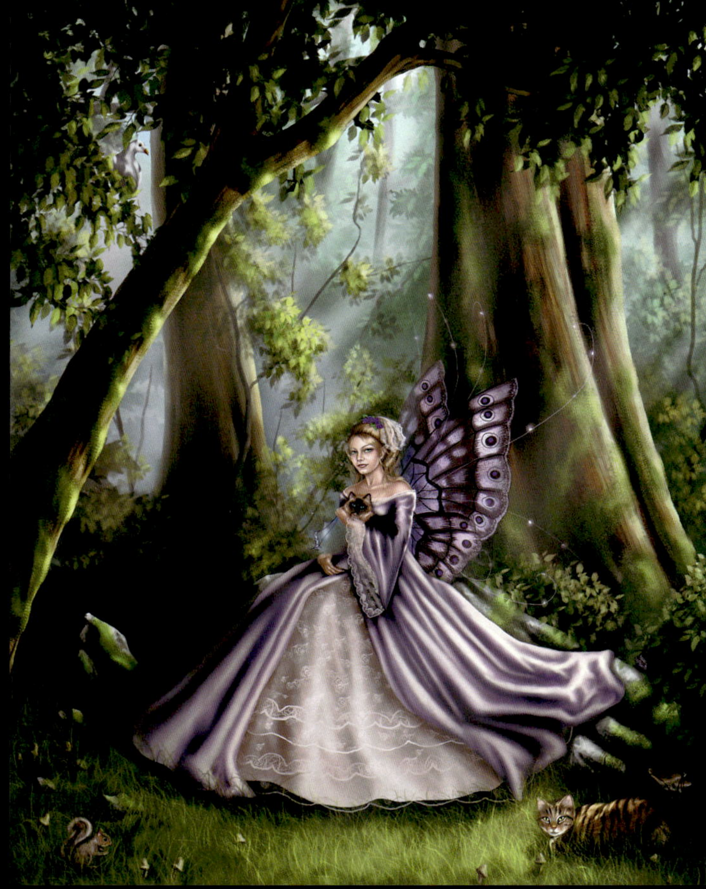

Lady Avalon
Photoshop
John Shannon, MALTA
[top]

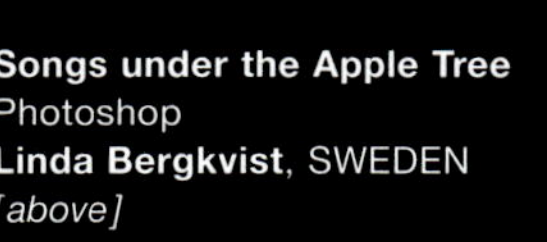

Songs under the Apple Tree
Photoshop
Linda Bergkvist, SWEDEN
[above]

Wildberries
Photoshop
Franz Steiner, GERMANY
[top]

Carrie
Photoshop
Laura Law, USA
[above]

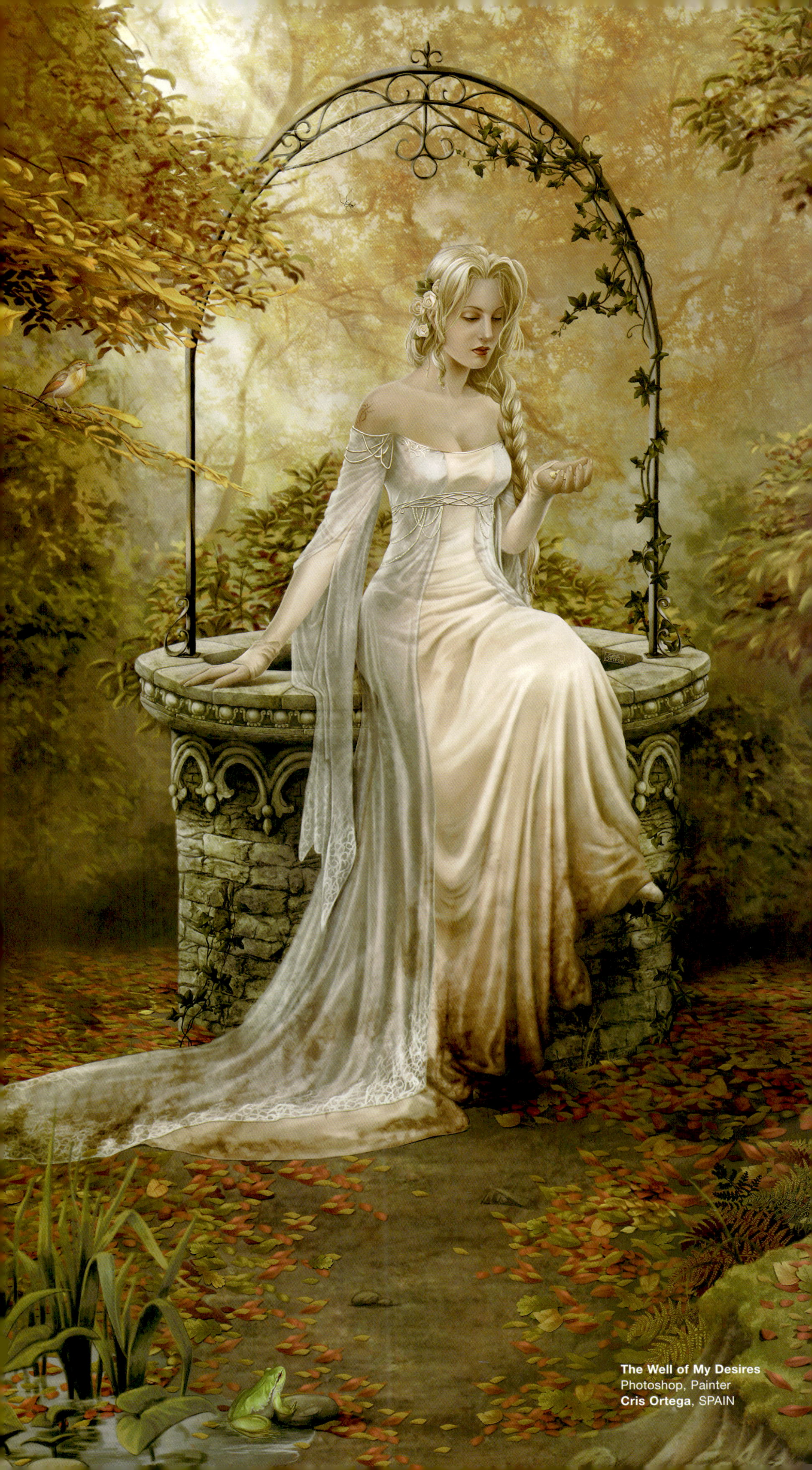

The Well of My Desires
Photoshop, Painter
Cris Ortega, SPAIN

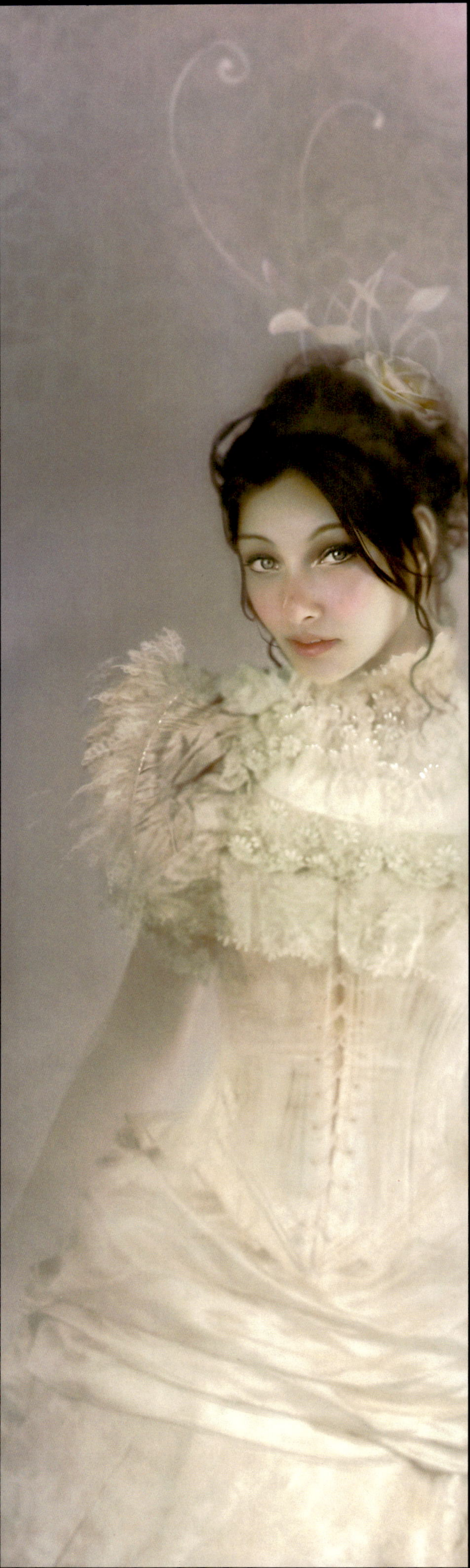

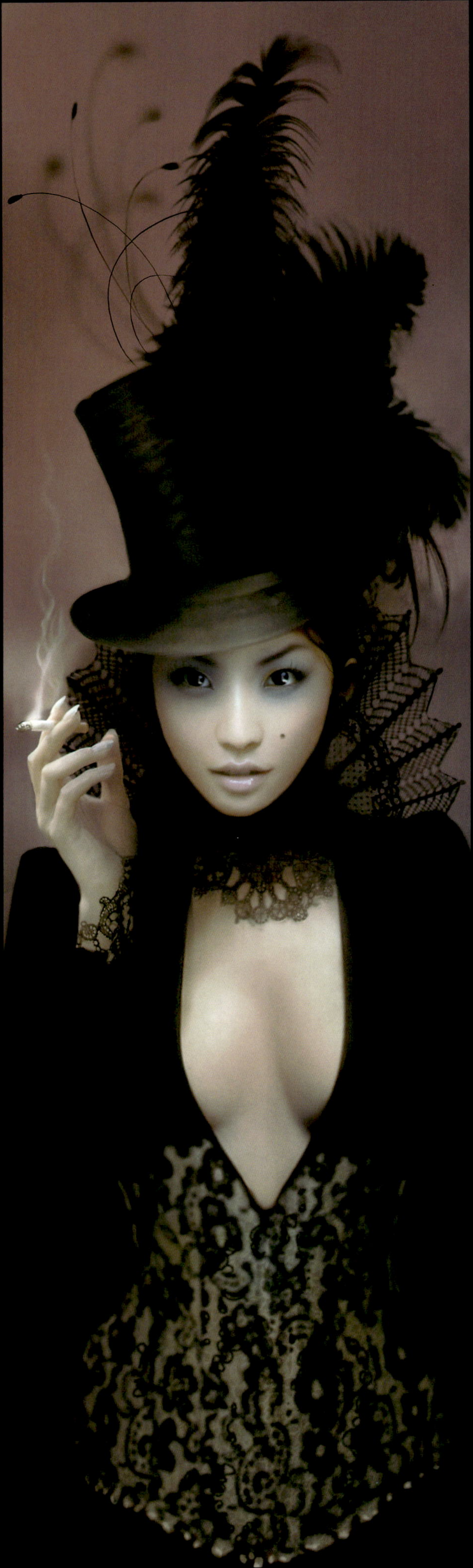

Ladies of London
Photoshop
Linda Bergkvist, SWEDEN
[left series]

Beautiful Killer
Photoshop
Hoang Le, VIETNAM
[right]

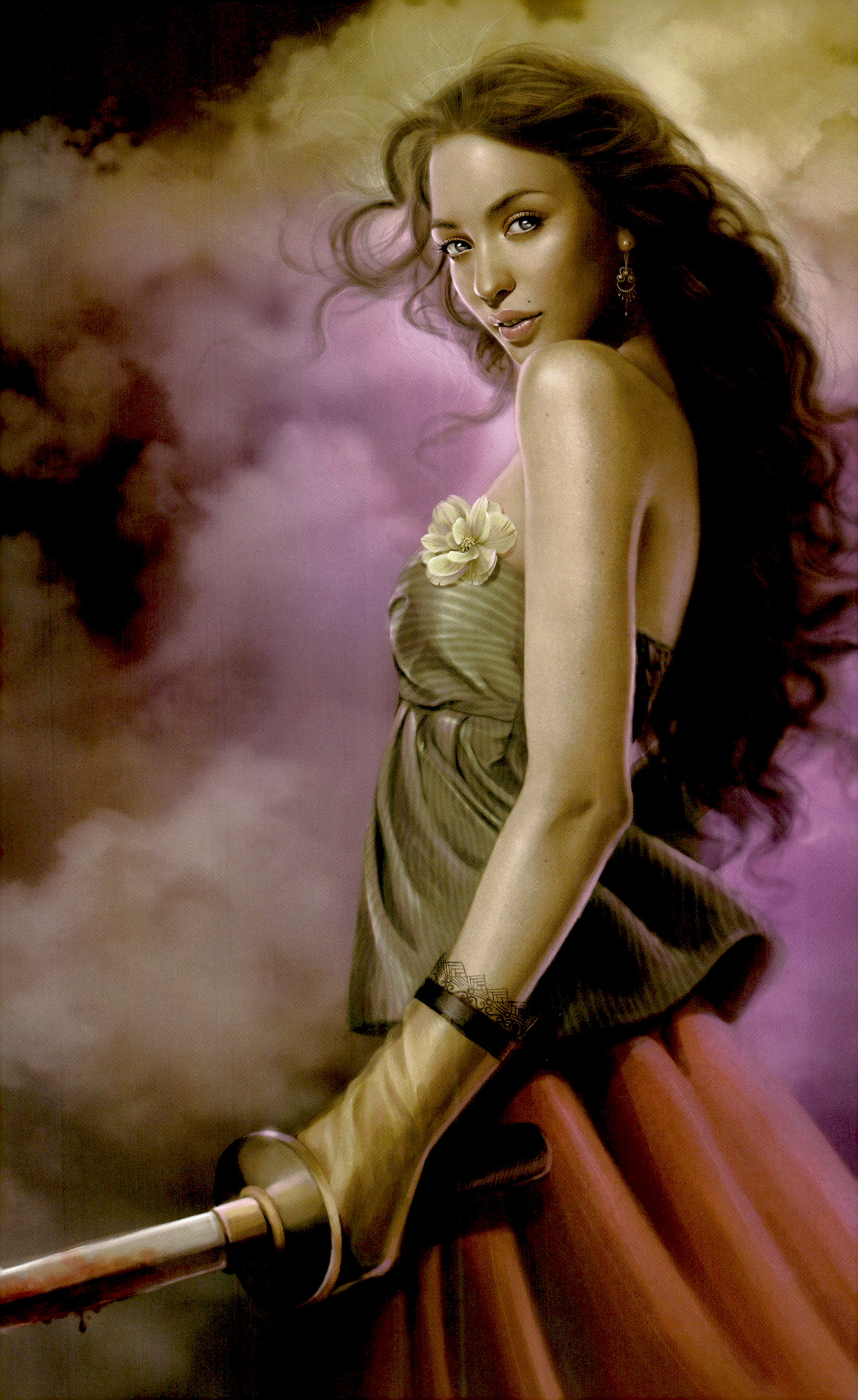

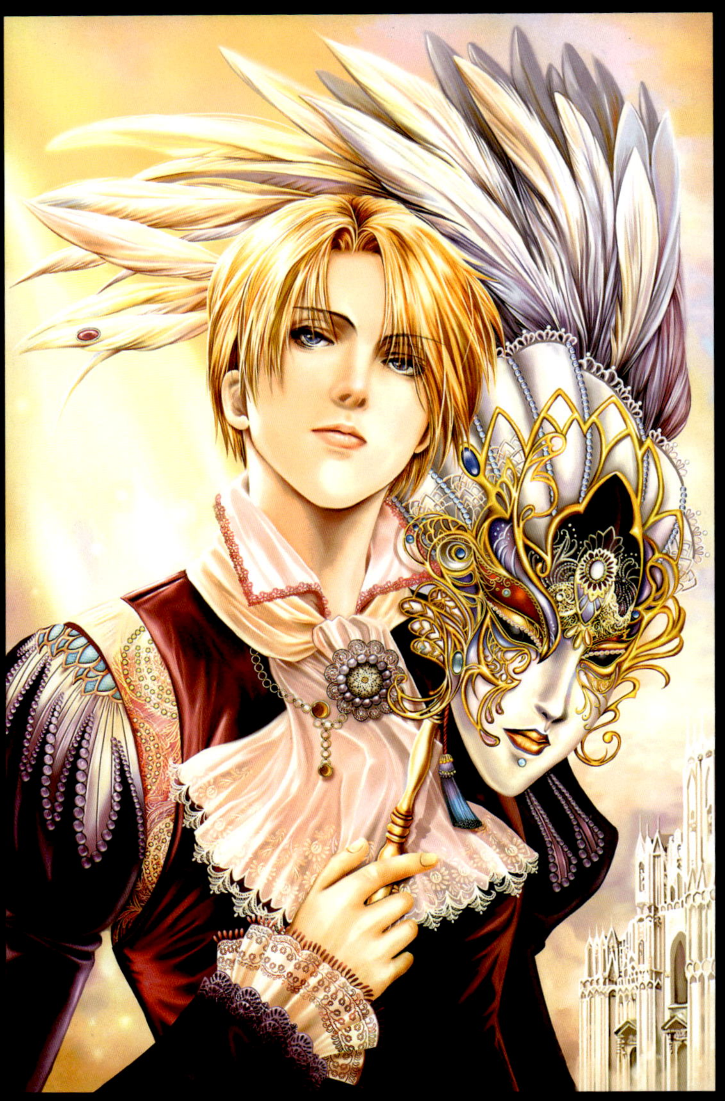

Mask of Venice
Photoshop
Fan Yang, USA
[above]

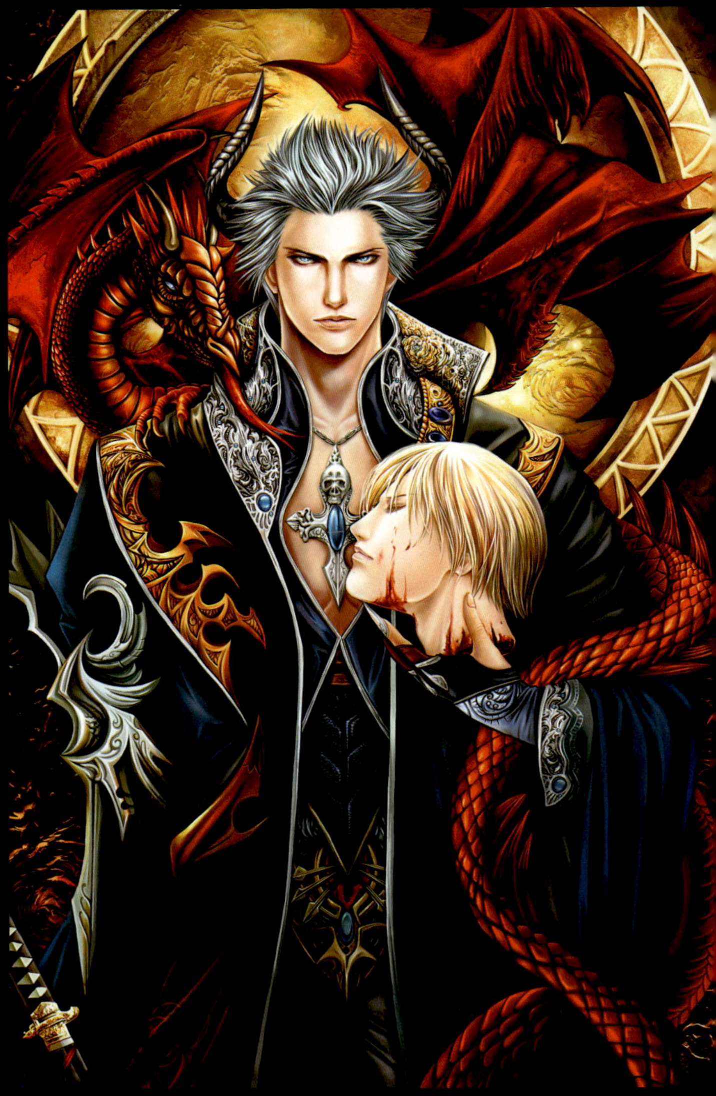

Devil
Photoshop
Fan Yang, USA
[above]

Queen
Painter, Photoshop
Chao Chin Kung, TAIWAN
[right]

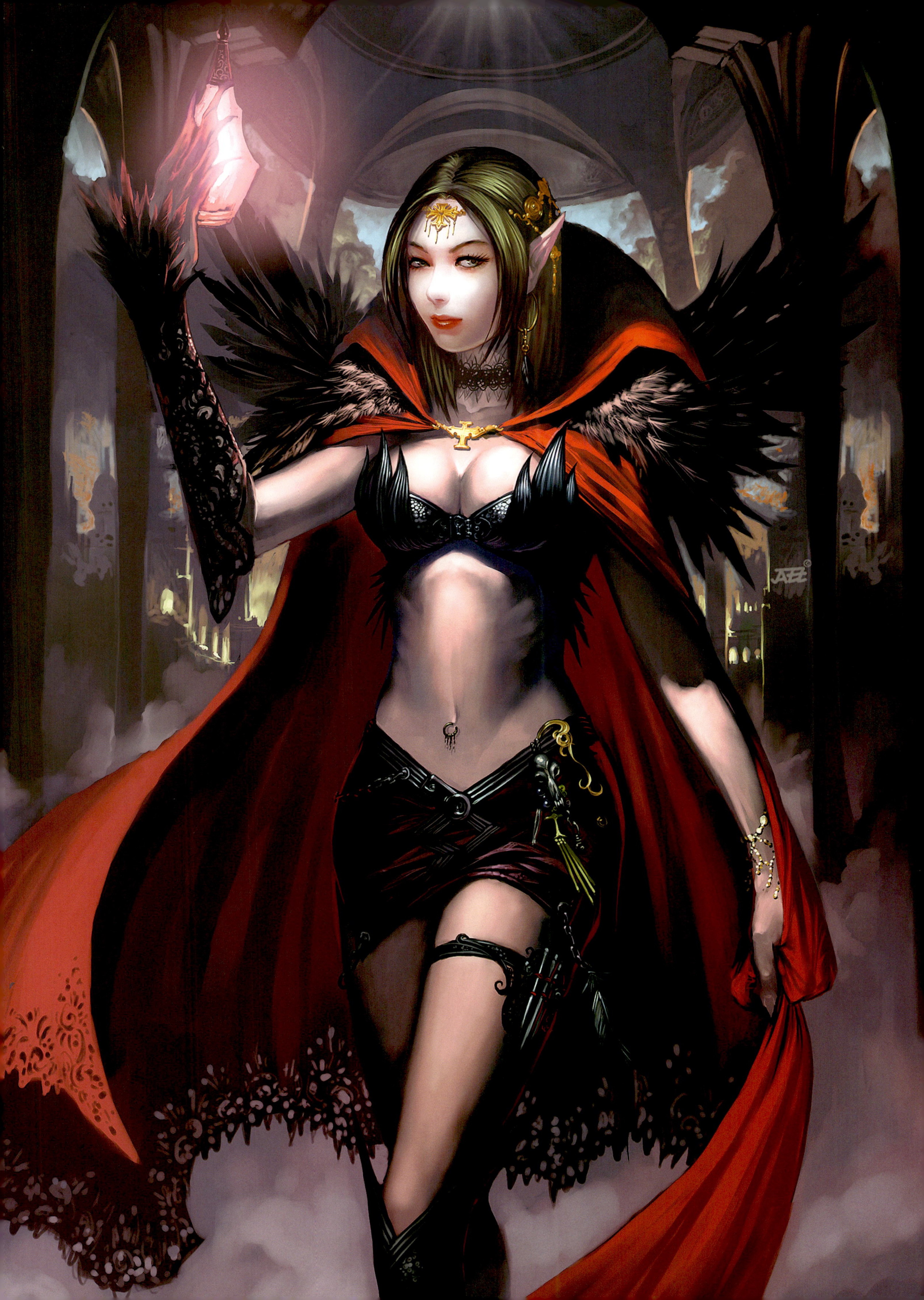

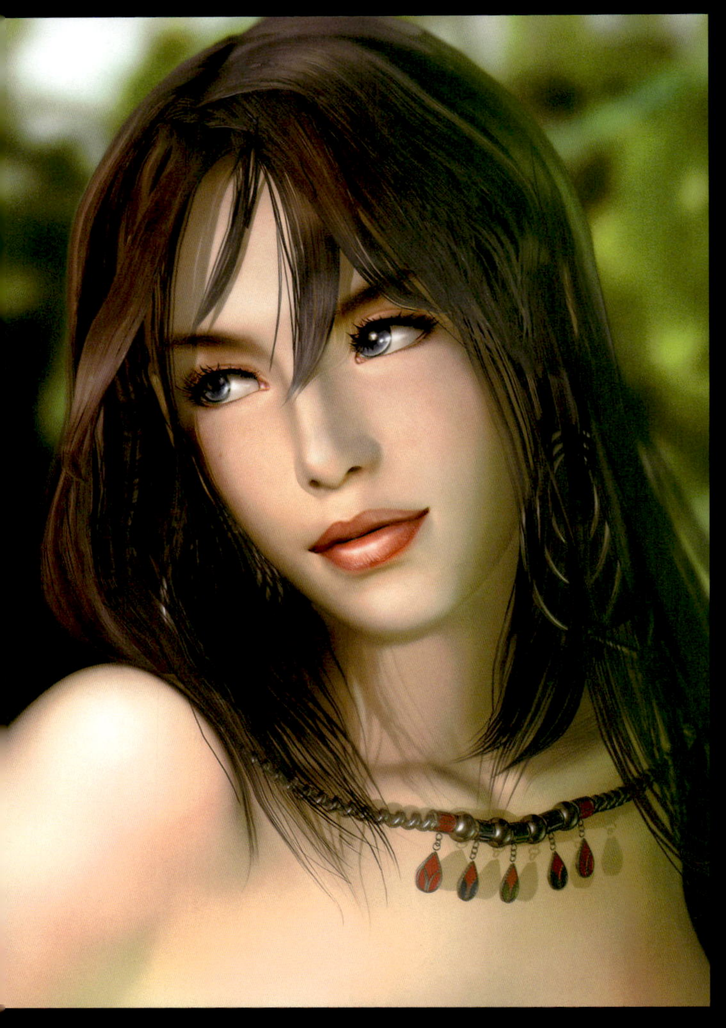

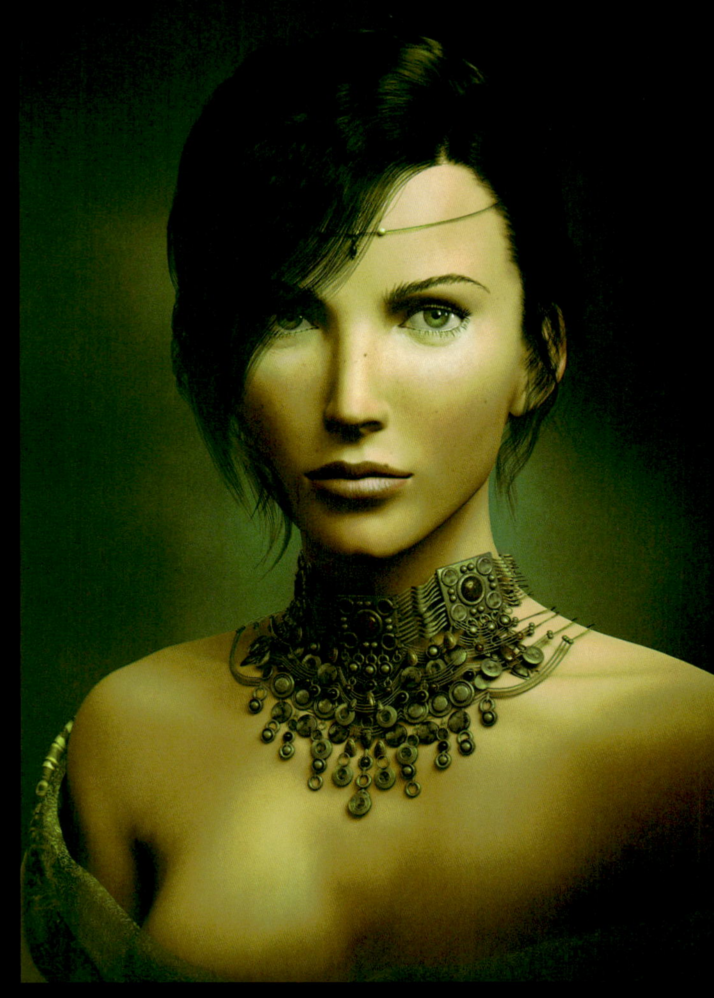

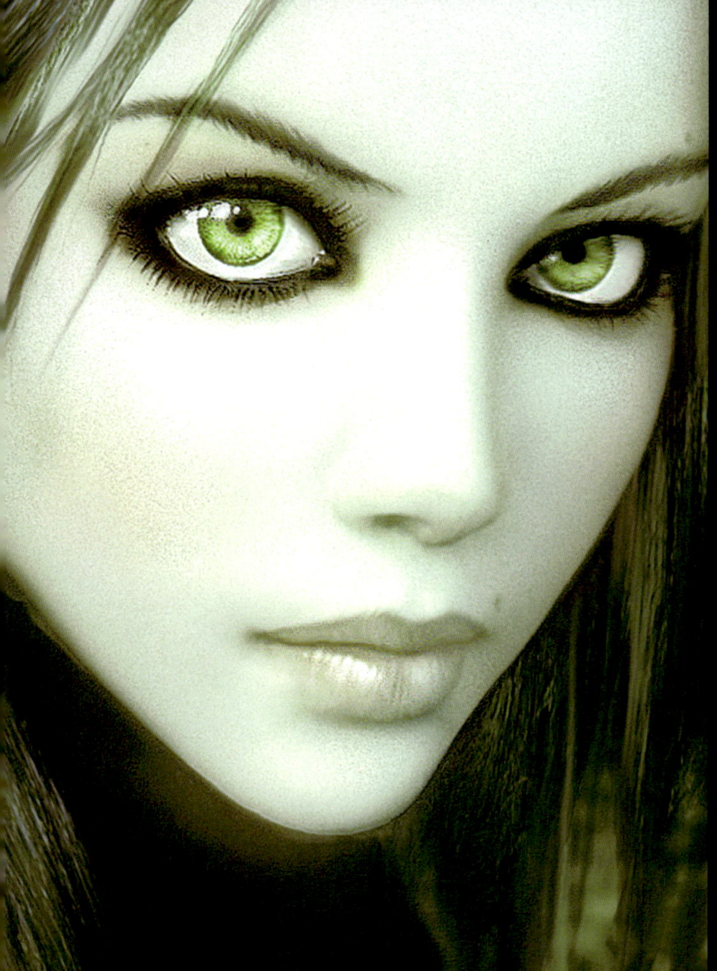

Redyan
Photoshop, 3ds Max
Client: Actoz soft
Soa Lee, KOREA
[above left]

Princess
3ds Max
Olivier Ponsonnet, FRANCE
[above]

Clio
LightWave 3D, Photoshop
Karl Poulson, USA
[left]

Smile with the Wind
3ds Max, Photoshop
Client: Actoz soft
Soa Lee, KOREA
[right]

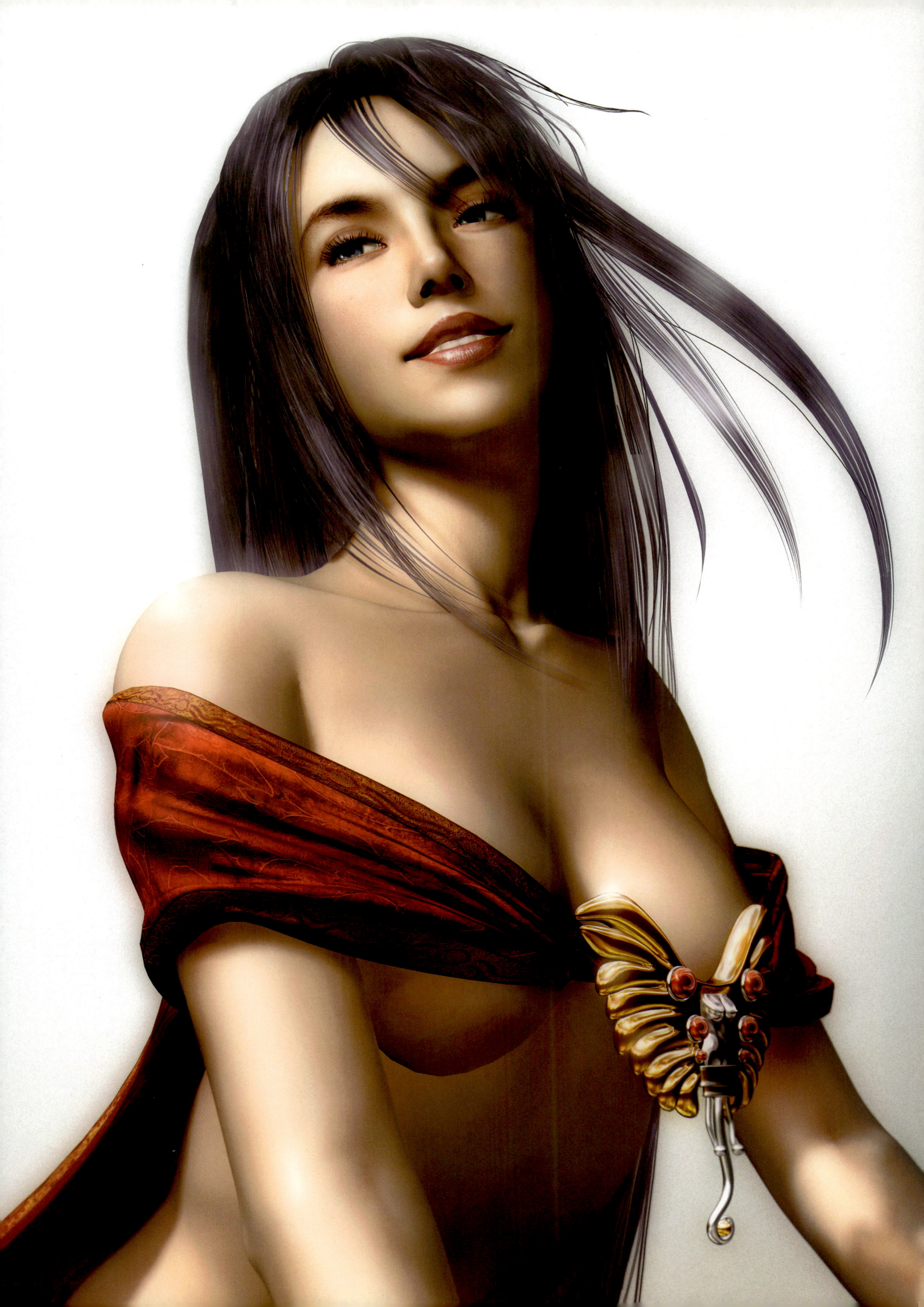

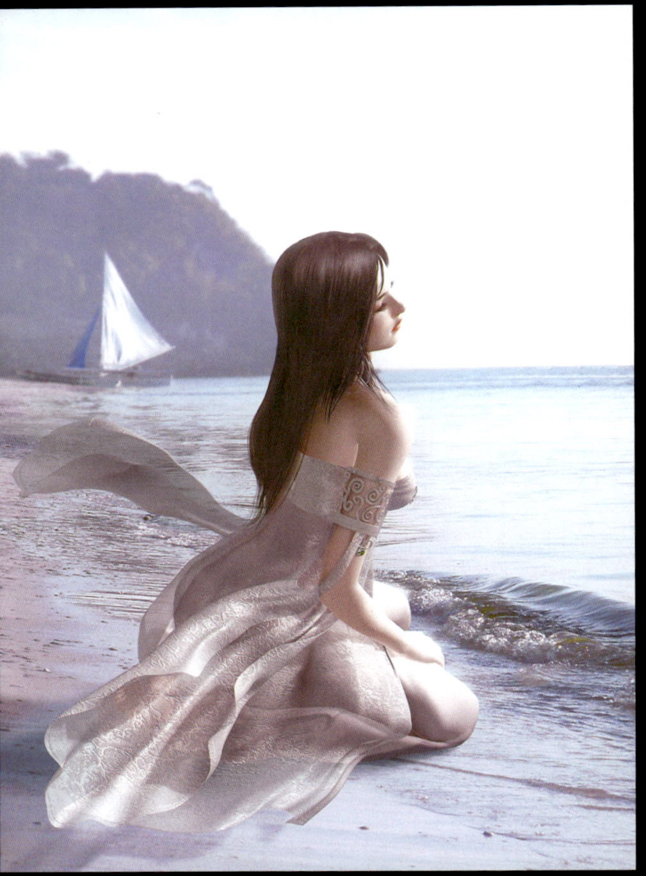

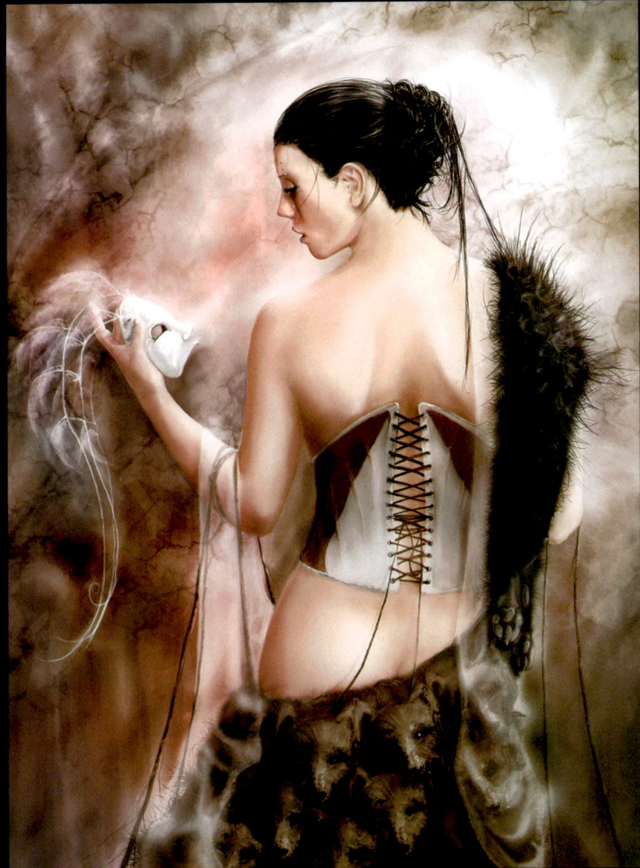

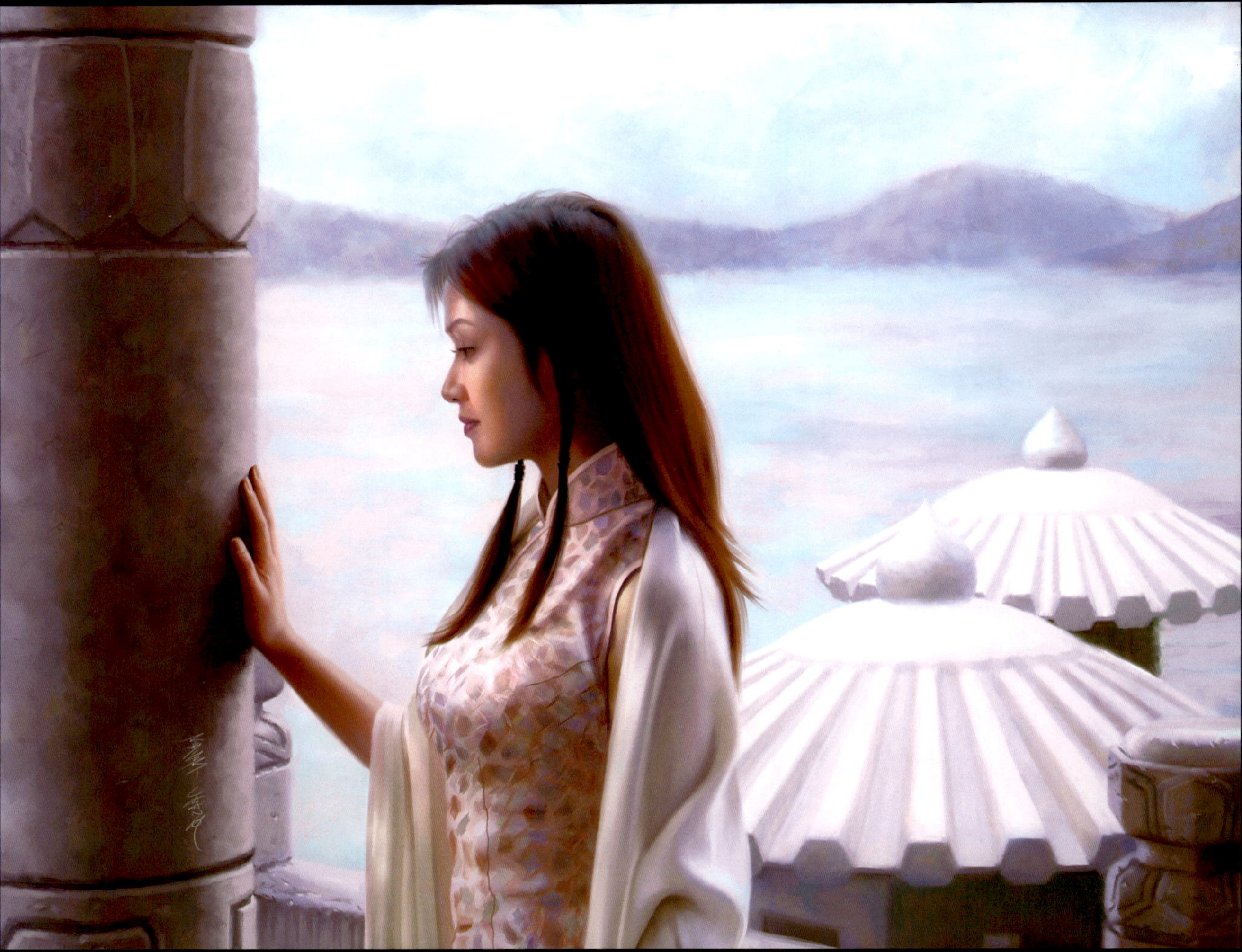

Beach
3ds Max
Soa Lee, KOREA
[top left]

Memories of Hangzhou
Photoshop, Painter
Robert Chang, USA
[above]

Masquerade
Photoshop
Egil Paulsen, NORWAY
[top right]

Spring Petals
Photoshop
Natascha Roeoesli, SWITZERLAND
[right]

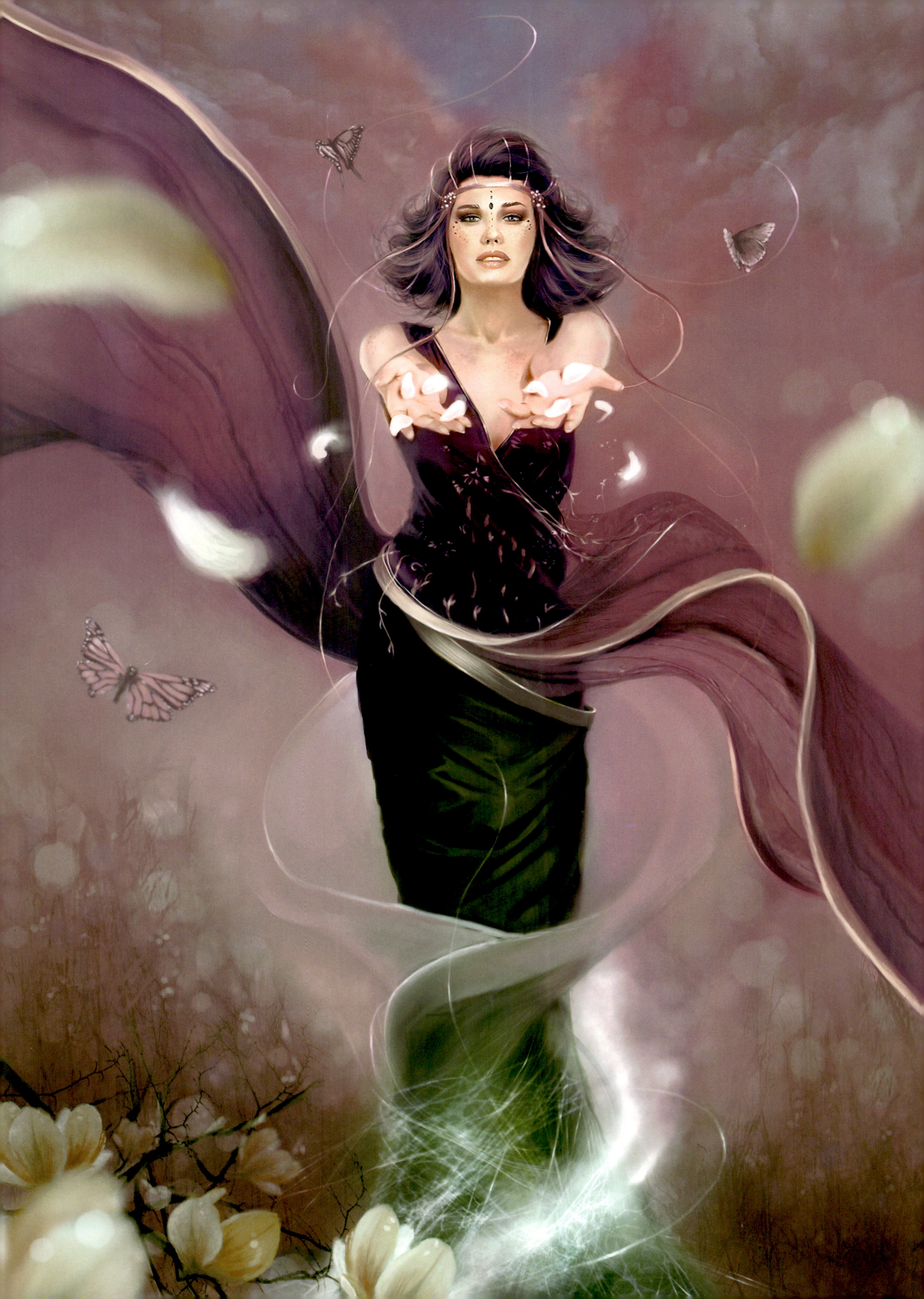

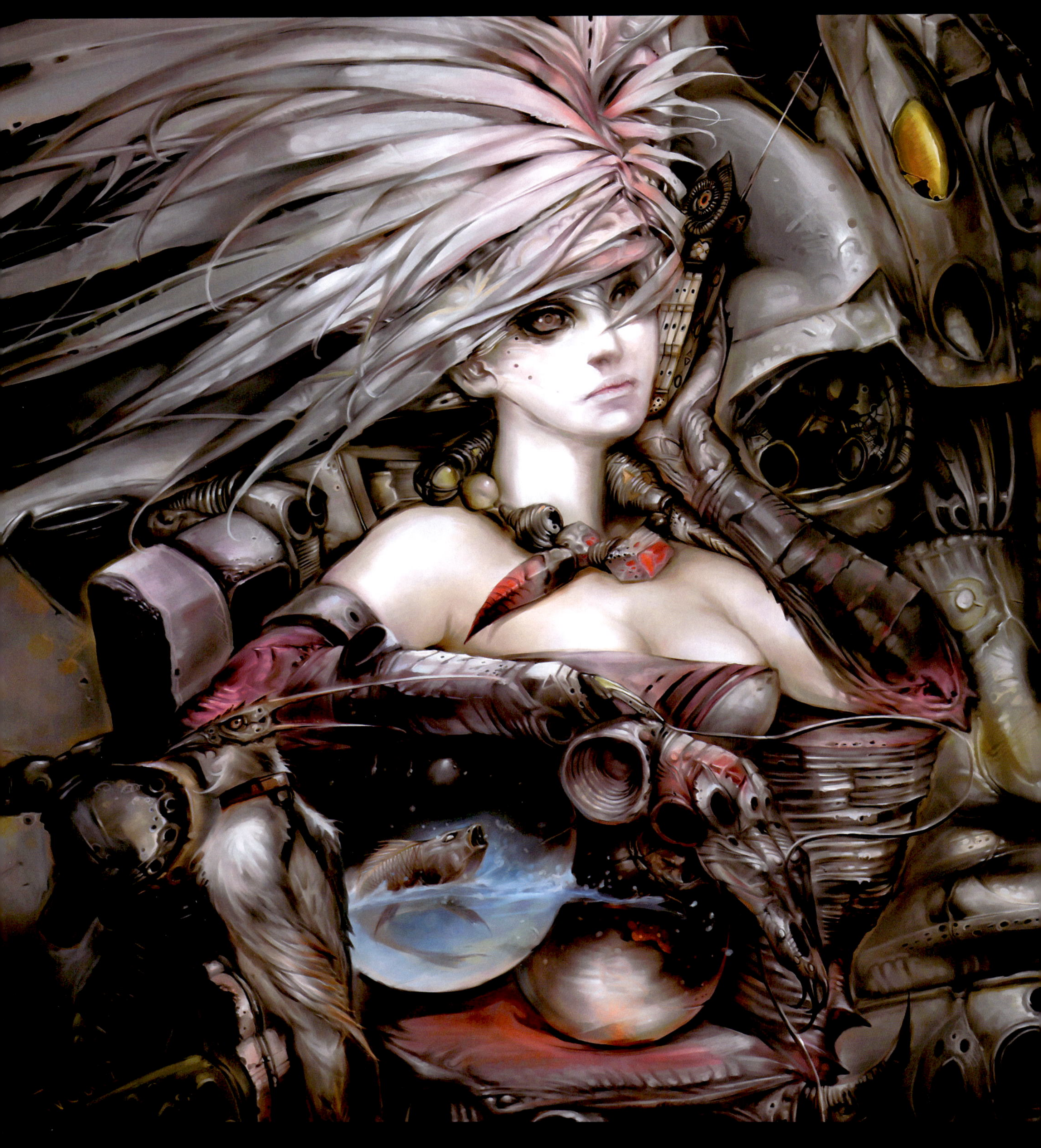

My World
Painter
Hong Kuang, SINGAPORE
[above]

Temple Guard Priestess
Photoshop
Oz Spiniello, AUSTRALIA
[right]

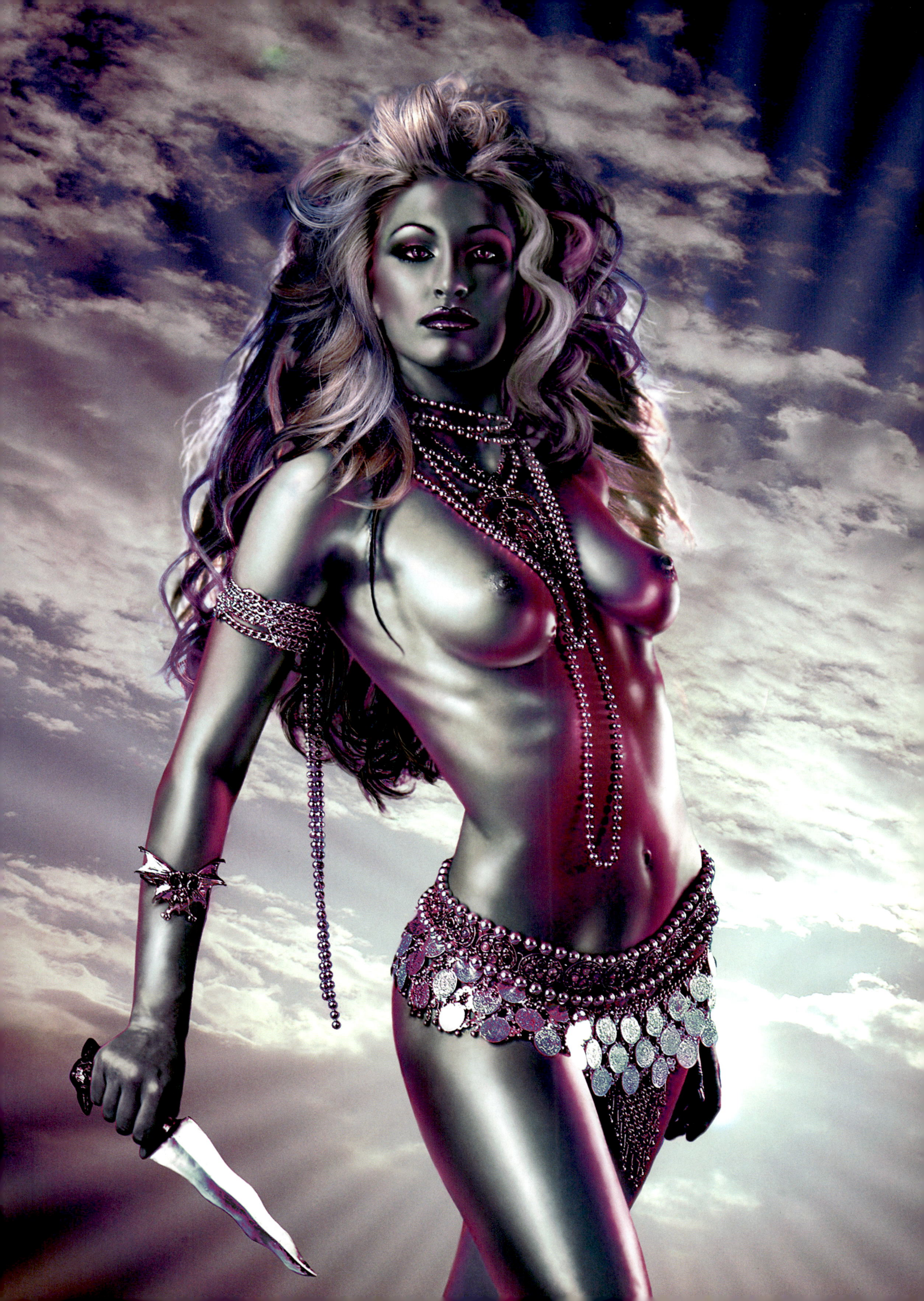

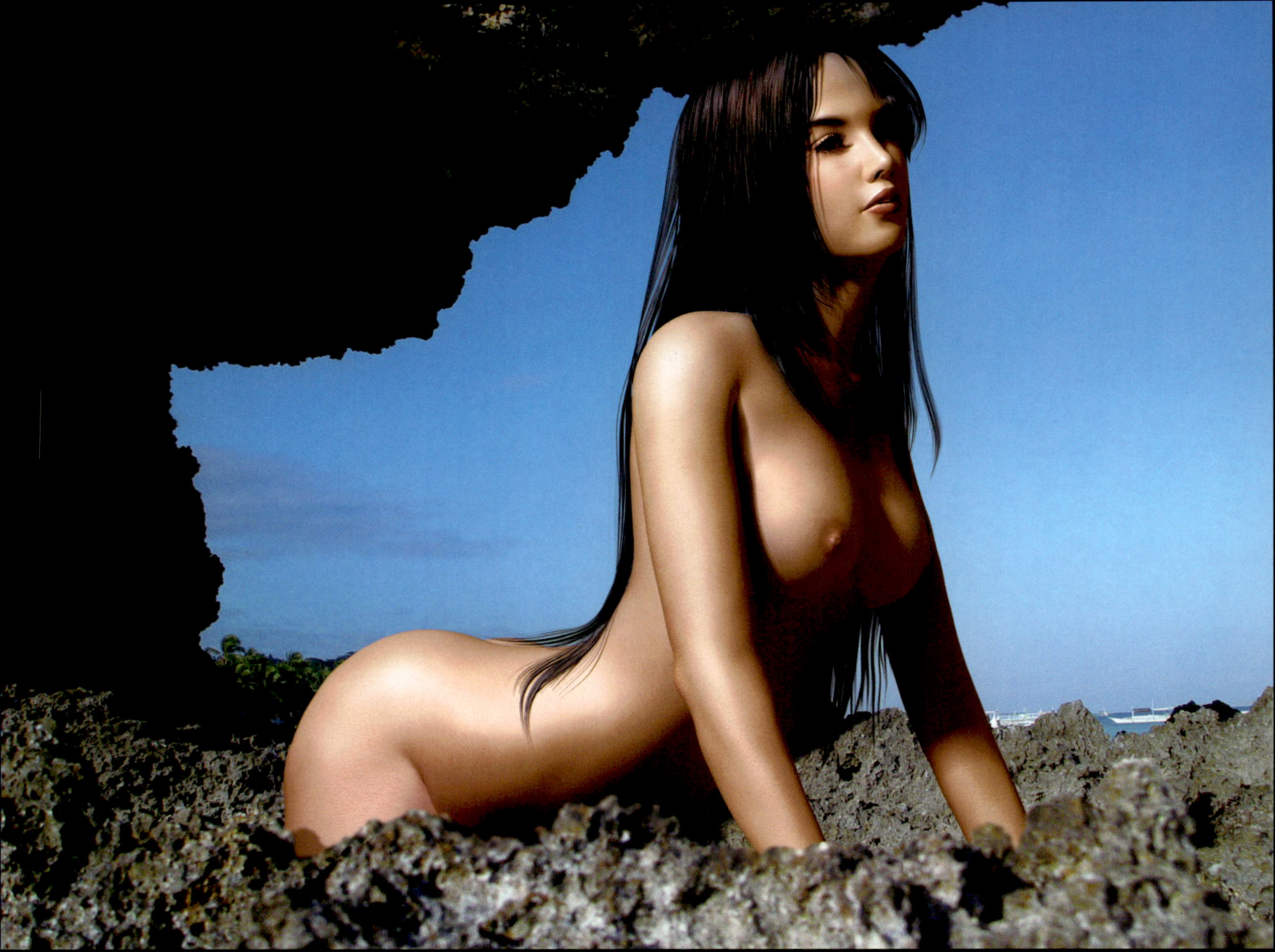

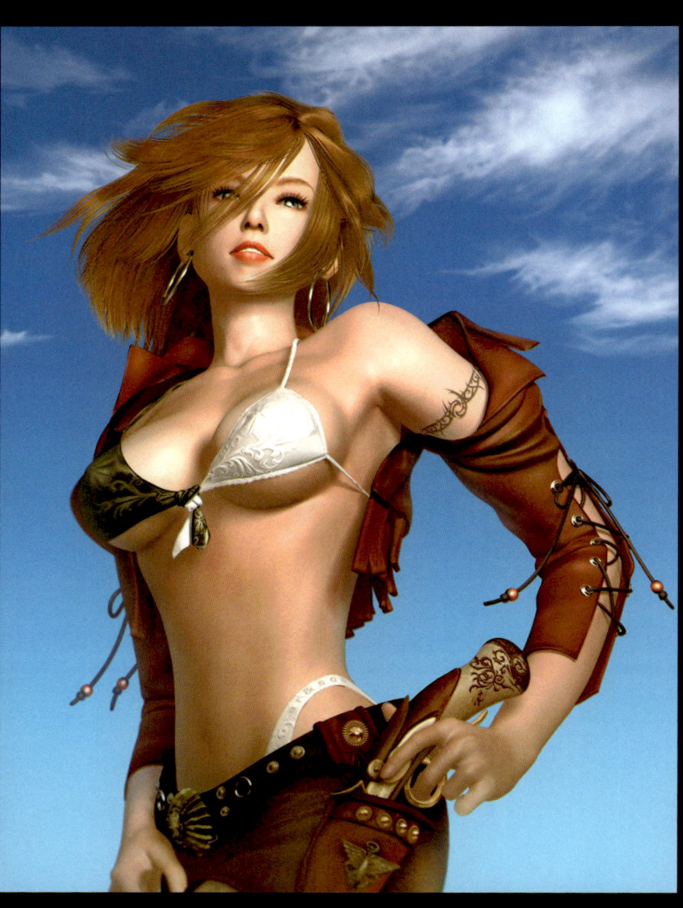

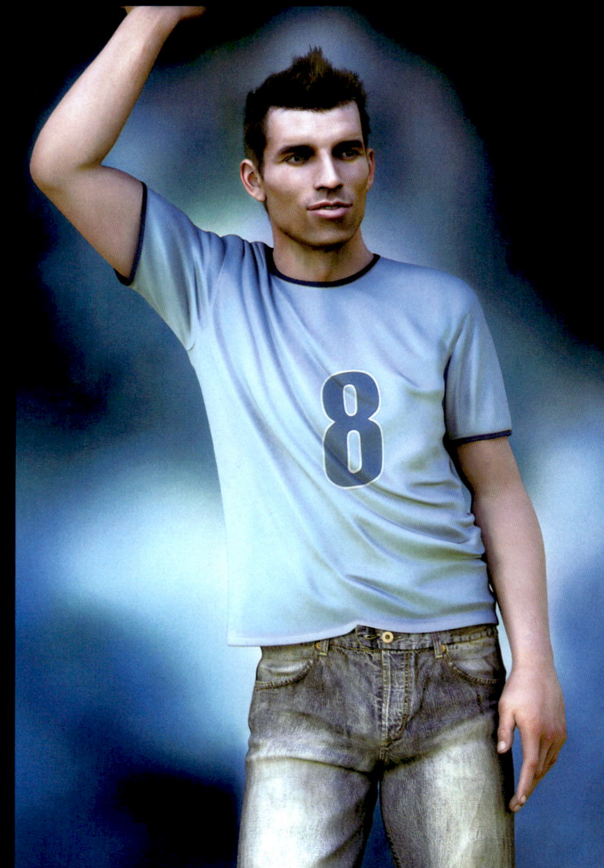

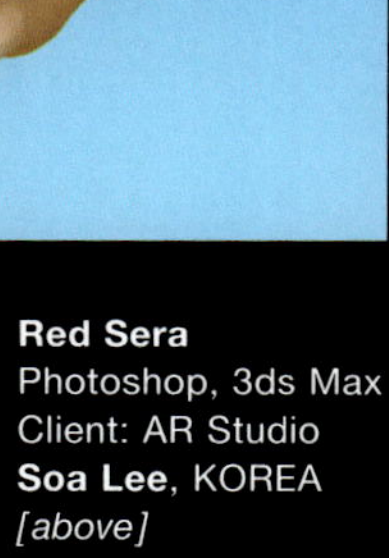

Borocay Venus
3ds Max, Photoshop
Soa Lee,
KOREA
[top]

Red Sera
Photoshop, 3ds Max
Client: AR Studio
Soa Lee, KOREA
[above]

Luke
3ds Max
Jiri Adamec,
CZECH REPUBLIC
[above]

Mamegal 2004
3ds Max, Character Studio,
Brazil r/s, Shag Hair
Koji Yamagami, Beans Magic, JAPAN
[right]

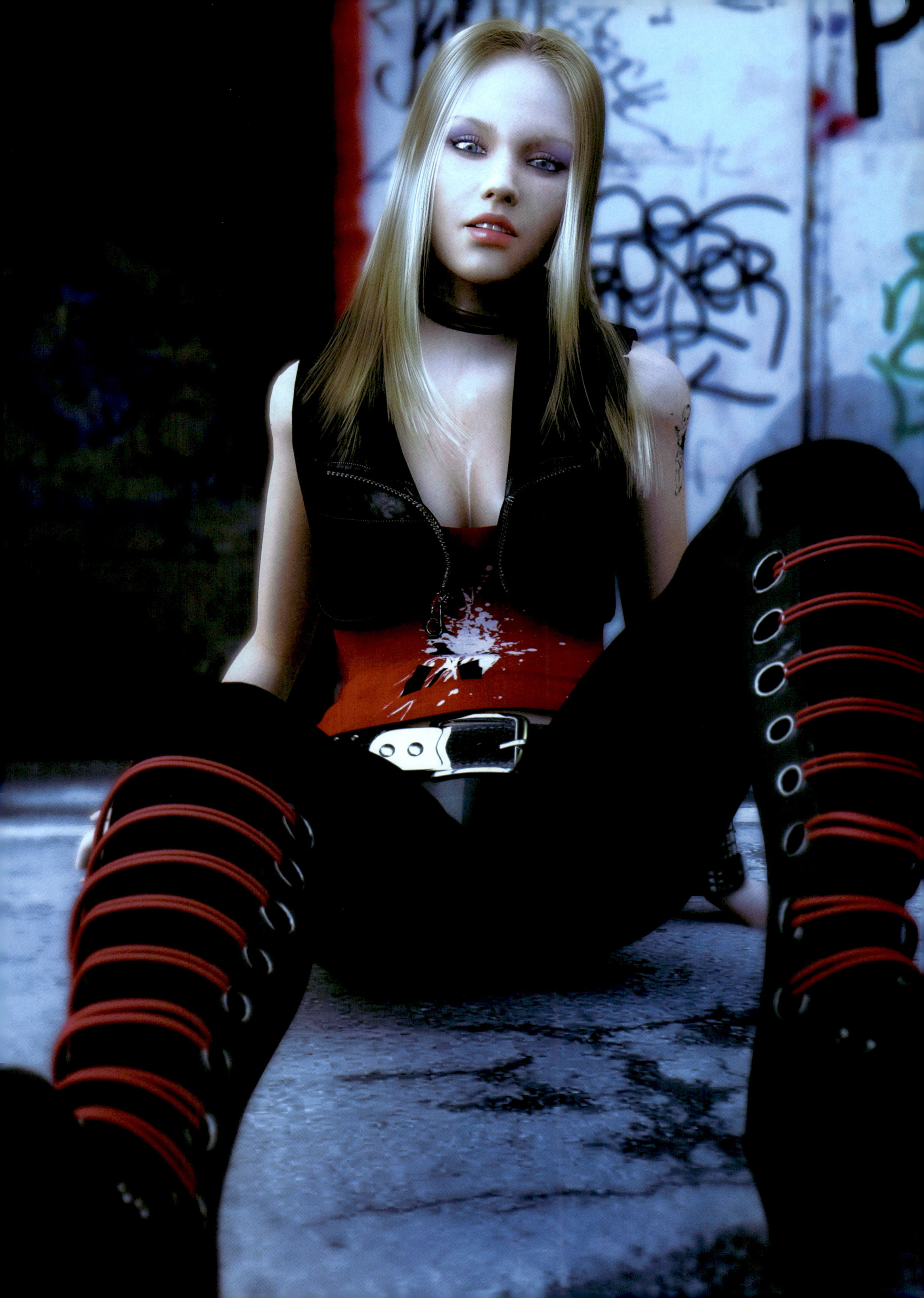

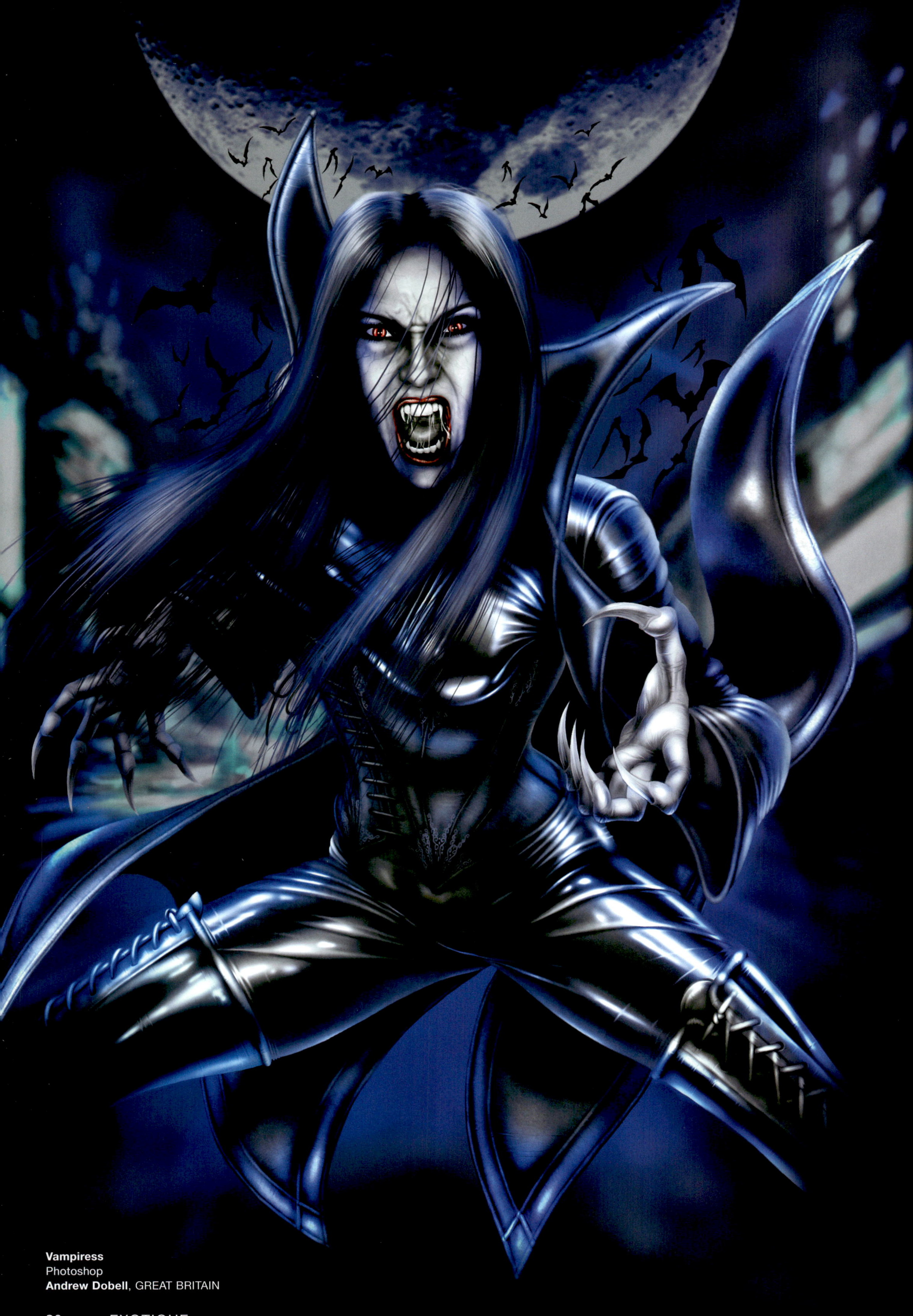

Vampiress
Photoshop
Andrew Dobell, GREAT BRITAIN

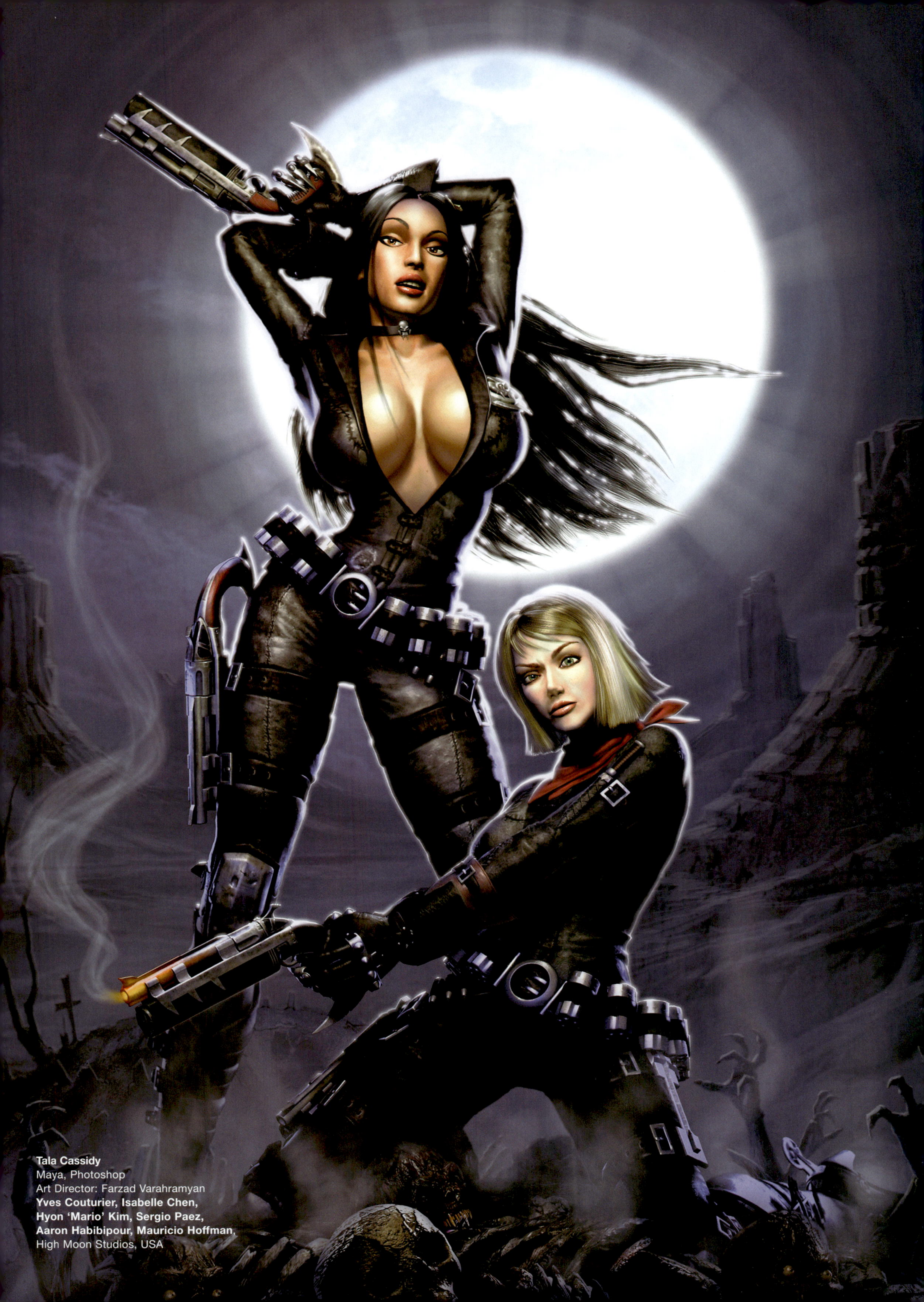

Tala Cassidy
Maya, Photoshop
Art Director: Farzad Varahramyan
Yves Couturier, Isabelle Chen, Hyon 'Mario' Kim, Sergio Paez, Aaron Habibipour, Mauricio Hoffman,
High Moon Studios, USA

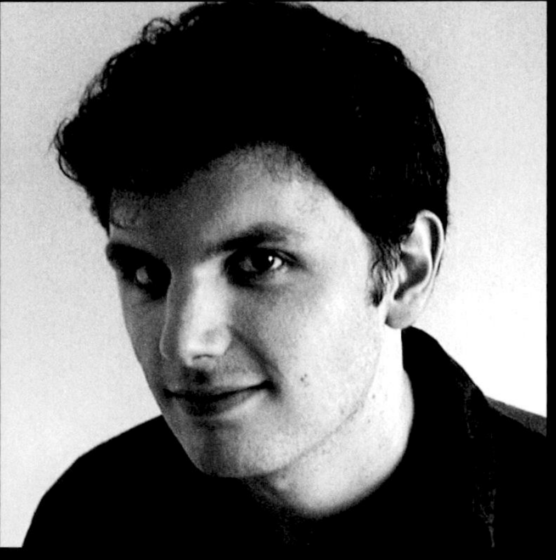

OLIVIER PONSONNET

www.reiv.fr.st
re1v@free.fr

"Everything can be a source of inspiration: somebody I've seen in the street, a TV ad, a movie."

Olivier is a student living in Bordeaux, France and studying programming (medical imagery) at Bordeaux University. "CG is my passion," he admits. "I don't study CG or even arts. I'm totally self-taught. I've learned everything in books and on the net. I always work freely, without methods or deadlines. I try several methods until I get something interesting. It's not uncommon to stumble on something completely different from my initial idea. I try to create pictures with personality and style. I attempt to produce pictures that make people feel something, like a mood or a feeling. I also search for aestheticism and beauty through all the female portraits that I create. Beauty is really fascinating, because it's really fragile: a little something can make your character beautiful. That's what I try to inject into my images. I work with 3ds Max for modeling, shading, lighting and rendering. For post-production and painting maps, I use Photoshop with a graphic tablet."

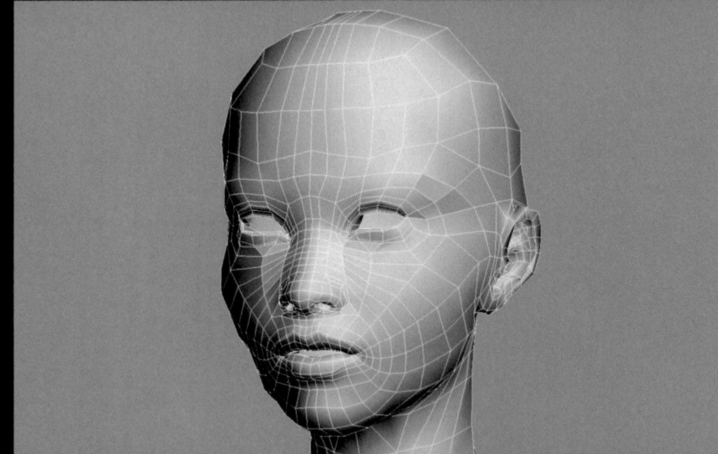

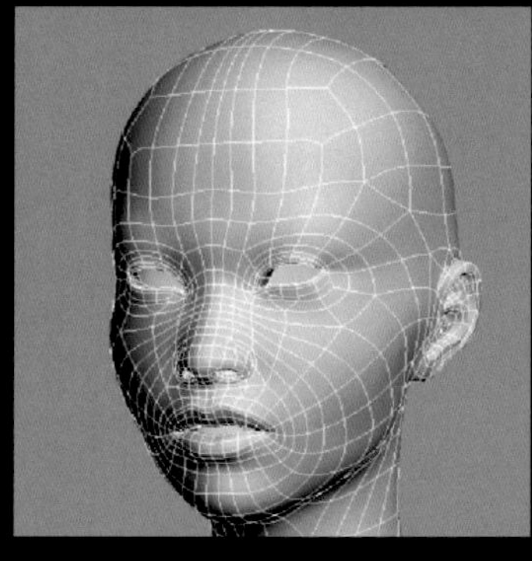

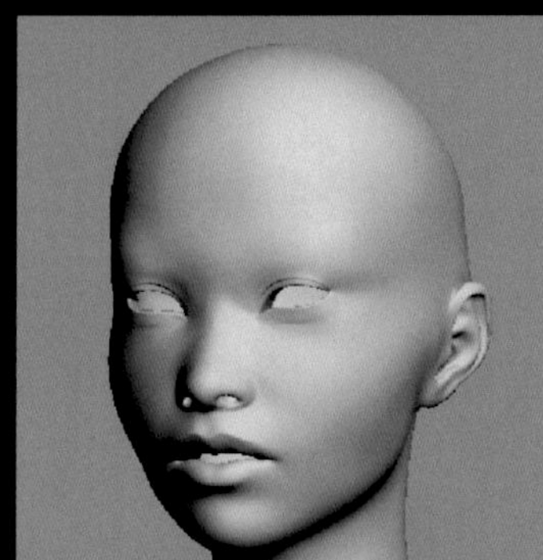

MODELING

I'm not a big fan of box modelling. I hate to start with a box and then add details until I get what I want. I always start from a simple quad. I then extrude its edges to get a rig of quad: this is the start of the character's eye. With a few more edges cuts and extrusions I get a correct eye area. Separately I do the same thing with the mouth area and then connect the two zones. I model the nose, extrude the edges of the bottom of the mouth area to get the chin. I finish the rest of the head, trying to keep a sort of concentric topology around the opened areas. This helps a lot when modifying the character's expression. I separately model the ears with the same technique (quad plus edges cuts and extrusions), and put everything together. I finally apply a meshsmooth modifier to my model.

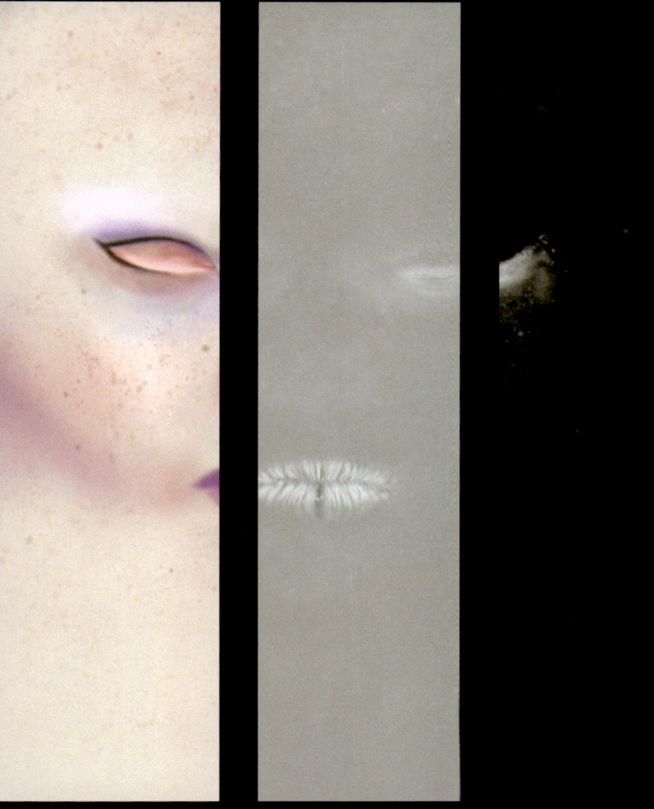

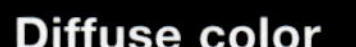

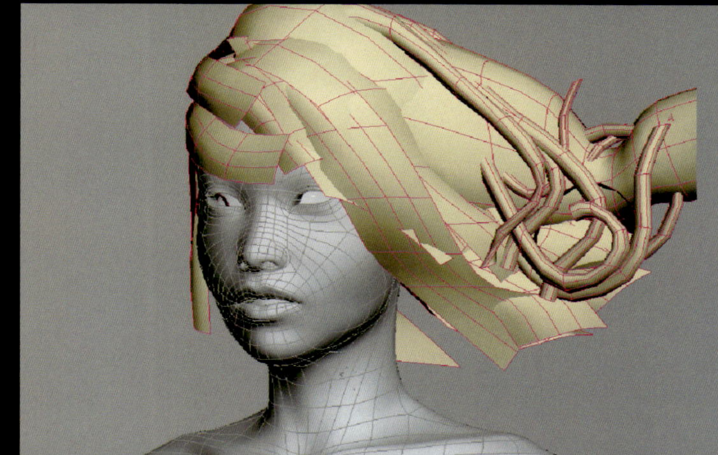

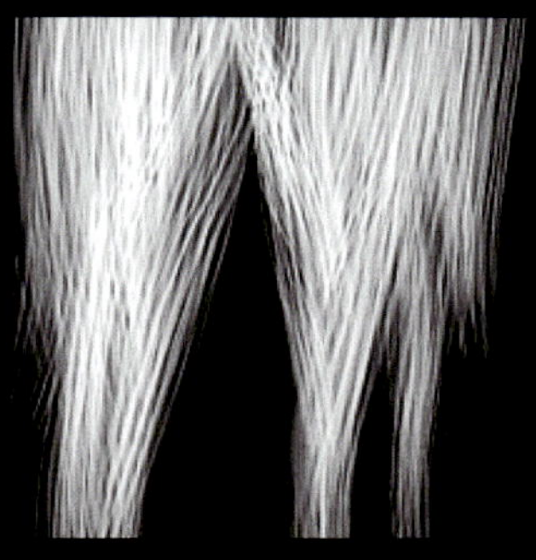

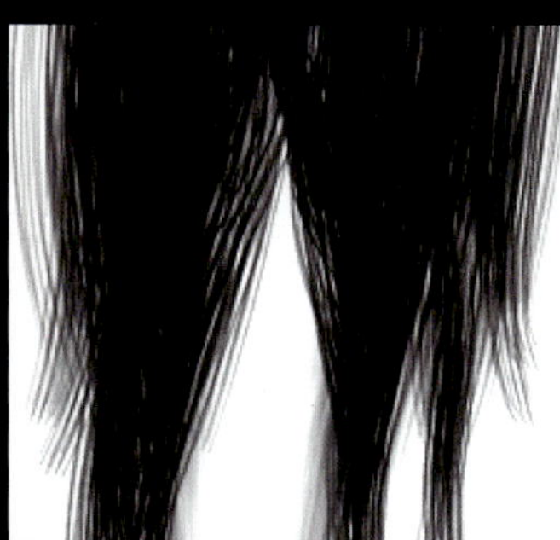

Diffuse color **Bump** **Specular** **Bump and Specular** **Transparency**

MAPPING

The next stage is the mapping. I usually apply a simple cylindrical mapping to the model and if there's too much overlapping I edit the UV coordinates to get something cleaner. The first map I usually paint is the diffuse map. Its global tint obviously depends on the character's ethnicity or suntan, but also on the sort of shader used. I use the mental ray Fast Skin Shader to get the diffuse and soft appearance of skin, and put my diffuse map in the overall diffuse channel. In this case, the skin colors are quite classical, but if you plug it into the unscattered diffuse color channel your map's going to be almost grey. Test both. As you can see the diffuse map is really classical. You just have to add irregularities and spots to get something natural. I use a greyscale version of this map as a base for the diffuse and bump map to create an irregular base. Skin is also slightly reflective, so I use the specular map as a reflection map which makes the skin particularly reflective on the lips and around the eyes and slightly on the rest of the face.

FINAL TOUCHES

The eyes are made of two concentric modified spheres. The inner one has a sub surface scattering material with the diffuse color of the eyes. The second sphere has a water-like material (reflective and fully transparent). I also add a sort of tear line that has the same material. It's a renderable spline placed along the junction of the ocular globe and the lower eyelid. This really gives a nice final touch to the eyes. You can also add a slight bump to its material with a simple noise map to deform the reflections. Eyebrows, eyelashes and hairs are using the same technique. They are basically modified polygonal planes or cylinders with a simple material. I paint a transparency map, and plug it into the transparency channel. Note that the material has an IOR set to 1. I invert this map and use it as a bump map to get some kind of volume effect. I also use it in the specular channel to get specular reflections only on the opaque parts of the mesh. For the hairs, if it's not dark, I also paint a diffuse color map with dark roots and brighter points. I finally set my lighting up generally with one main light and two backlights. I also place big white and self-illuminated boxes (the output value of the diffuse color set higher than 1). These boxes are only visible through reflections in order to get bright reflections, particularly on the lips and eyes.

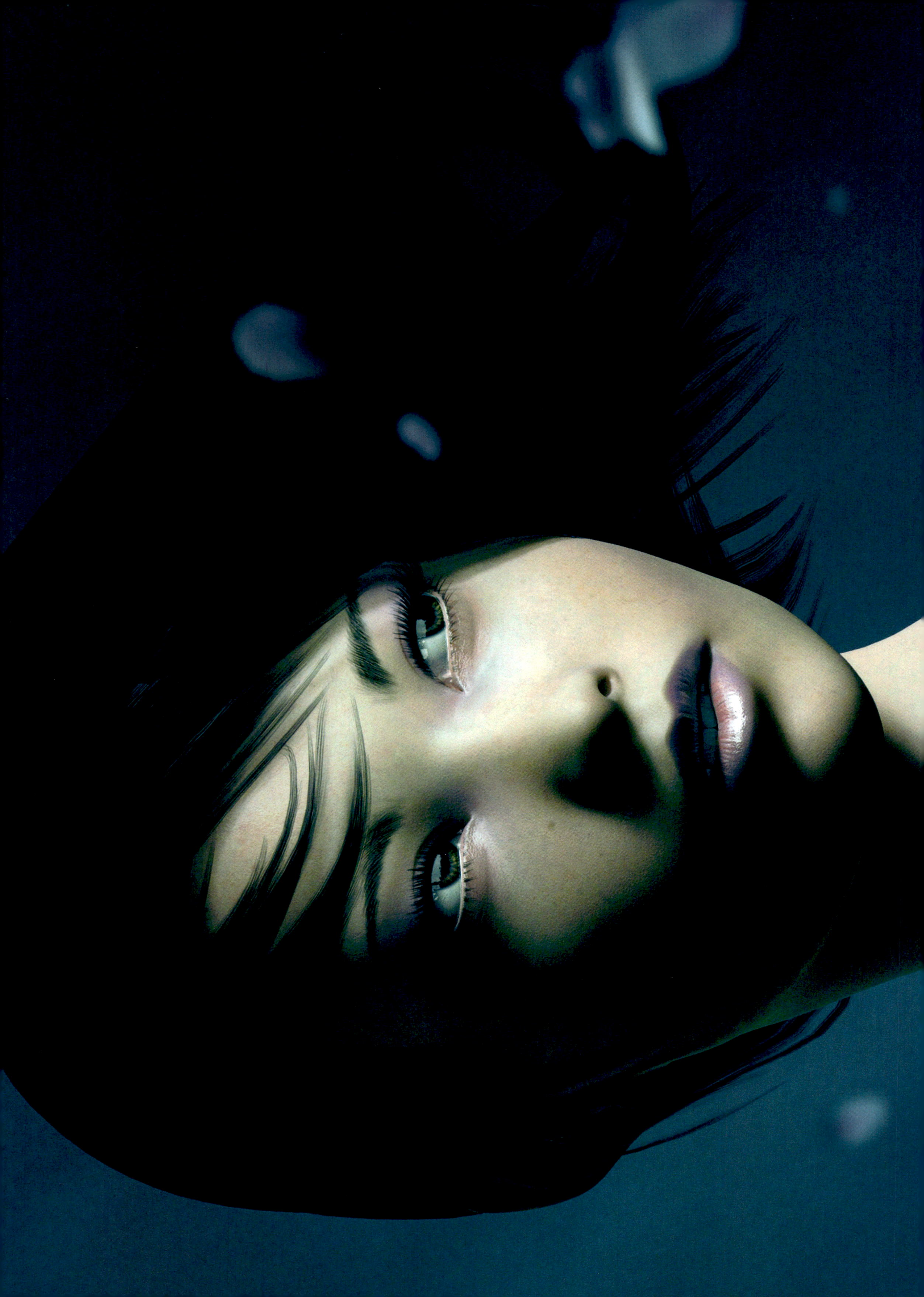

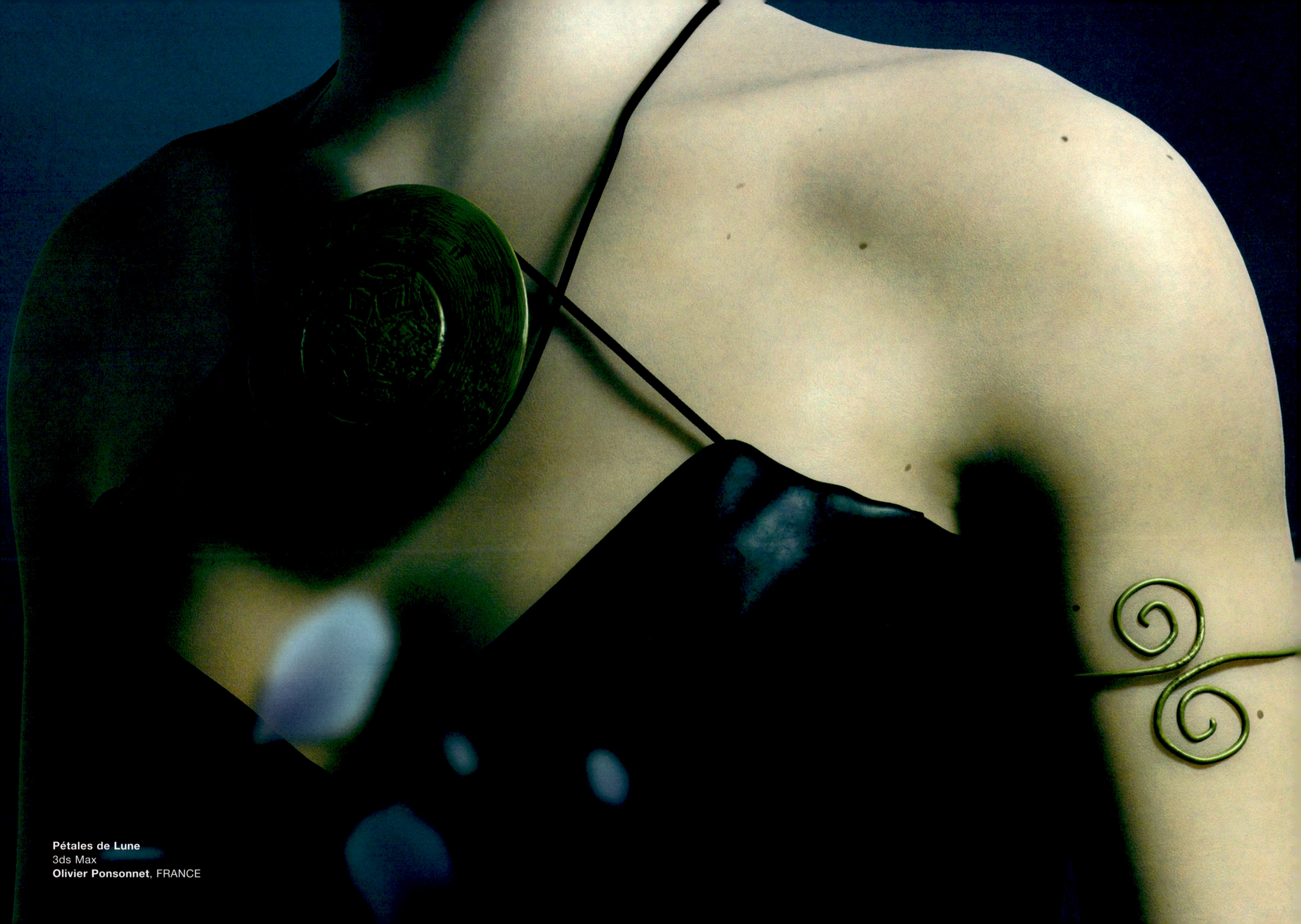

Pétales de Lune
3ds Max
Olivier Ponsonnet, FRANCE

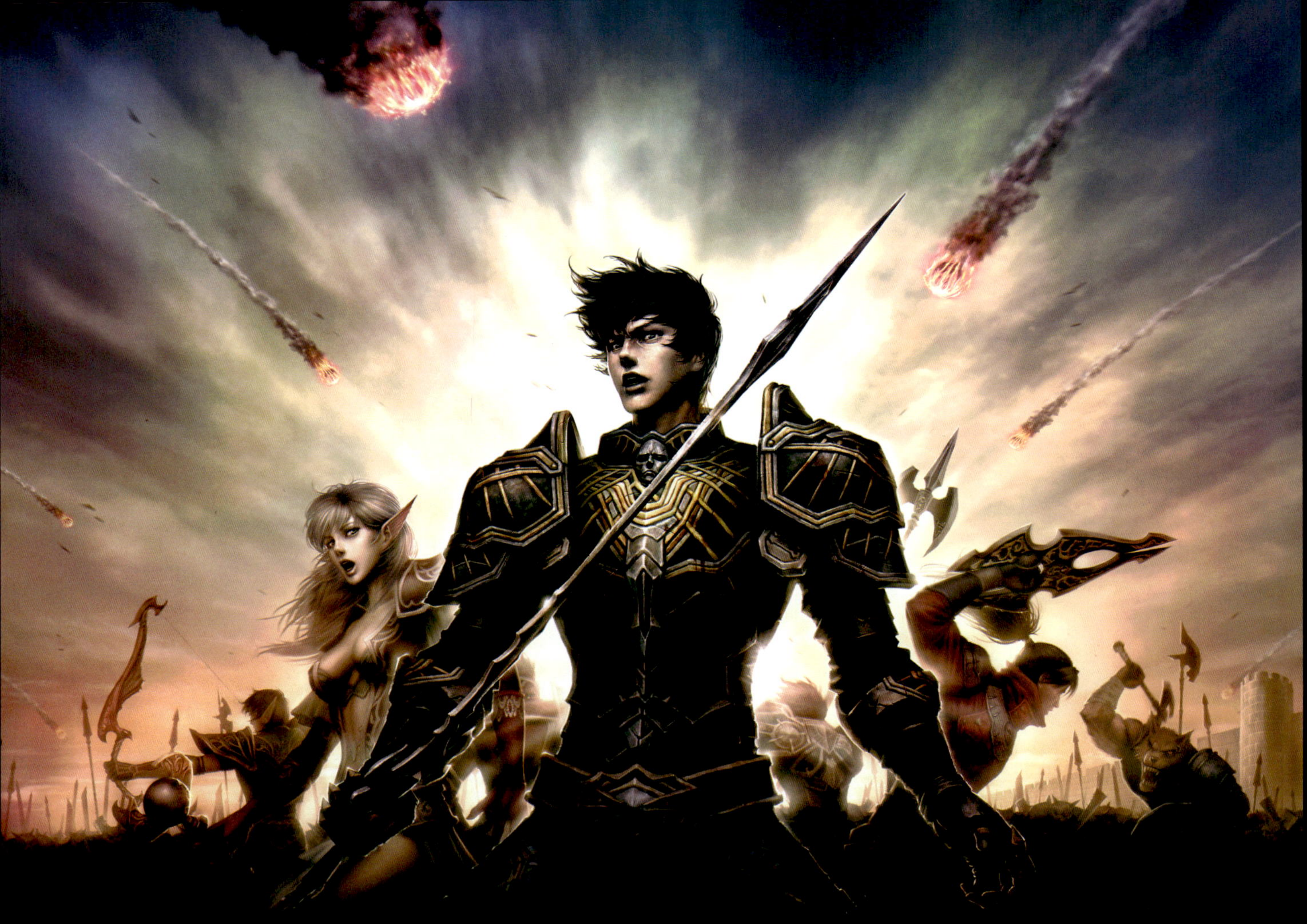

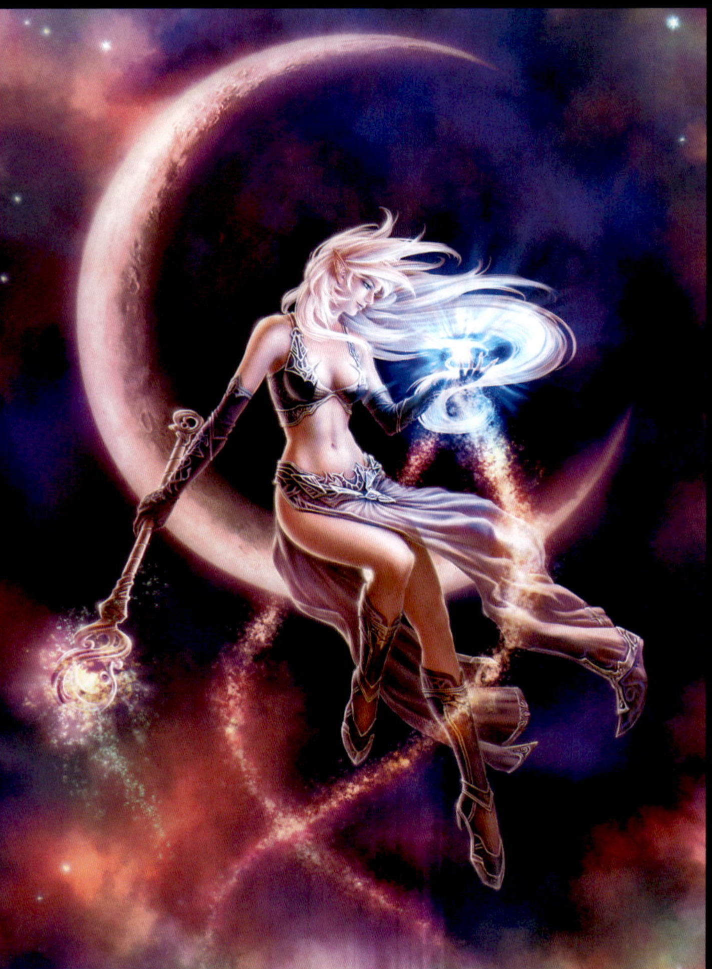

Hope
Photoshop, Painter
Client: Giomind
Cho Kyoung-min, KOREA
[above]

Goddess of moonlight
Photoshop, Painter
Client: Giomind
Cho Kyoung-min, KOREA
[left]

Follow me
Photoshop, Painter
Client: Giomind
Cho Kyoung-min, KOREA
[right]

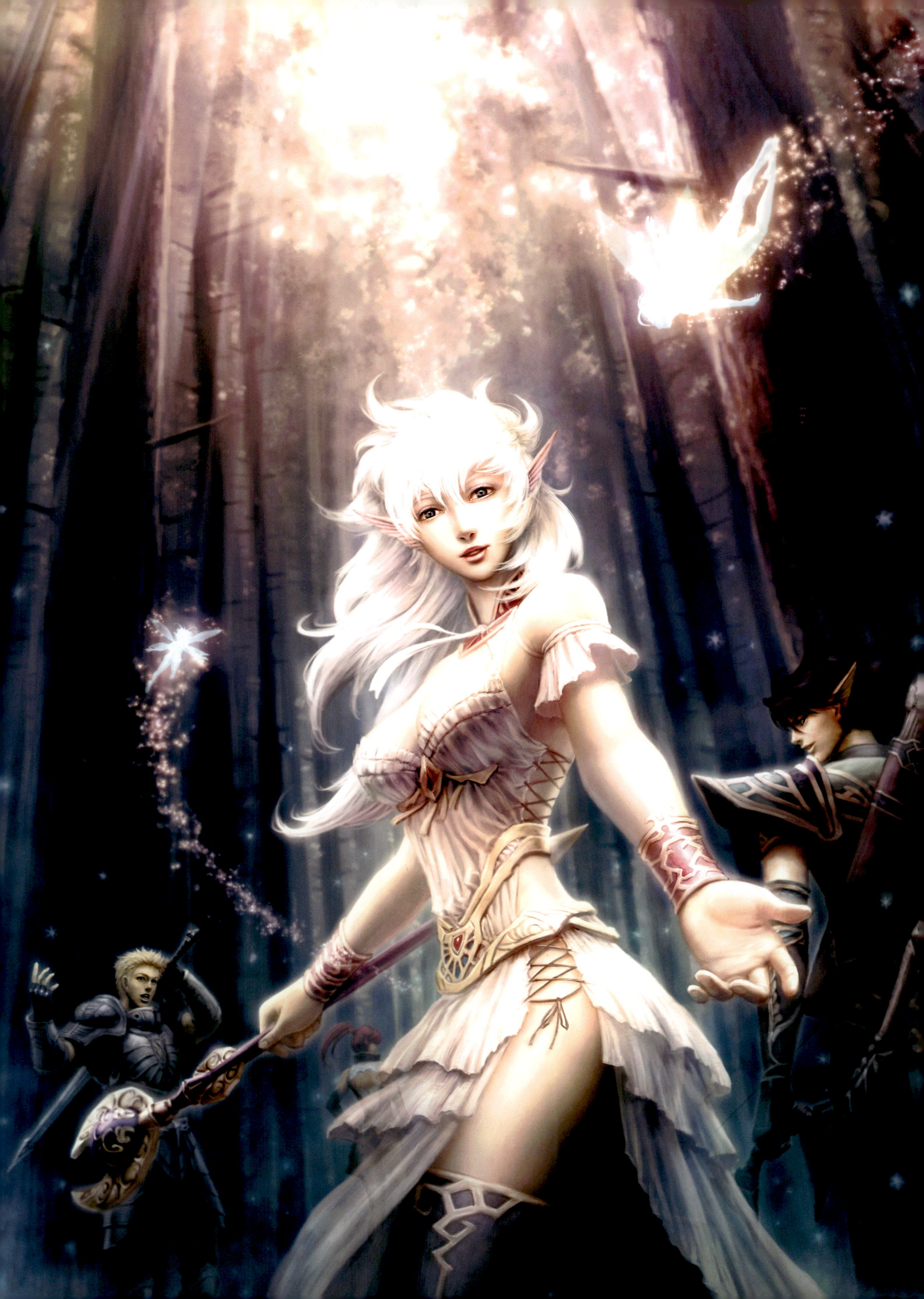

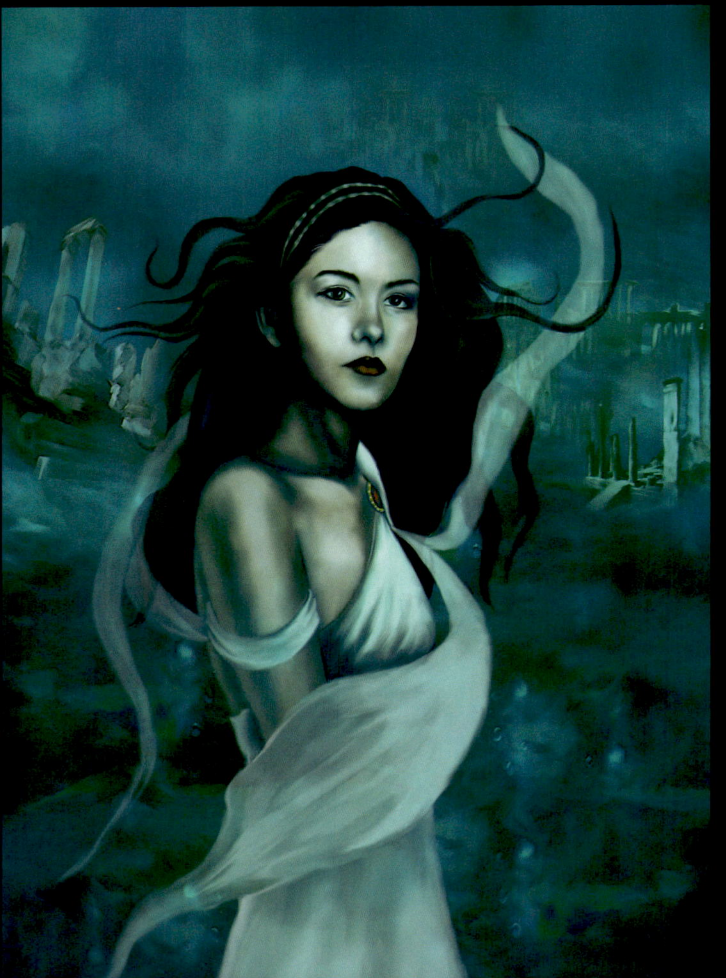

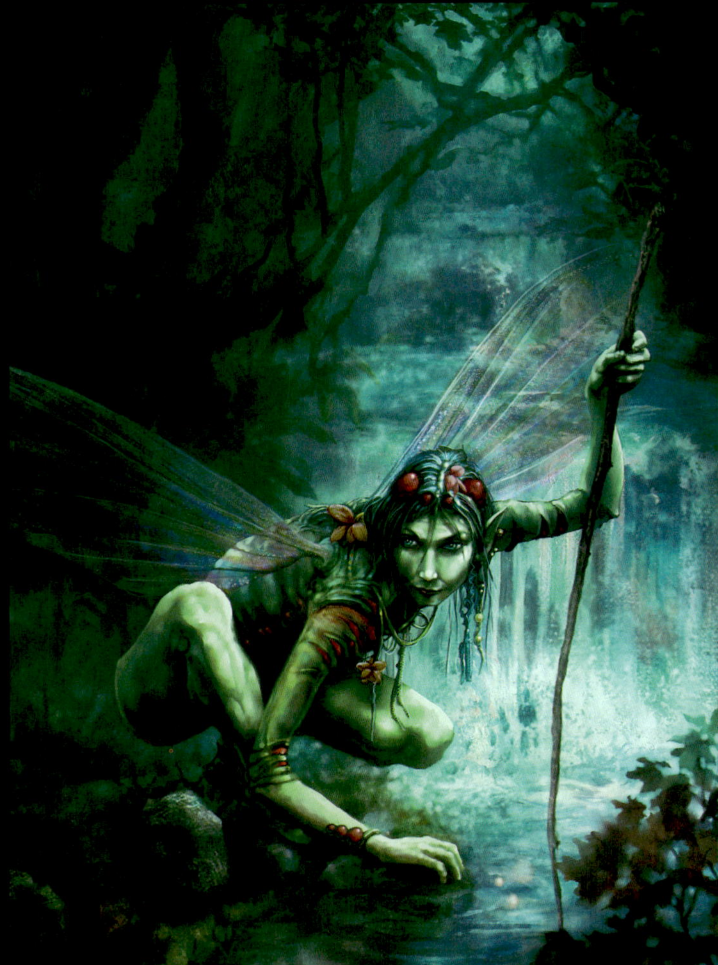

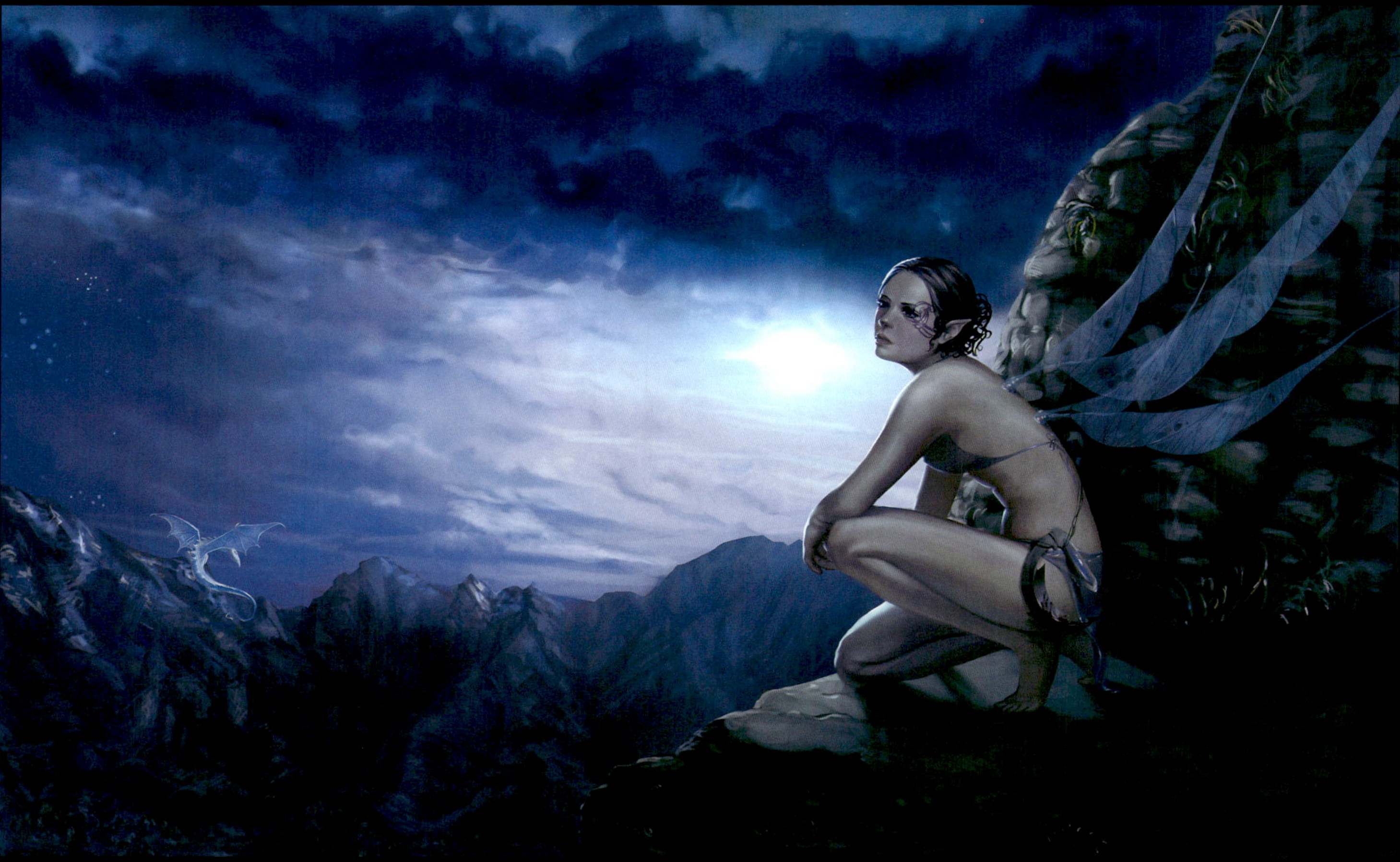

Ghosts of Atlantis
Photoshop
Kelly Carter, USA
[top left]

The Next Prey
Photoshop, Painter
Linda Tso, NEW ZEALAND
[above]

Waterfall Fairy
Photoshop, Painter
Chris Young, GREAT BRITAIN
[top right]

Redemption
Painter, Photoshop
Jason Chan, USA
[right]

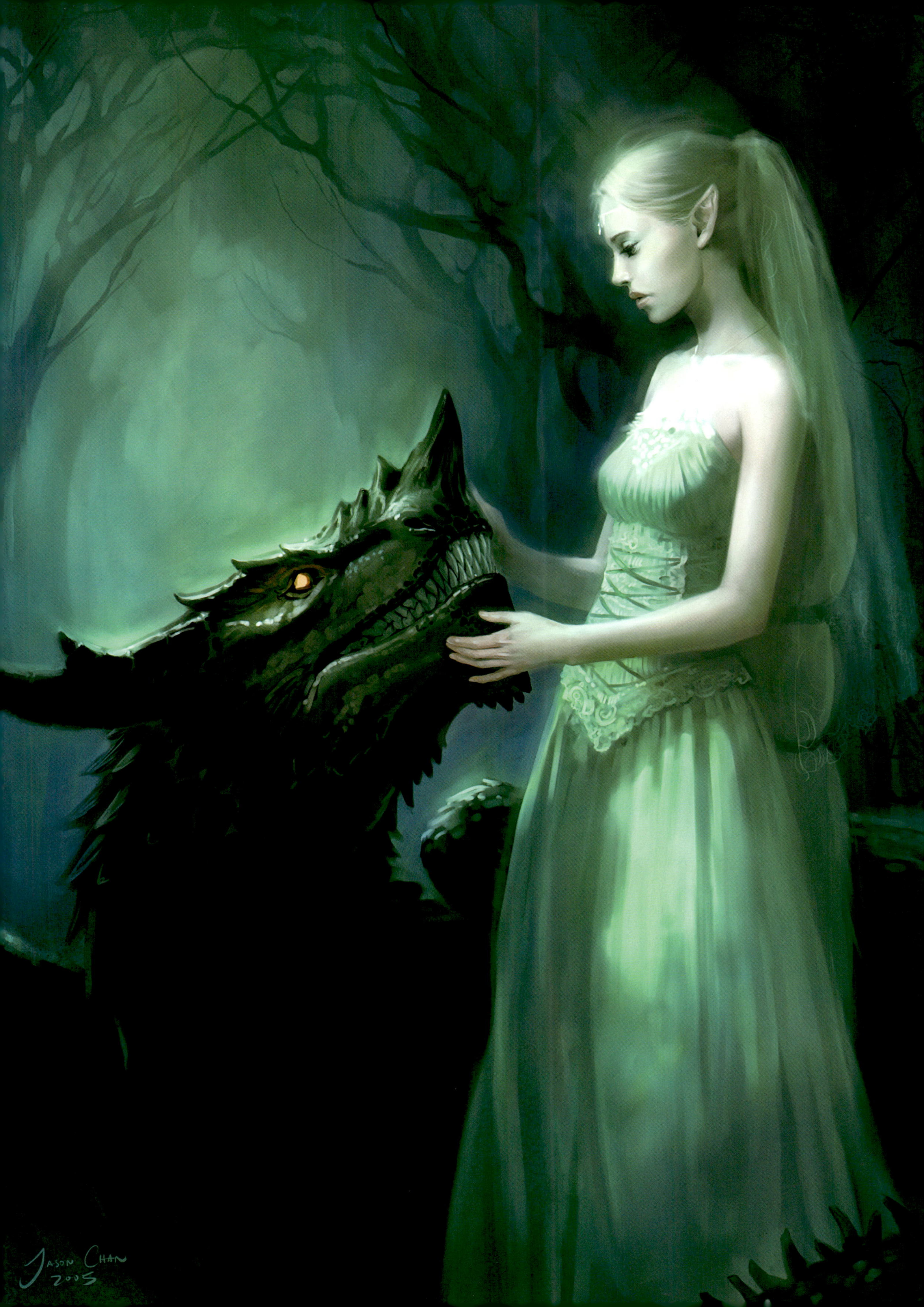
Jason Chan
2005

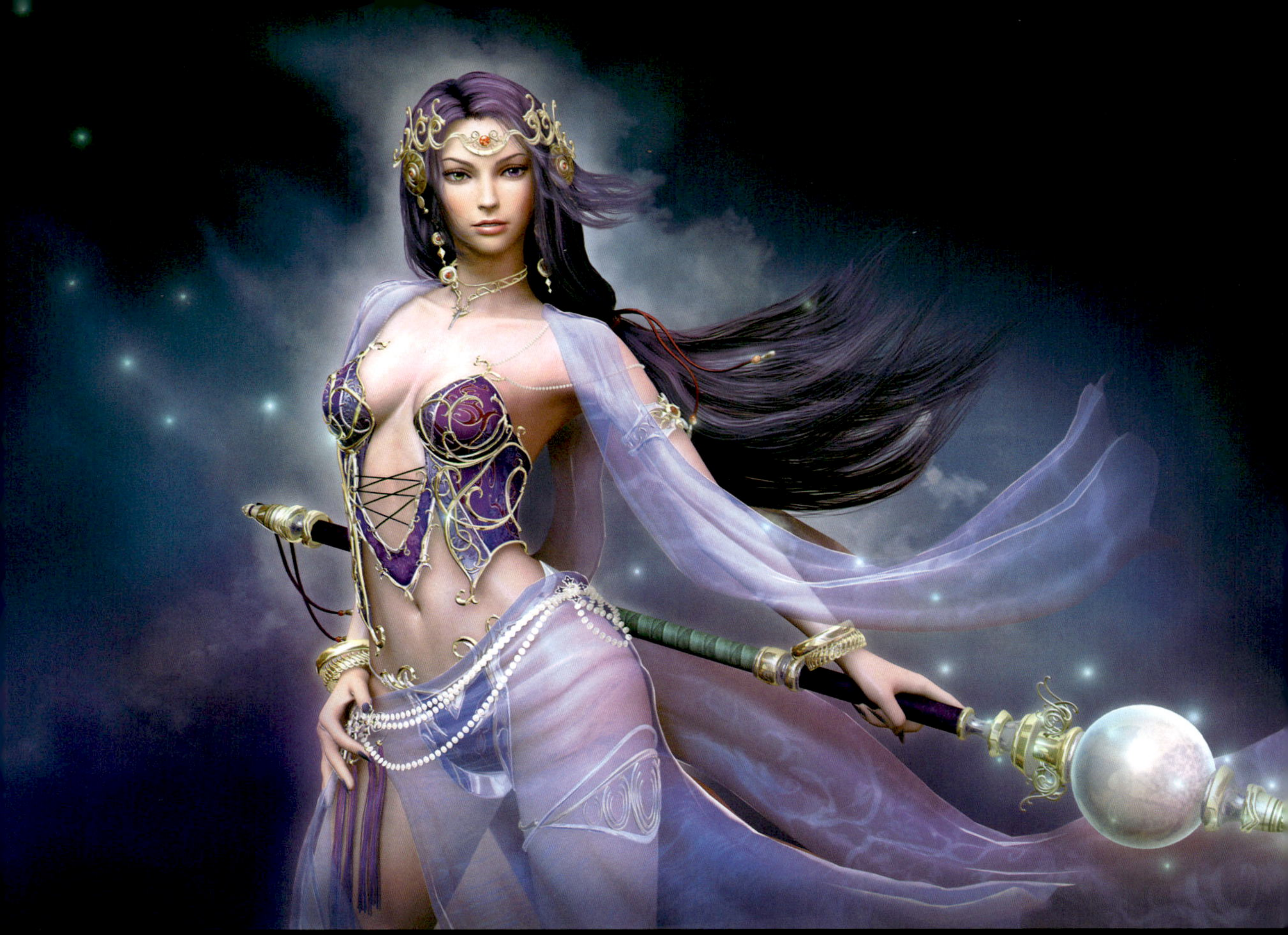

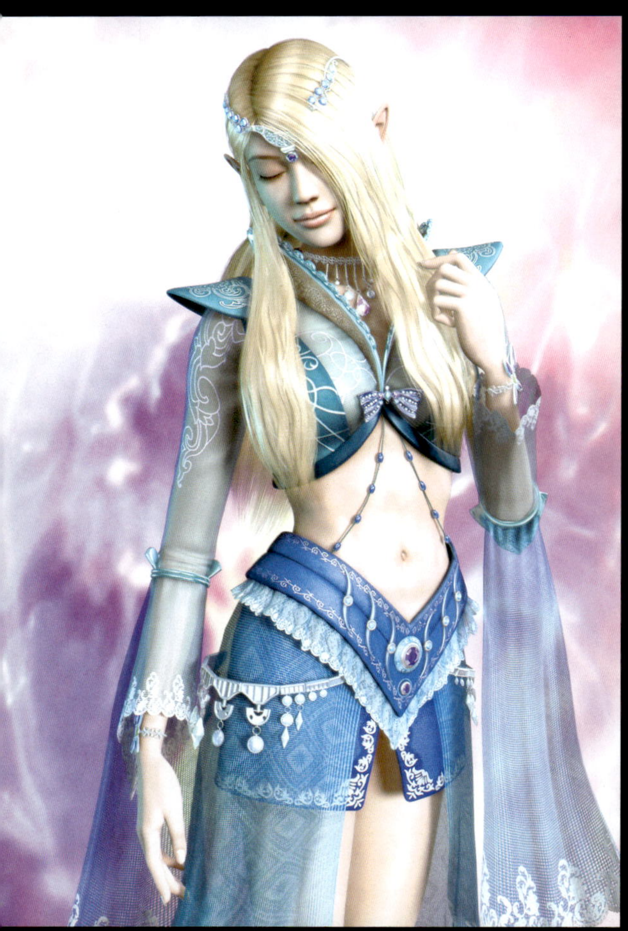

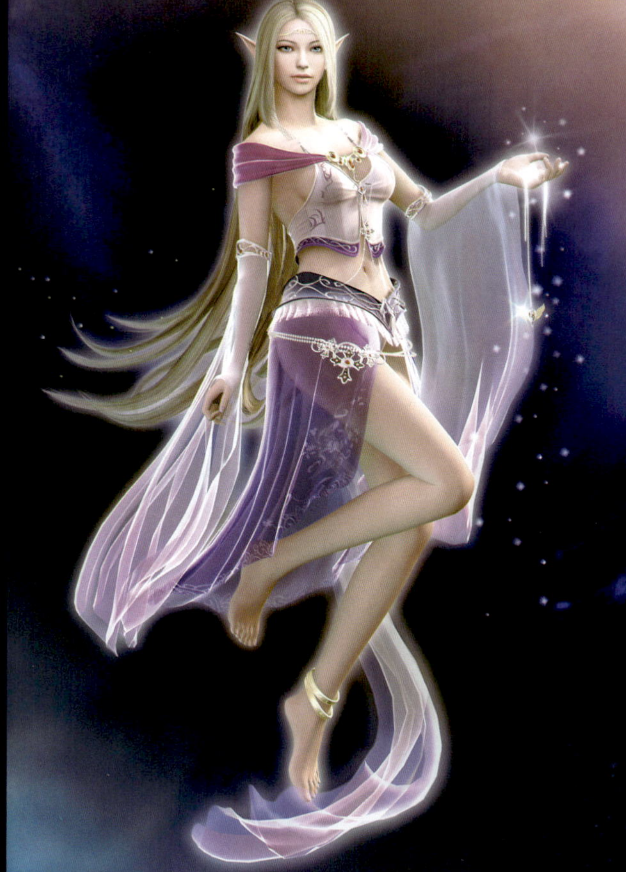

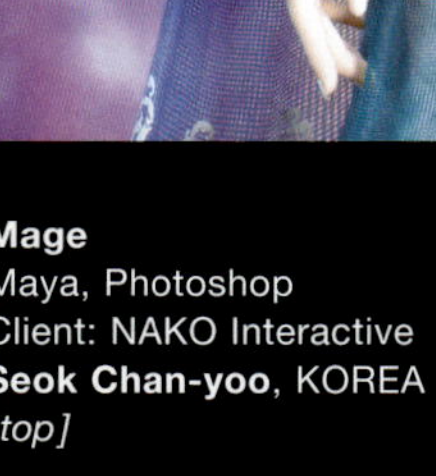

Mage
Maya, Photoshop
Client: NAKO Interactive
Seok Chan-yoo, KOREA
[top]

Elf
Softimage|XSI, Photoshop
Sang Hyun Bang,
KOREA
[above left]

Healer Elf
Maya, Photoshop
Client: NAKO Interactive
Seok Chan-yoo, KOREA
[above right]

Tears
3ds Max, Photoshop
Client: Actoz soft
Soa Lee, KOREA
[right]

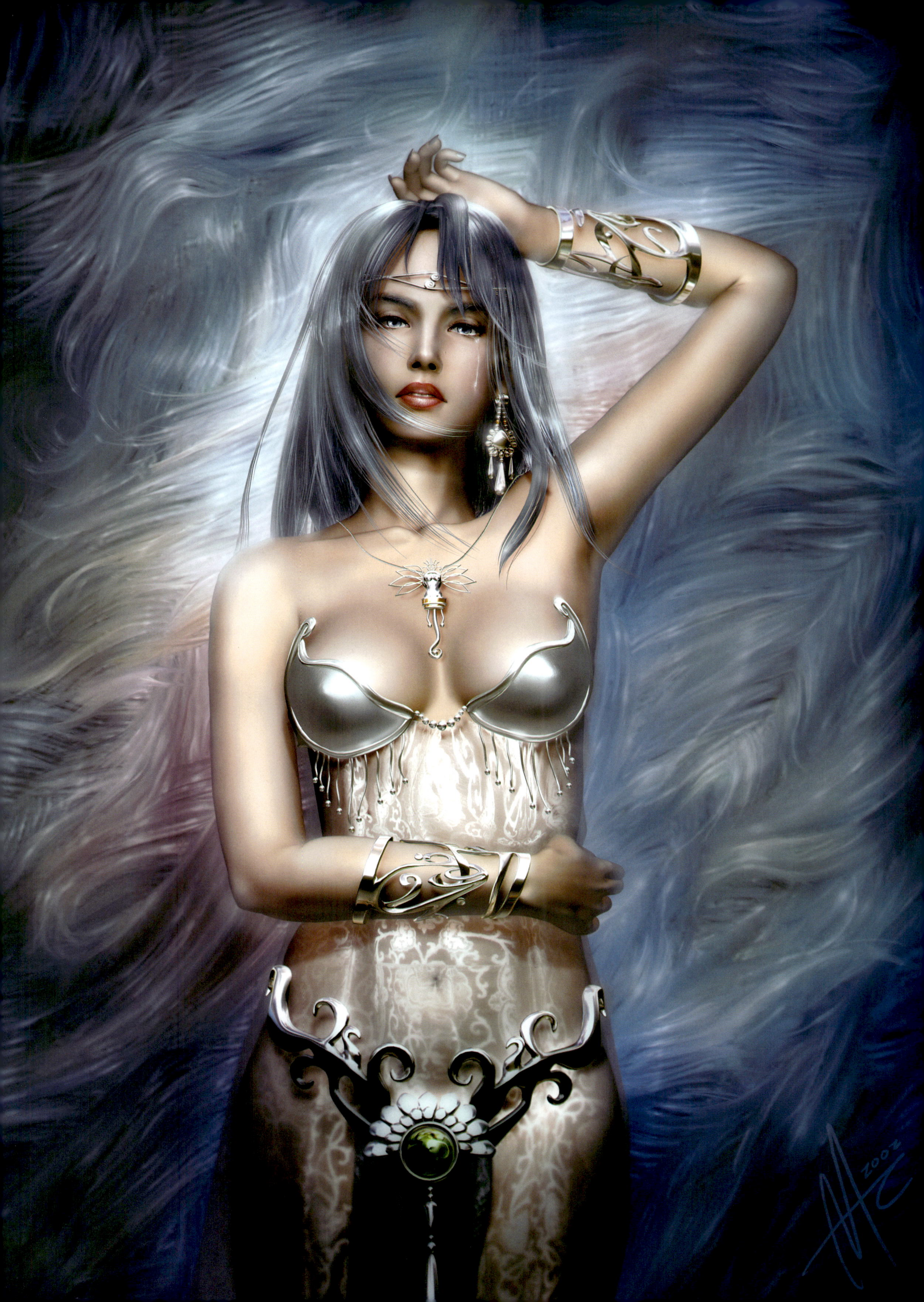
2002

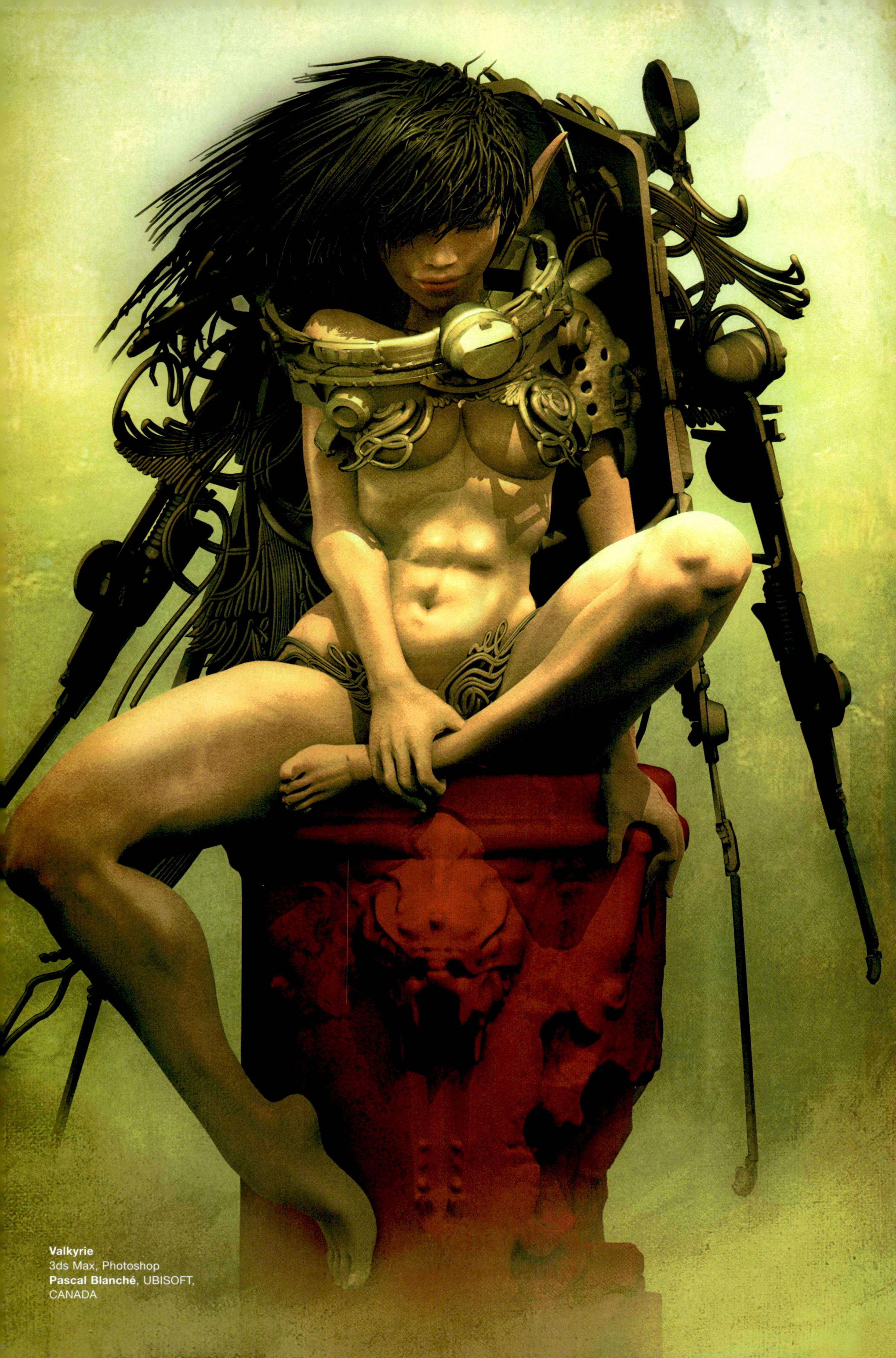

Valkyrie
3ds Max, Photoshop
Pascal Blanché, UBISOFT, CANADA

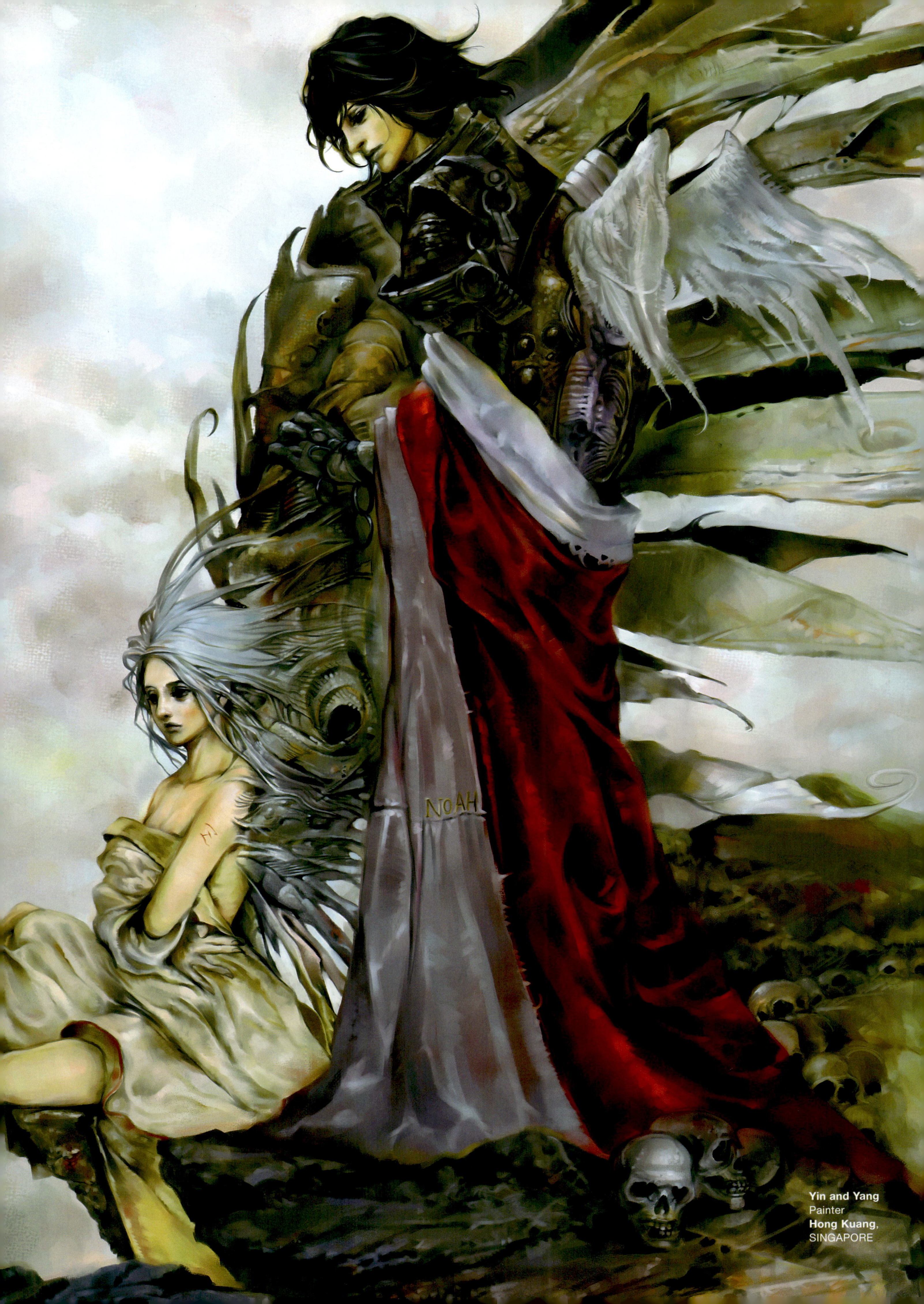

Yin and Yang
Painter
Hong Kuang,
SINGAPORE

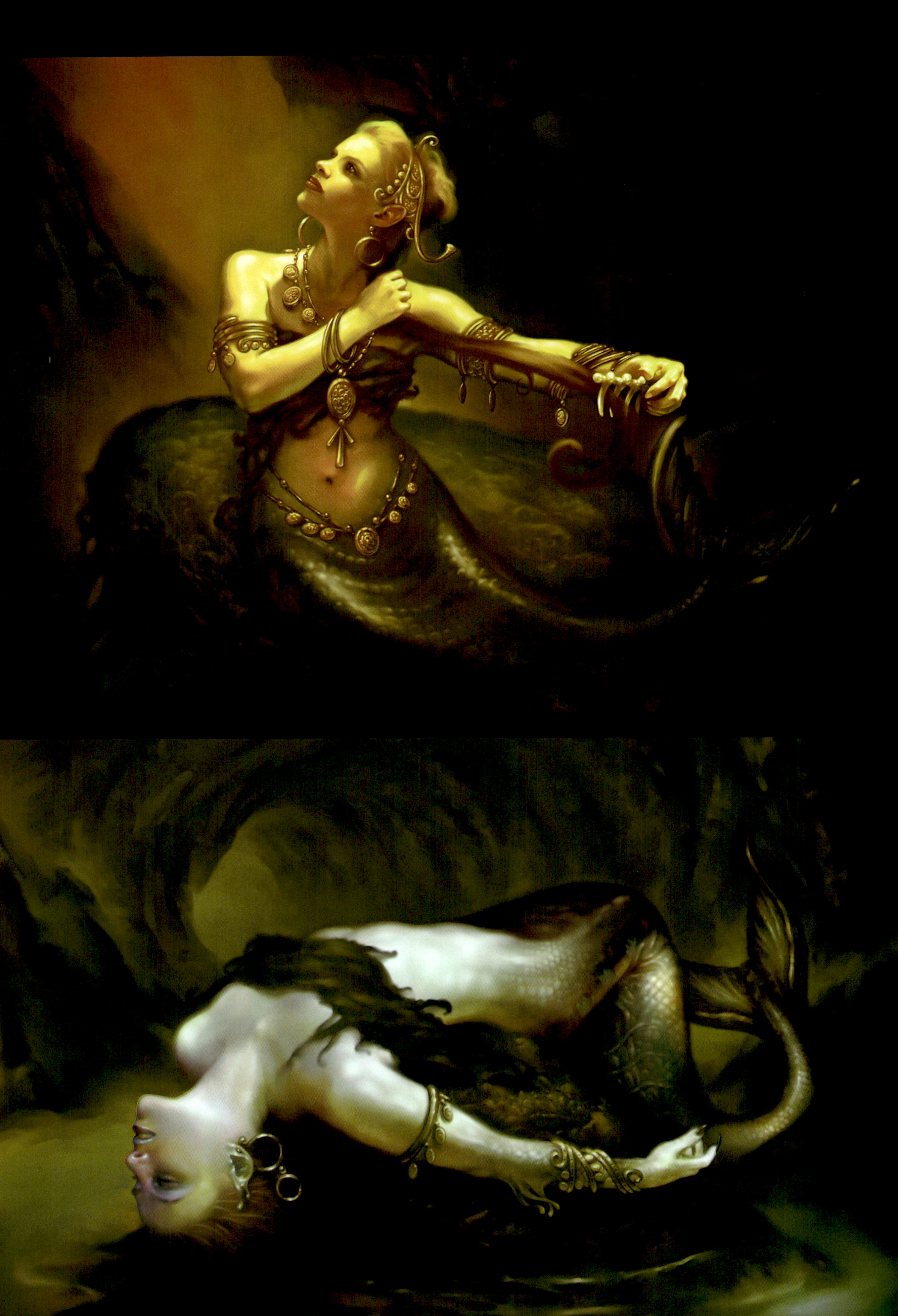

Siren
Painter
Patrick Jones,
AUSTRALIA
[left]

QIN 2
Photoshop,
Painter, ArtRage
Client: le 7éme Crecle
Aleksi Briclot, FRANCE
[right]

Darkdreamer
Painter
Patrick Jones,
AUSTRALIA
[left]

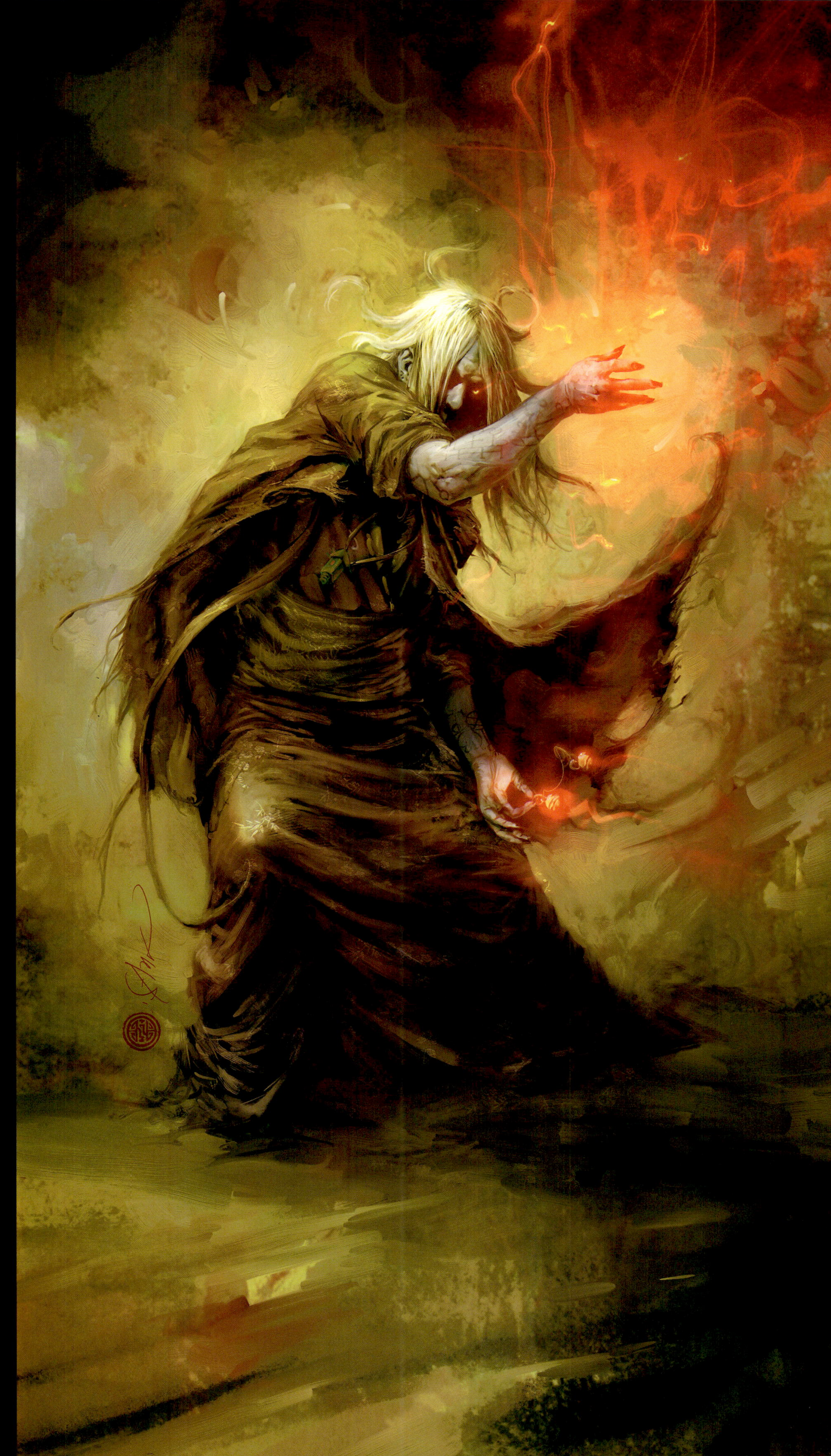

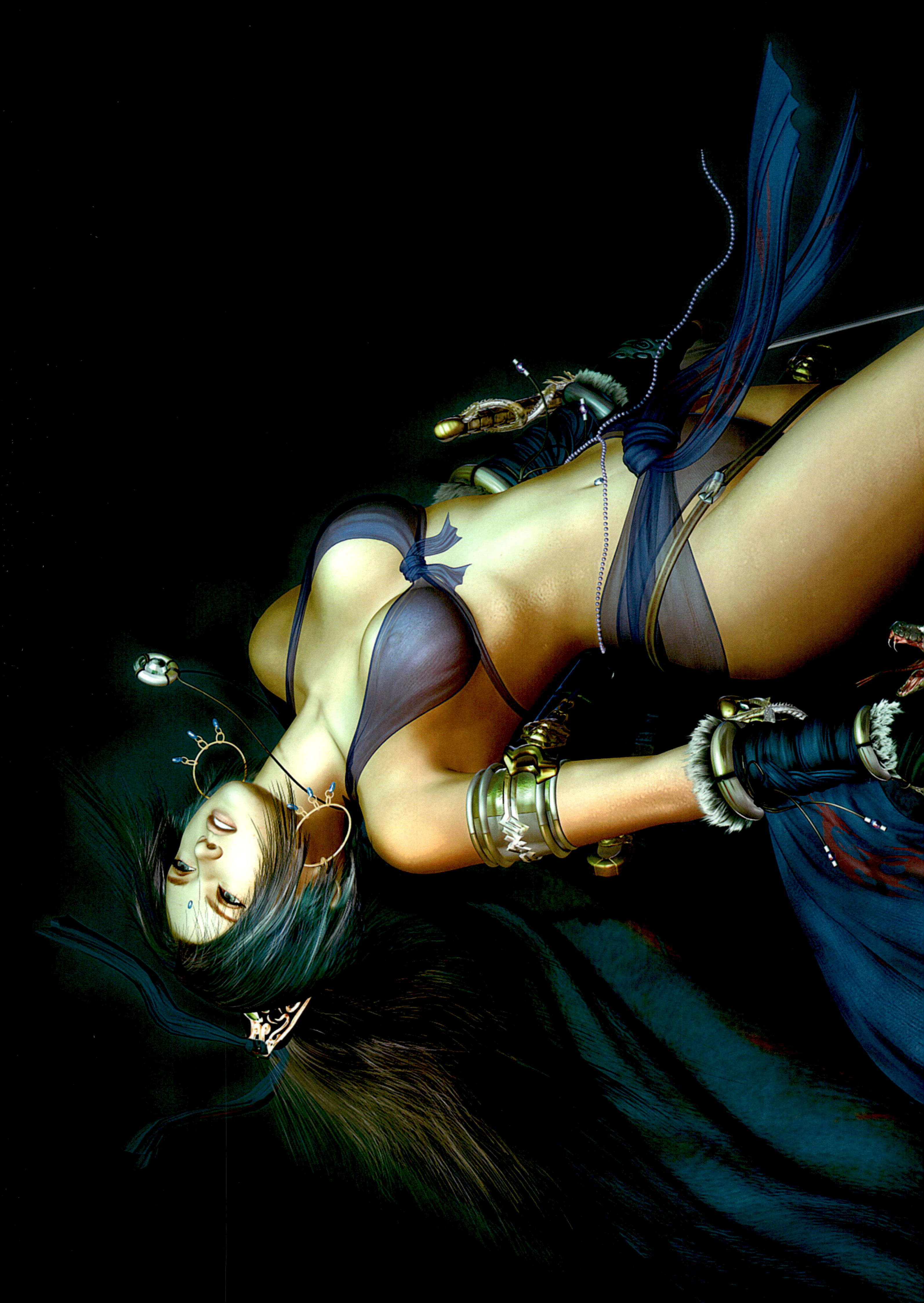

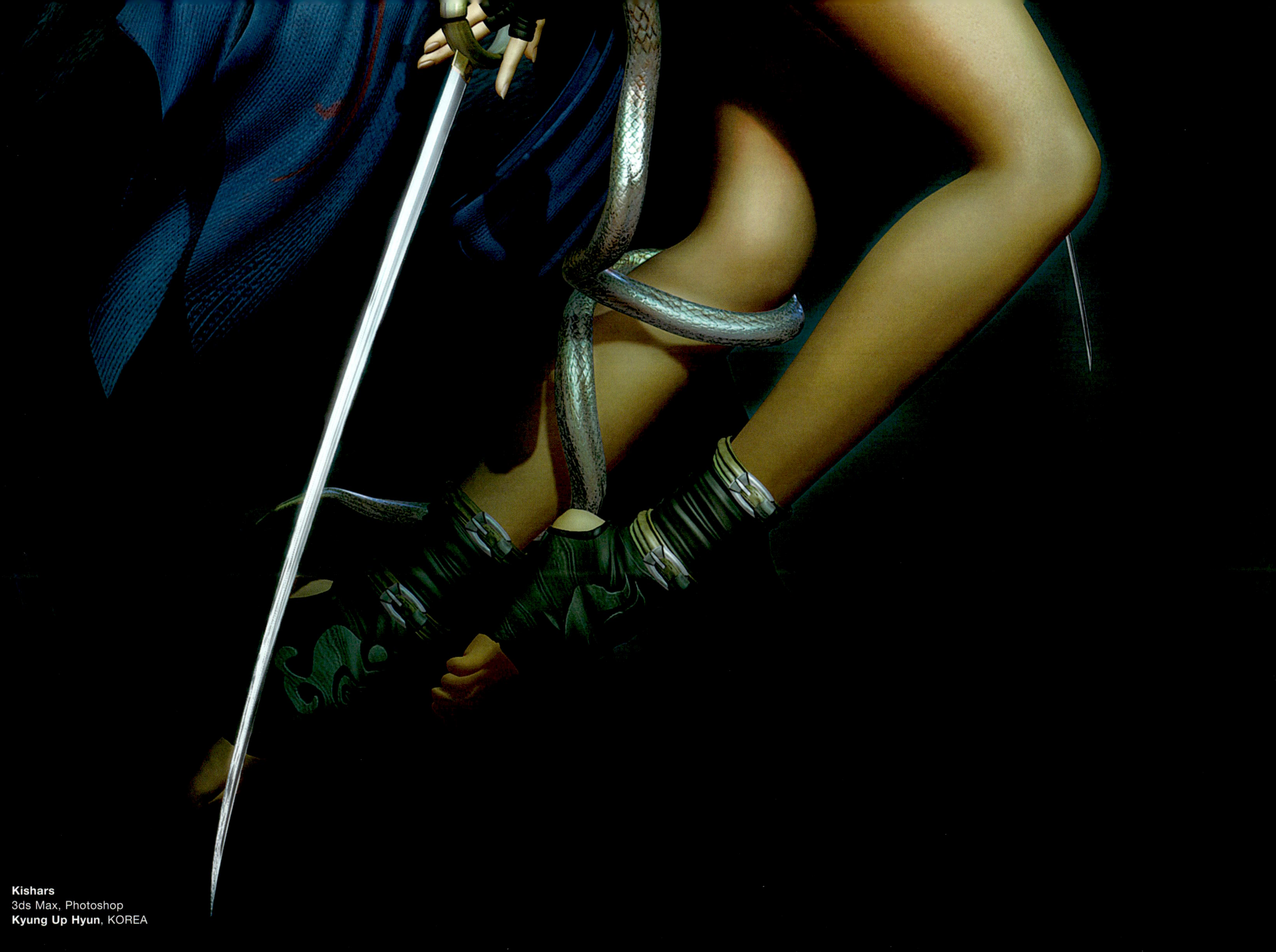

Kishars
3ds Max, Photoshop
Kyung Up Hyun, KOREA

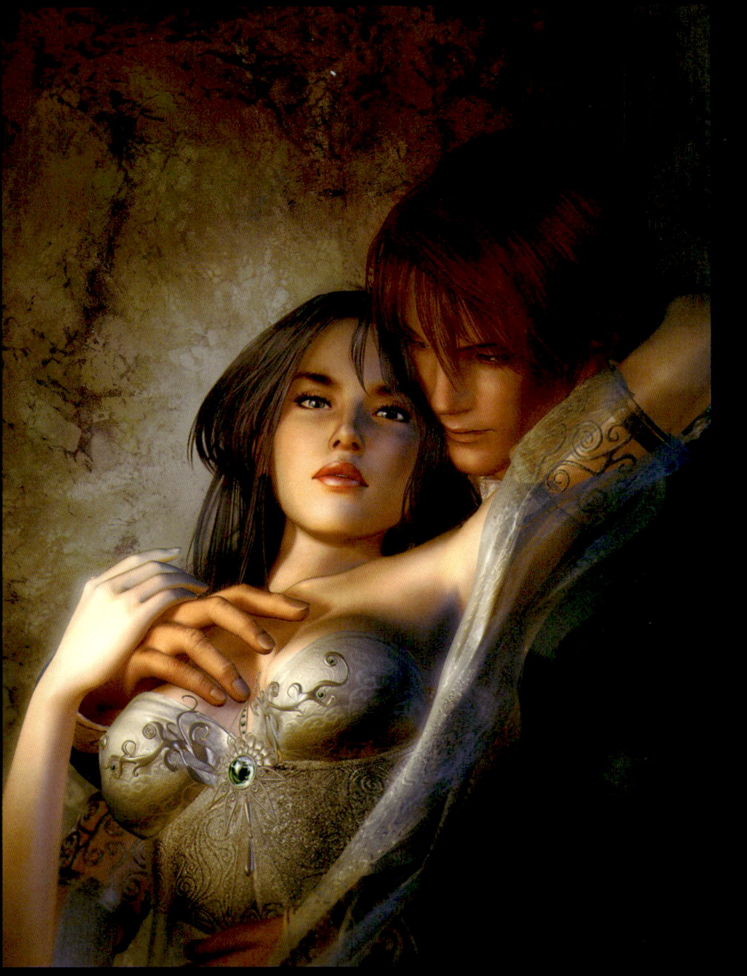

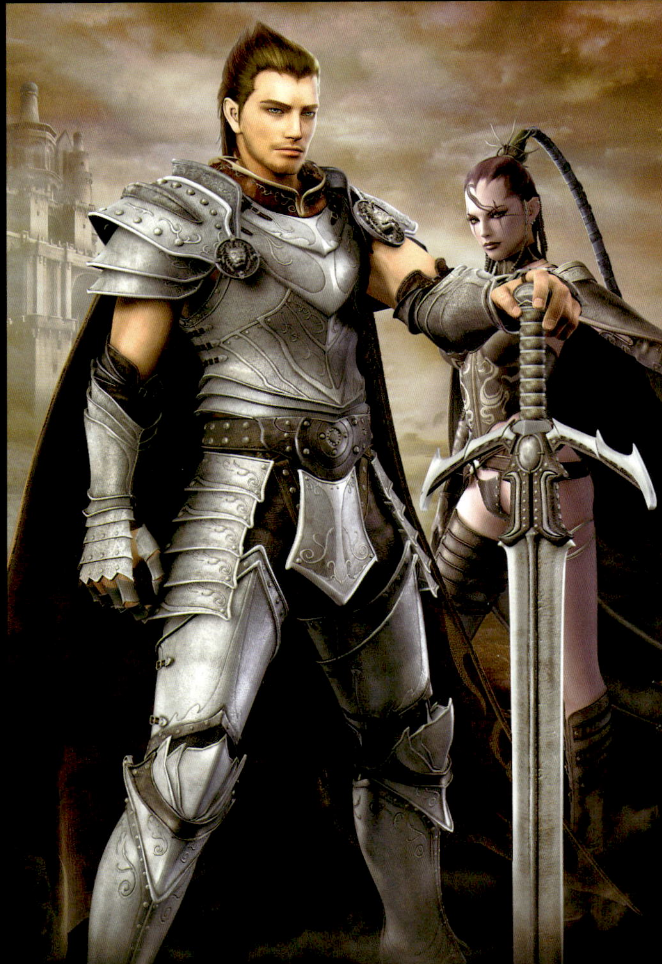

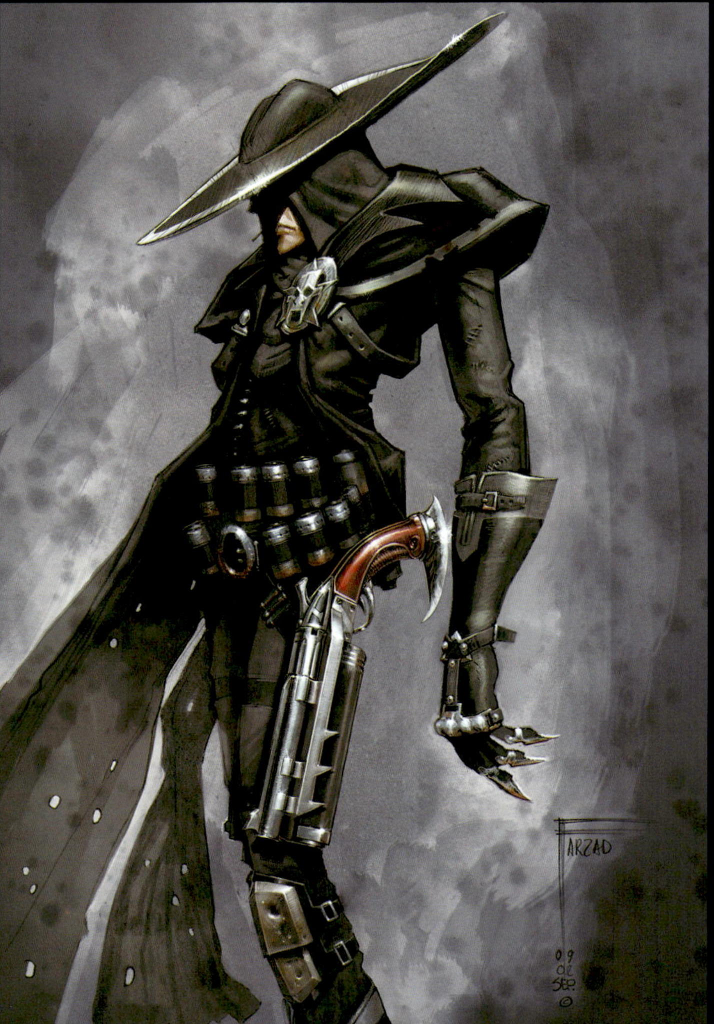

Temptation of Darkness
3ds Max, Photoshop
Soa Lee, KOREA
[above left]

Knight Mage
Maya
Client: NAKO Interactive,
Seok Chan-yoo, KOREA
[above]

Jericho Cross
Photoshop
Farzad Varahramyan,
High Moon Studios, USA
[left]

Enemy of God Cover Art
Photoshop
Client: Phoenix Publishing
Kerem Beyit, TURKEY
[right]

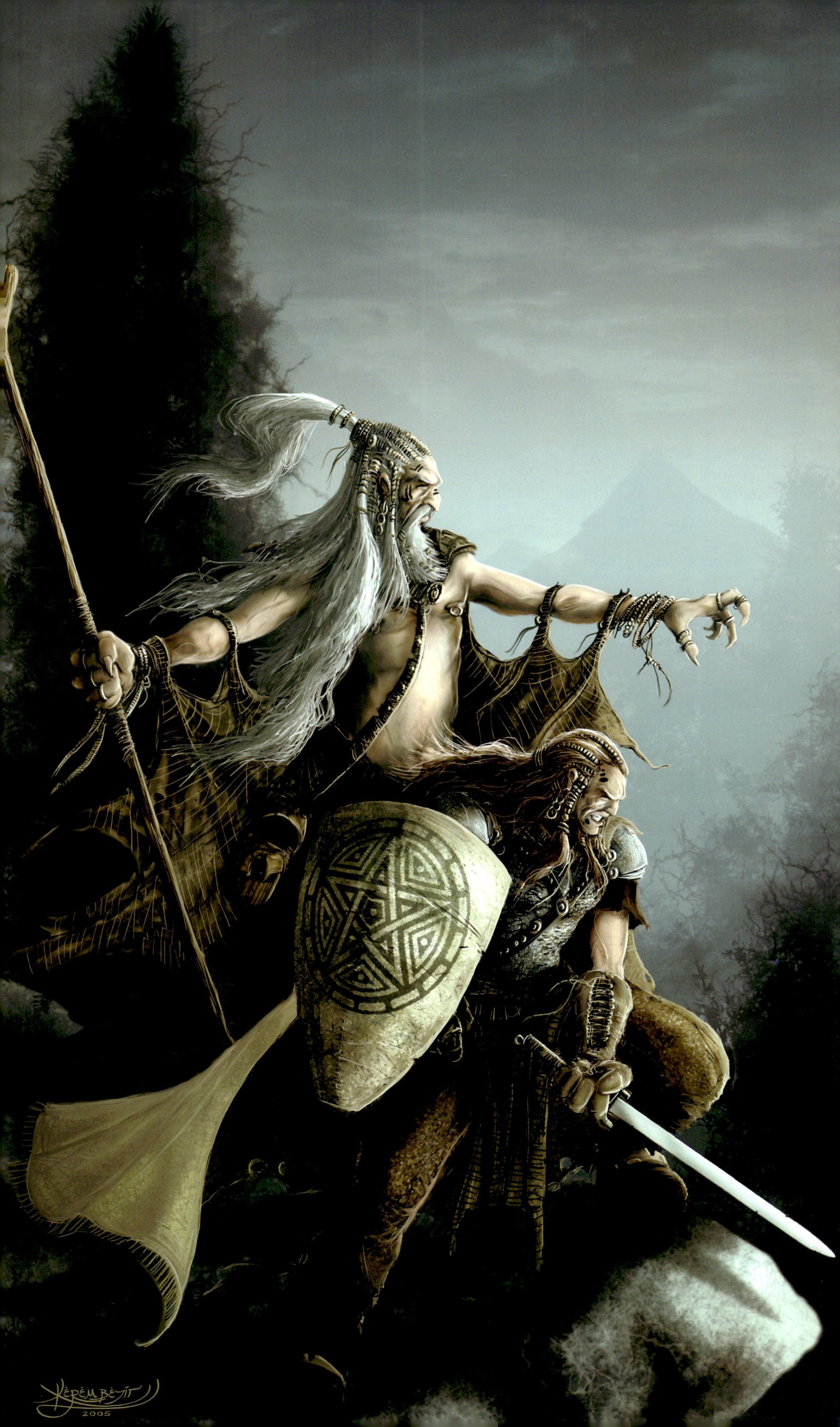
KEREM BEYIT
2005

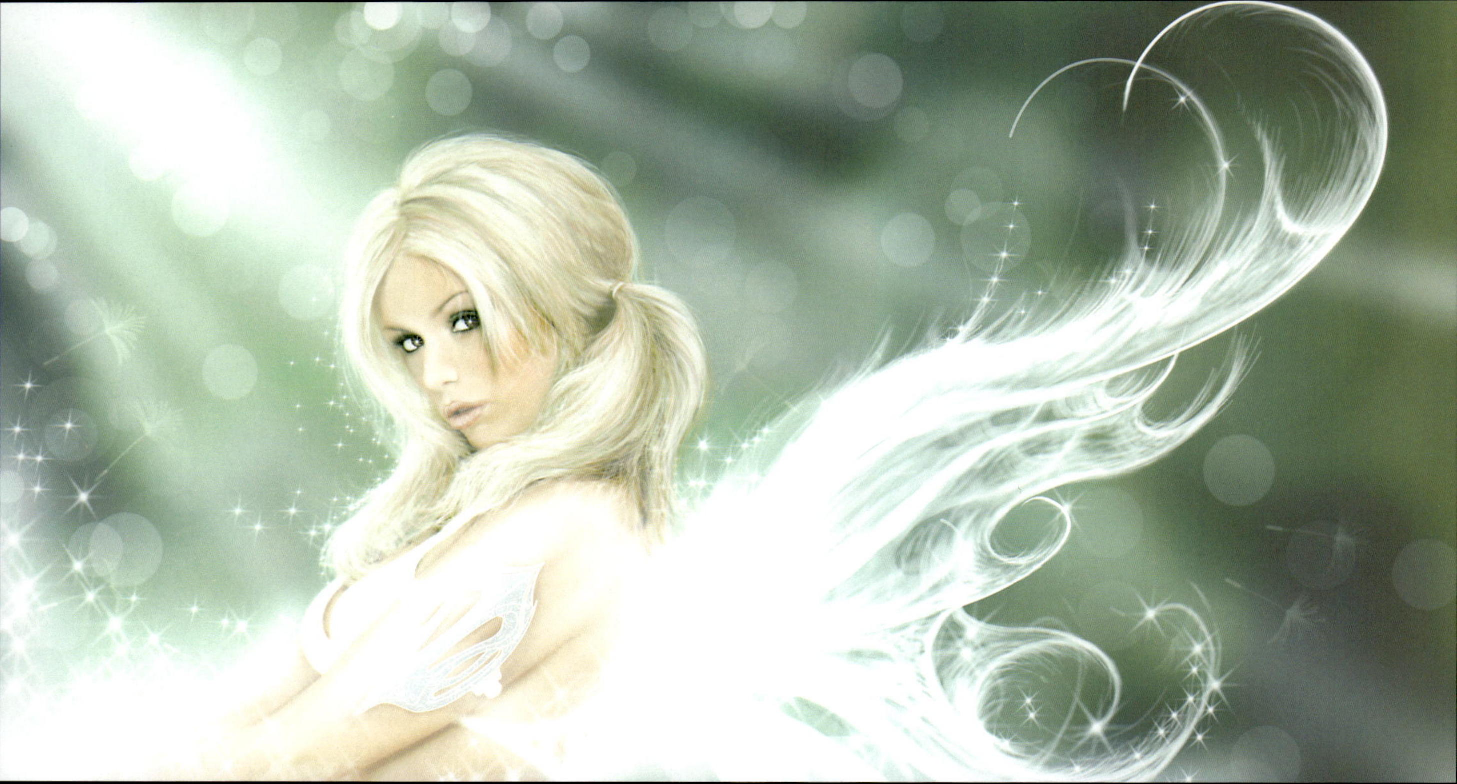

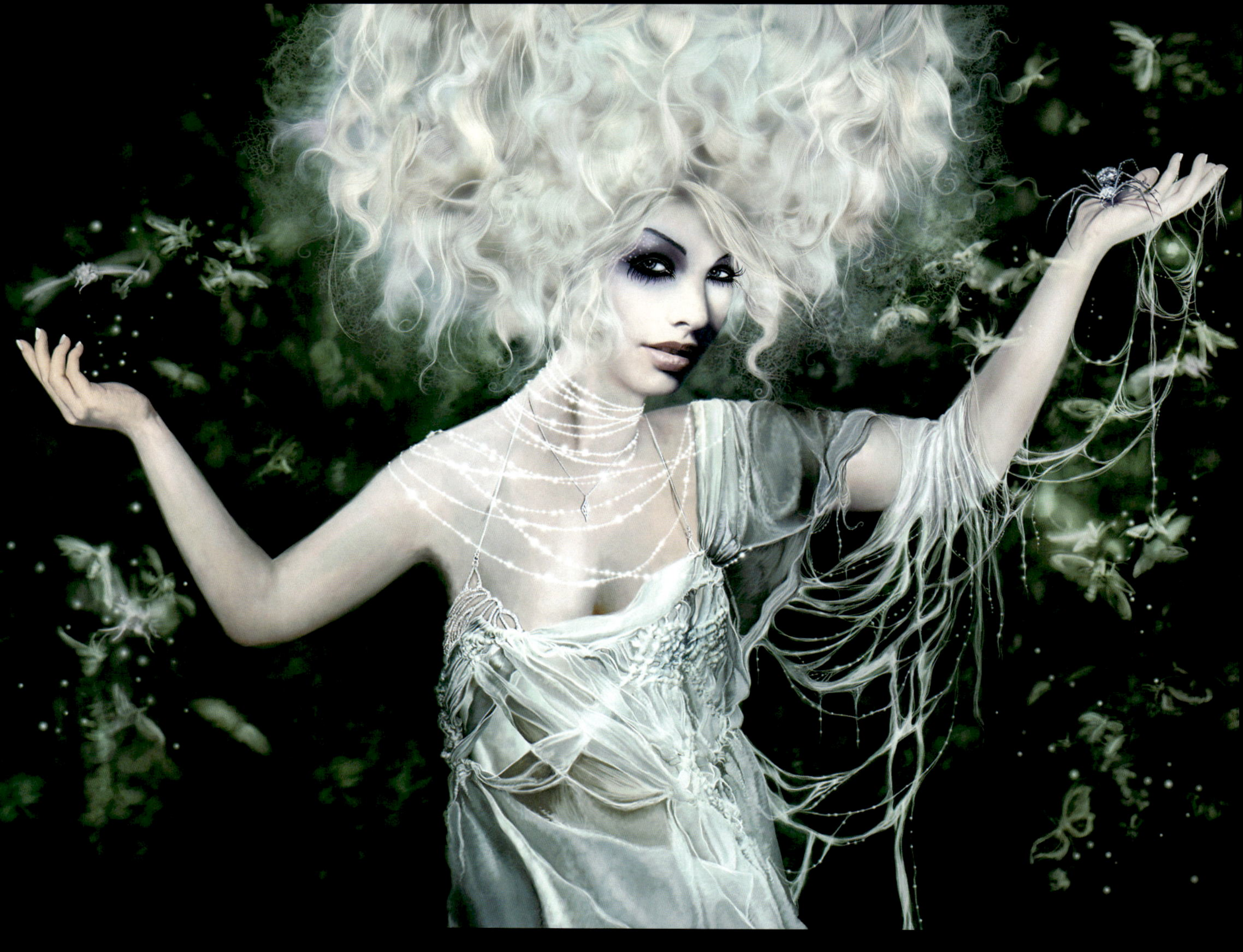

Simone Linsell Fairy
Photoshop
Edward Draper, GREAT BRITAIN
[top]

Darjaleene
Painter, Photoshop
Katarina Sokolova, UKRAINE
[above]

Sinner
Painter
Hong Kuang, SINGAPORE
[right]

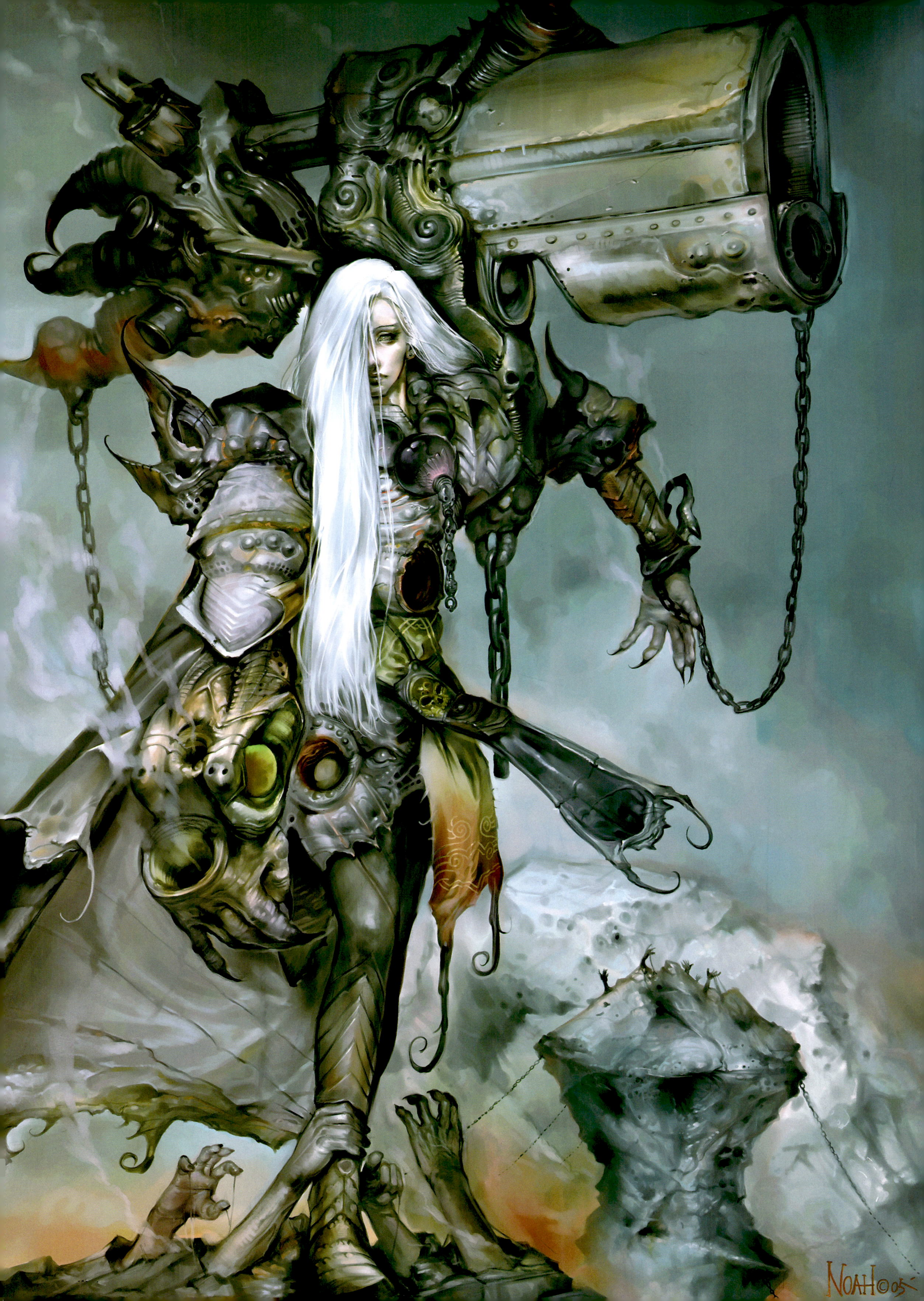
NOAH©05

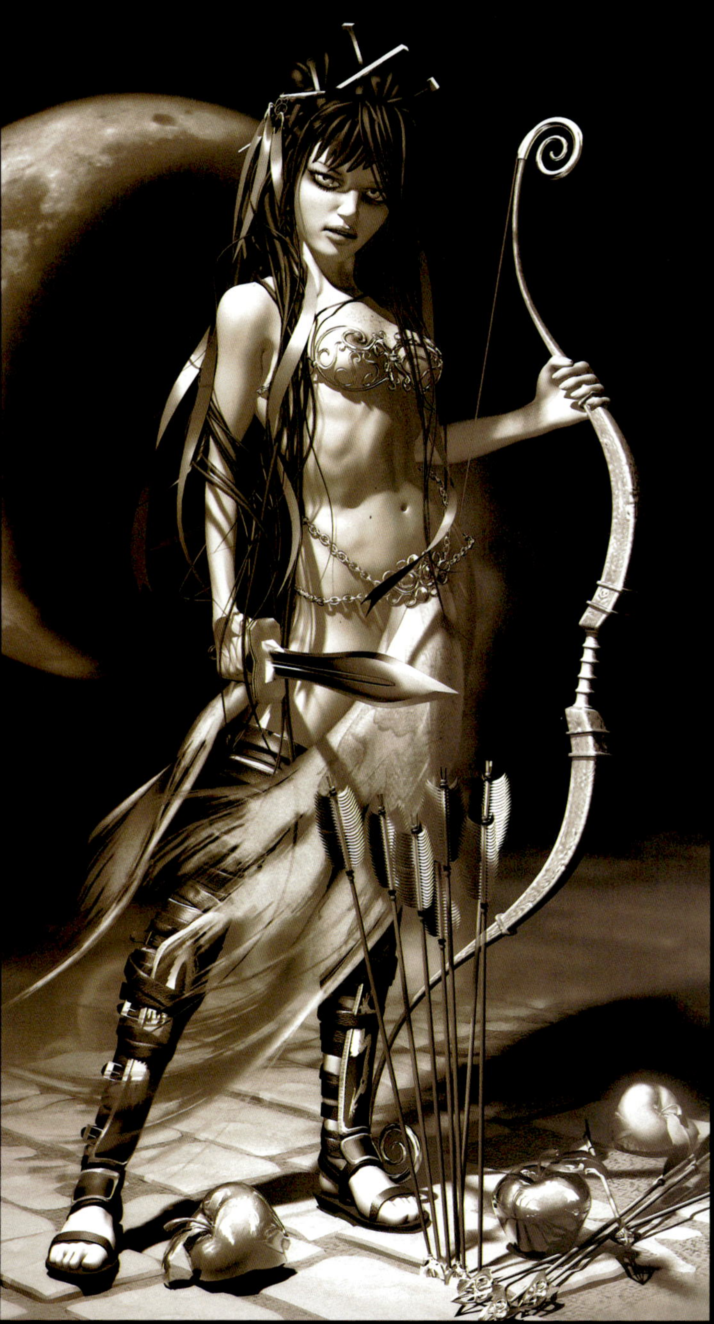

Atalanta's Proposal
SoftimageIXSI, Photoshop
Bryan Eppihimer, USA
[above]

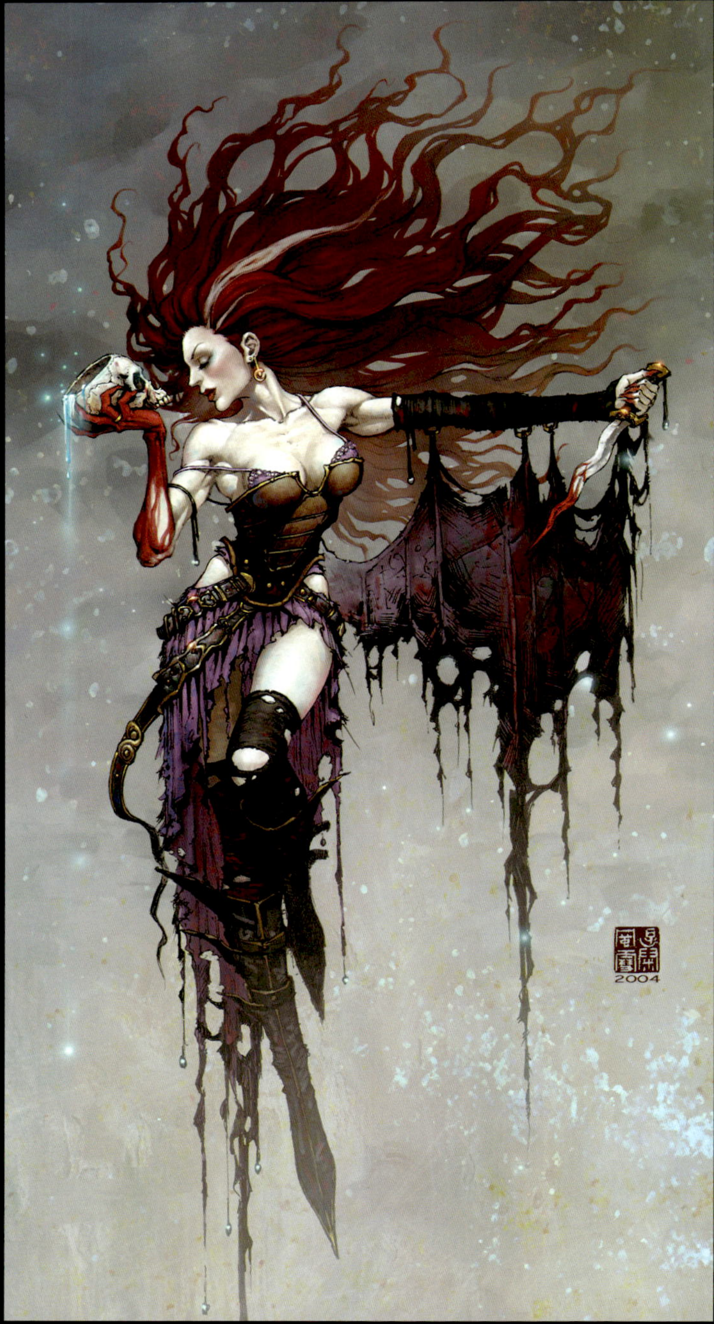

Witch
Painter, Photoshop
Wei Wang, CHINA
[above]

Essventacha Sadensa - Letter
Photoshop
Friedric Petrequin,
Heavydarkness Studio, FRANCE
[right]

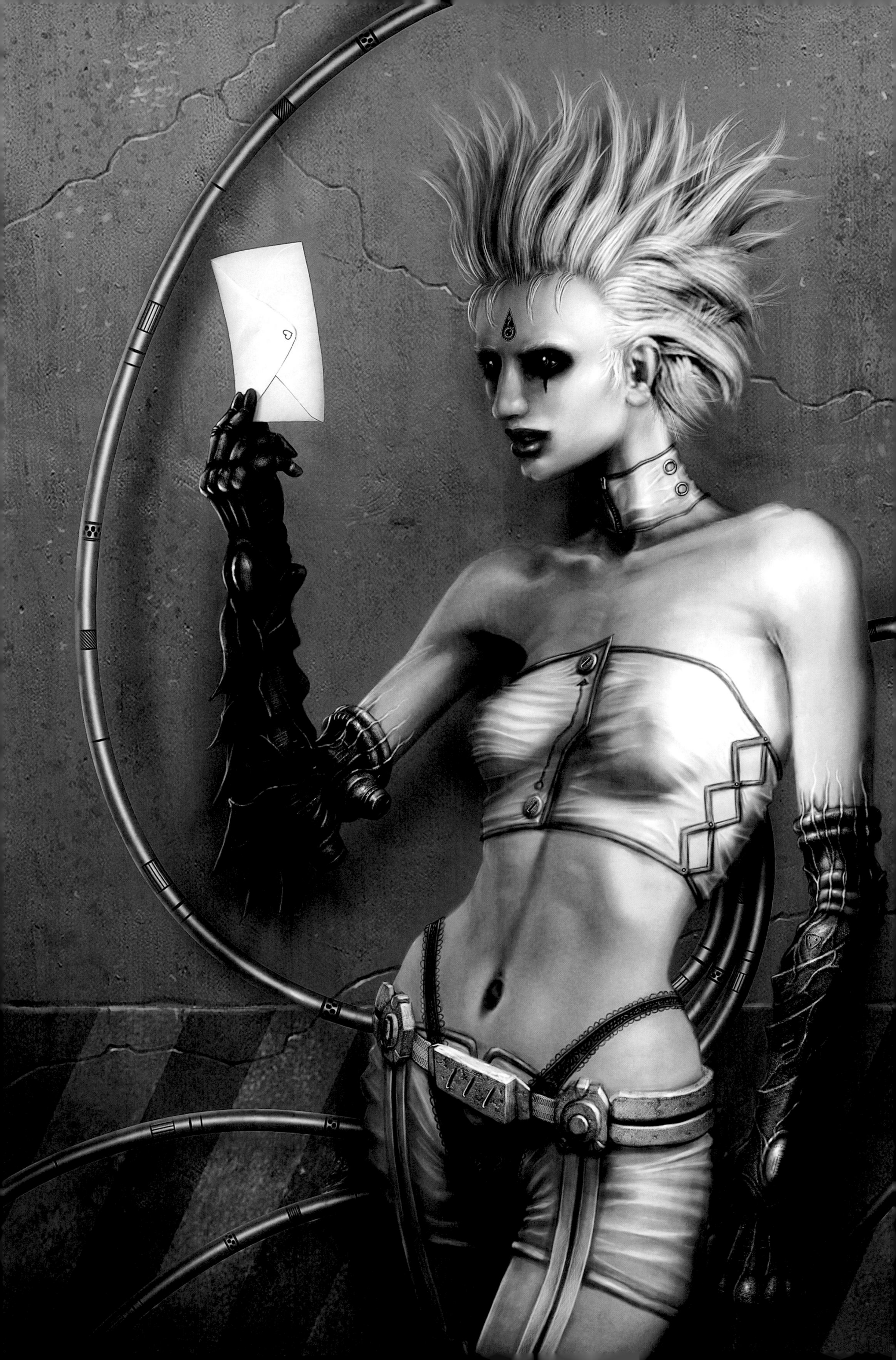

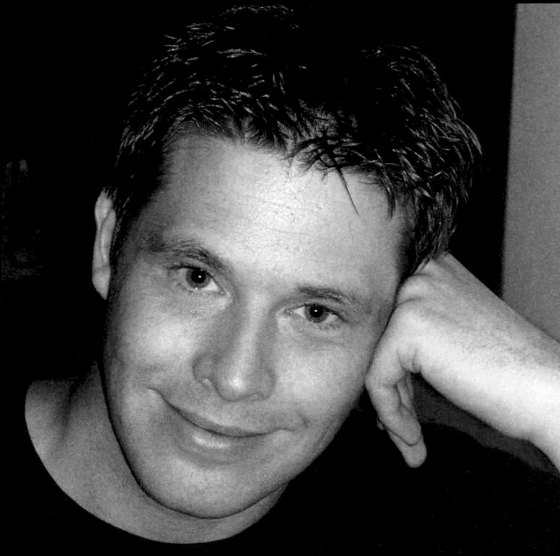

HENNING LUDVIGSEN

www.henningludvigsen.com
henlu@online.no

"It was in Athens I realized that I'd been working for ten years without doing what I really wanted to do in life—paint."

Henning grew up in Holmestrand, a small town in the south of Norway. In Norway, art school can be joined at quite an early age, and this is where he learned the basics of traditional art. "The Amiga was the first computer which opened my eyes to digital art," explains Henning. "I realized the tremendous opportunities available when working digitally. After ten years of working my way up through the ranks of the ad agency industry, I got the opportunity to use my skills in computer game development. With this opportunity, came an invitation to move to sunny Greece, which I immediately accepted. It was in Athens I realized that I'd been working for ten years without doing what I really wanted to do in life—paint." Since 2004, Henning has focused on developing workflow skills and creating fantasy-related 2D art. He is currently working as the Art Director of a Norwegian/Greek computer game development company in Athens.

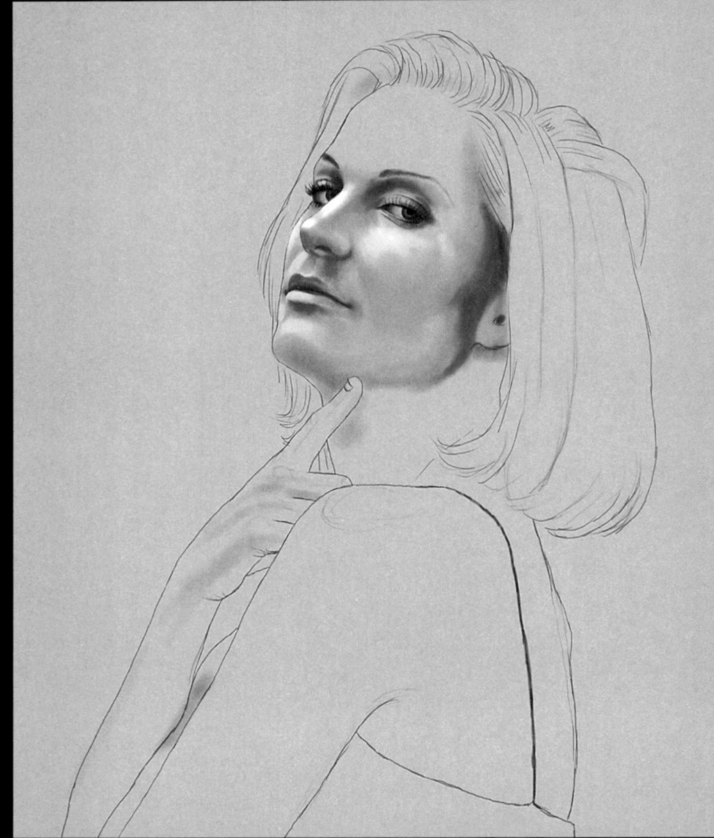

SKETCHING

I started off by making a simple sketch. As a fan of realism, I used a grid on top of the reference picture I was looking at while painting. I copied the same grid onto a blank canvas and then drew a rough and simple base. I did this to avoid major proportional mistakes at an early stage in the process as I could easily see where a line in the photo broke with the grid. As soon as I had a decent looking sketch, I got rid of the grid and added a simple greyscale background to the painting. I kept the sketch in a separate layer on top of the others. Next I got some rough shapes up to catch the overall feeling. For some reason, I always start off with the eyes. If the eyes don't feel right, it can break the piece. One reason for having a greyscale background is that I can toggle easily between black and white while applying shadows and highlights, and not be limited by working from one side of the black or white greyscale range. It is only at this stage in the process that I apply rough shades with a semisoft brush set to medium. The other reason why I work with grey tones in the beginning is that it allows me to focus on getting the shape up and running before even thinking about colors.

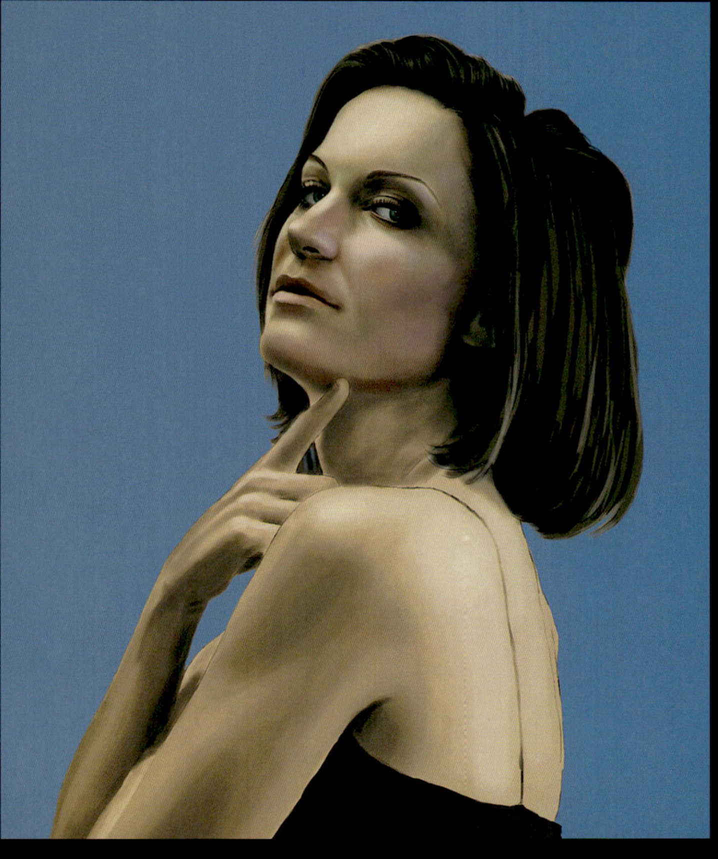

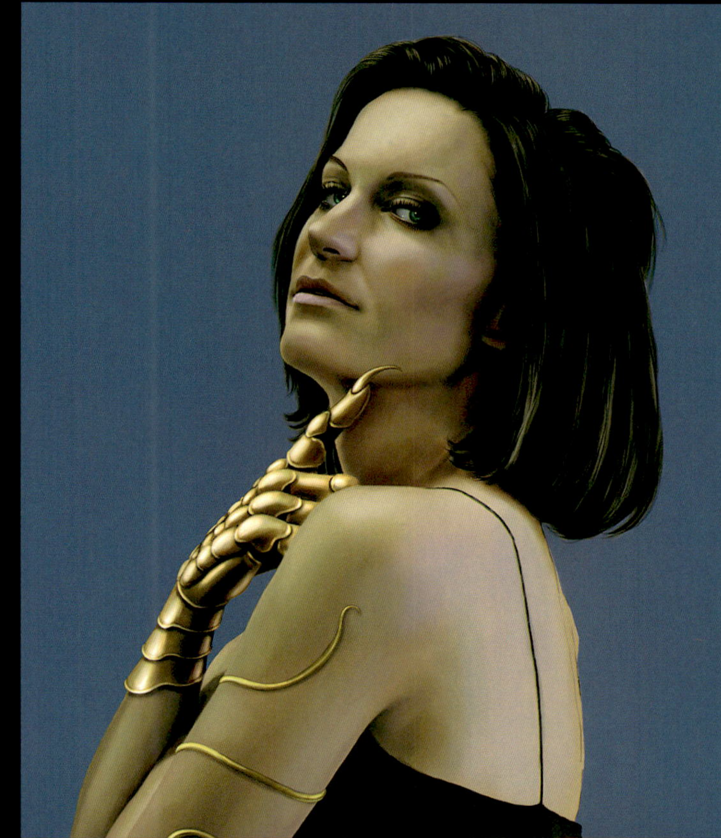

BLOCKING-IN COLOR

When a rough greyscale version was ready, I merged the shaded base layer with the sketch. I then applied some very rough base colors using the brush tool with Color mode enabled. When the basic colors were applied, I began adding some more details—still pretty rough, but I usually prefer starting with messy brush strokes before working my way into more details. While I still had a lot of detailing to do, I continued adding features in the girl's face. From then on, I used the ordinary hard-edged brush on Normal mode only. I think using sharp brushes with dense spacing feels closer to painting the "old fashioned way". This painting was an experiment in using hard-edged brushes, and it was my first step away from smooth, airbrush-style paintings. I am a strong believer in using reference pictures for paintings, as I simply don't think the human mind can emulate realism well enough to compete with the real thing. When making paintings, I normally use friends as reference models, and I consider it a challenge to make the art resemble the model as closely as possible, like with this painting.

DETAILS

Still using the hard-edged brush, I went over the entire piece area by area applying more details and correcting the skin tones. When the base colors are placed, I prefer to mix colors as I go along and directly onto the piece. This makes it all more fun, and the end result looks more natural. Knowing that skin has all kinds of colors depending on the area of the body, I made sure that areas like the nose, the bits around the eyes, shoulders, neck, and forehead got a vague tint of red. In other places, the skin might be thinner and should appear more blue or grey. Even green and yellow are colors I use for skin tones, and in the shadows purple and blue made sense because I wanted to use cold ambient light. At this stage, I added the metal gauntlet and applied smooth and rough metal shading. I wanted the gauntlet to look feminine and delicate, which is why I painted the hand first, and then replaced it. I painted the gauntlet a little thicker to give the metal the right build and thickness. The hair started to shape up at this point, and I went on from here until I felt that the painting was done. On this occasion I stopped earlier than usual to maintain the feeling and impression that this is a traditional painting with human artistic errors, and not a typical digital painting.

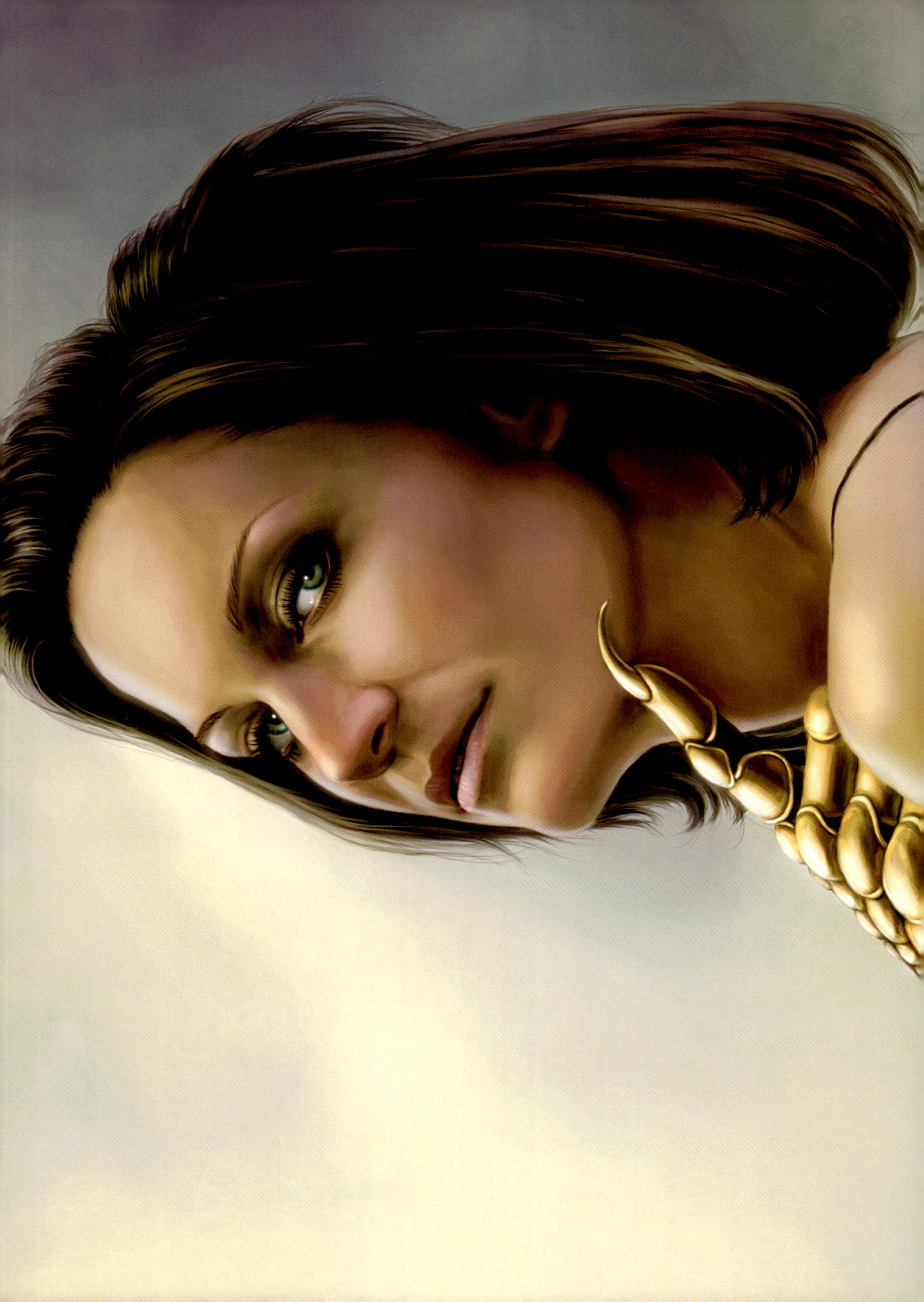

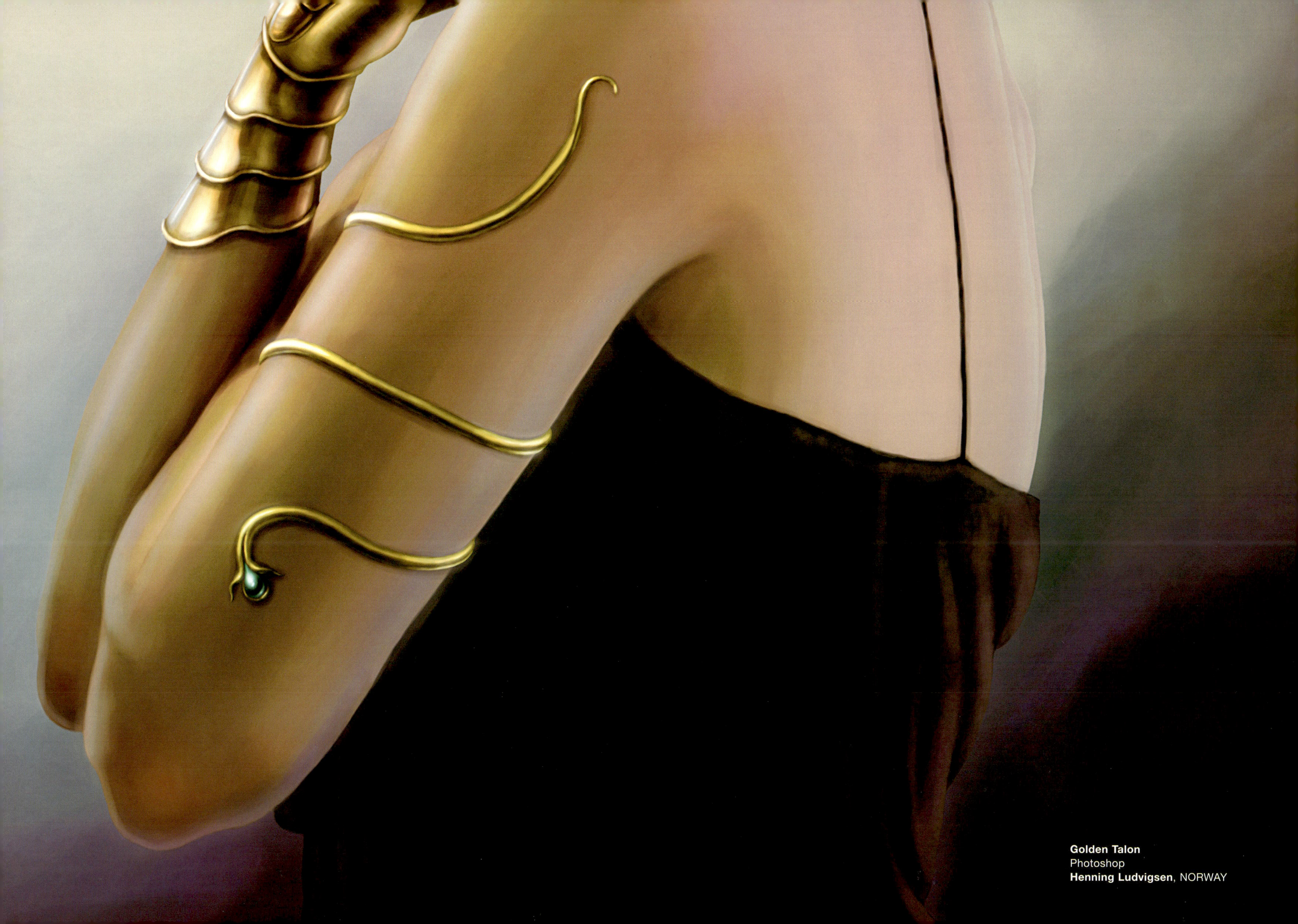

Golden Talon
Photoshop
Henning Ludvigsen, NORWAY

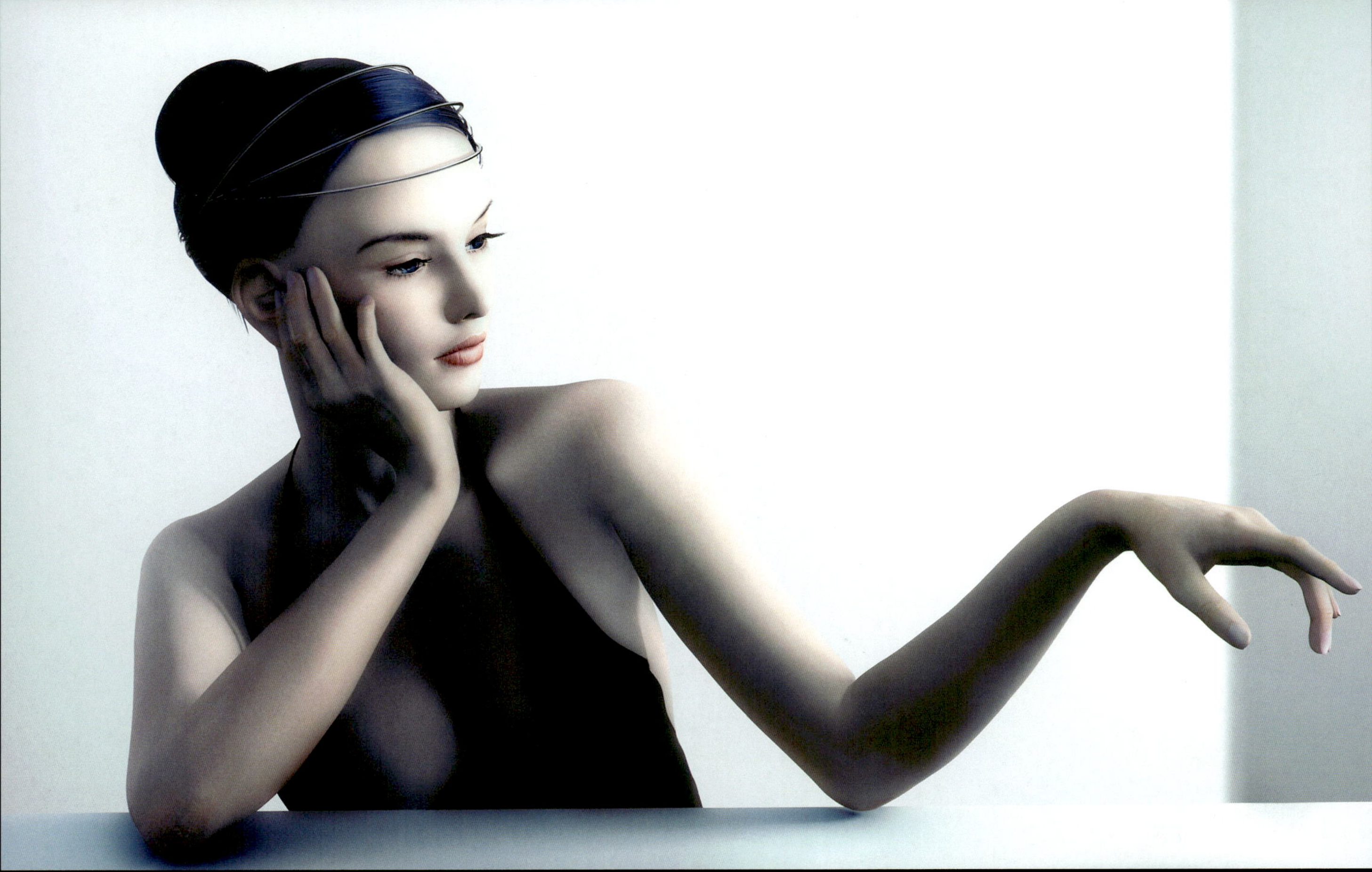

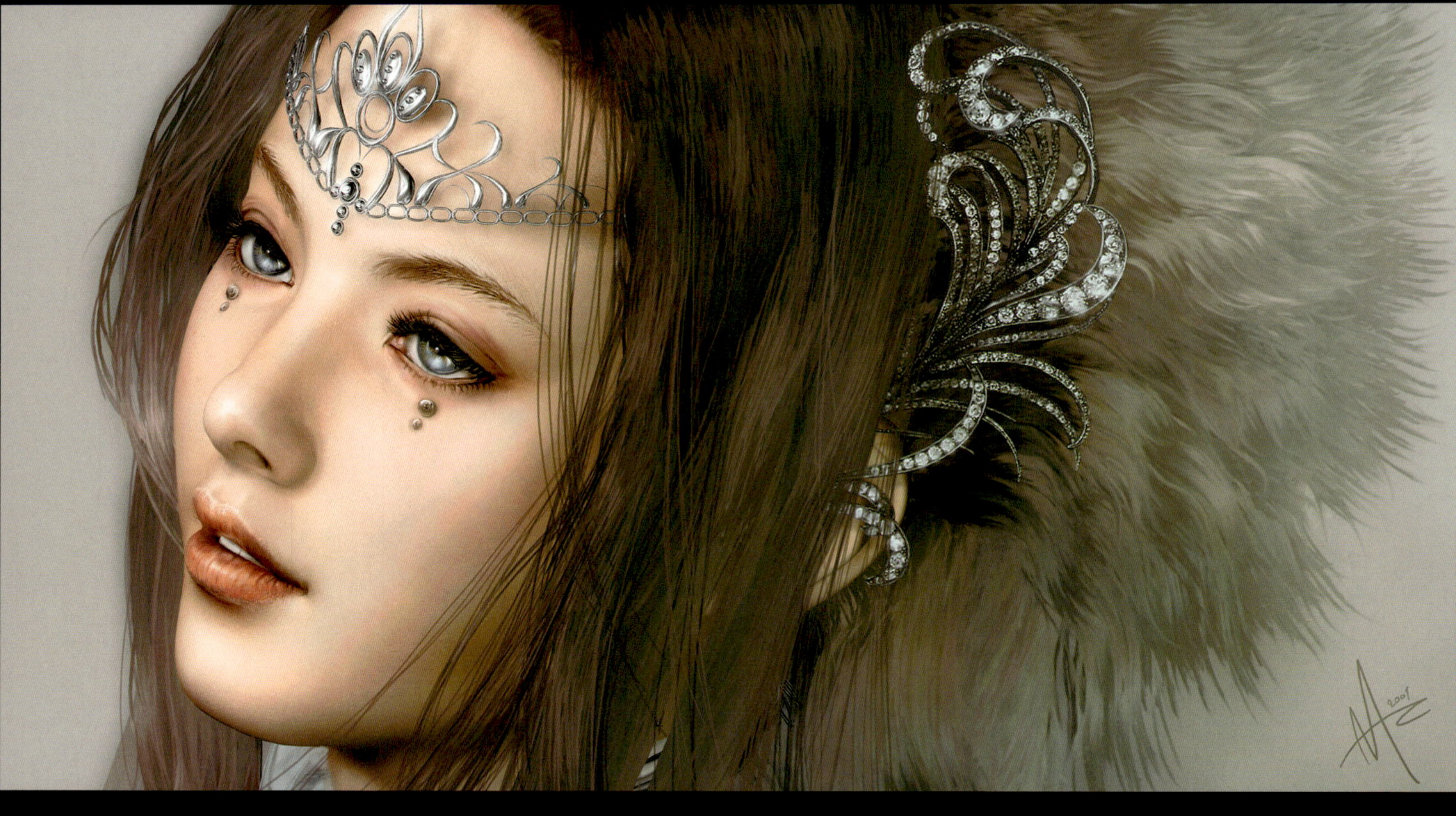

Wine
3ds Max, Photoshop
Soa Lee, KOREA
[top]

Suphia
3ds Max, Photoshop, Paintshop Pro
Soa Lee, KOREA
[above]

Inaé
3ds Max
Olivier Ponsonnet, FRANCE
[right]

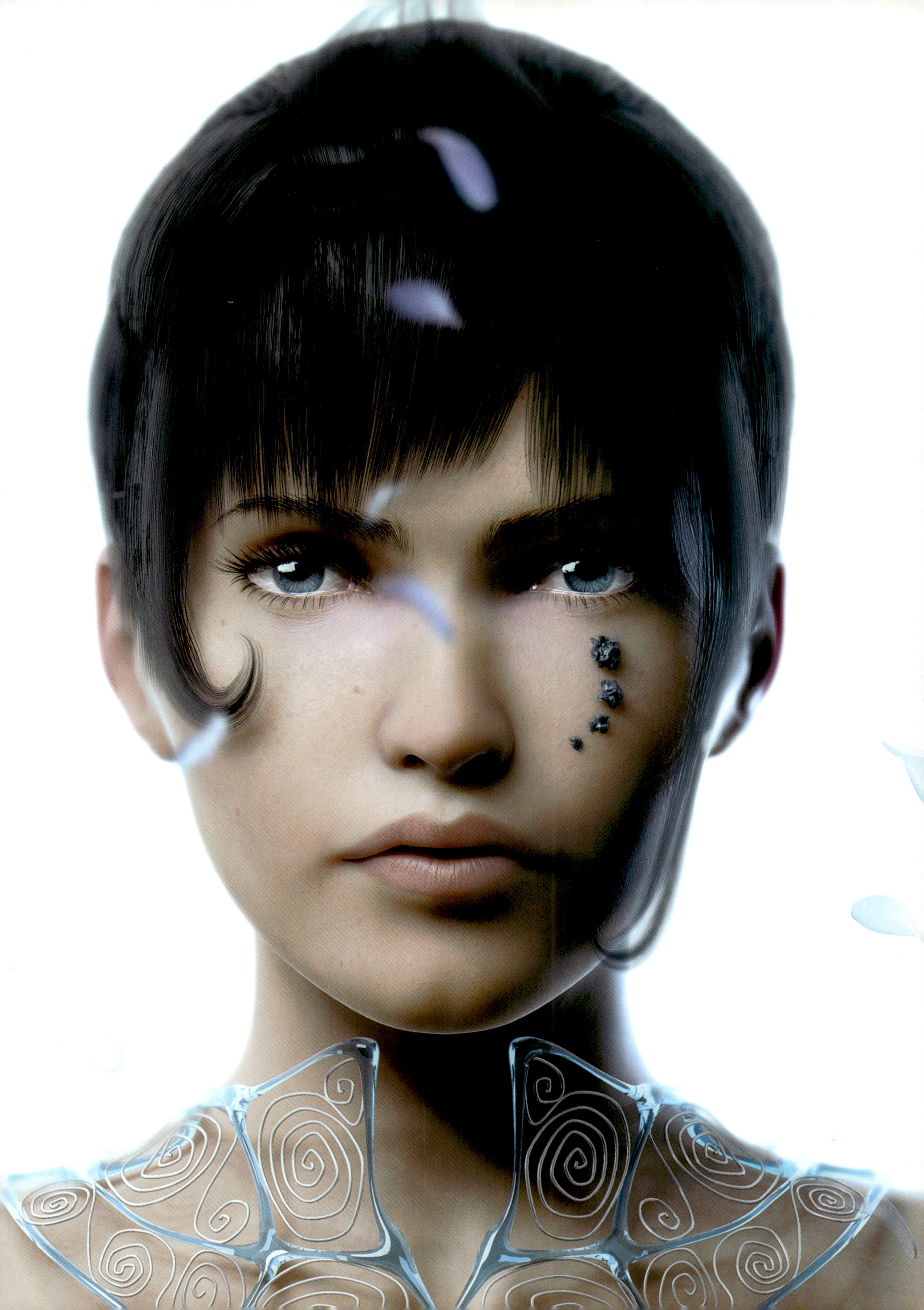

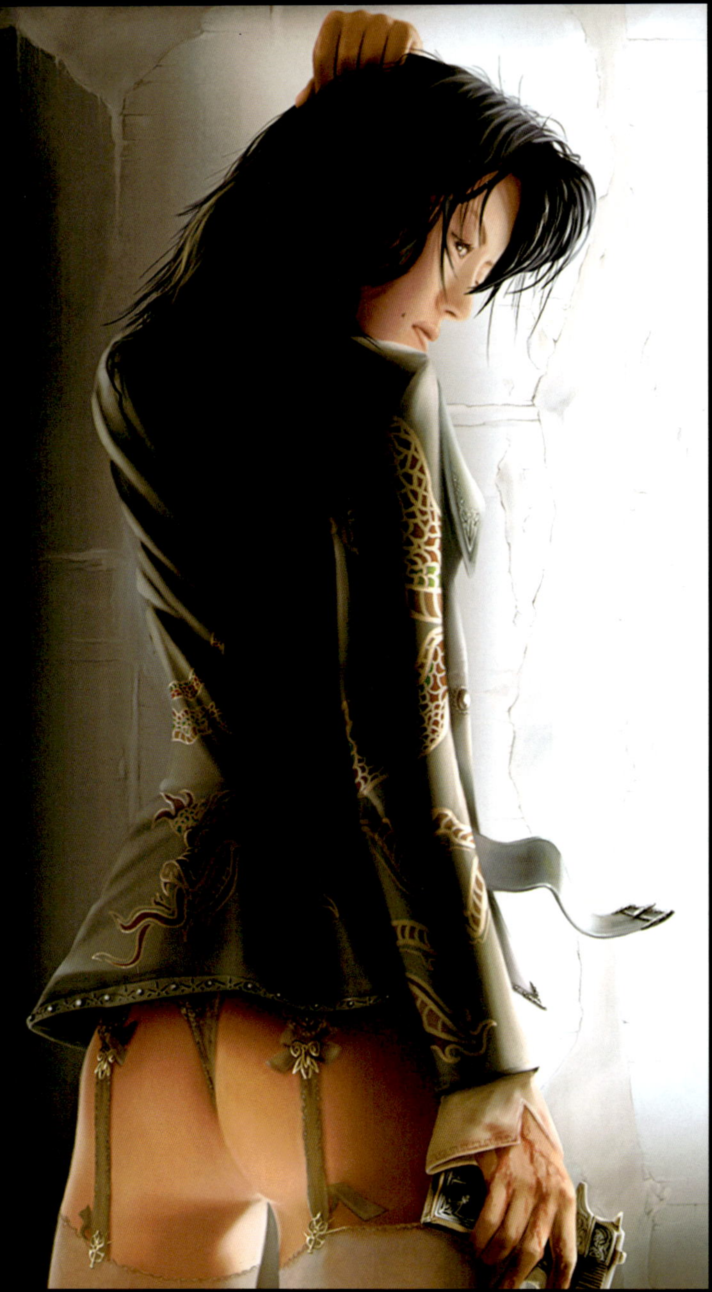

The Crane
Photoshop, Painter
Mark Jordan, SLOVENIA
[above]

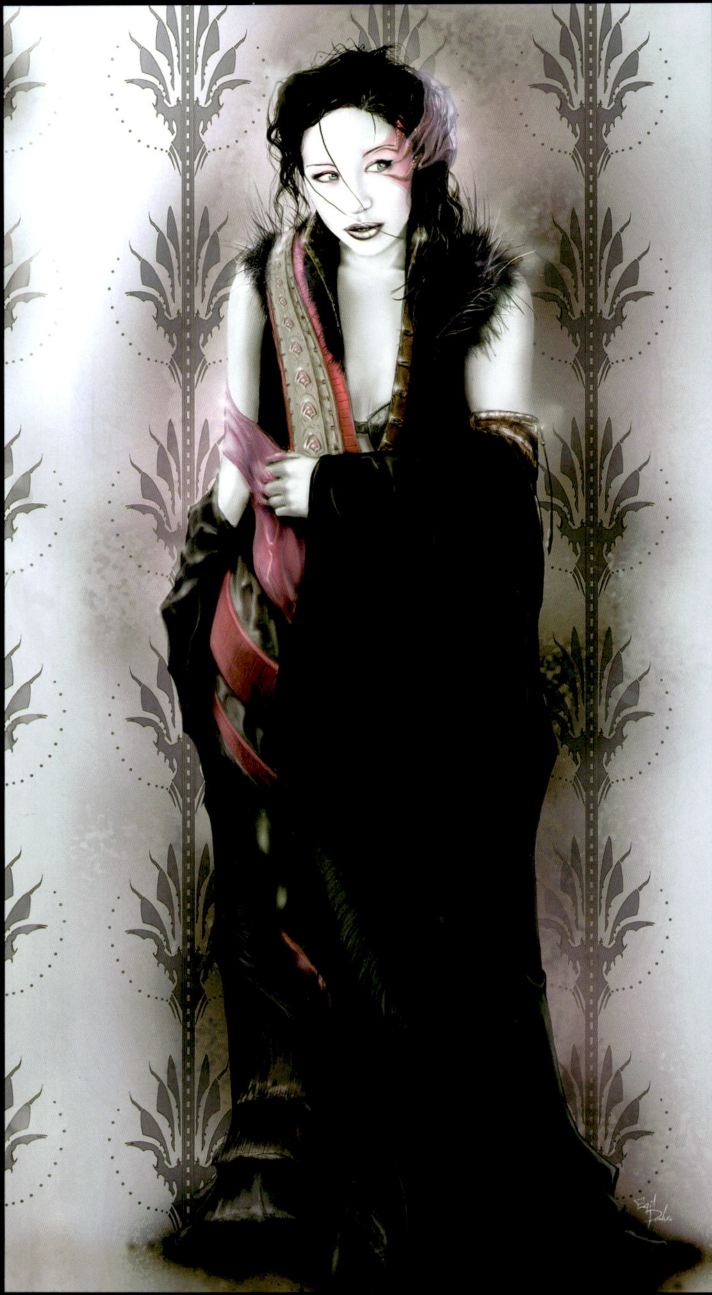

Papillon
Photoshop
Egil Paulsen, NORWAY
[above]

Devastation
Painter
Anry Nemo, RUSSIA
[right]

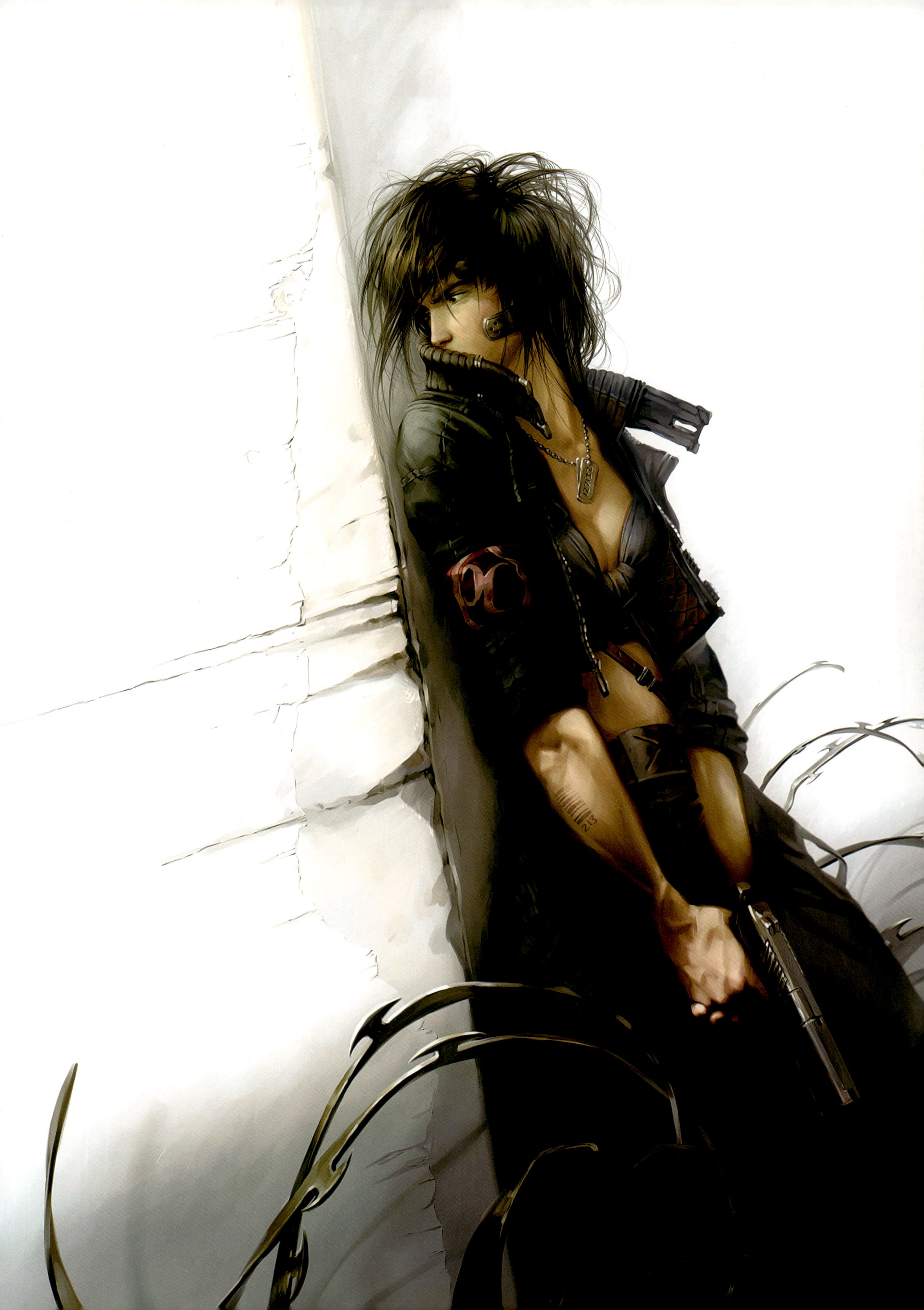

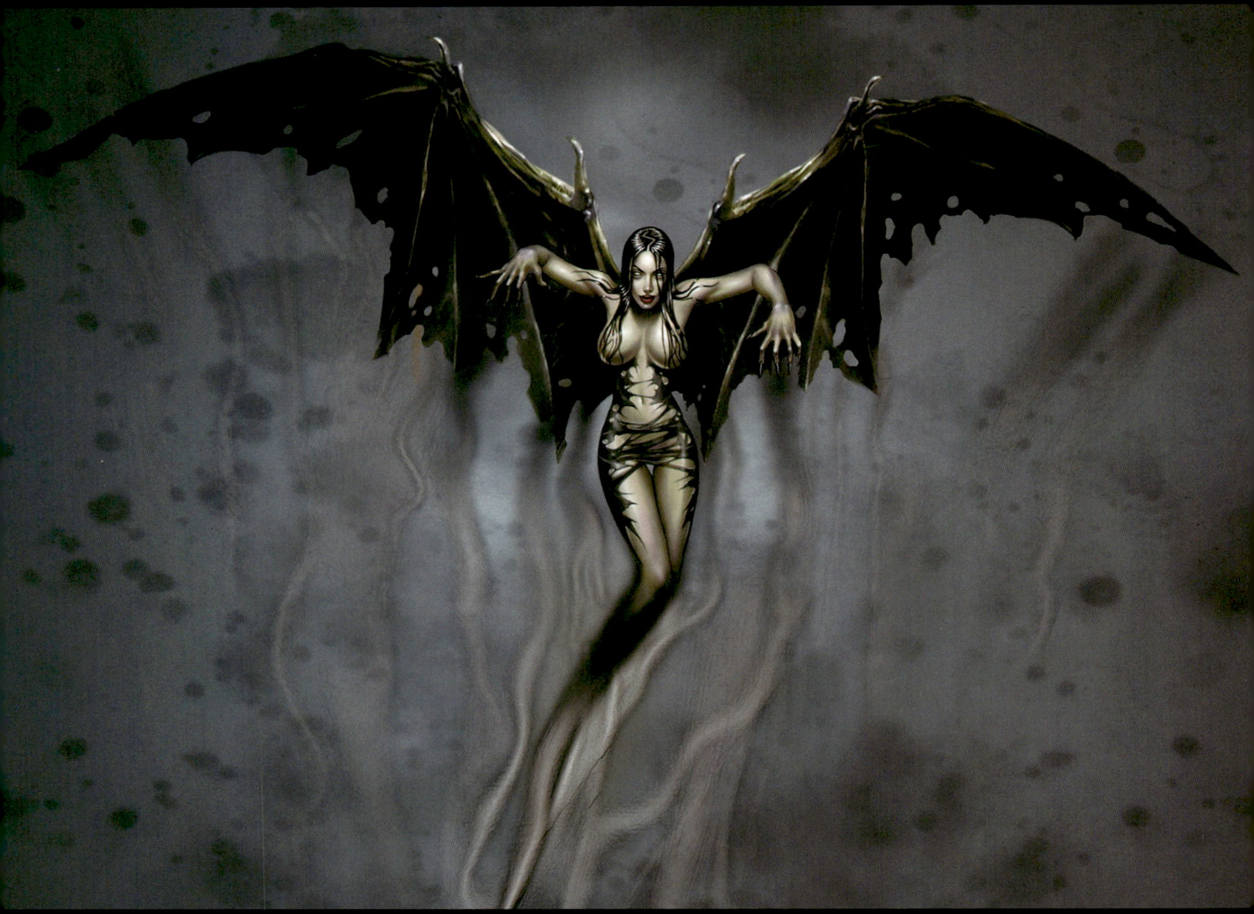

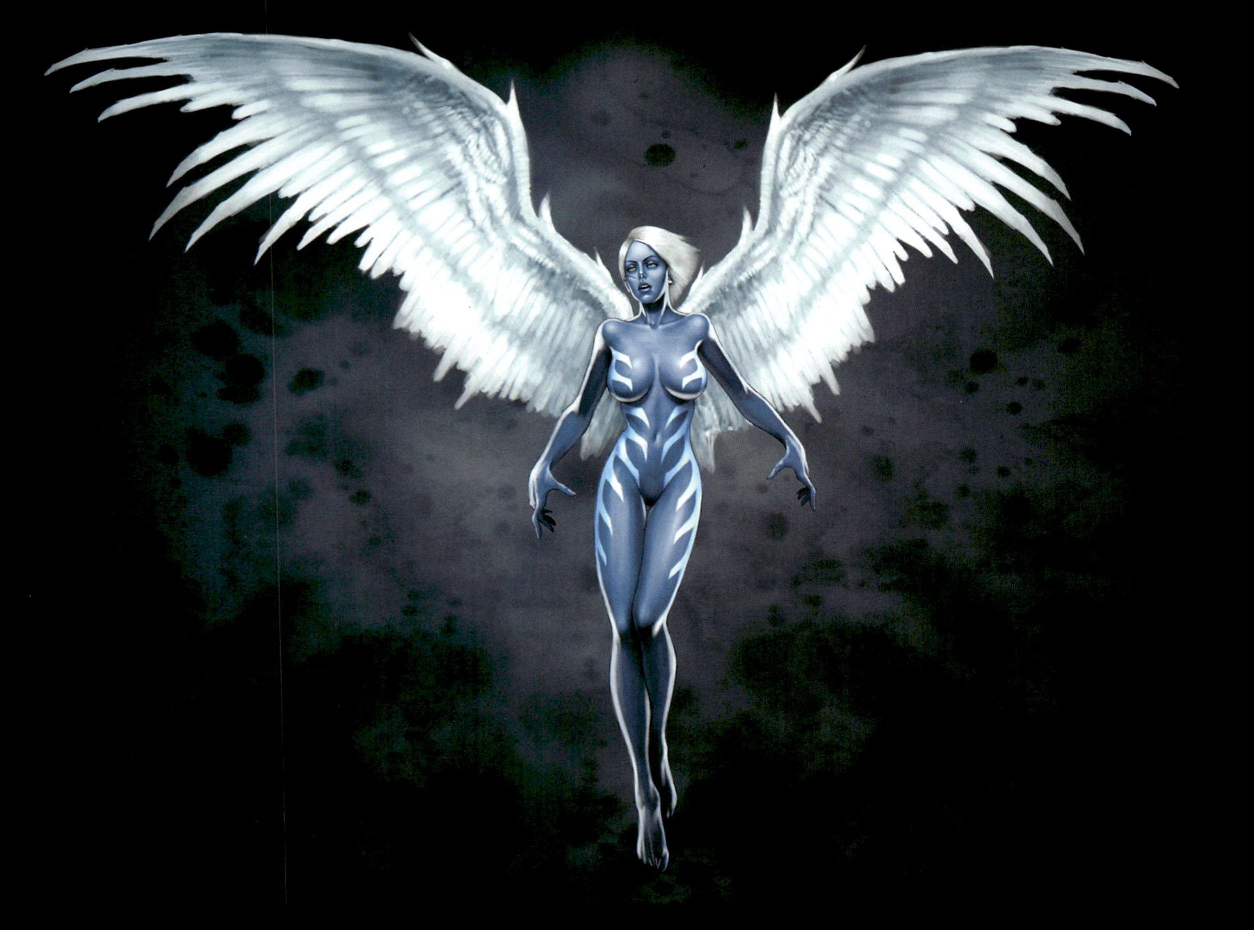

ala: Boss
Photoshop
rt Director: Farzad Varahramyan
Steve Jung, High Moon Studios, USA
top]

Cassidy Sharp: Boss
Photoshop
Art Director: Farzad Varahramyan
Steve Jung, High Moon Studios, USA
[above]

Elven Warrior
Photoshop, Painter
Cho Kyoung-Min, KOREA
[right]

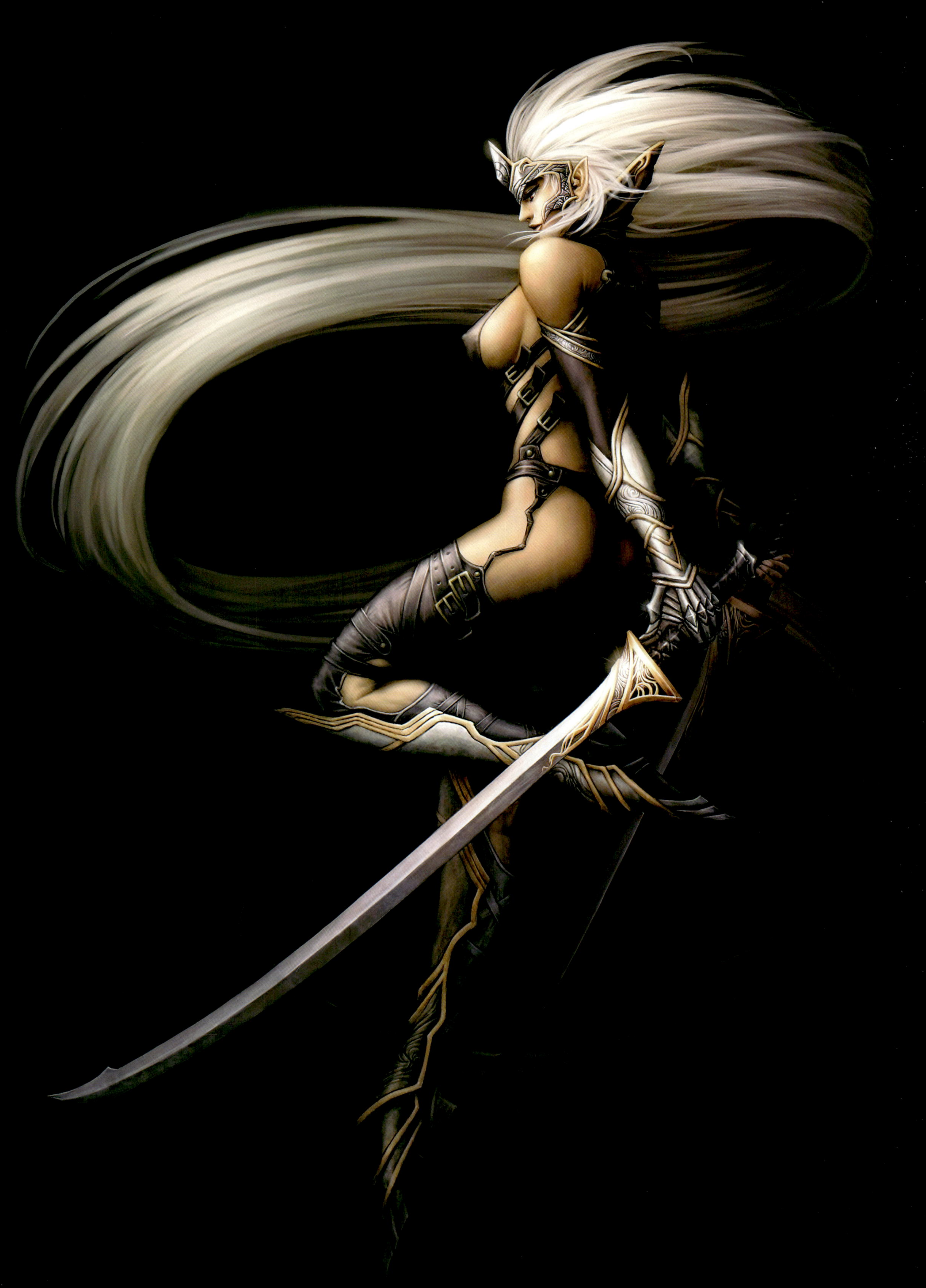

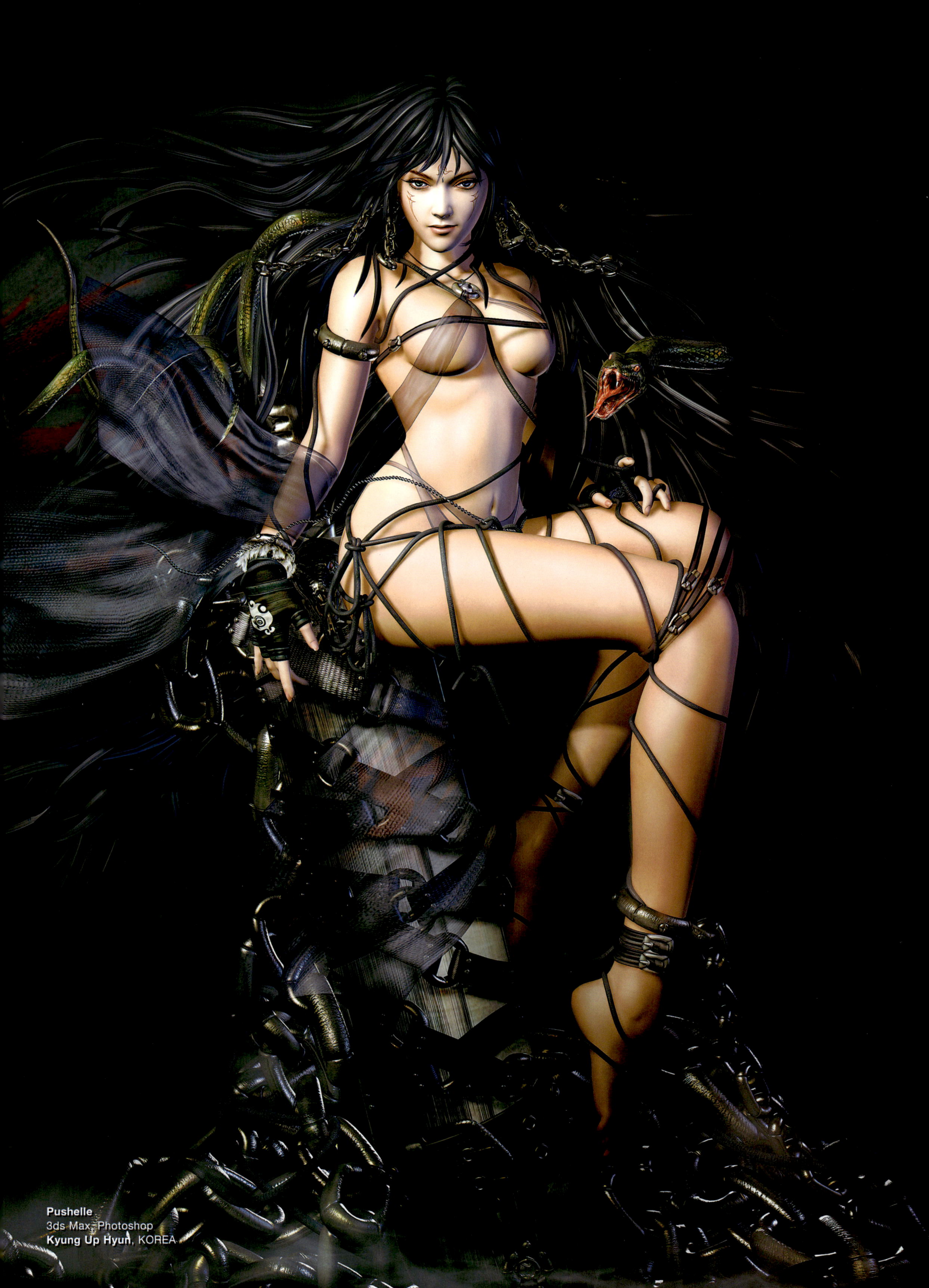

Pushelle
3ds Max, Photoshop
Kyung Up Hyun, KOREA

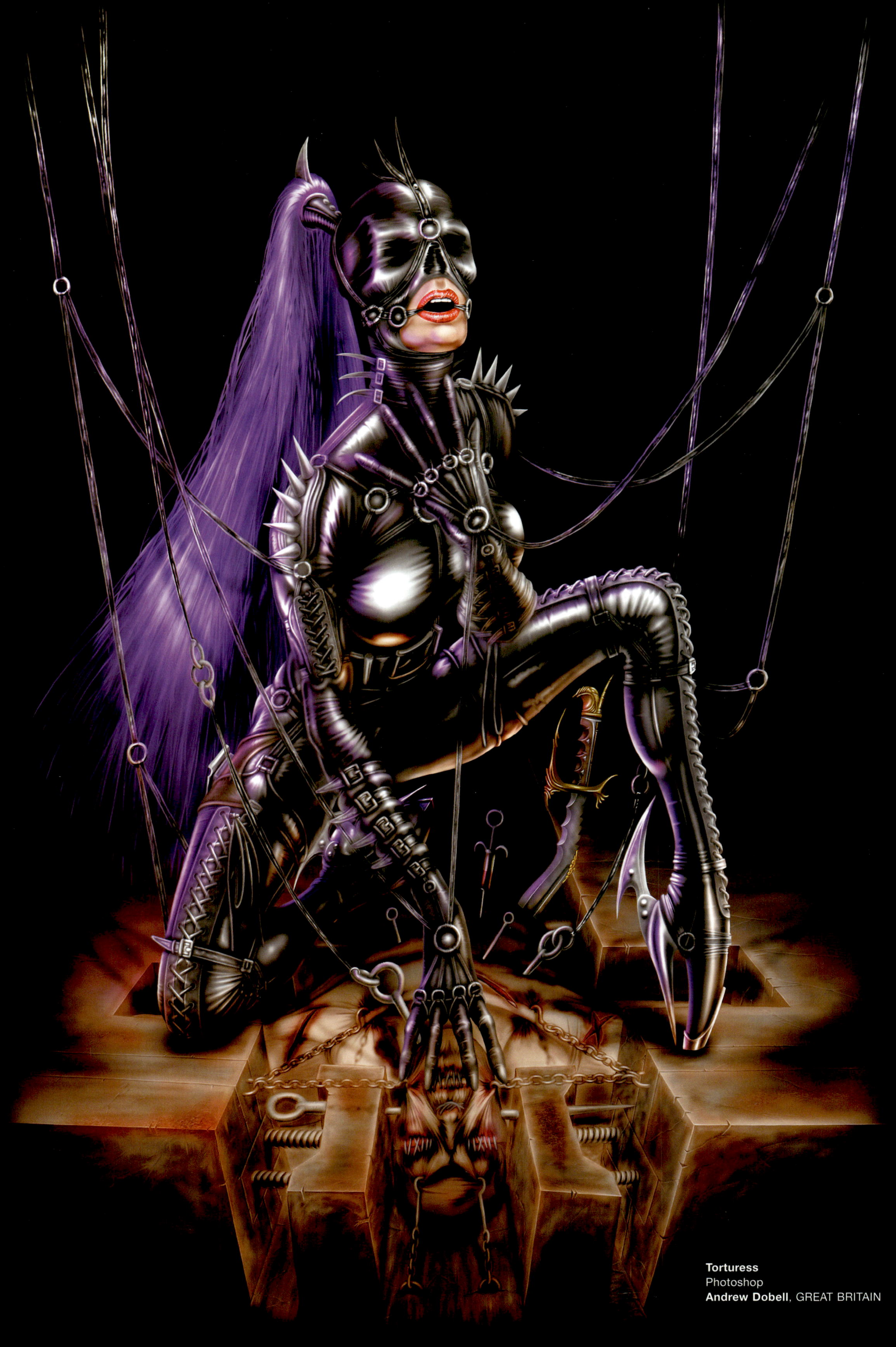

Torturess
Photoshop
Andrew Dobell, GREAT BRITAIN

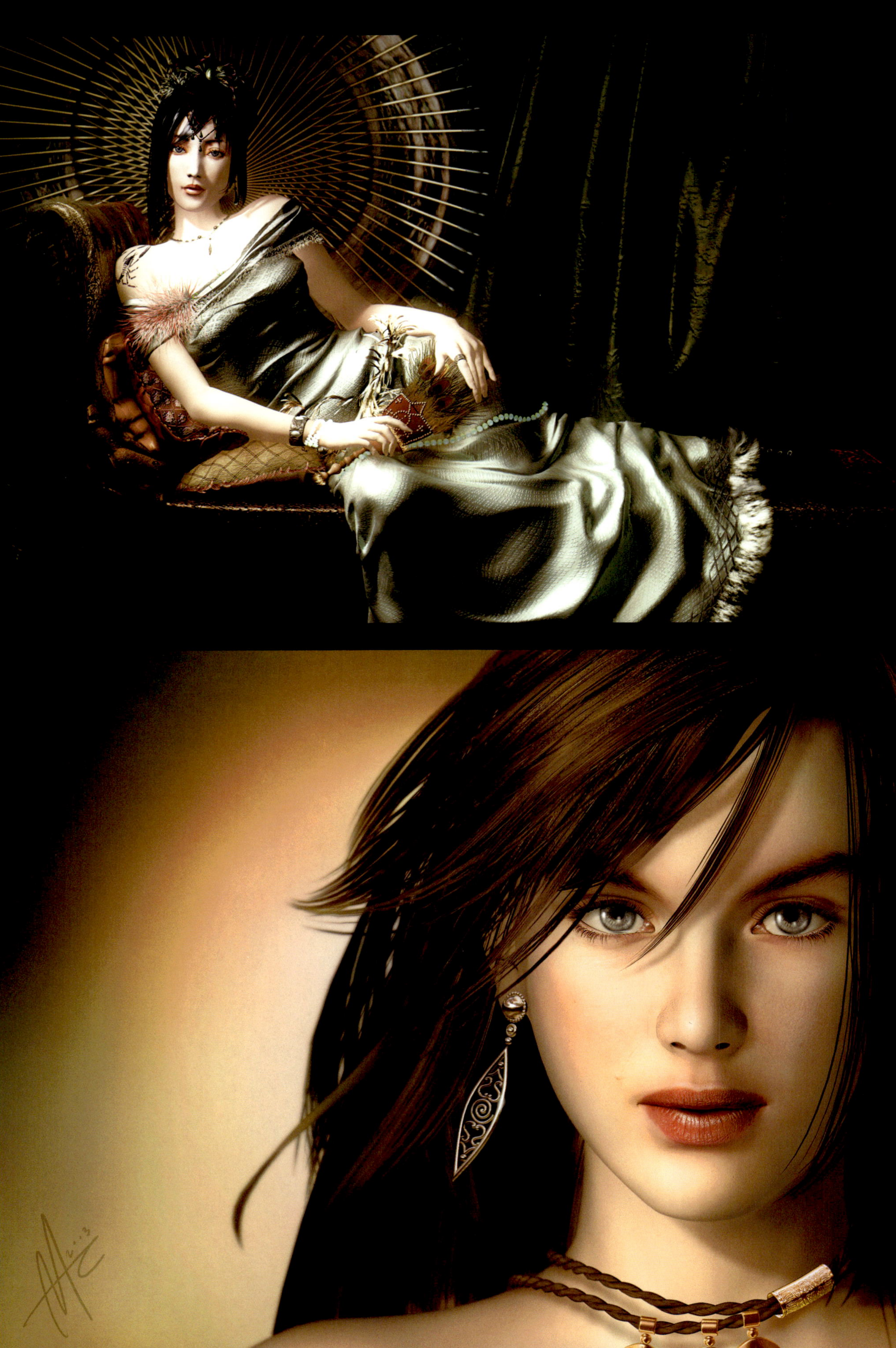

Moona
Maya
Soa Lee, KOREA
[top]

Elene
3ds Max, Photoshop
Soa Lee, KOREA
[above]

When the Wind Blows
Photoshop
Christine Griffin, USA
[right]

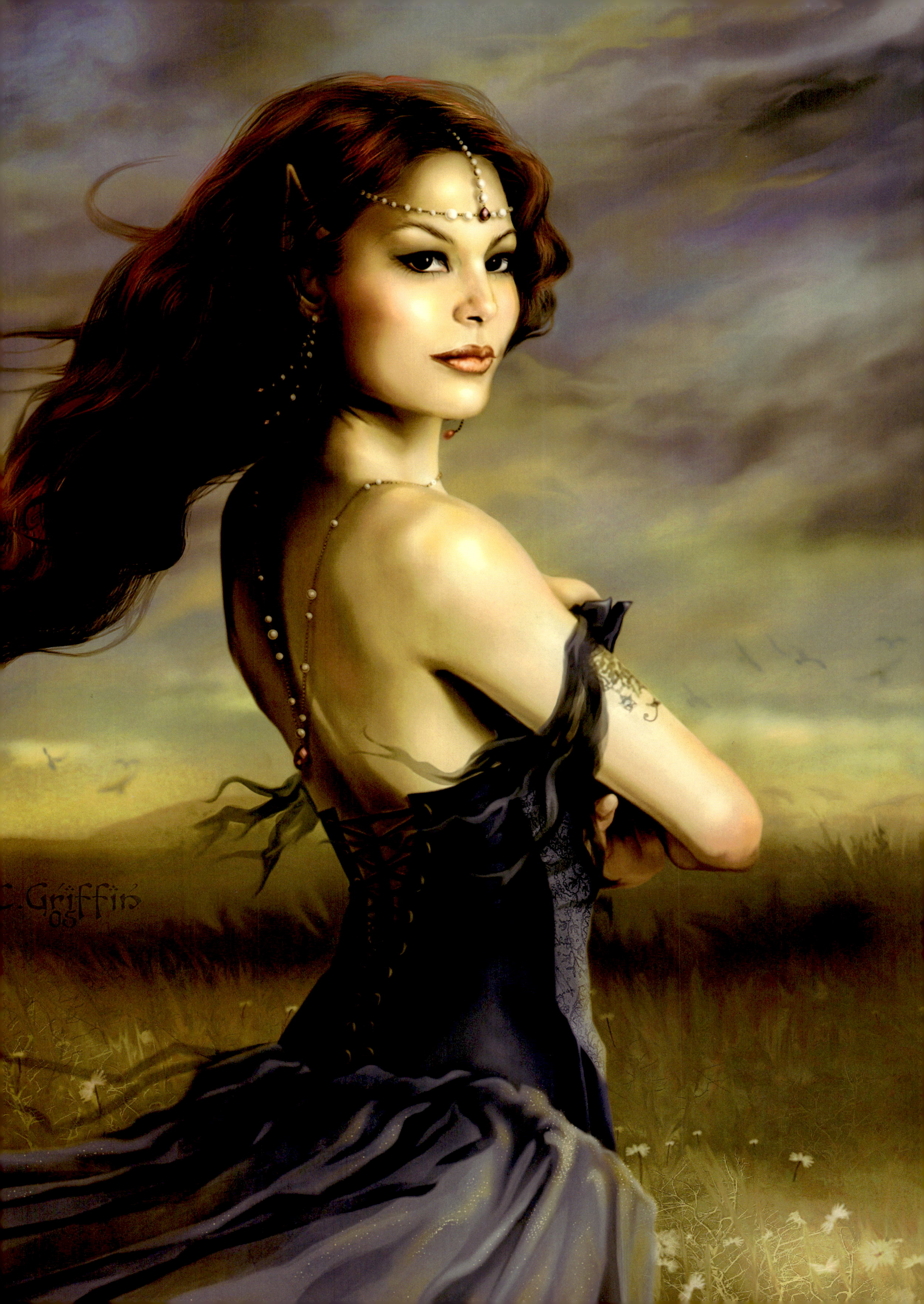
C. Griffin
05

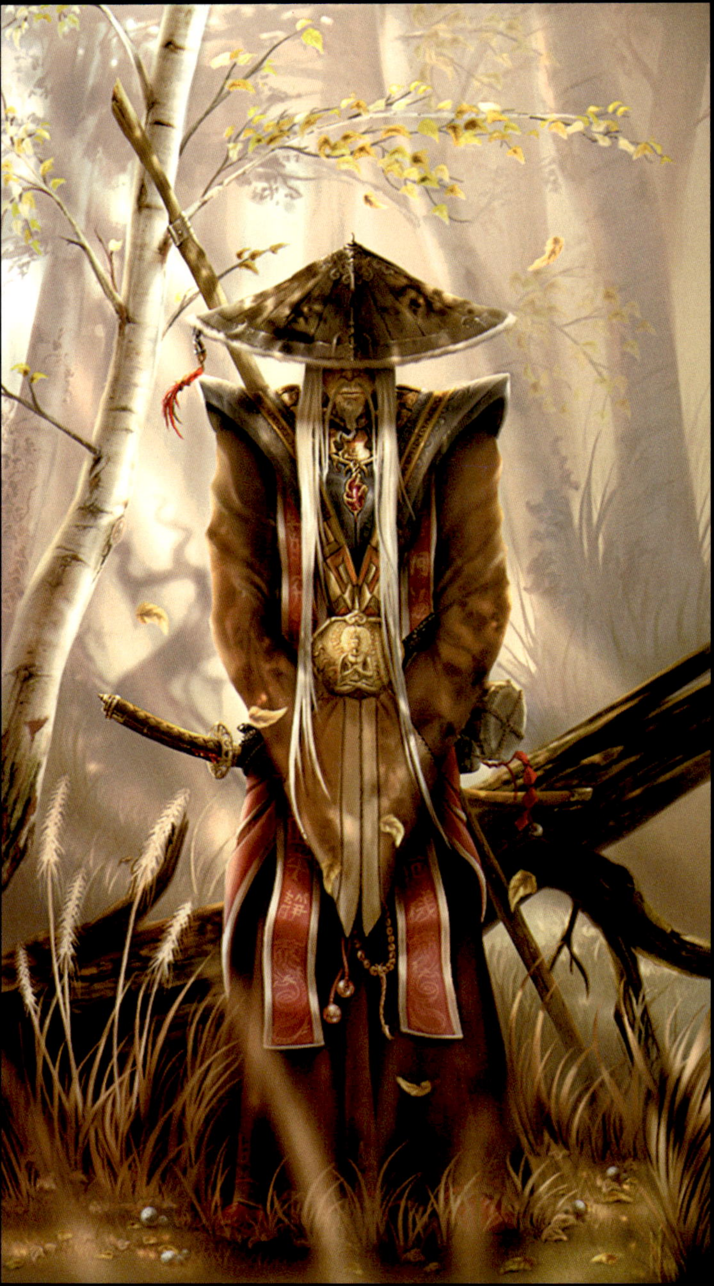

Shao-Leen
Photoshop, Painter
Mark Jordan, SLOVENIA
[above]

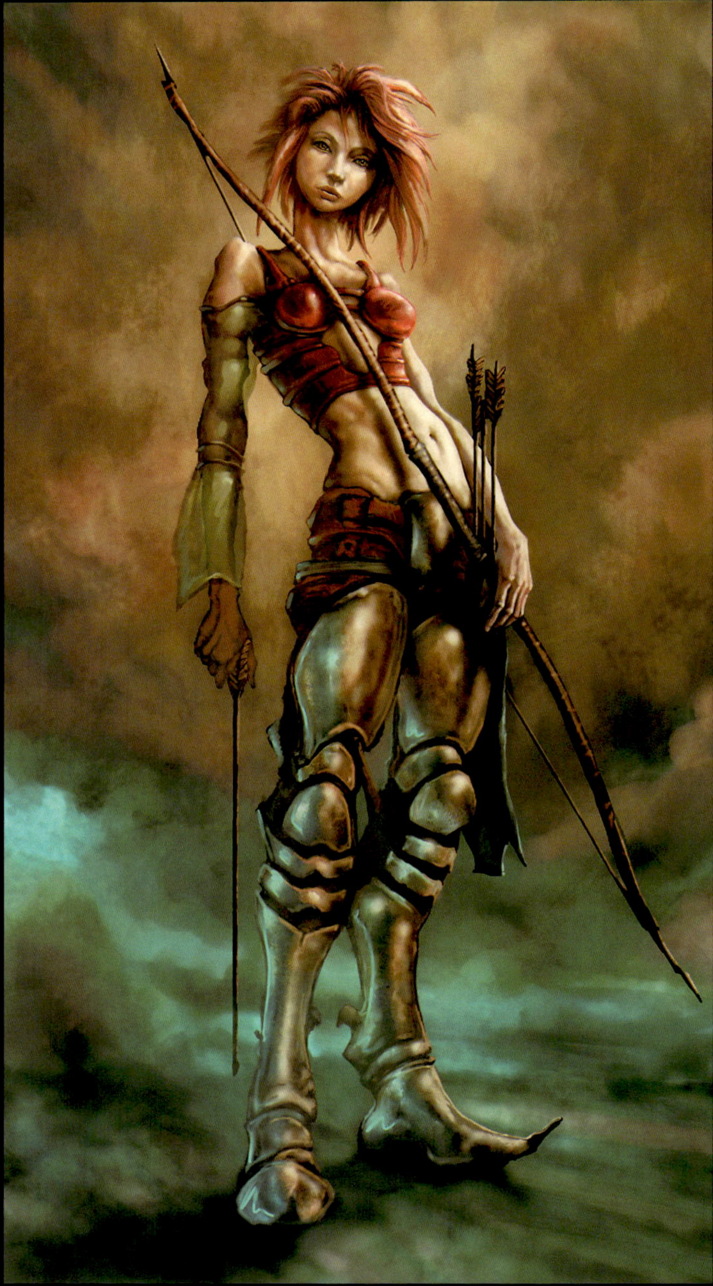

Archer
Photoshop, Painter
Chris Young, GREAT BRITAIN
[above]

Naga Dance
Photoshop
Camille Kuo, TAIWAN
[right]

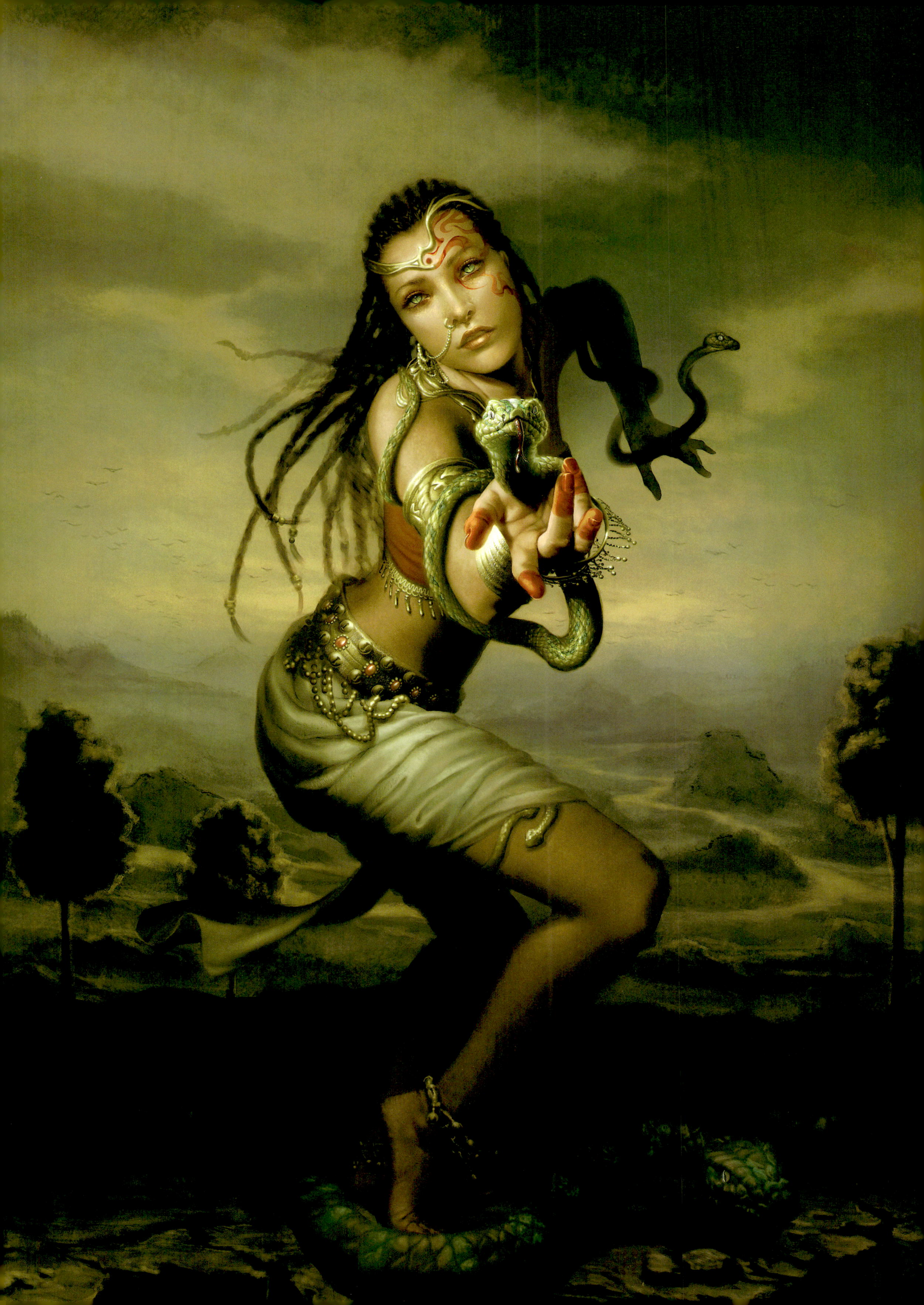

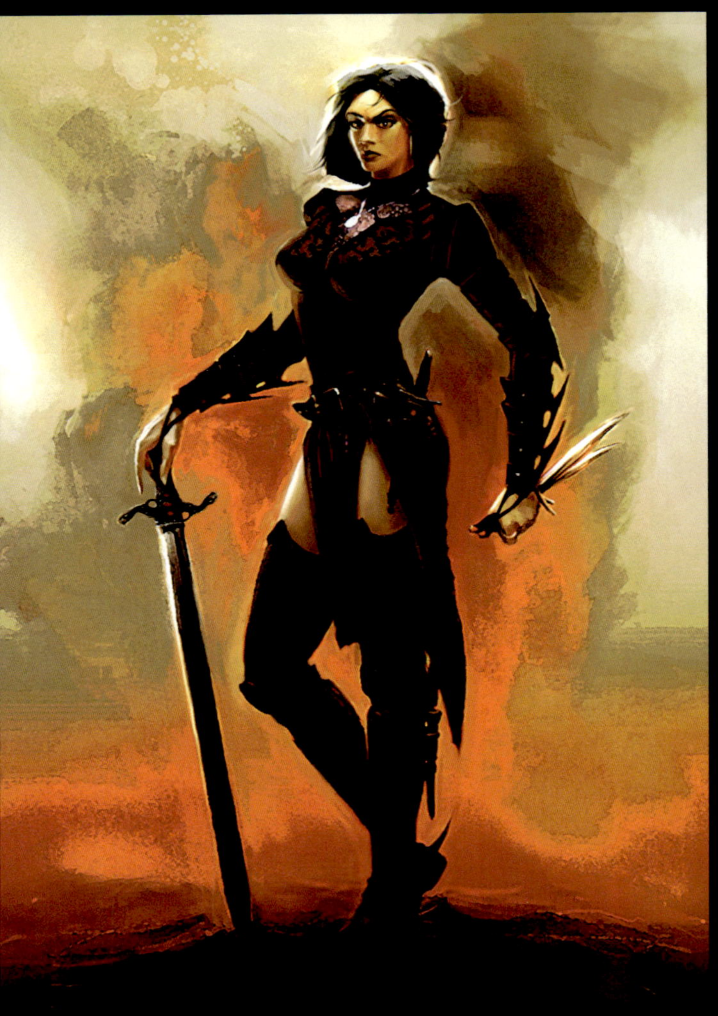

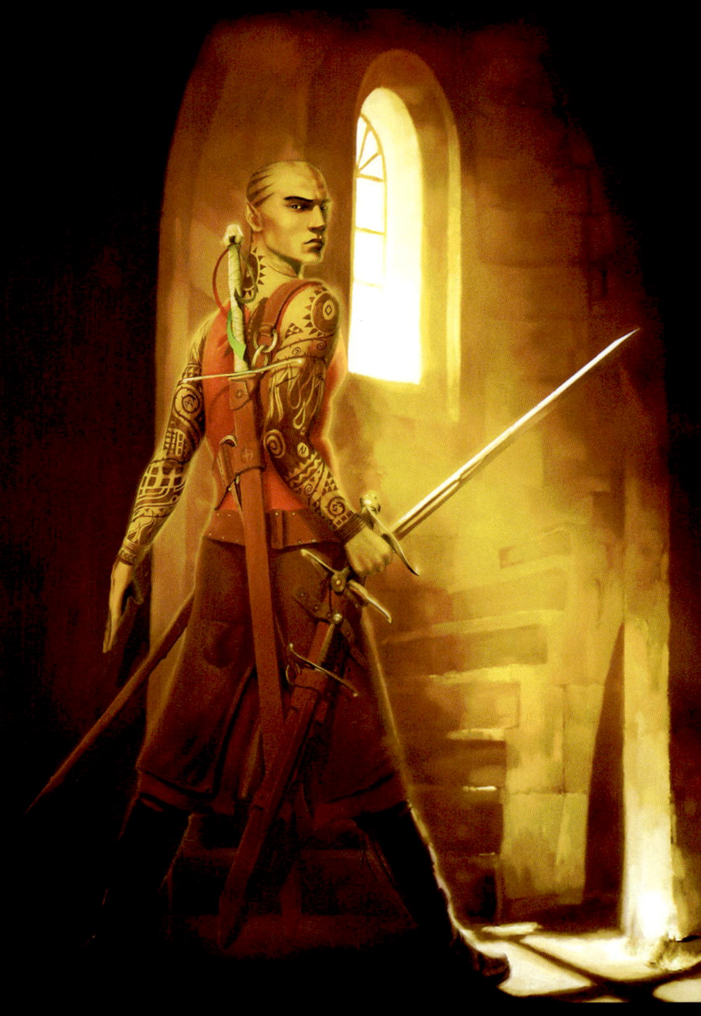

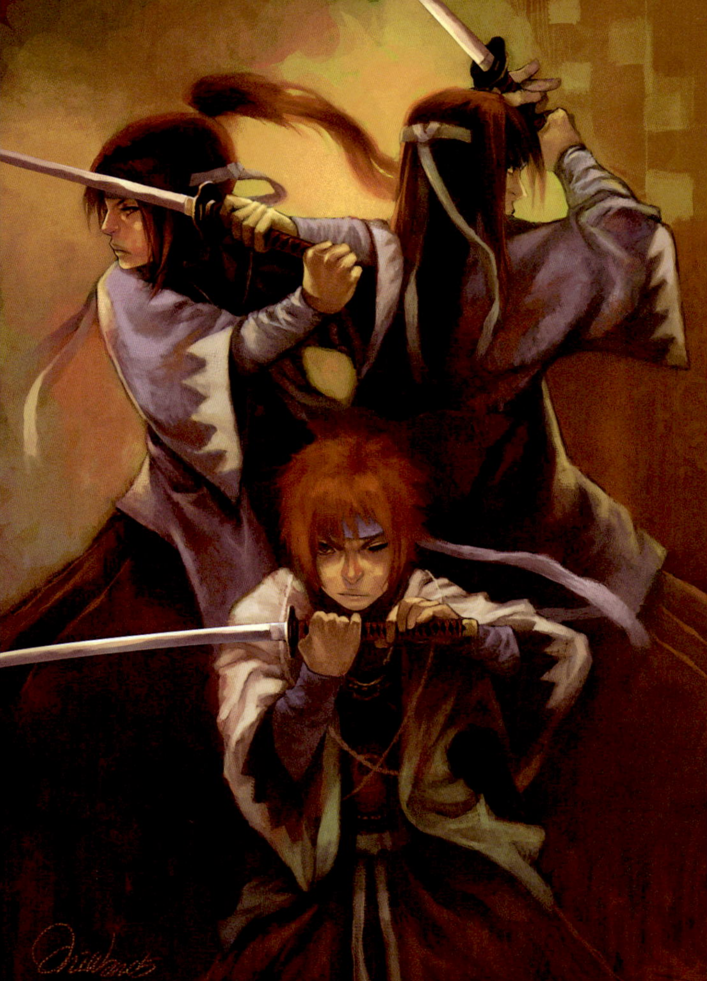

Dark Fire
Painter, Photoshop
John Dickenson,
Carbon Canyon Studios,
USA
[above left]

Cardil Shan Imadrîl
Photoshop, Painter
Oliver Wetter, Fantasio Fine Arts,
GERMANY
[above]

Shinsengumi
Photoshop
Leung Chun Wan,
HONG KONG
[left]

Queen of the Eternity
Painter
Hong Kuang,
SINGAPORE
[right]

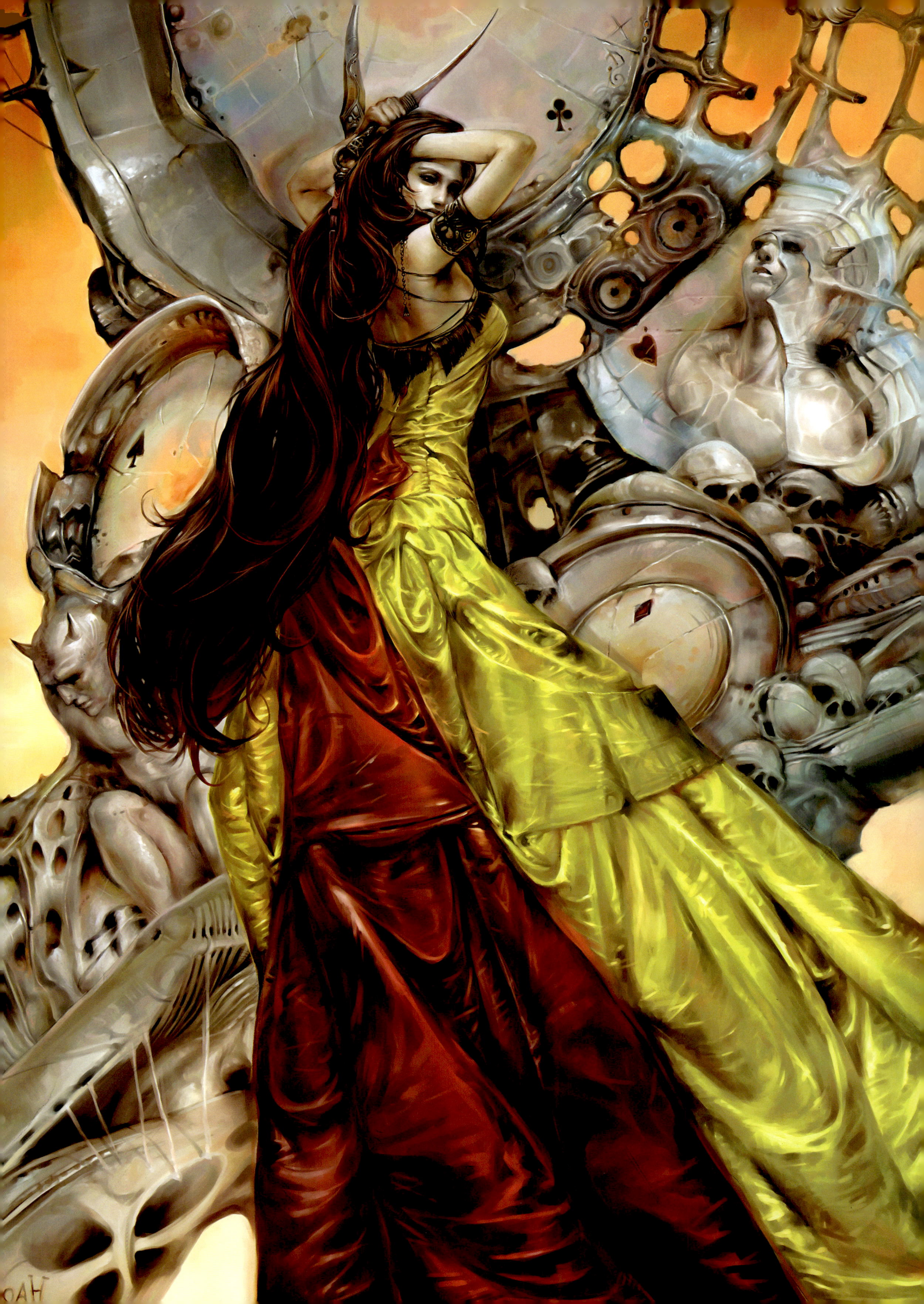

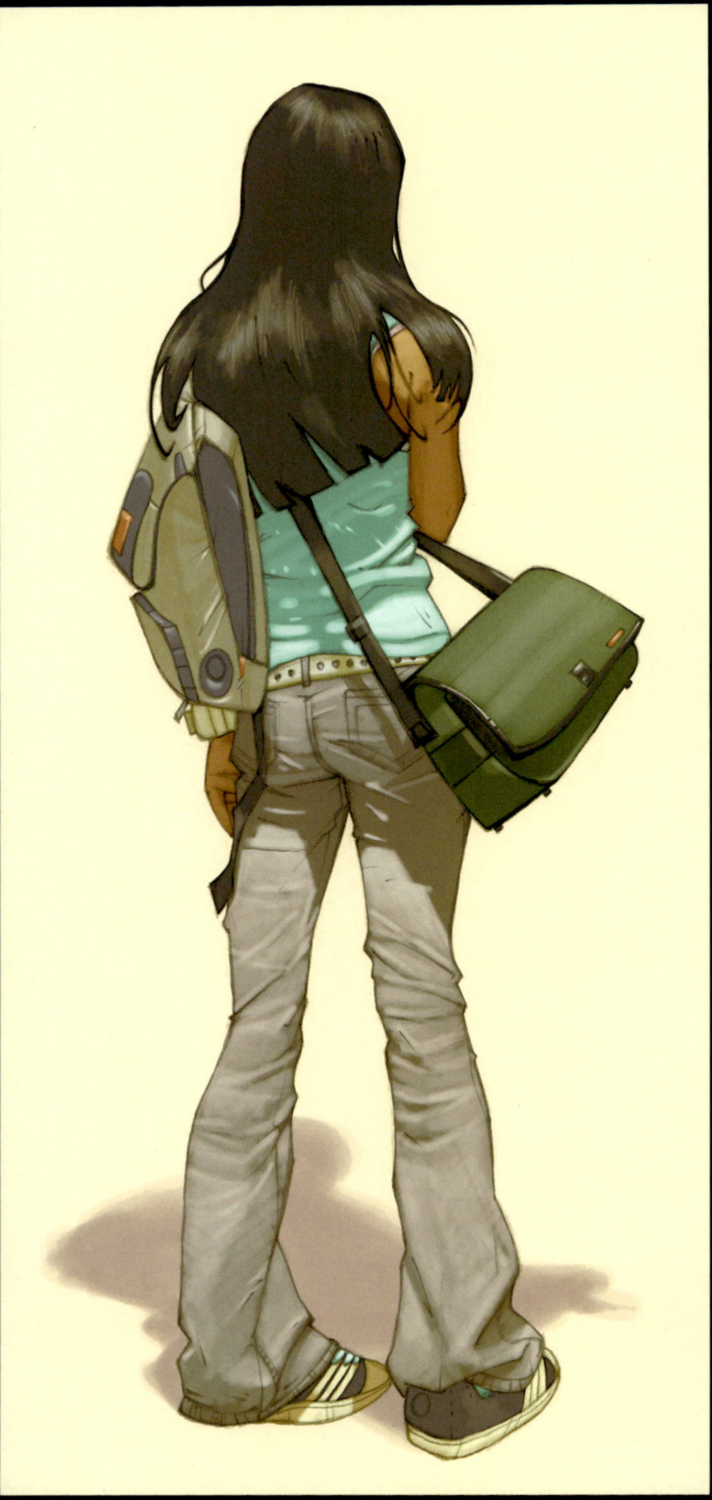

1-2-3
Photoshop
Francisco Perez, USA
[above]

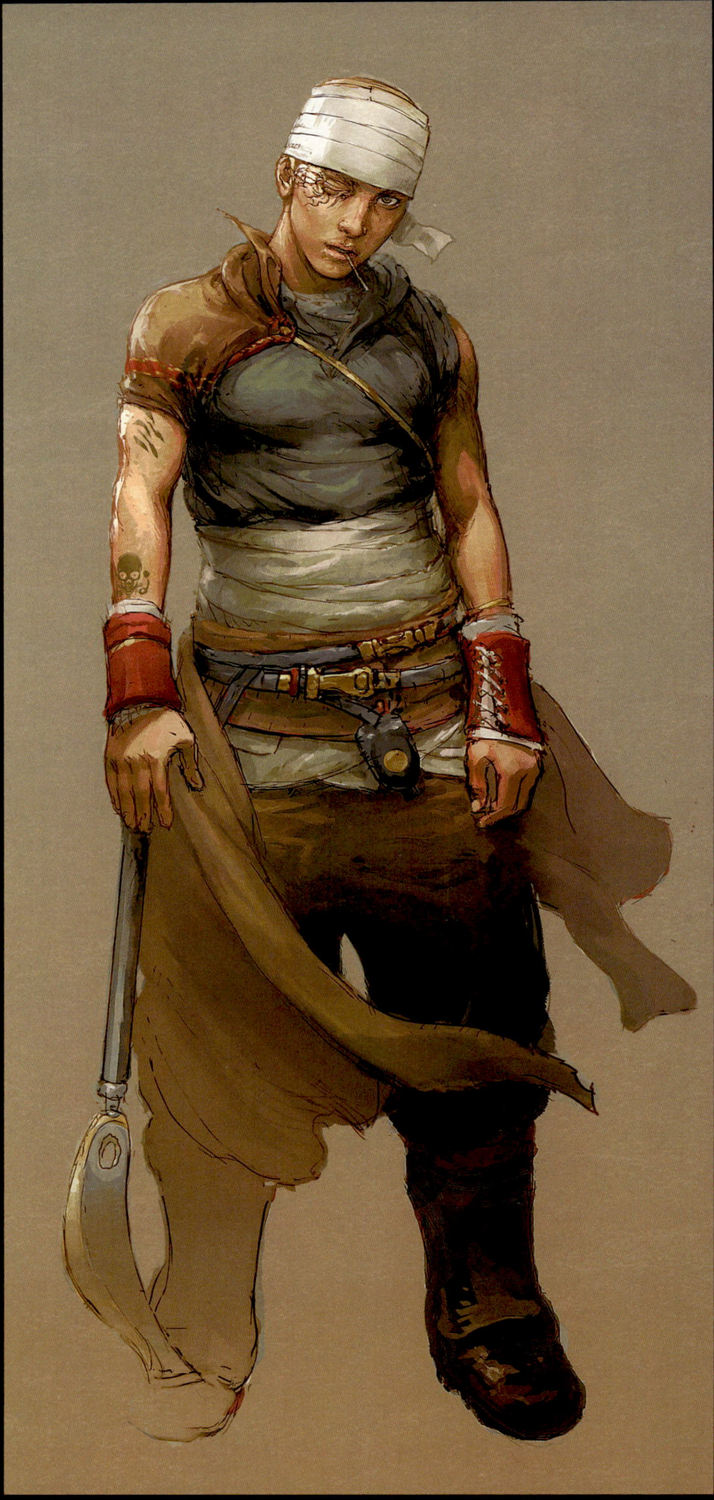

White Buffalo - Reeve
Photoshop
Gez Fry, JAPAN
[above]

Winter
Photoshop
Gez Fry, JAPAN
[right]

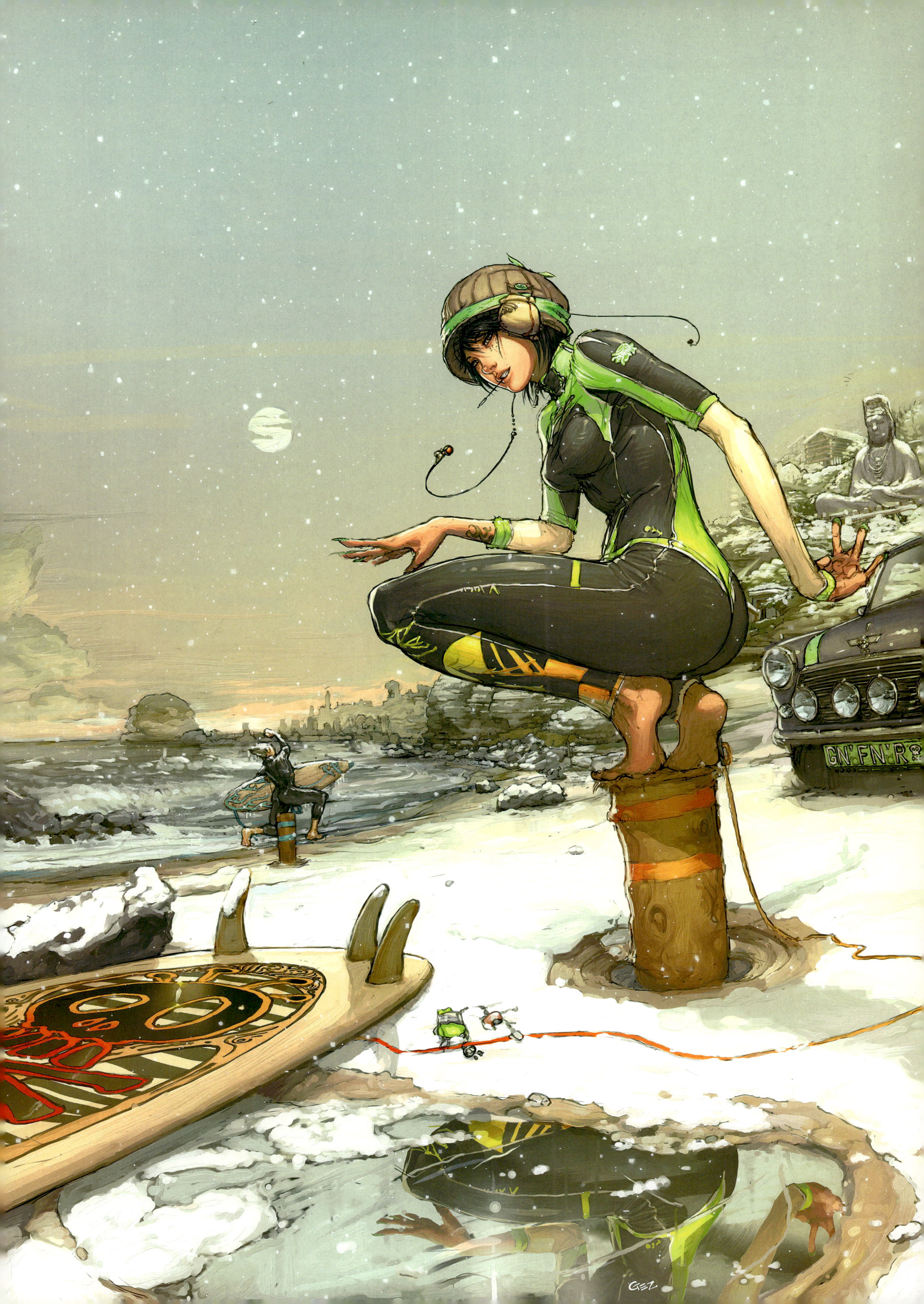
GN'FN'R
GEZ

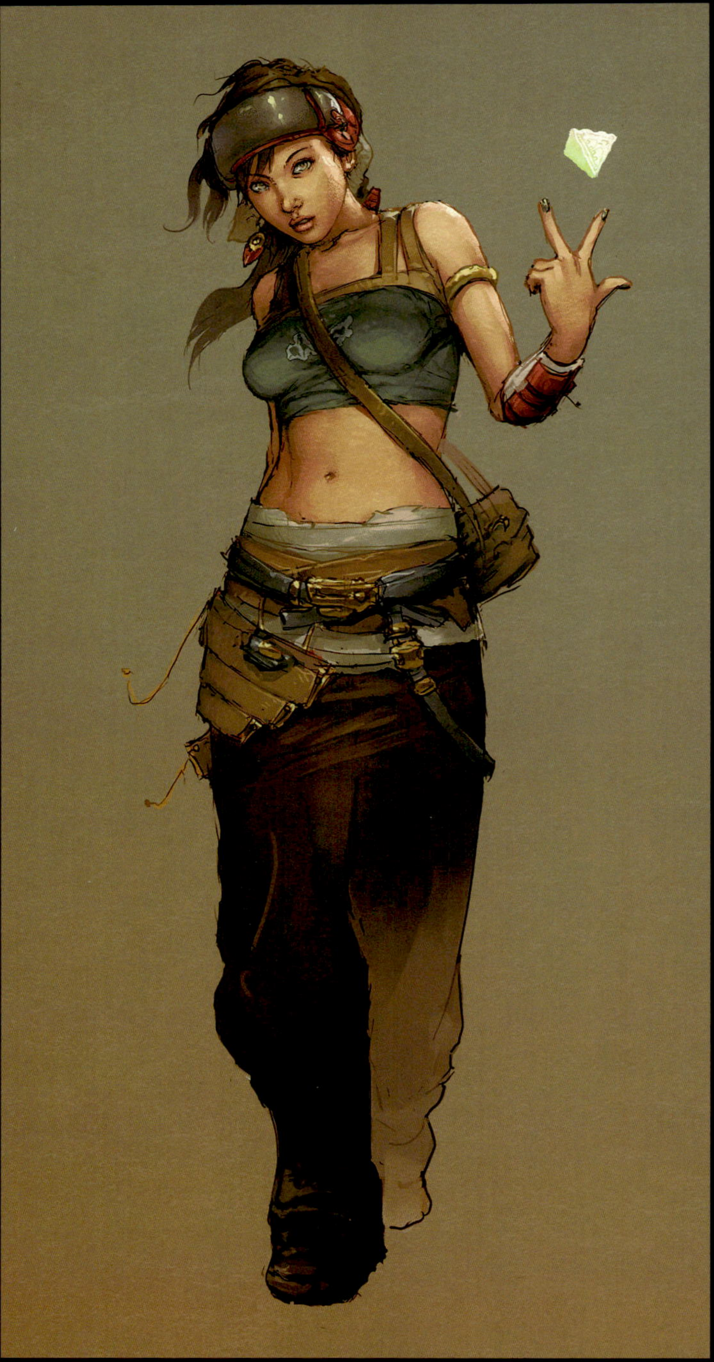

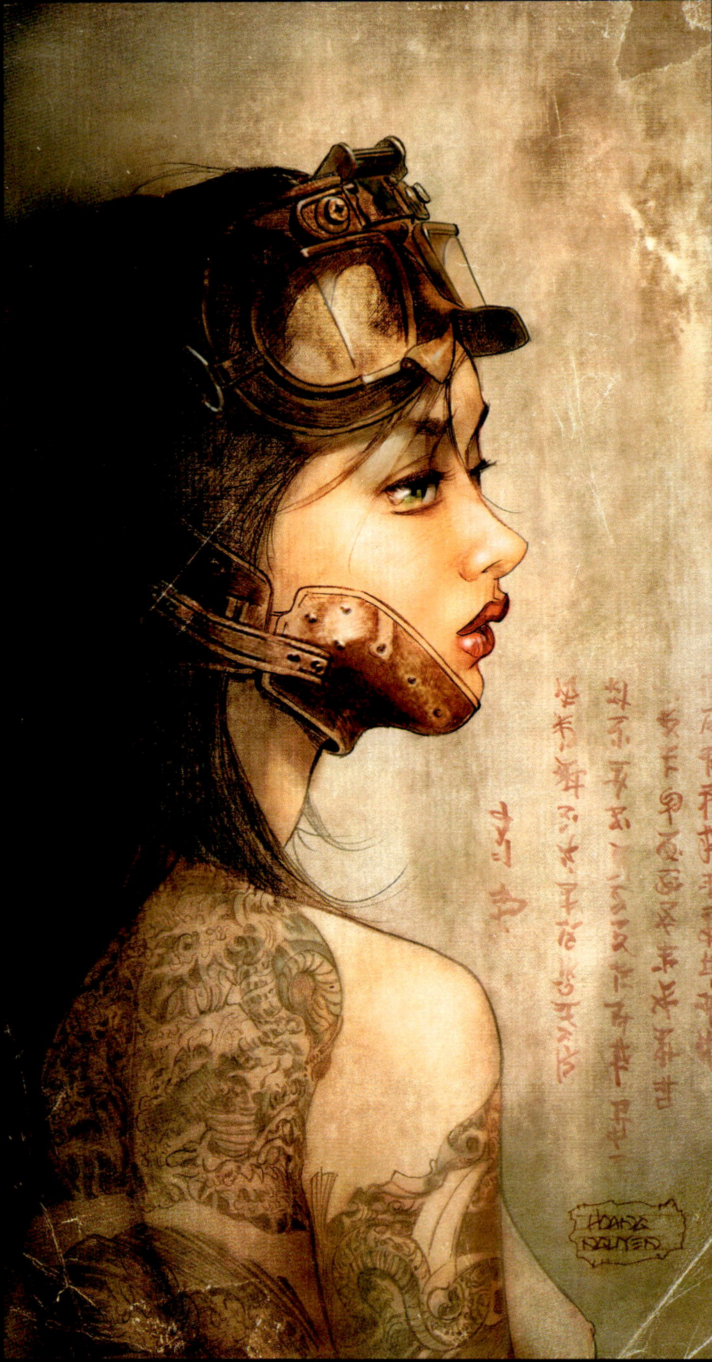

White Buffalo - Kay
Photoshop
Gez Fry, JAPAN
[above]

Memories Lost
Photoshop
Hoang Nguyen, USA
[above]

Swordsman
Photoshop
Leung Chun Wan, HONG KONG
[right]

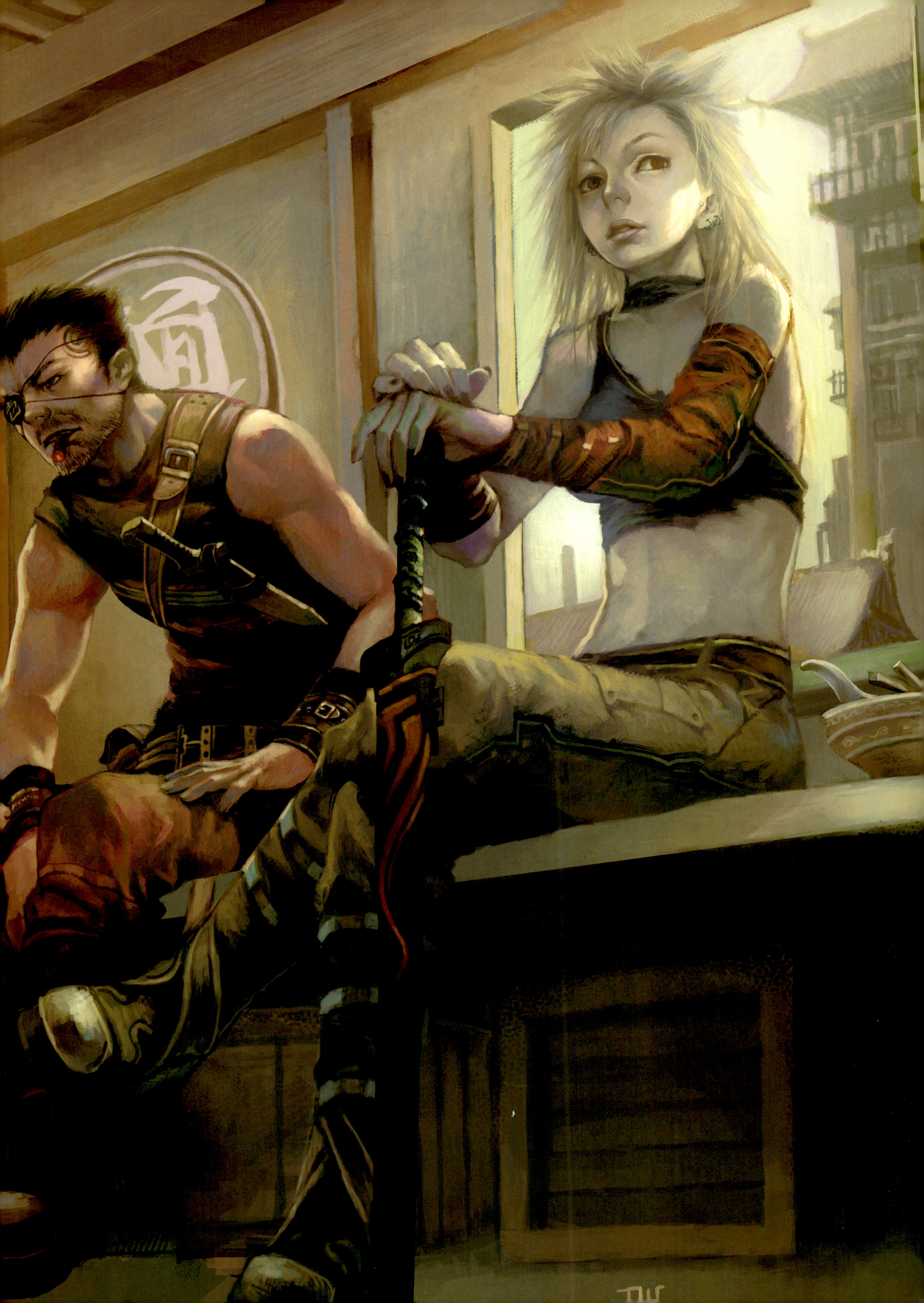

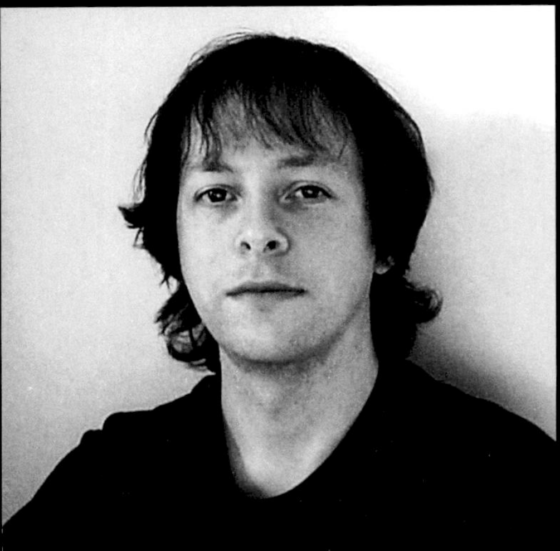

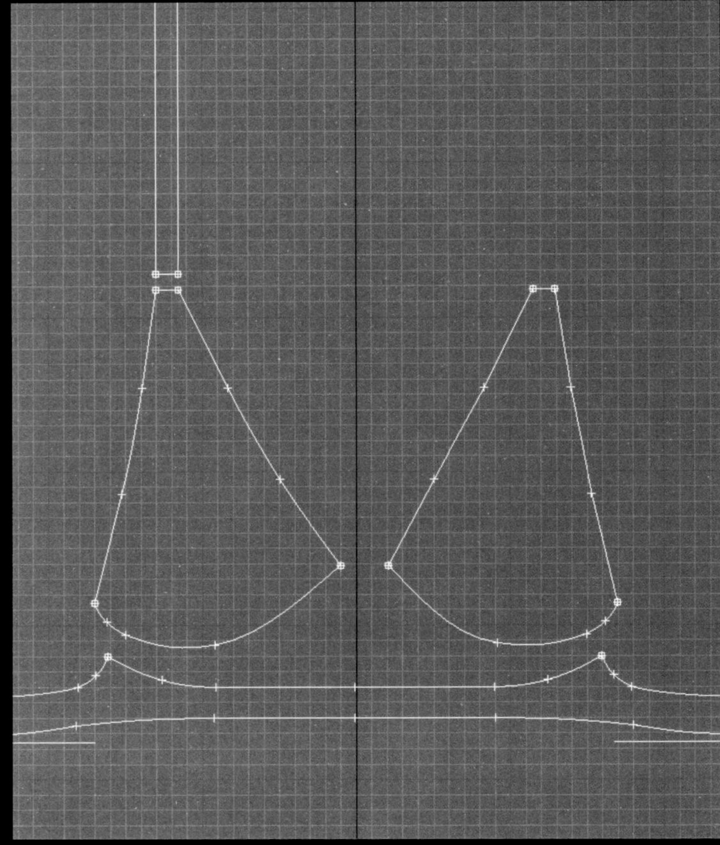

LIAM KEMP

www.this-wonderful-life.com
Liam@this-wonderful-life.com

"I didn't know anyone who knew anything about 3D and I had no Internet access, so all my learning was done the hard way."

After leaving school, Liam envisaged a career in illustration. This proved to be more difficult than he'd anticipated, and after a couple of years with little success he decided it was time to learn how to use a computer. "My next door neighbor had 3ds Max (but didn't know how to use it)," explains Liam. "He showed me some of its capabilites, which I was sufficiently impressed with to want to start learning how to use the program myself. I didn't know anyone who knew anything about 3D and I had no Internet access, so all my learning was done the hard way. I even learned nurbs before I knew how to model with polygons! Within a couple of years I had made two animated shorts: 'When Statues Dream' and 'Telly'. It was my third short 'This Wonderful Life' that got me recognition on the festival circuit. It was shown at Siggraph, 3D festival and Imagina. In August 2004 I left my job to work full-time on my next self-funded animated short 'The Normals'."

CLOTH

The costume was created using the ClothFX plug-in, where splines are drawn to create panels that form each section of the garment. The panels are then arranged around the body in the appropriate positions before the simulation pulls all the separate pieces together, wrapping them around the body and into place. For texturing the garment, a planar map was projected onto the whole spline layout of the cloth panels, and a screenshot was taken. Because the clothing was created using flat panels, this made texturing much easier as there was no need for UV tweaking, and texture streaking became non-existent. For the surface of the garment, a bump map was created using a 50% blend between hand-painted texture (for the creases and seams) and a fine noise map (for the roughness of the fabric). Another noise map was used in the Specularity channel to break up the uniformity of the highlights. To recreate the look of velvet, in the Diffuse channel I created a falloff map and increased the RGB value for the fresnel component so that the maroon color would appear brighter at glancing angles.

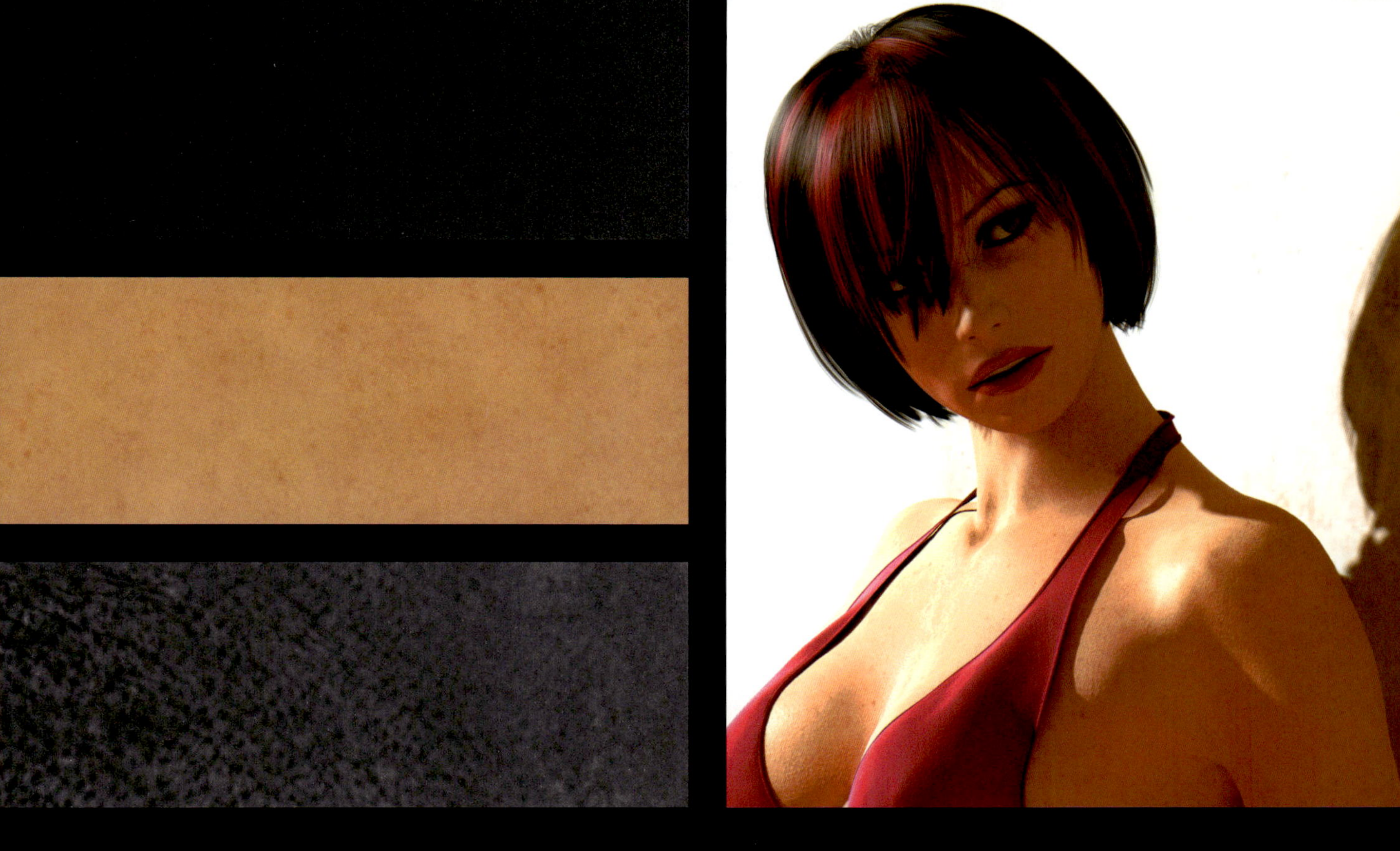

SKIN

To create the skin texture, I made several UV projections over various parts of the body. Arms, legs, body, hands and neck all received separate projections which were then loaded into a Composite material. A greyscale map was then used to blend between each projection so that underlying textures in the Composite material would show through. For the diffuse component, I started off by scanning a patch of skin which I then brought into Photoshop to duplicate, mirror, rotate, and rubberstamp across the surface of the texture map. Additional modifications to the brightness, contrast and hue were made to reduce the tiling effect. On top of this base I hand-painted smaller details such as veins and blemishes to complete the diffuse layer. The bump map was drawn by hand—I would initially concentrate upon a small area where I would create the goose-pimples, cracks and pores, and then rubberstamp this to other areas, adding in extra detail as required. The Specularity and Glossiness maps were black bitmaps. I used Photoshop's Grain filter to create the irregularities of the reflected surface.

LIGHTING

I wanted the image to appear sunlit and have a warm feel, so I created a spotlight with a slight yellow tint that shone directly across her body in order to pick out her curves. The environment was a simple box, about the size of a large room, with a weathered-looking texture placed upon the walls. For the flooring, I used a texture map of wooden floorboards and gave it a golden tint in order to soften the reflected light up onto her skin. For all the mesh objects, Global Illumination was used with photons to bounce the light and give an even warm tint across the whole image. As the hair was not a geometric object, it couldn't respond effectively to bounced light and so a separate lighting set-up was used for this. In order to match the illumination of the rest of the image, I placed spotlights in positions where light would reflect off the walls and onto her body.

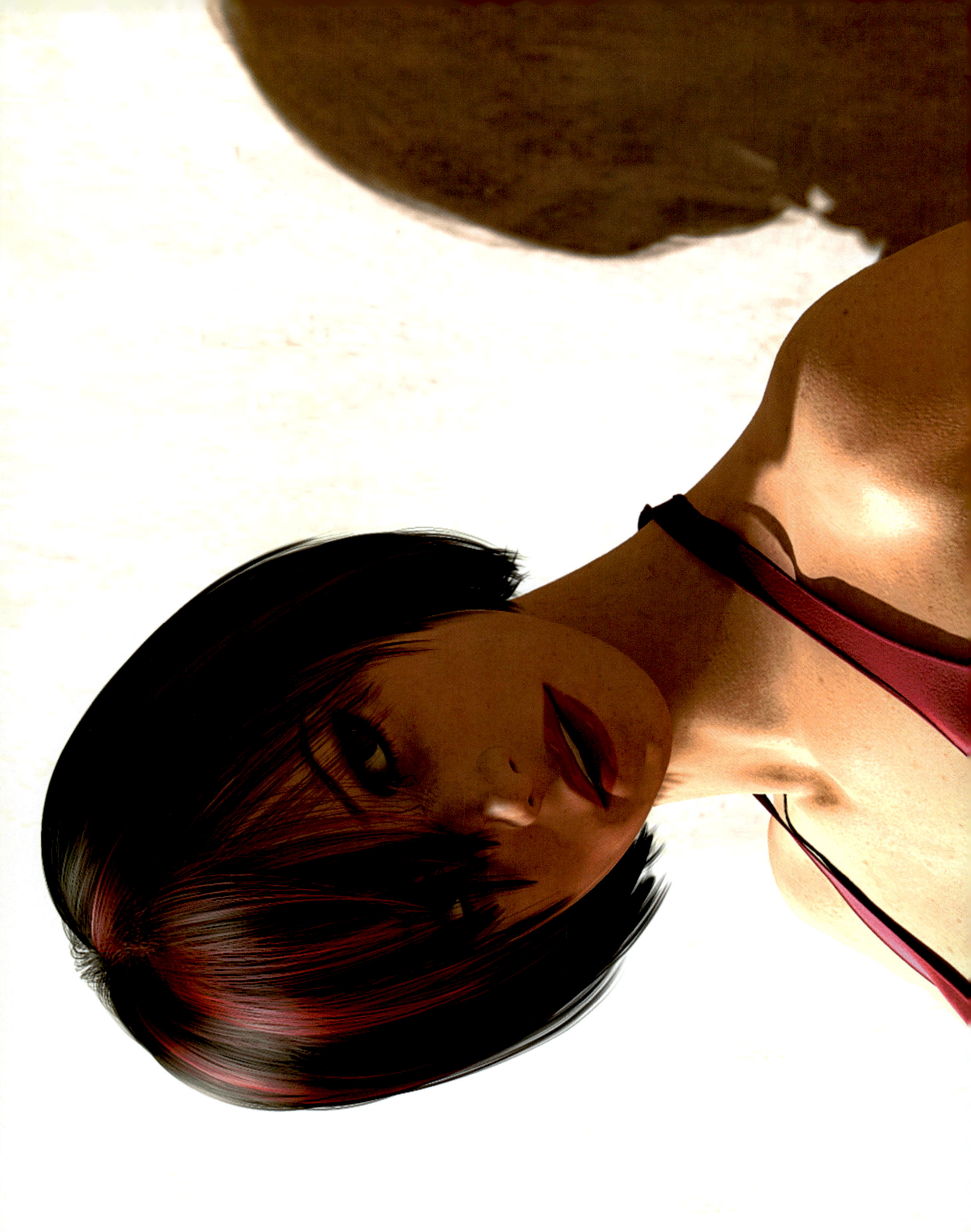

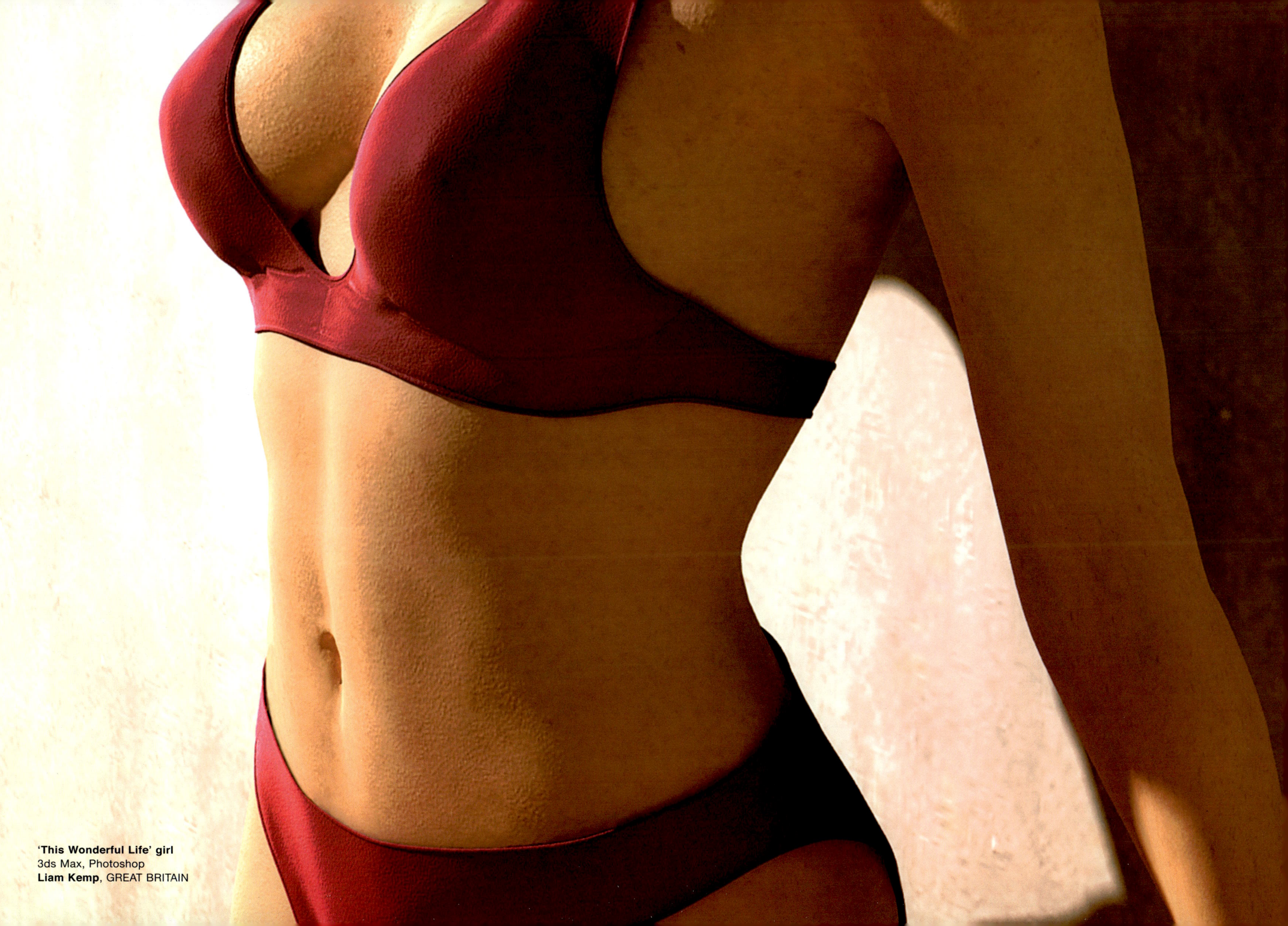

'This Wonderful Life' girl
3ds Max, Photoshop
Liam Kemp, GREAT BRITAIN

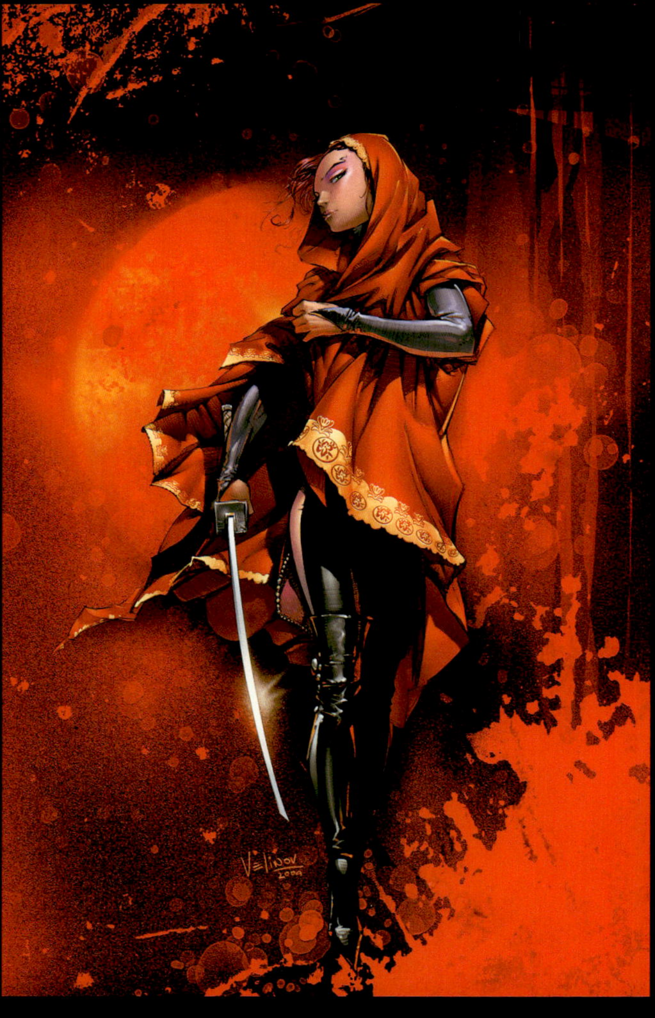

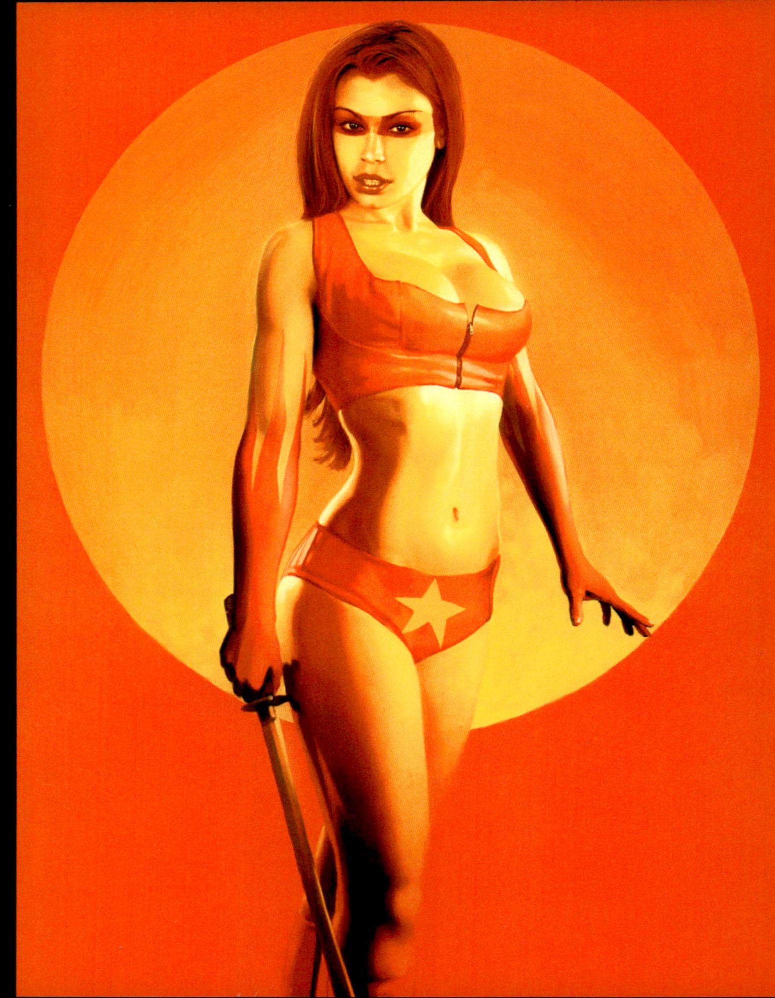

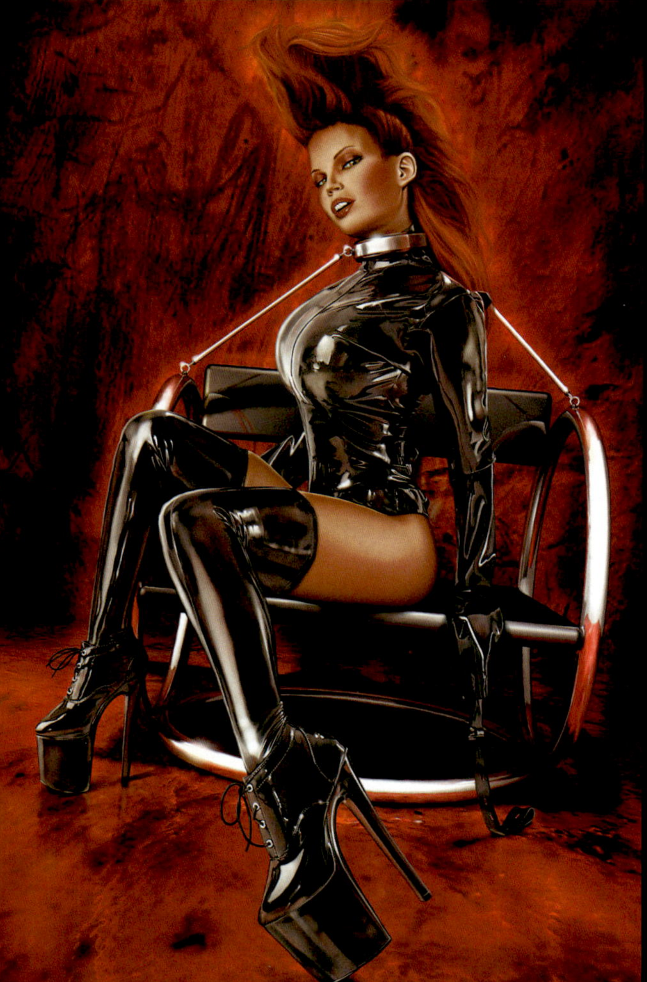

Red Moon
Photoshop
Svetlin Velinov, BULGARIA
[above left]

Ronin Girl
Painter
Oliver Wetter, Fantasio Fine Arts, GERMANY
[above]

Bianca
Photoshop, 3ds Max
Model: Bianca Beauchamp
Jean-Yves Lelcercq,
JYL Computer Art,
BELGIUM
[left]

Drop Red Gorgeous
CINEMA 4D, Poser, Photoshop
Client: 3D World magazine/
Future Publishing
Adam Benton, GREAT BRITAIN
[right]

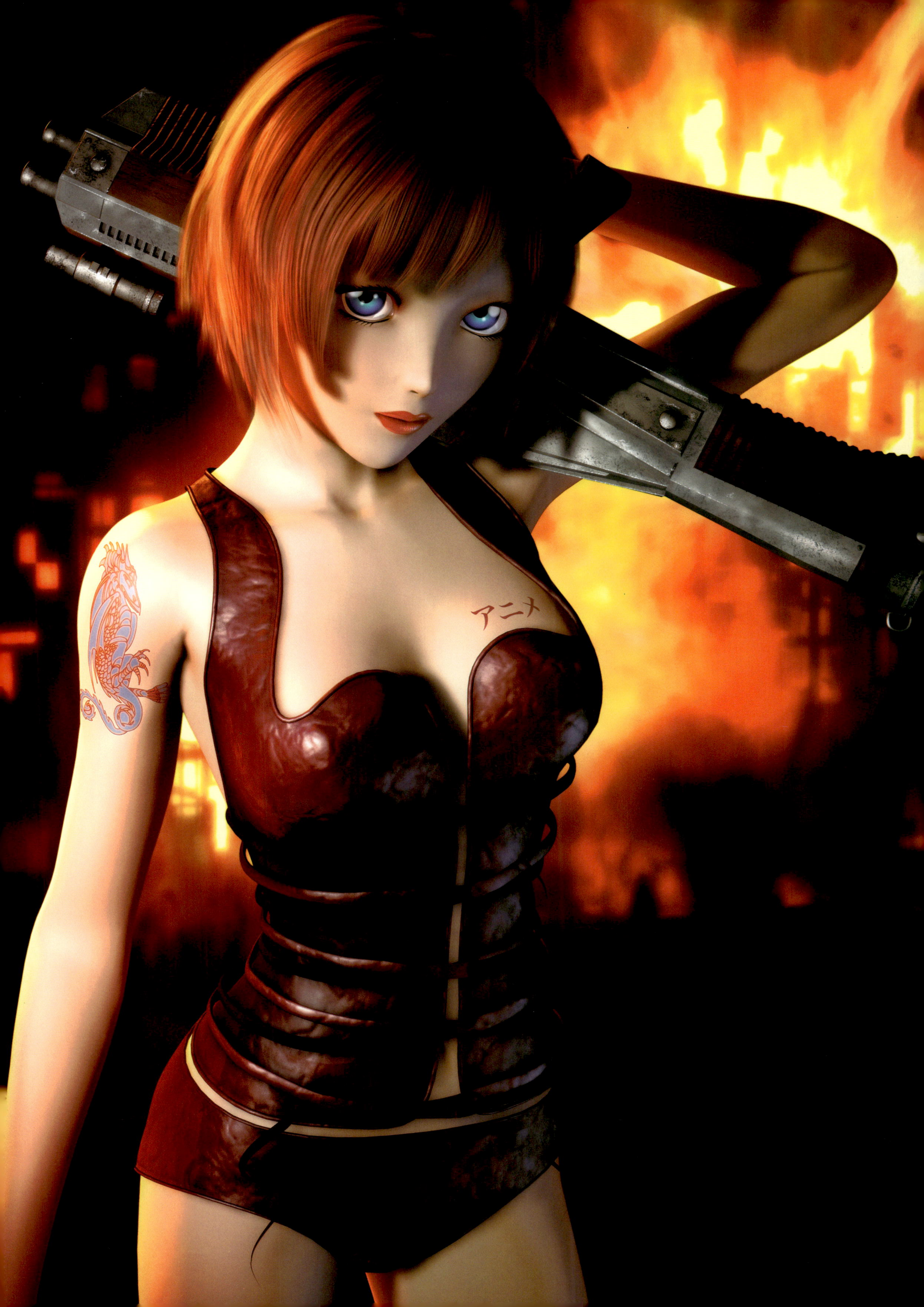
アニメ

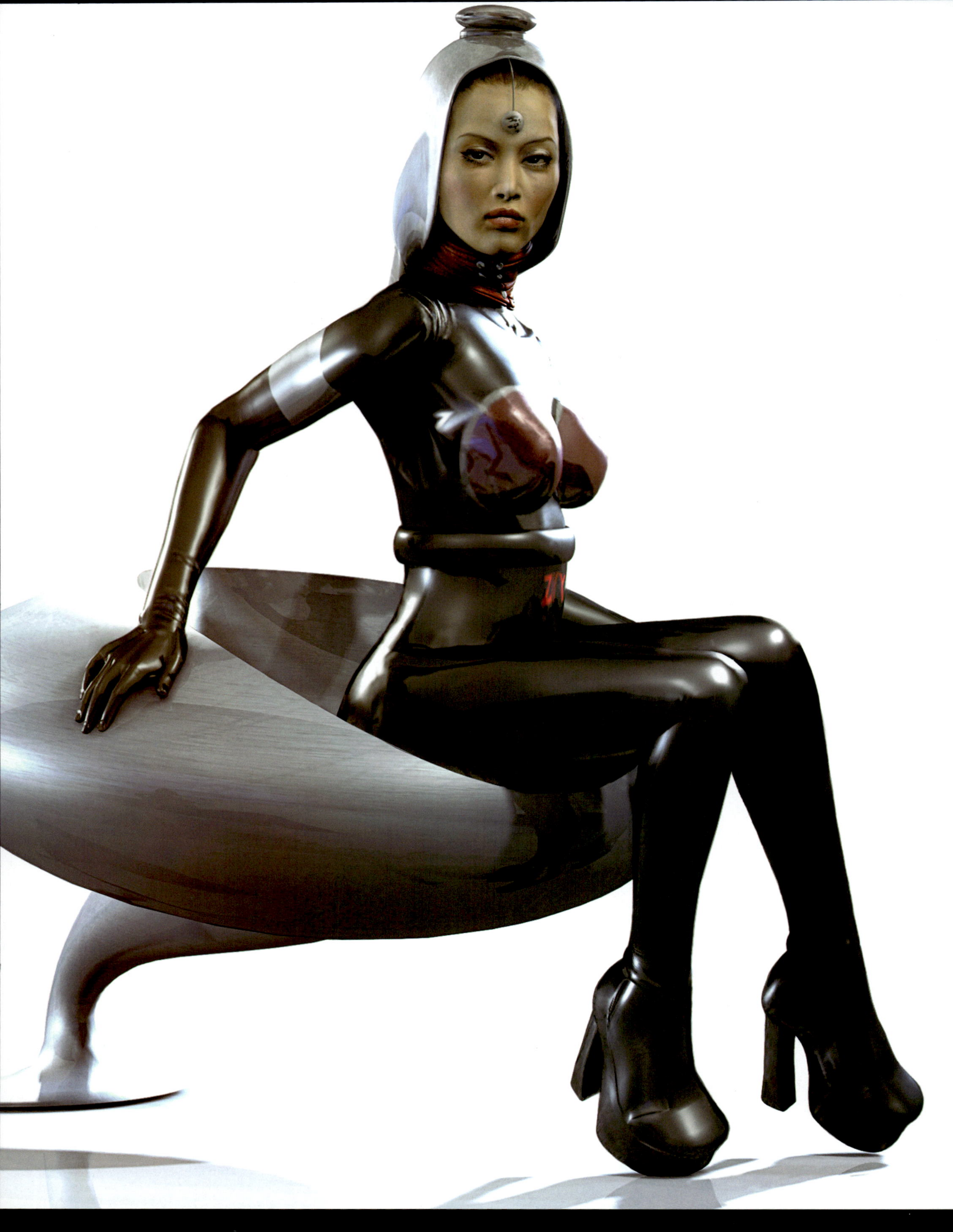

Karma
Maya, Photoshop
Rene Morel, CANADA
[above]

FG
Photoshop, CINEMA 4D
Benedict Campbell, GREAT BRITAIN
[right]

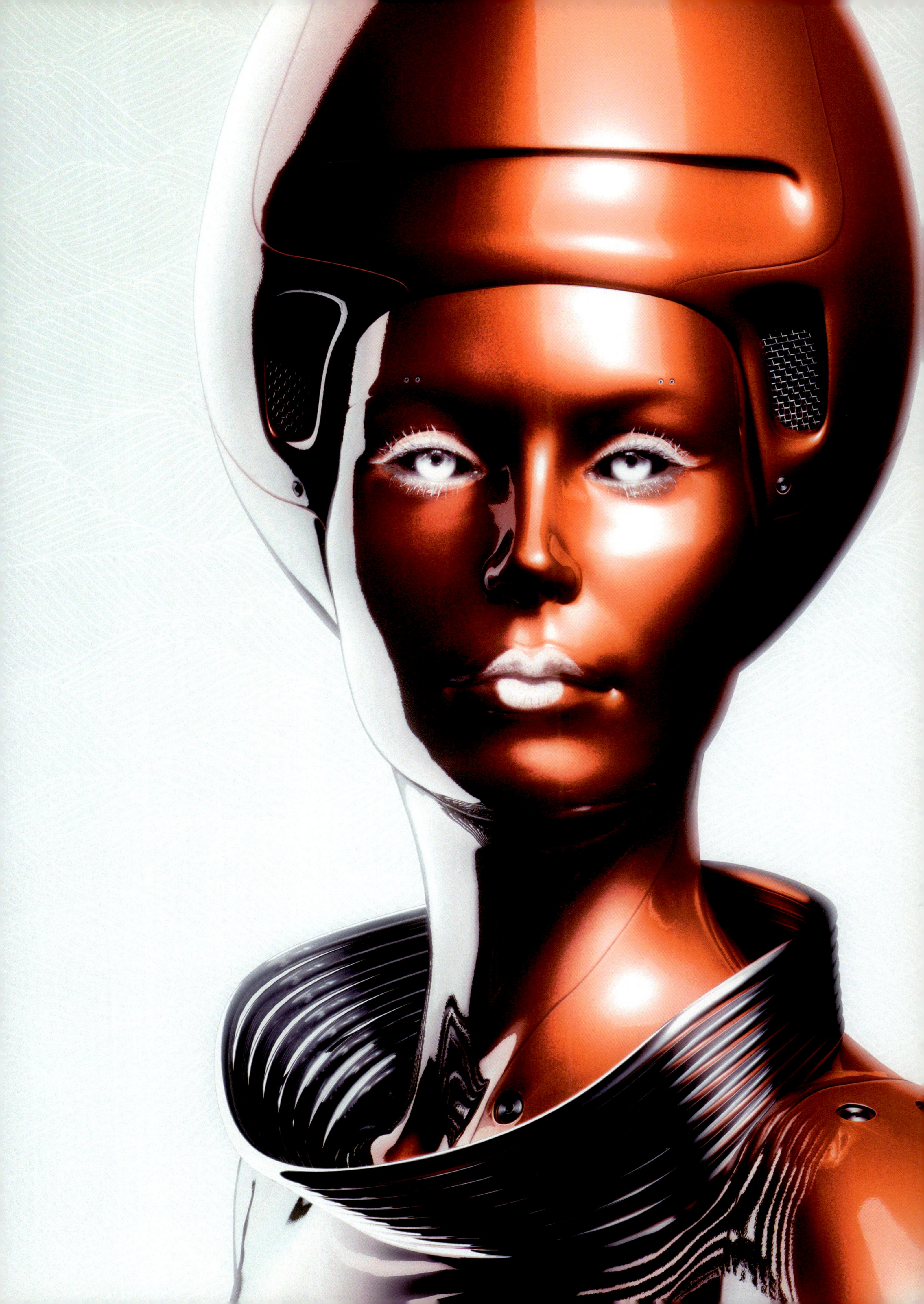

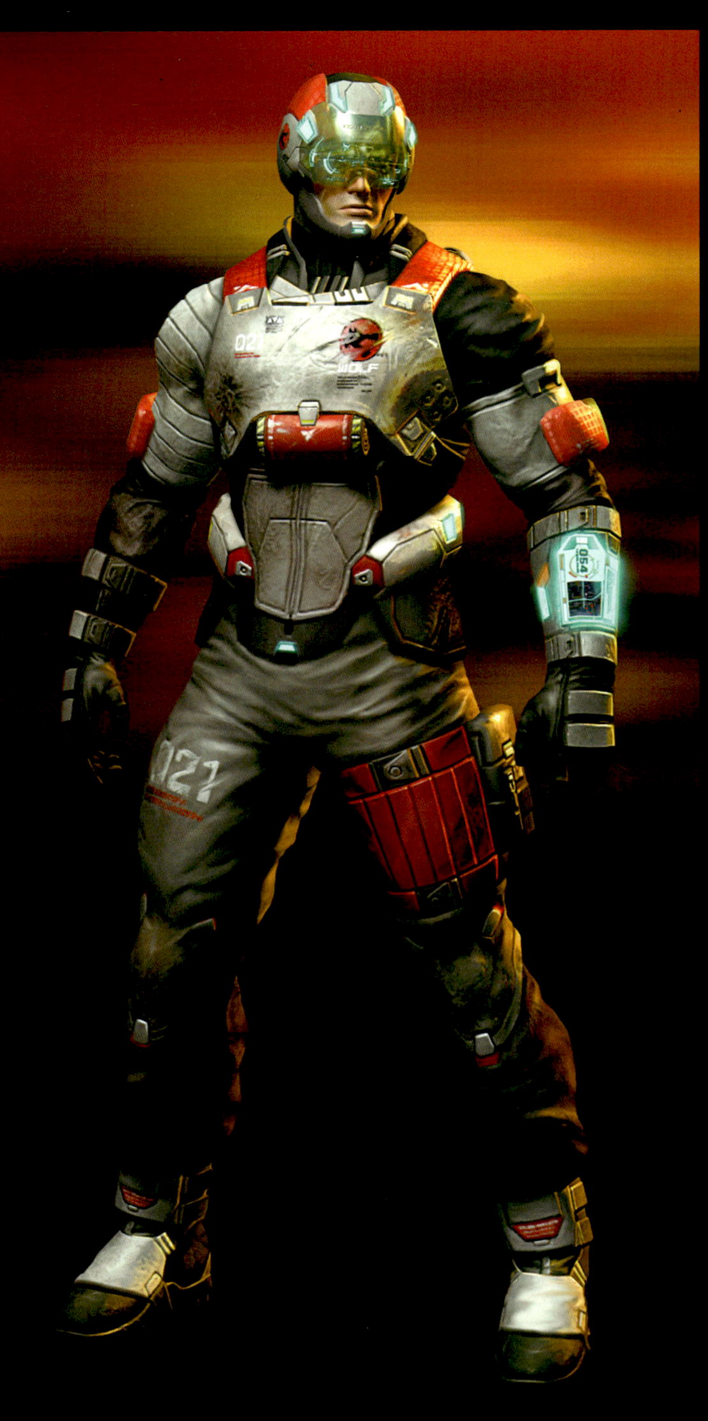

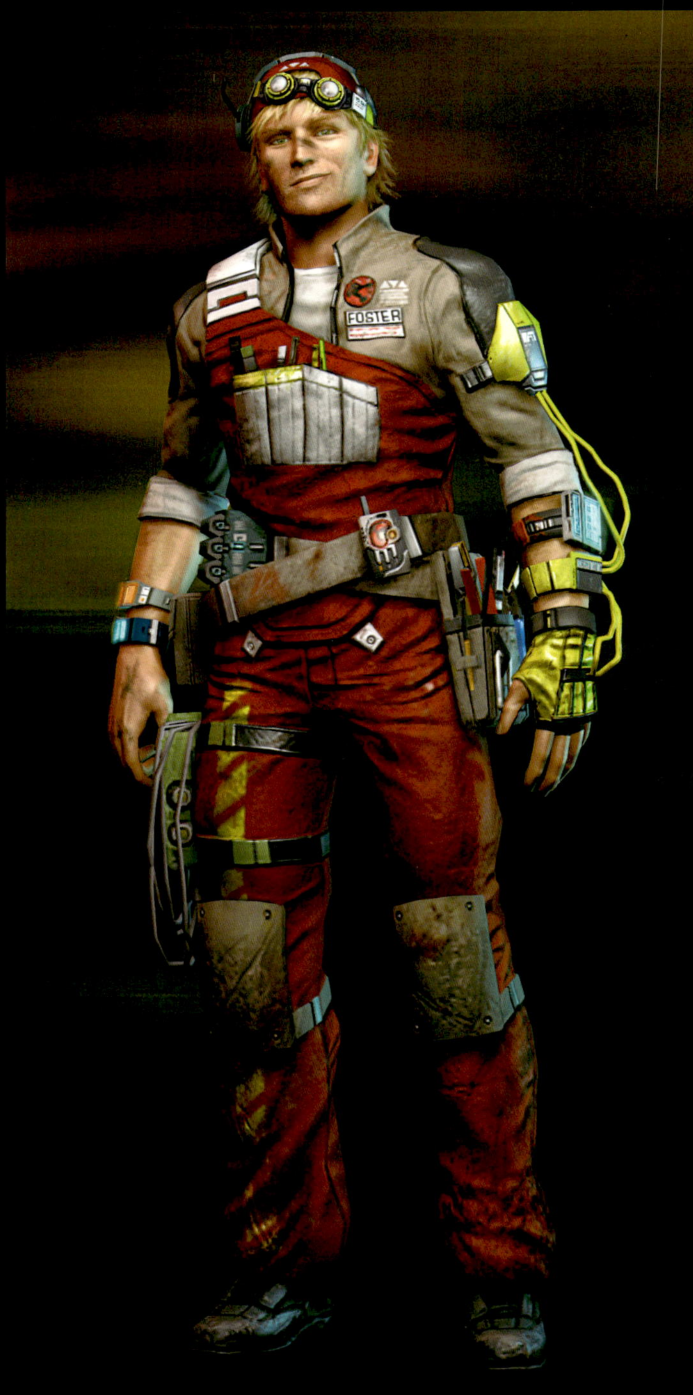

Mech Warrior, MechAssault 2
3ds Max, Photoshop
Josh Nizzi, Day 1 Studios, USA
[above]

Foster, MechAssault 2
3ds Max, Photoshop
Josh Nizzi, Day 1 Studios, USA
[above]

Natalia Magazine Cover, MechAssault 2
3ds Max, Photoshop
Josh Nizzi, Day 1 Studios, USA
[right]

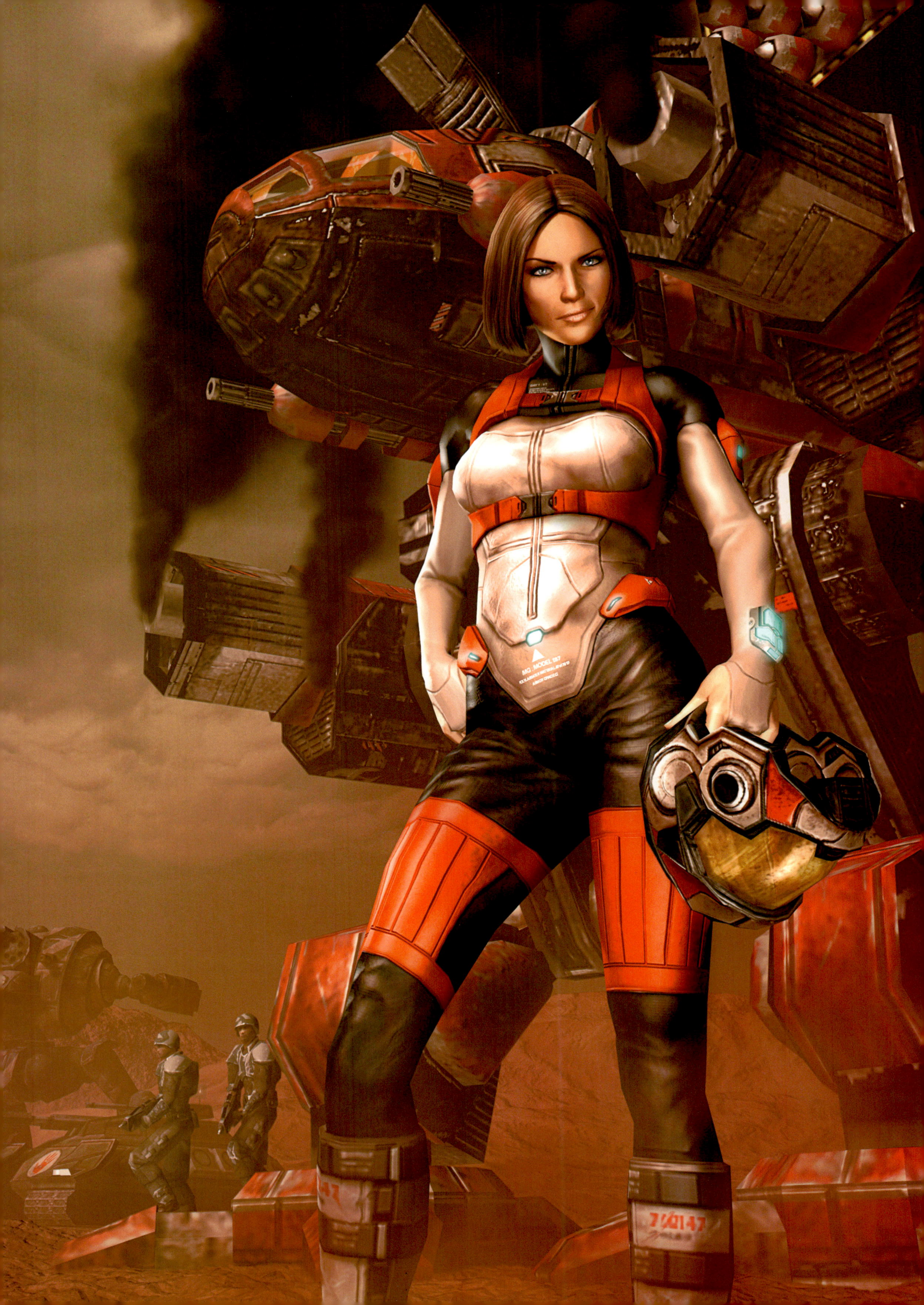

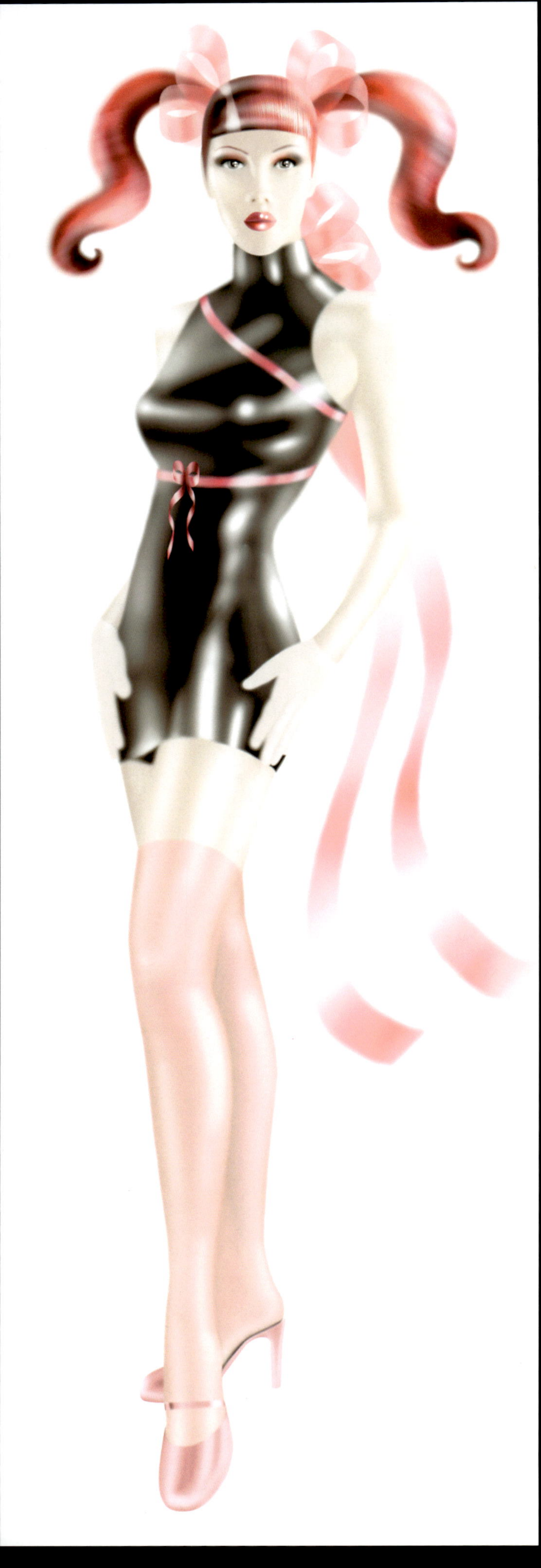

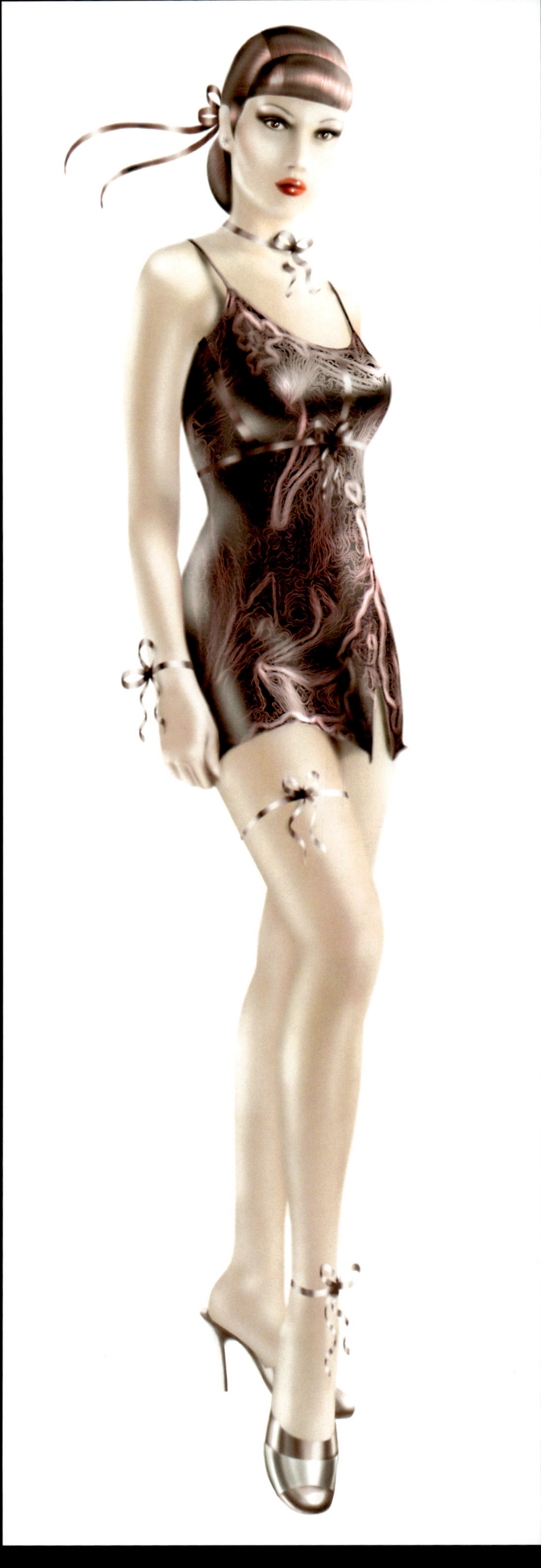

Pretty (Strawberry Dream)
Photoshop
Lisa Bertnick, USA
[far left]

Sasha
Photoshop
Lisa Bertnick, USA
[left]

Shoot
Photoshop, Poser, BodyPaint, CINEMA 4D
Benedict Campbell, GREAT BRITAIN
[right]

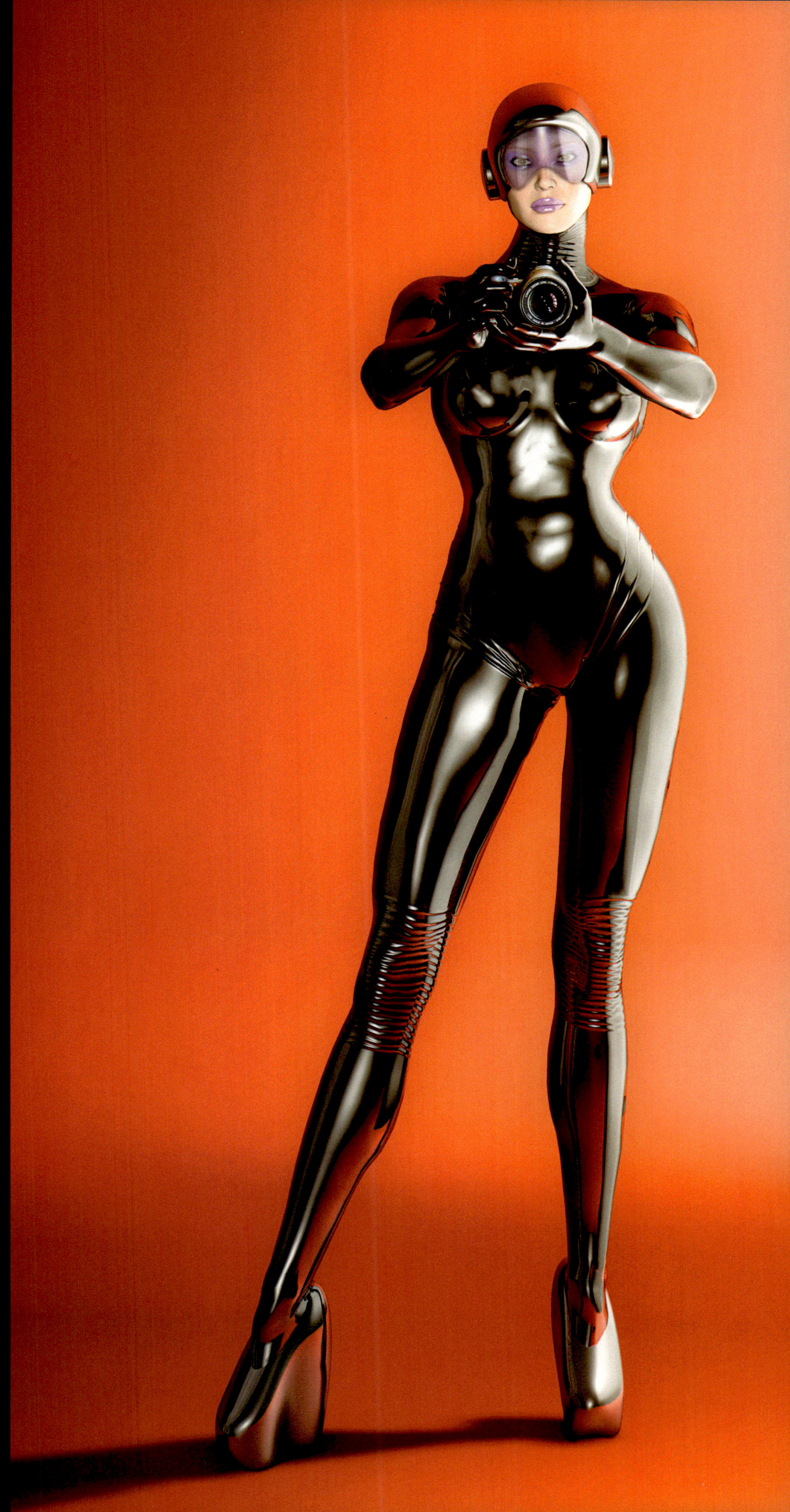

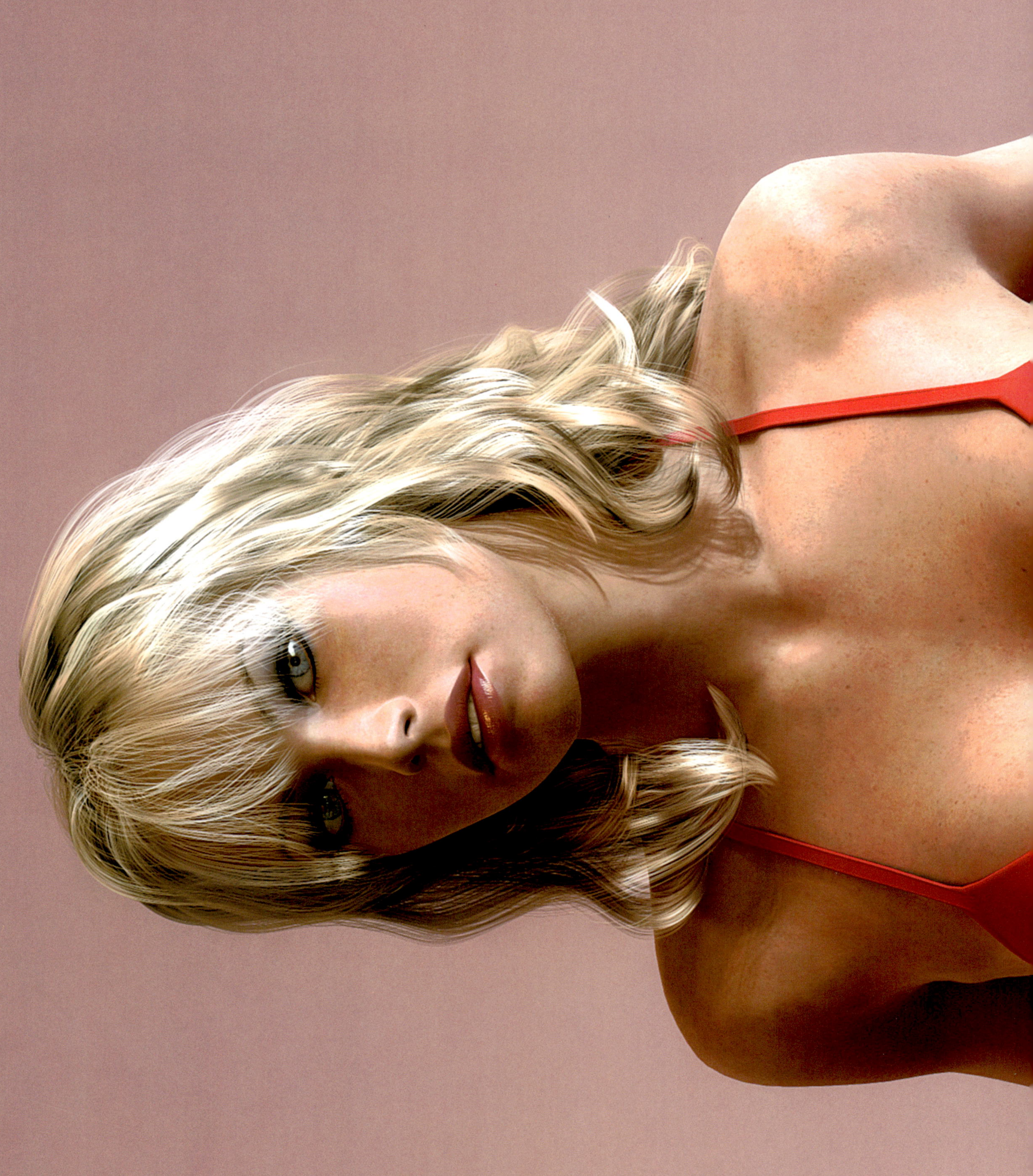

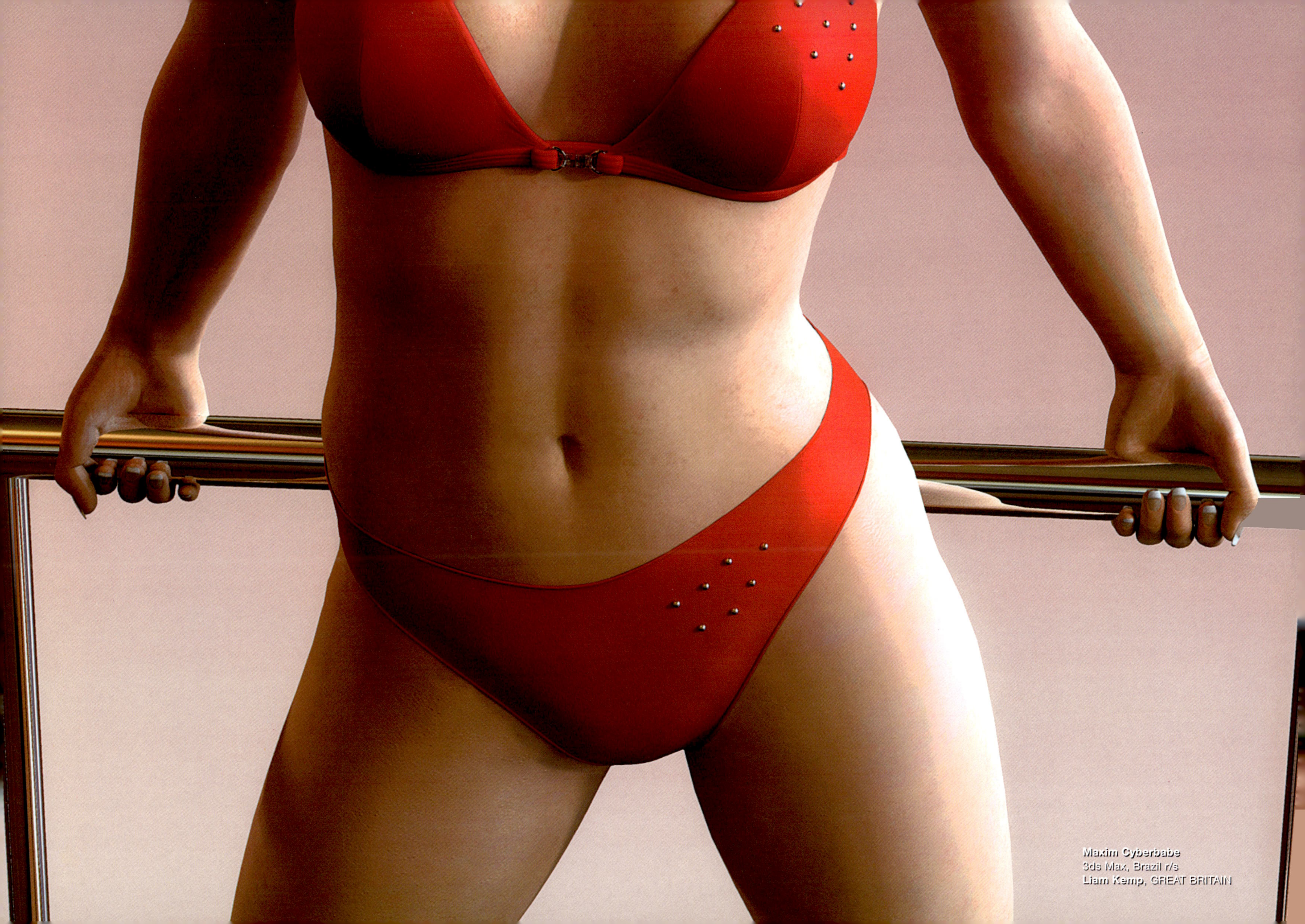

Maxim Cyberbabe
3ds Max, Brazil r/s
Liam Kemp, GREAT BRITAIN

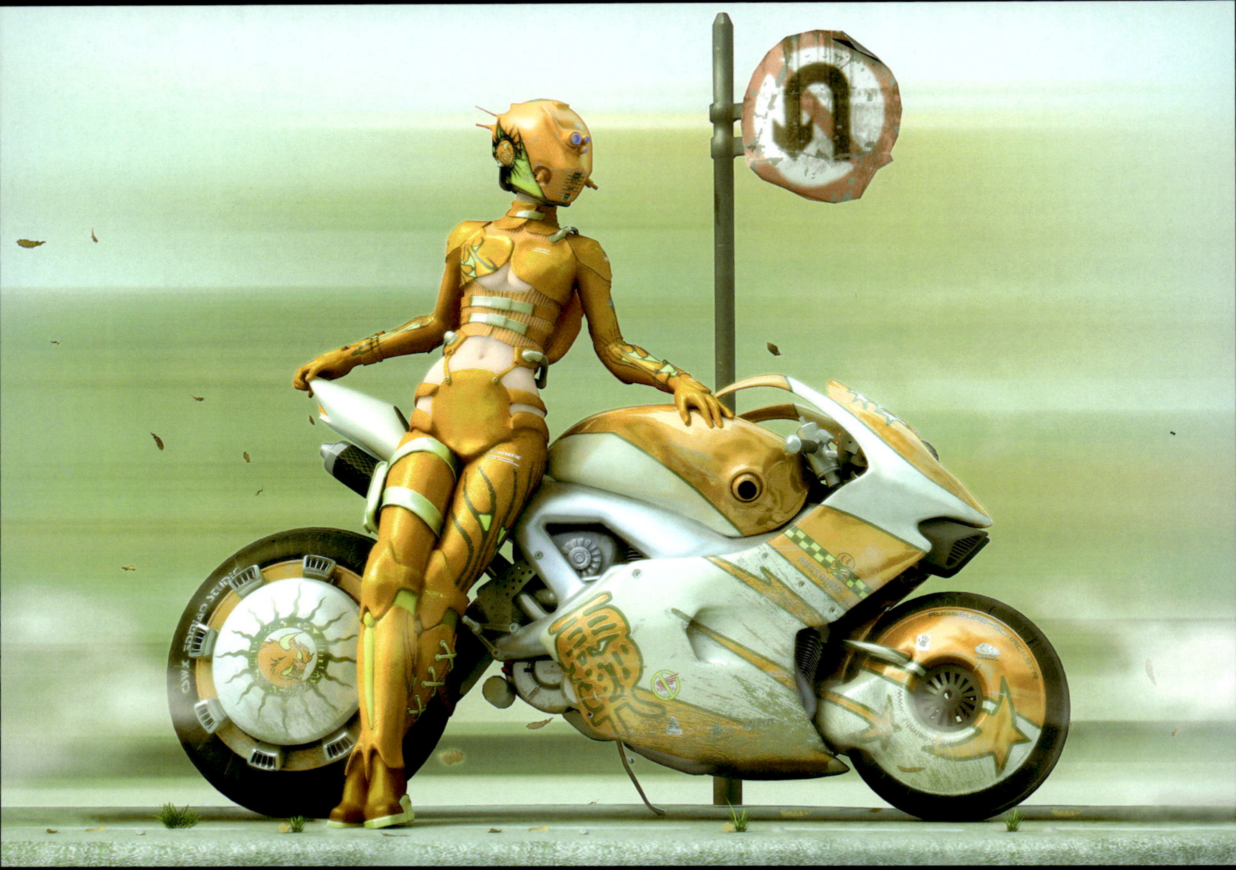

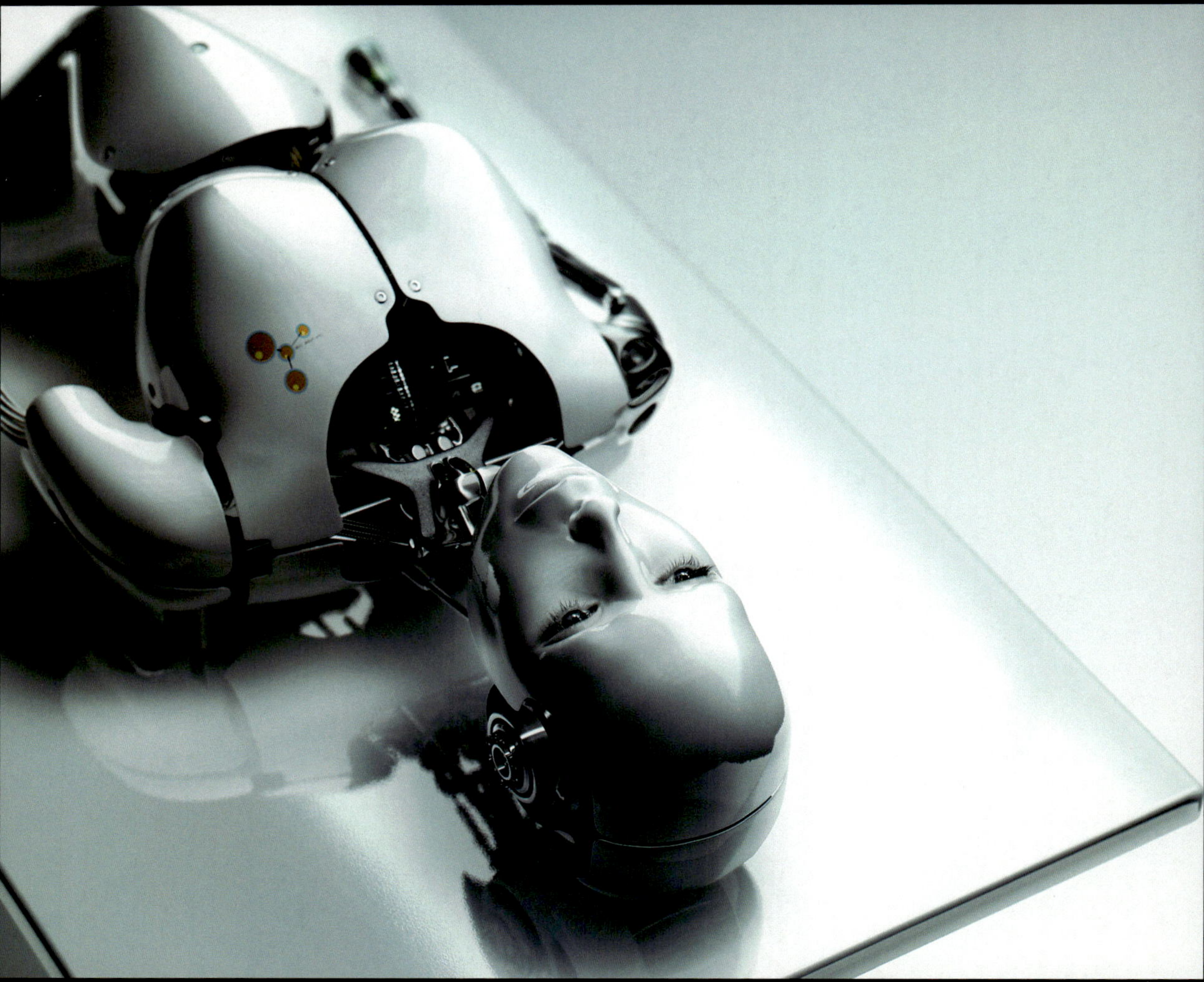

Cyclone Girl
3ds Max, VRay, Photoshop
Miao He, GERMANY
[top]

T3 bot
Photoshop, BodyPaint, CINEMA 4D
Benedict Campbell, GREAT BRITAIN
[above]

MM
Photoshop, CINEMA 4D, Poser
Benedict Campbell, GREAT BRITAIN
[right]

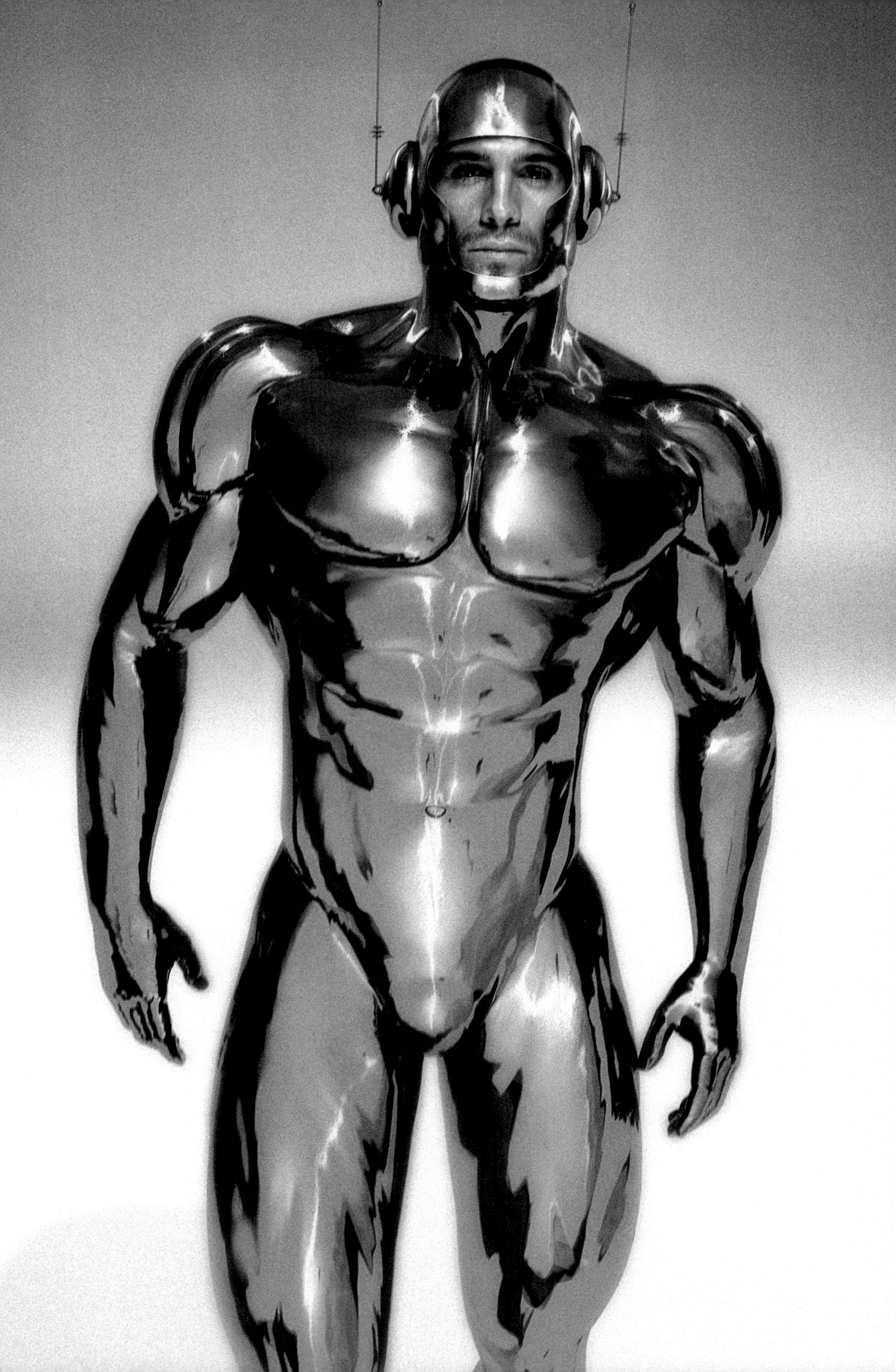

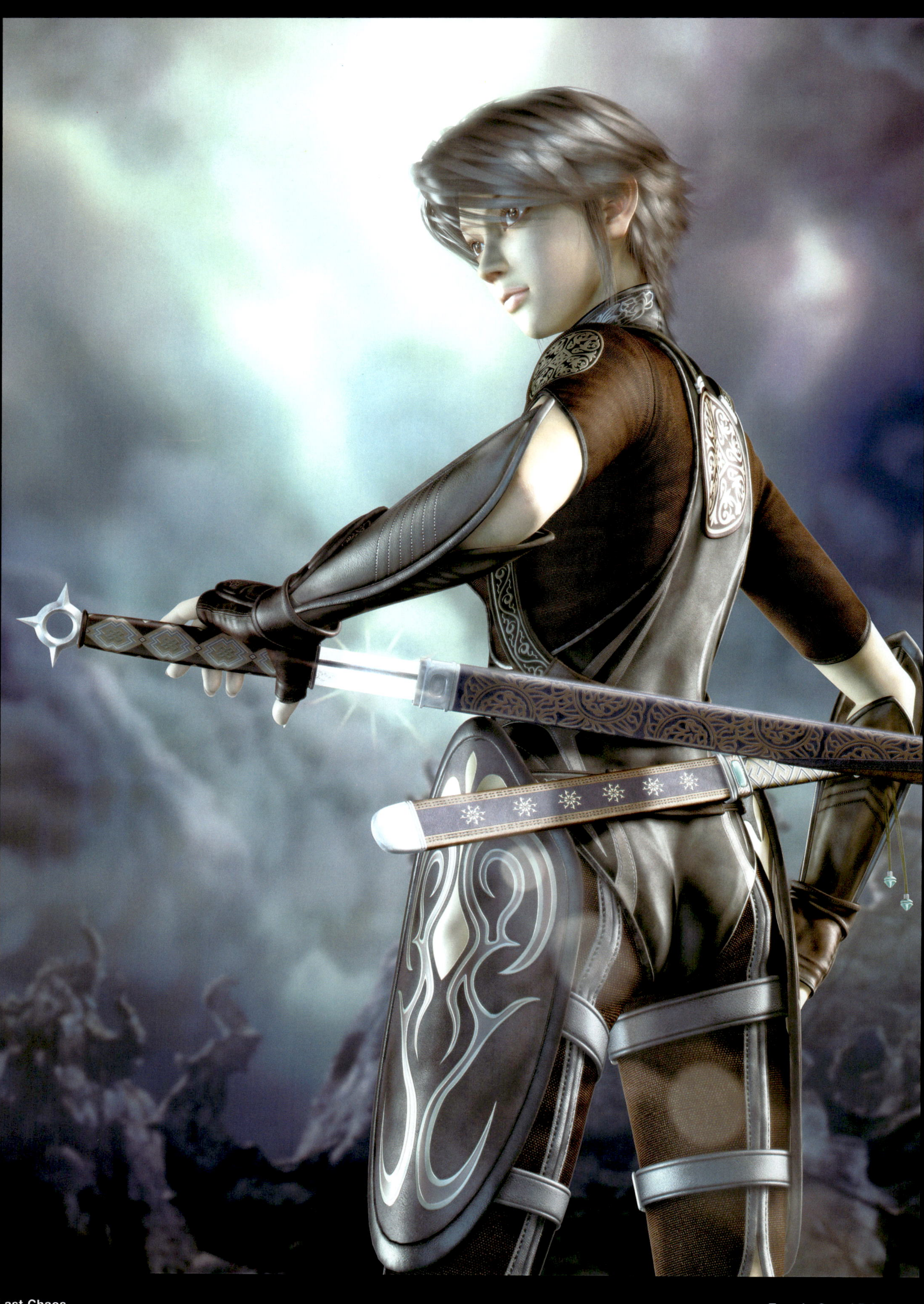

Last Chaos
Softimage|XSI, Maya, Photoshop
Sang Hyun Bang, KOREA
[above]

Temple Guard Priestess
Photoshop
Oz Spiniello, AUSTRALIA
[right]

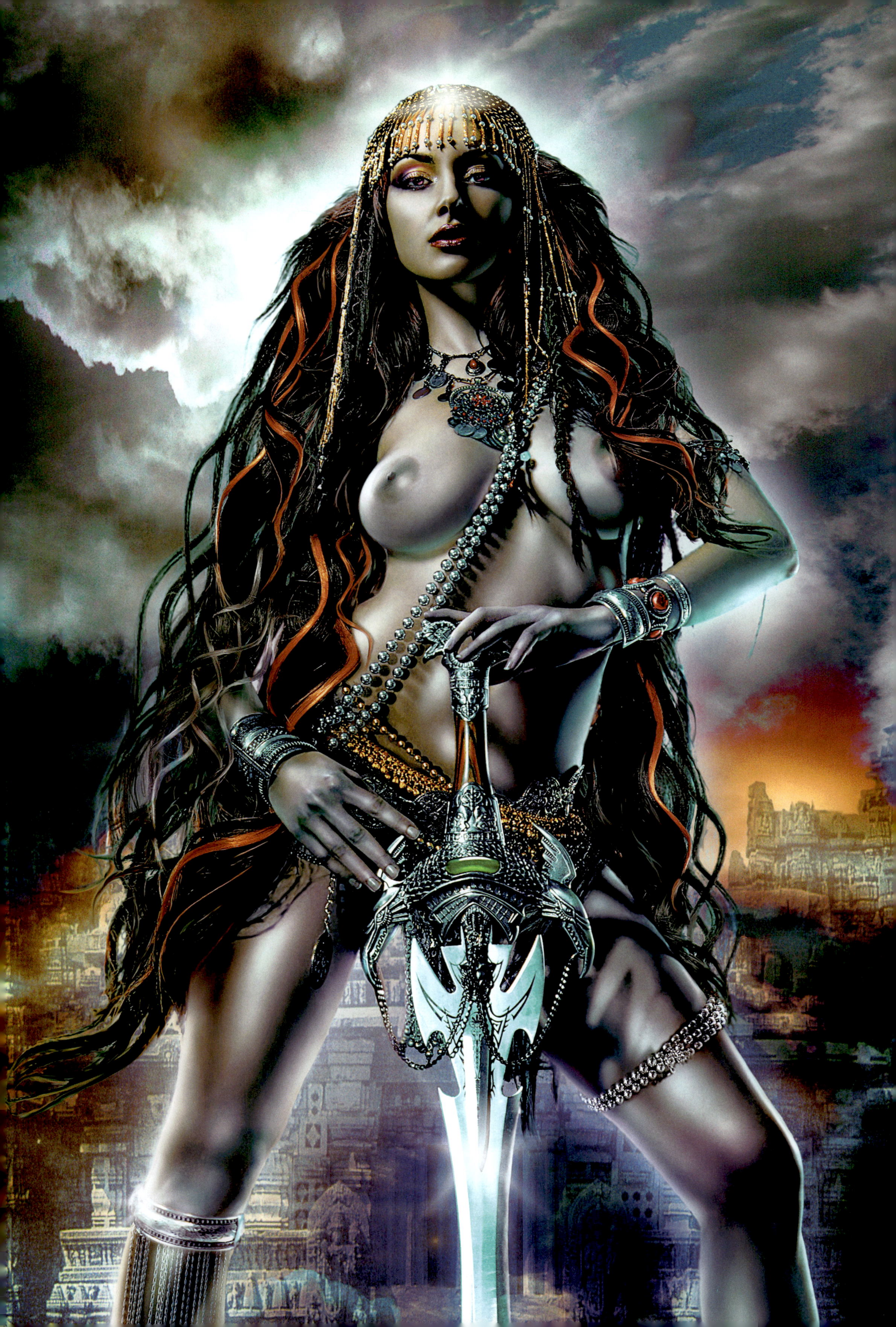

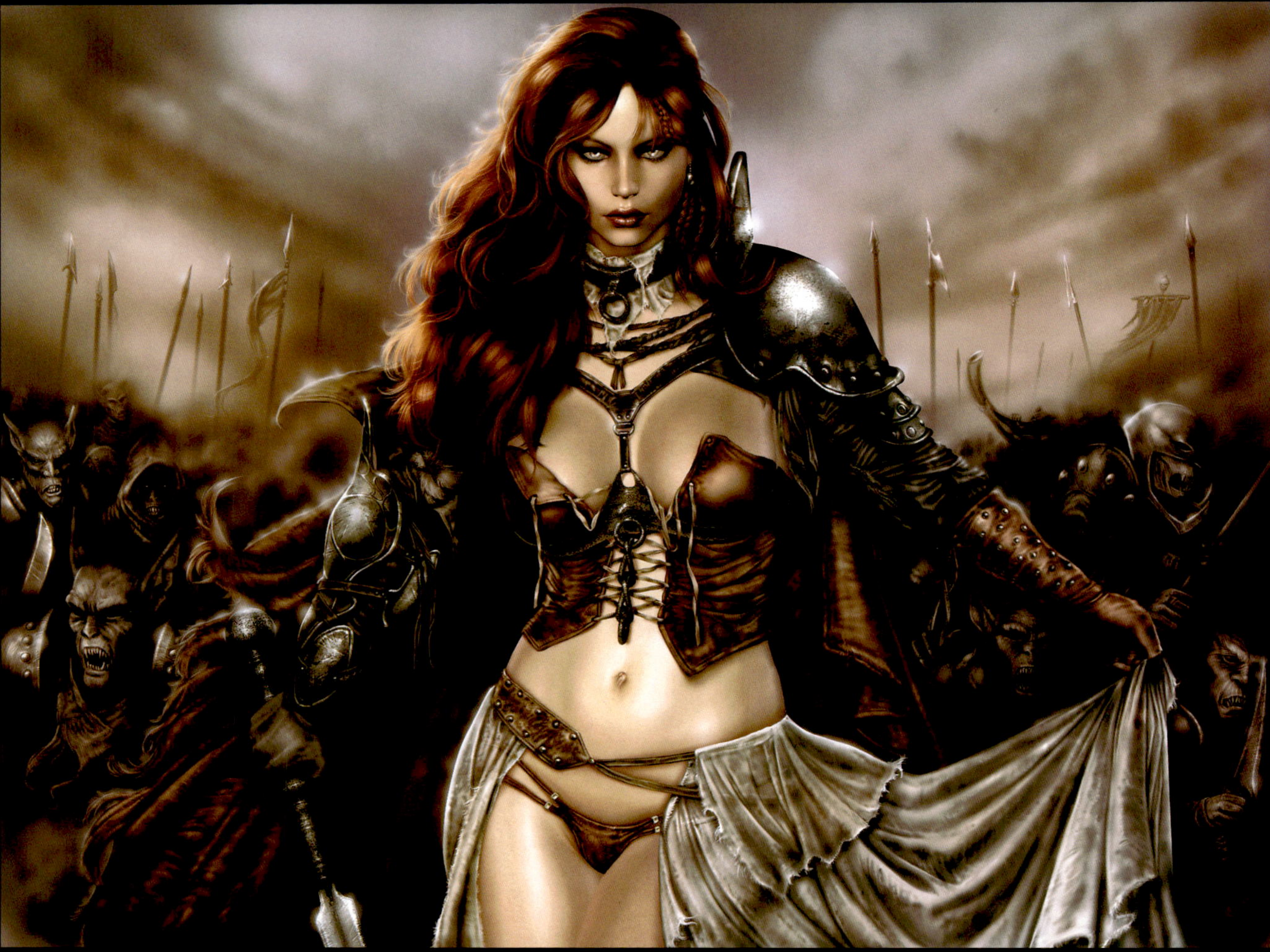

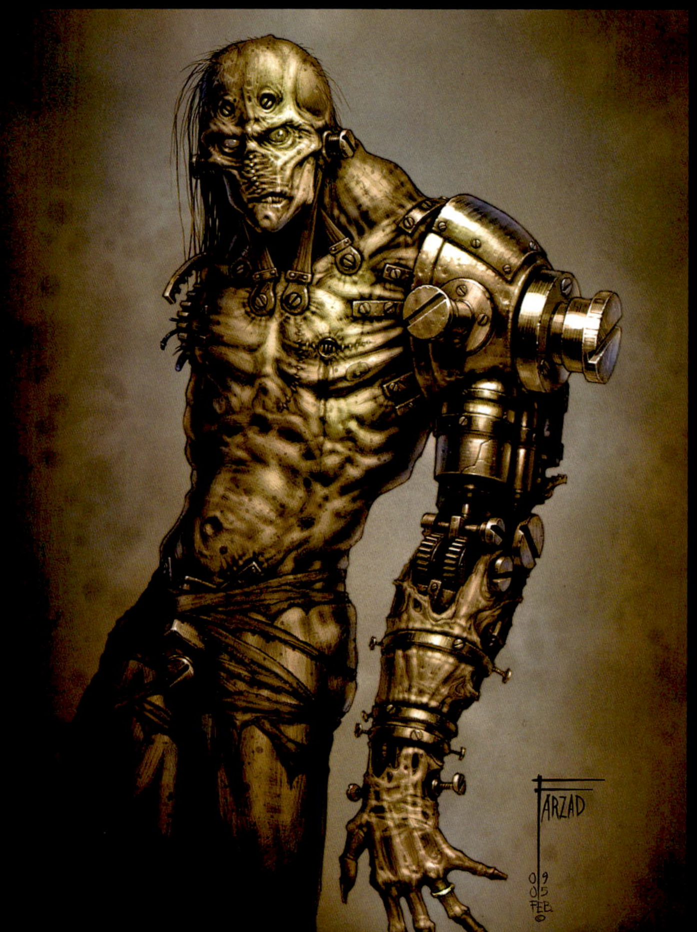

Might
Poser, Photoshop
Mark Coulson, GREAT BRITAIN
[above]

Mechbeth
Photoshop
Farzad Varahramyan, USA
[left]

S-girl (punisher)
Maya, Photoshop
Client: NAKO Interactive
Seok Chan-yoo, KOREA
[right]

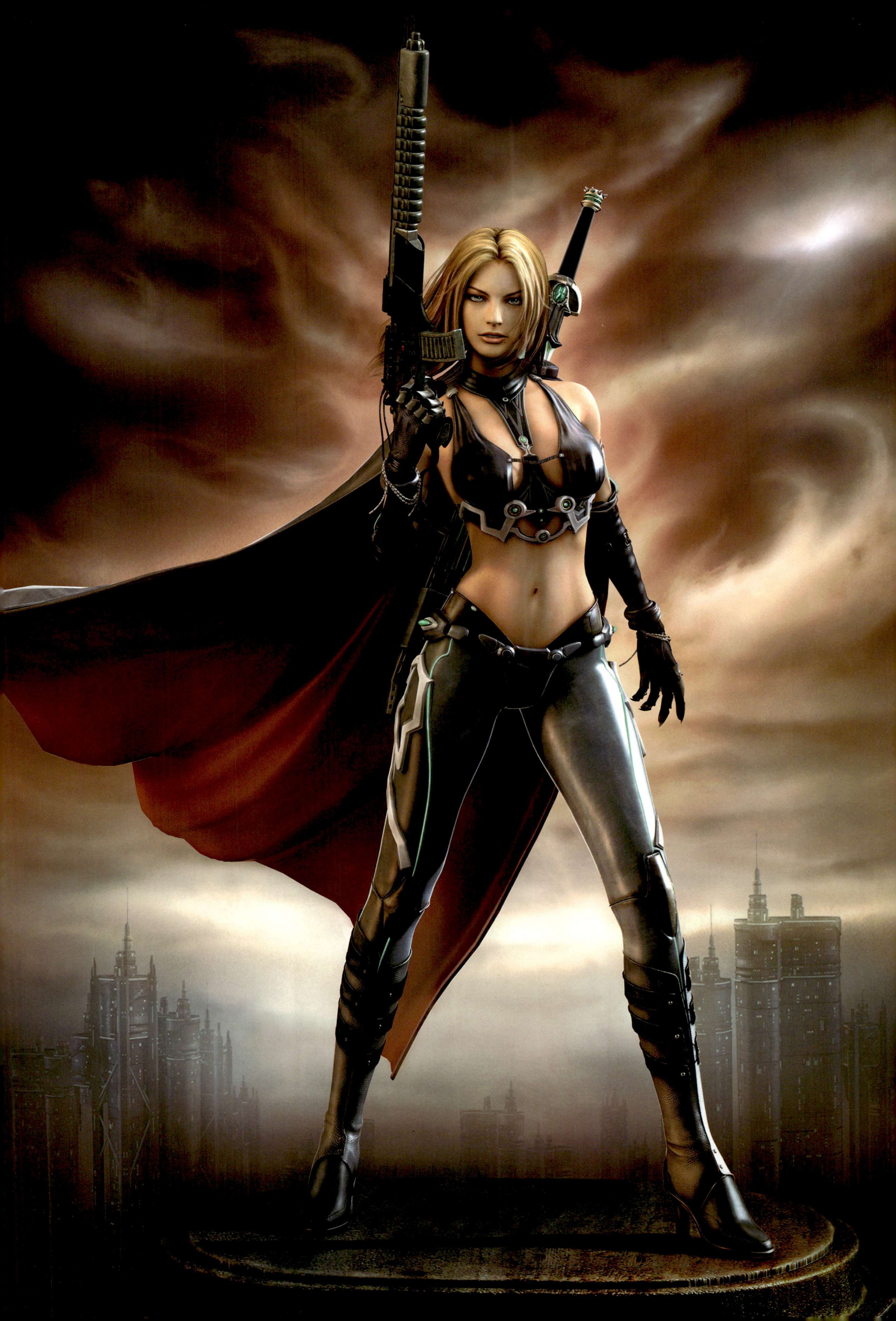

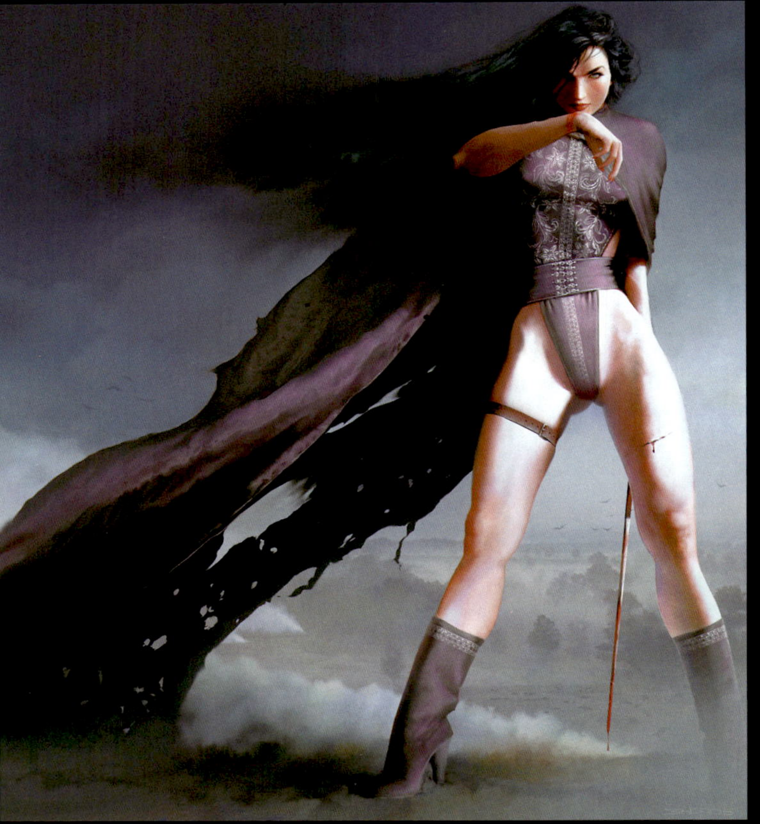

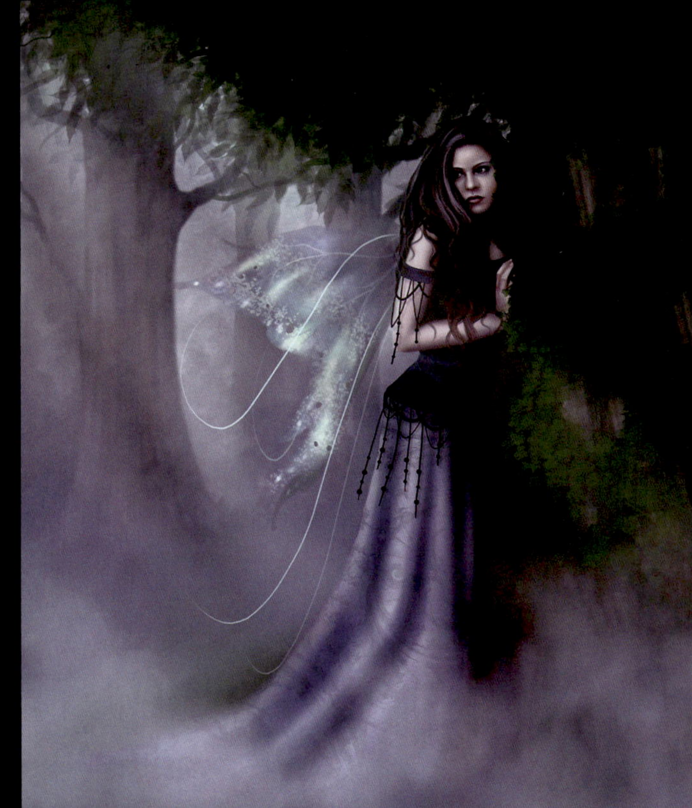

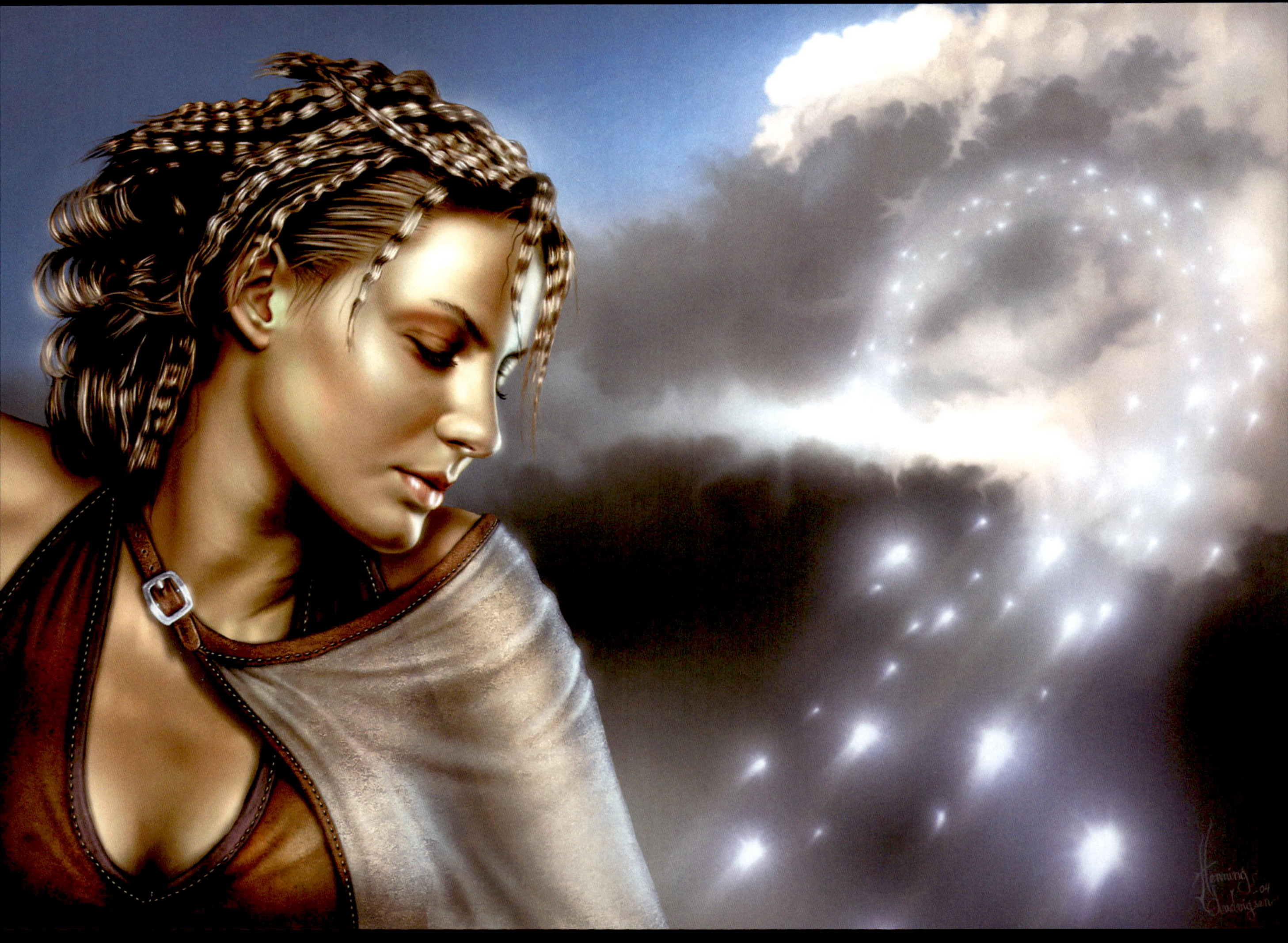

Countess2
Photoshop
Steven Stahlberg, MALAYSIA
[top left]

The Ascent
Photoshop
Henning Ludvigsen, NORWAY
[above]

Nedda
Photoshop
Laura Law, USA
[top right]

Dawn
3ds Max, Photoshop
Soa Lee, KOREA
[right]

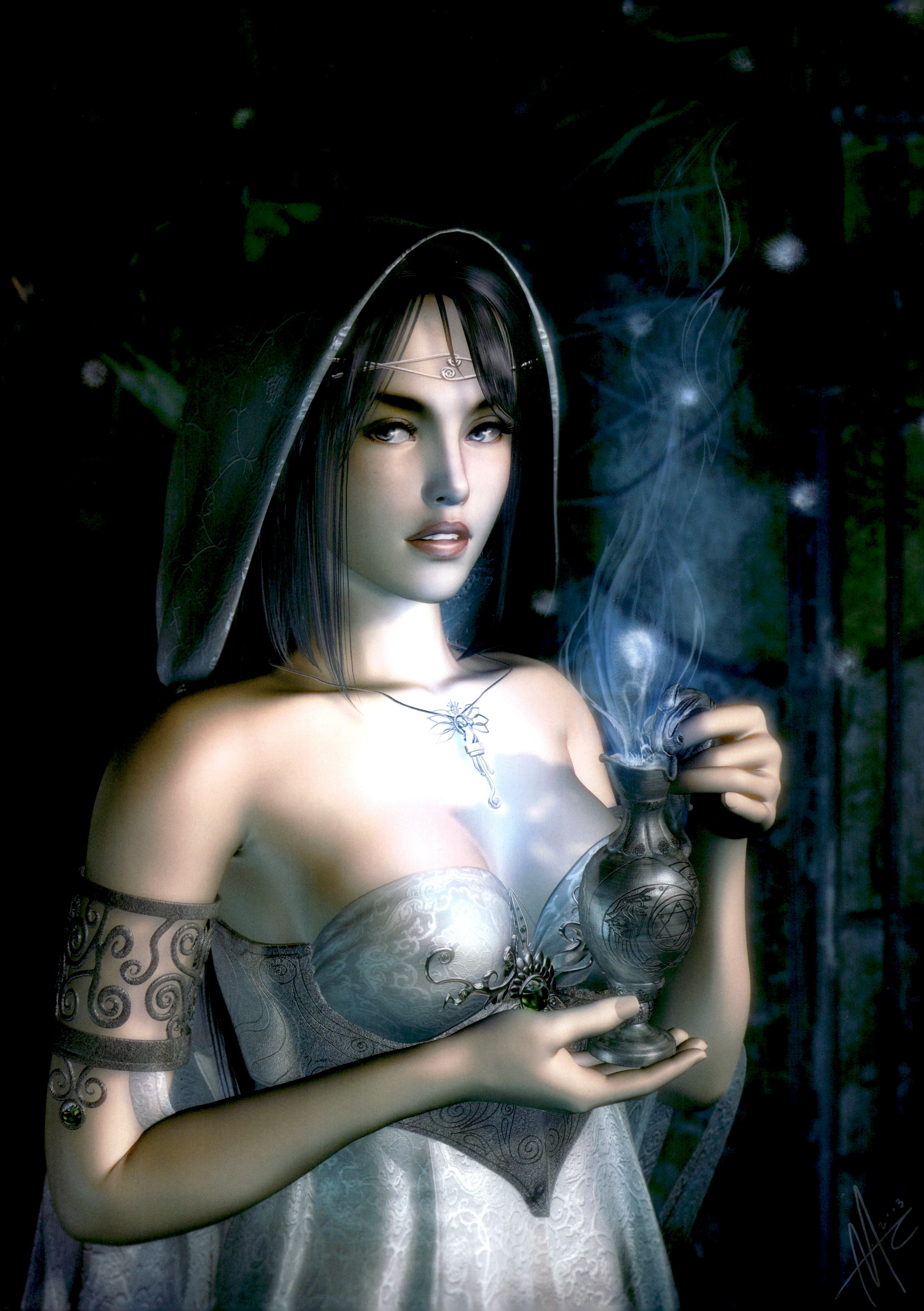

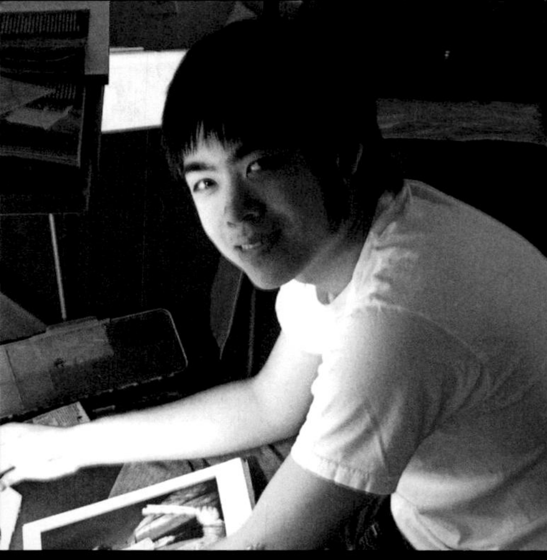

JASON CHAN

www.jasonchanart.com
jason@jasonchanart.com

"During high school I began frequenting online art forums and using those as inspiration and learning from people there."

Jason Chan was born September 24, 1983 in Stockton California. Ever since he could hold a pencil, he has been drawing. "I learned all over the place," admits Jason. "Both my parents, as well as some of my uncles all have artistic talent. They were my first teachers." What began as a childhood hobby soon developed into a passion. His interest in video games, fantasy and science fiction, and anime lead him in a particular path with his work and before he knew it, he was freelancing. "I frequently visit art forums to keep learning while I'm not at school and see what other people are up to", explains Jason. He is currently pursuing a BFA in Illustration at the Academy of Art University in San Francisco. He is due to graduate in the Spring of 2006.

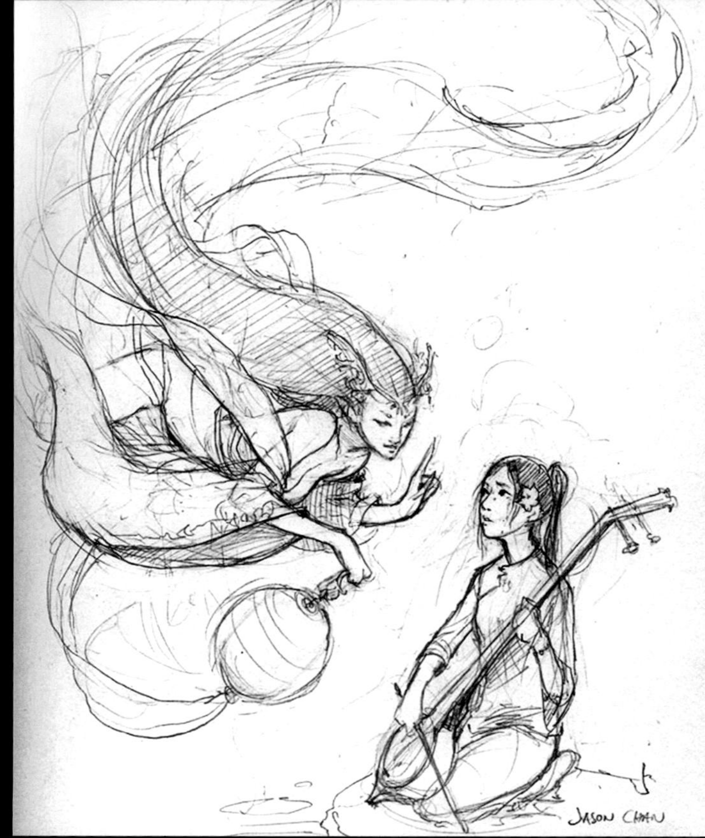

SKETCHING

Digital art is a funny thing. It gives you unlimited control of your image allowing you to step back in time when you make a mistake, zoom in to do the tiniest detail or zoom out to do the largest stroke. The one thing it lacks is a sense of physical reality. You can't hold your artwork. Because of this, sometimes the mood strikes me to begin with something I can touch, like piece of paper and a pencil. I will normally start out by drawing a series of quick thumbnails to find a working composition. From there I will do a more detailed sketch and possibly do some character designs. In this particular piece, I made the mistake of going to paint without working out the background beforehand in my sketch. I was a little too eager to add color, and I paid for it later. Ideally, you would want to know exactly what you are going to be doing when you go to paint—it's just a lot faster and easier.

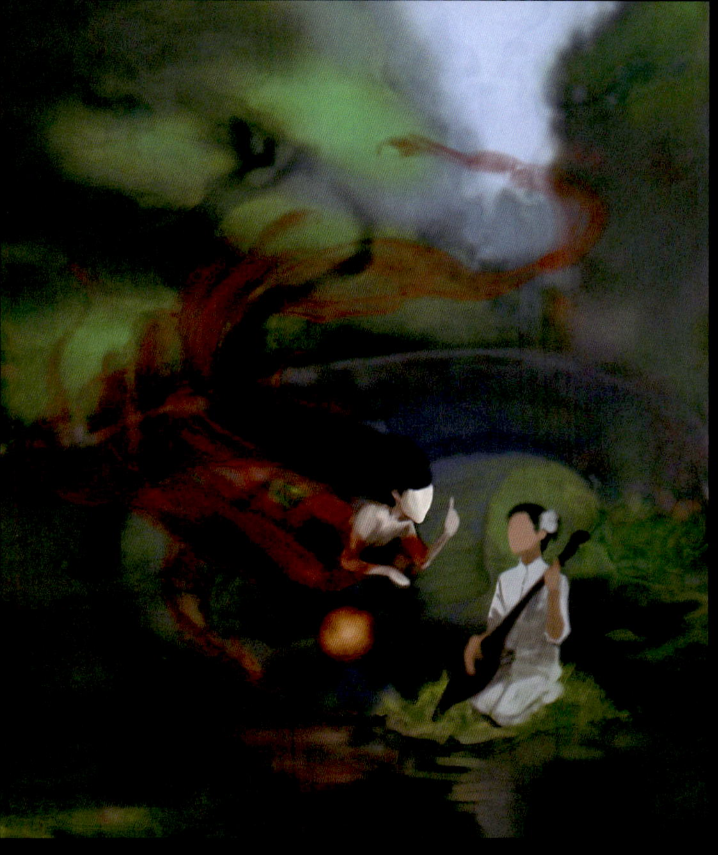

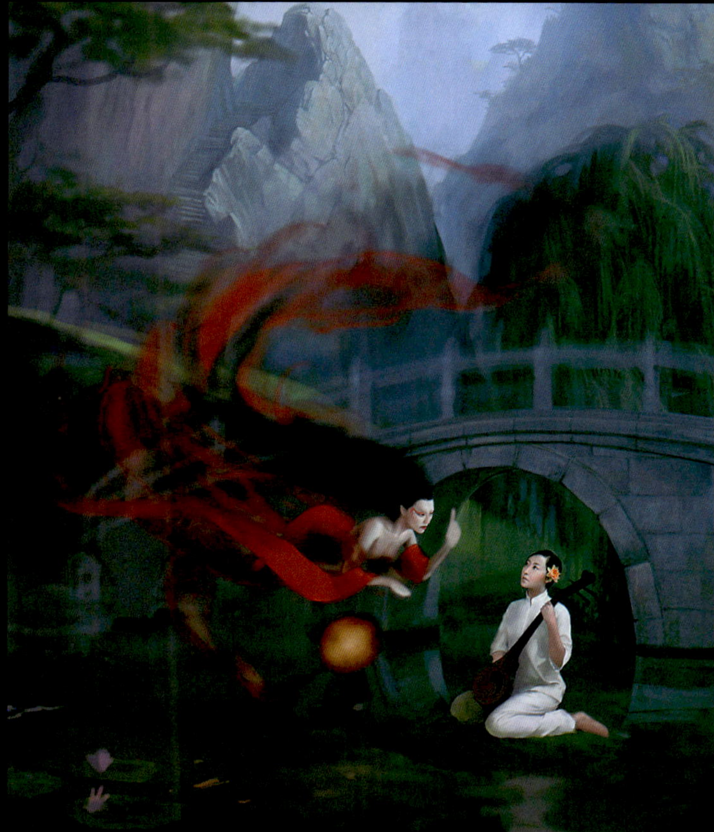

BLOCKING-IN

Once I have the image scanned, I begin by blocking in colors. In this image, I was going for a more photorealistic look for the characters so I didn't bother saving the lines under the initial block-in. All I needed was the initial idea and gesture. The sketch was then laid on my desk where I could look at it when I needed to. I don't like to work on a white canvas, so I try to get the whole image in some sort of color. It's important to try to get your values correct so that you can see the overall impact of the image. Colors come second to value normally, but I really needed to get that intense red in from the get-go. The whole time I knew that I wanted a green image with a brilliant red character. I ran into trouble with this image because I didn't resolve the background in my initial sketch. I went through numerous different trees, fiddled with the bridge, and did various changes to the mountains before I was happy with how the background was working.

DETAIL

Finally, after much struggle with the background, I was able to start adding details to the background, and my favorite part, the characters. For this image, I wanted things to look fairly realistic so I took some photos for reference. If I had been going for a more stylized look, I would probably have skipped that step. I also had to do a little research into Chinese architecture and art aesthetics. I love the great vertical paintings of mountains in the mist that you see on scrolls, and I tried to mimic that a little in this image. I applied the detail in multiple passes. I added some general detail to the image as a whole so that it read and then added more and more detail to areas I wanted to pop out. This leaves a looser look to areas that are less important, which draws your eyes to the areas that you have detailed and are most important to you. It also allows you to stop at any point and still have the whole image read. Normally, I don't like to render the image until every inch is photorealistic, so I left parts of the image somewhat loose. Once I was happy with the way the image looked I took it into Photoshop for some color balancing for the final touches. At that point, with any luck, hours of intense work will have hopefully come to fruition.

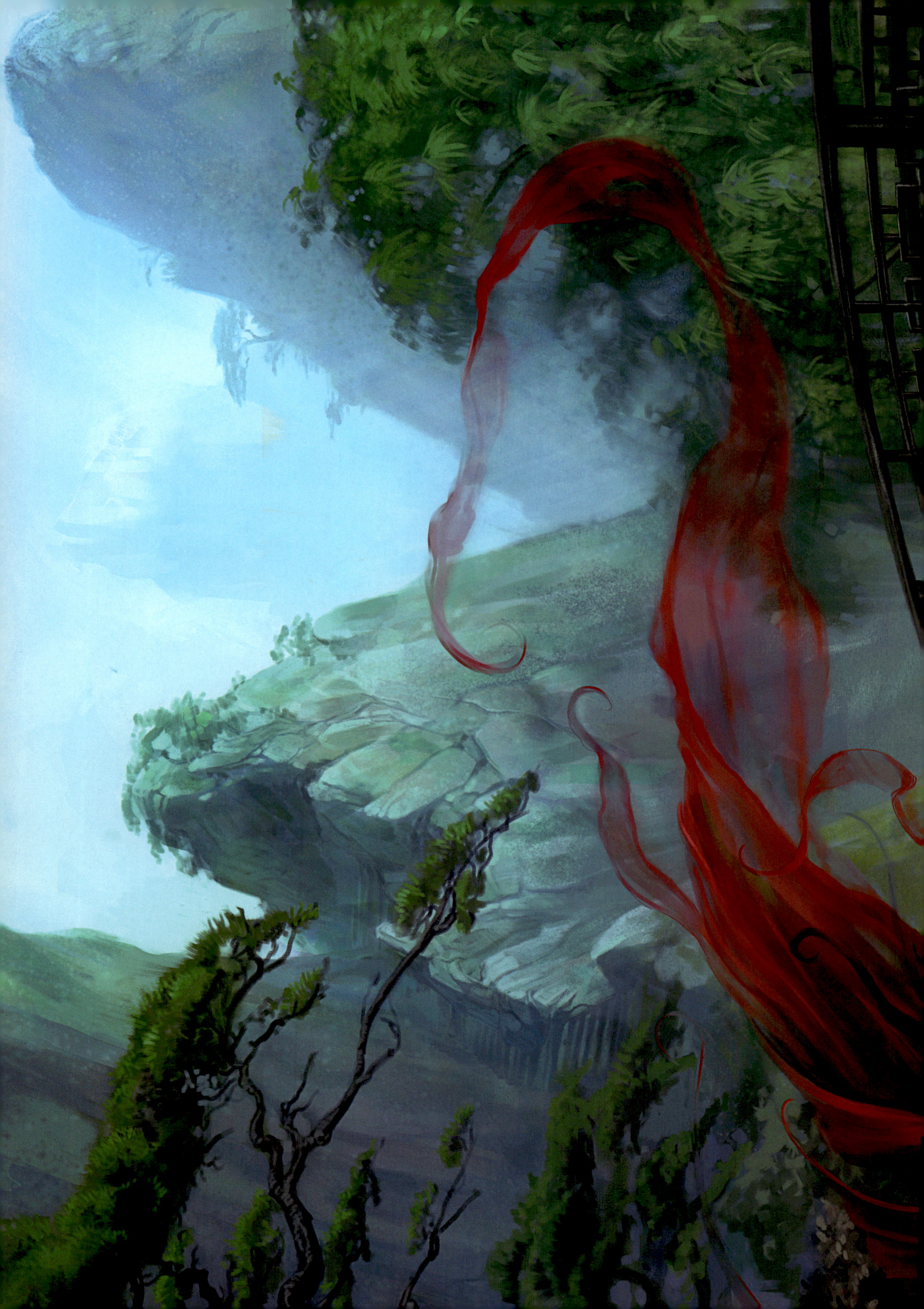

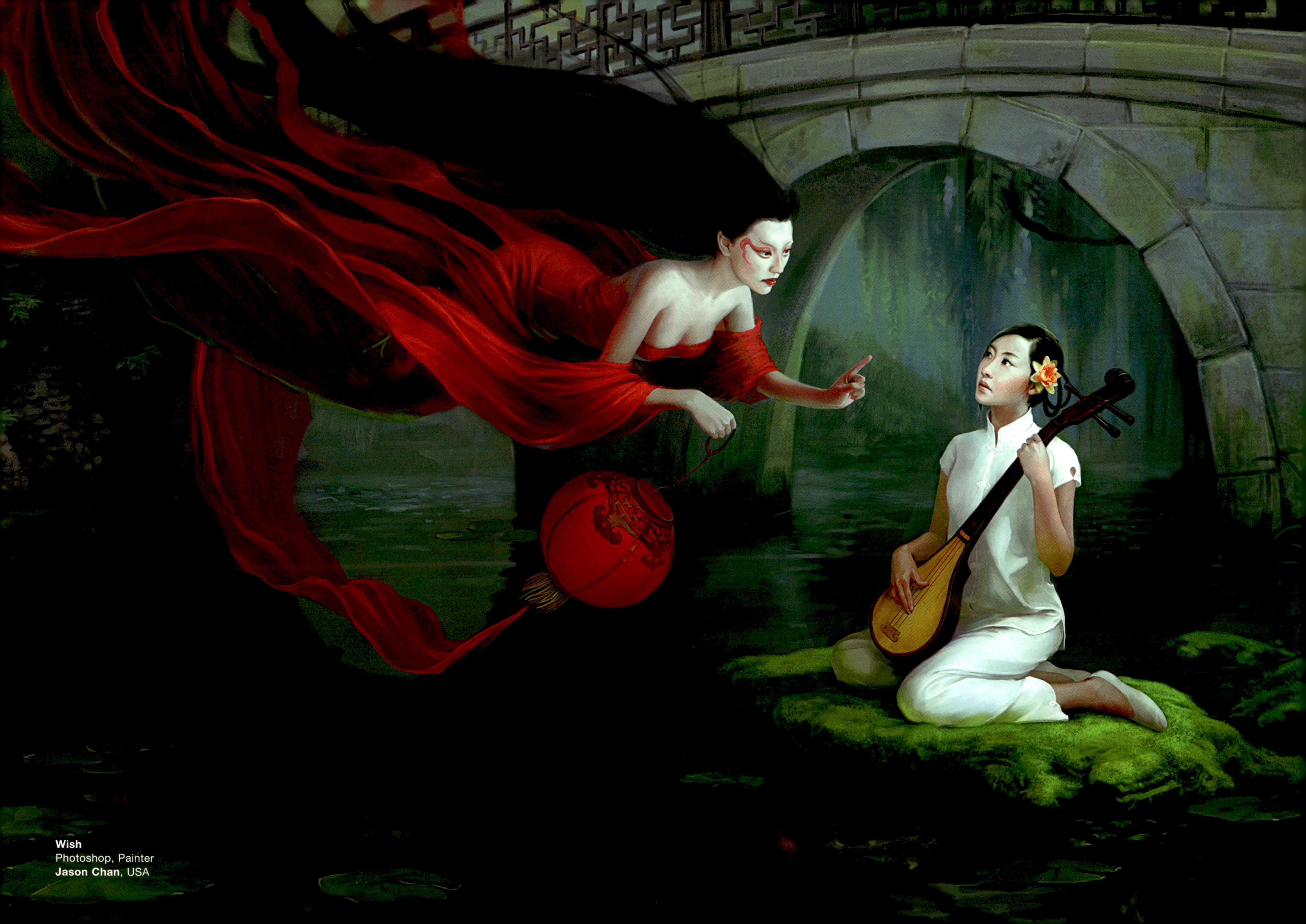

Wish
Photoshop, Painter
Jason Chan, USA

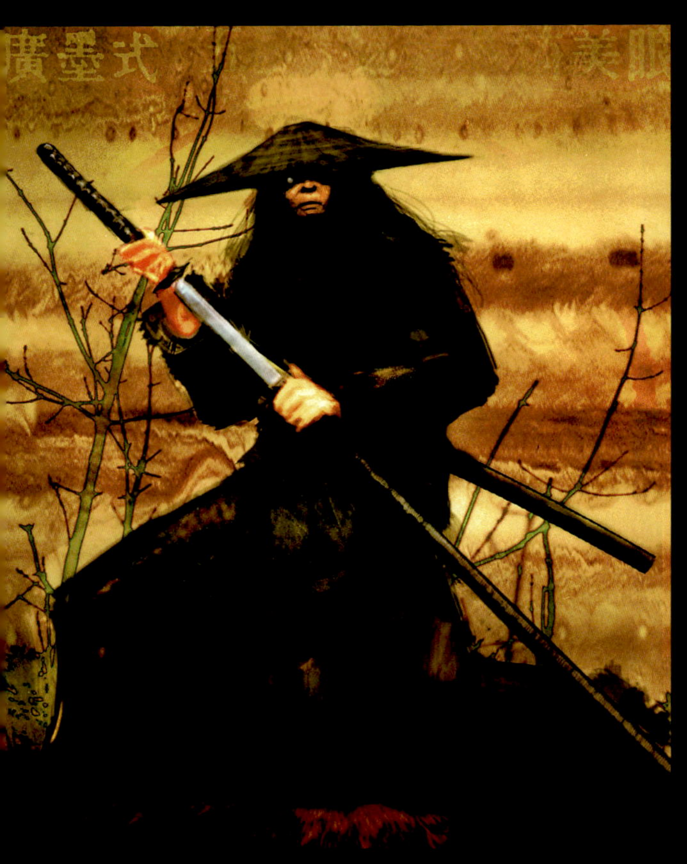

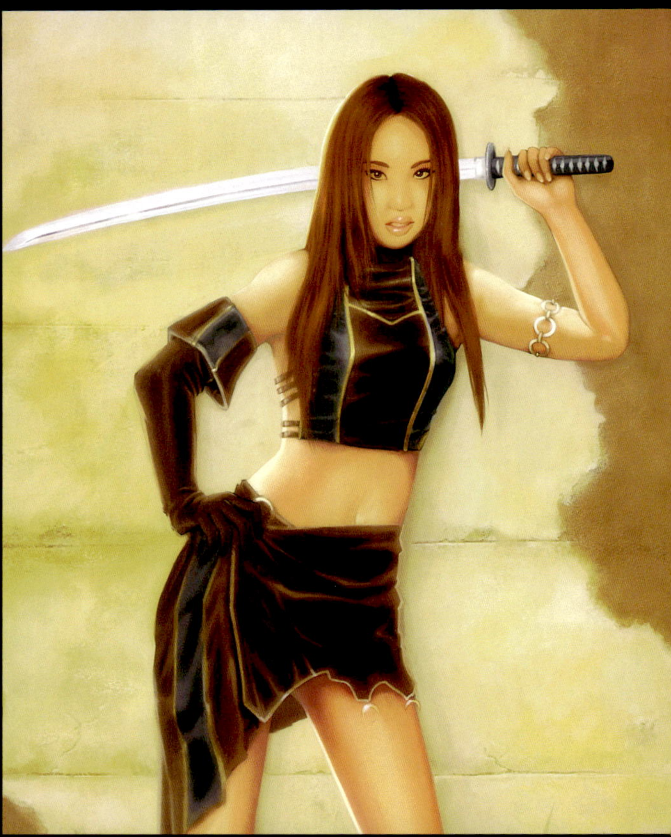

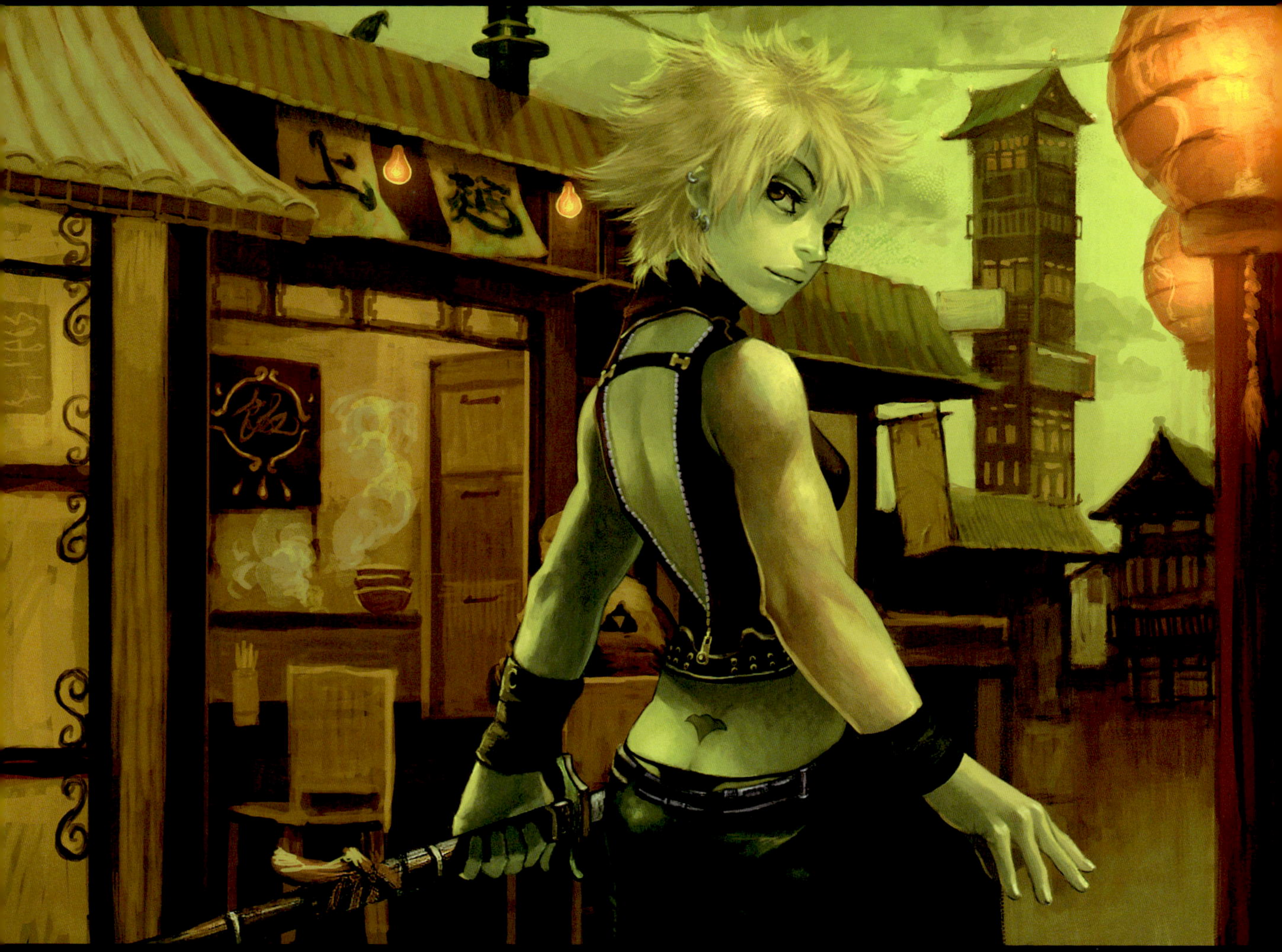

Samourai
Photoshop
Damien Chanez,
FRANCE
[top left]

Huang Rong
Photoshop
Leung Chun Wan,
HONG KONG
[above]

Fantasy Female Character
Photoshop
Daniel P. Ferreira,
USA
[top right]

QIN 1
Photoshop, Painter, ArtRage
Client: le 7éme Crecle
Aleksi Briclot, FRANCE
[right]

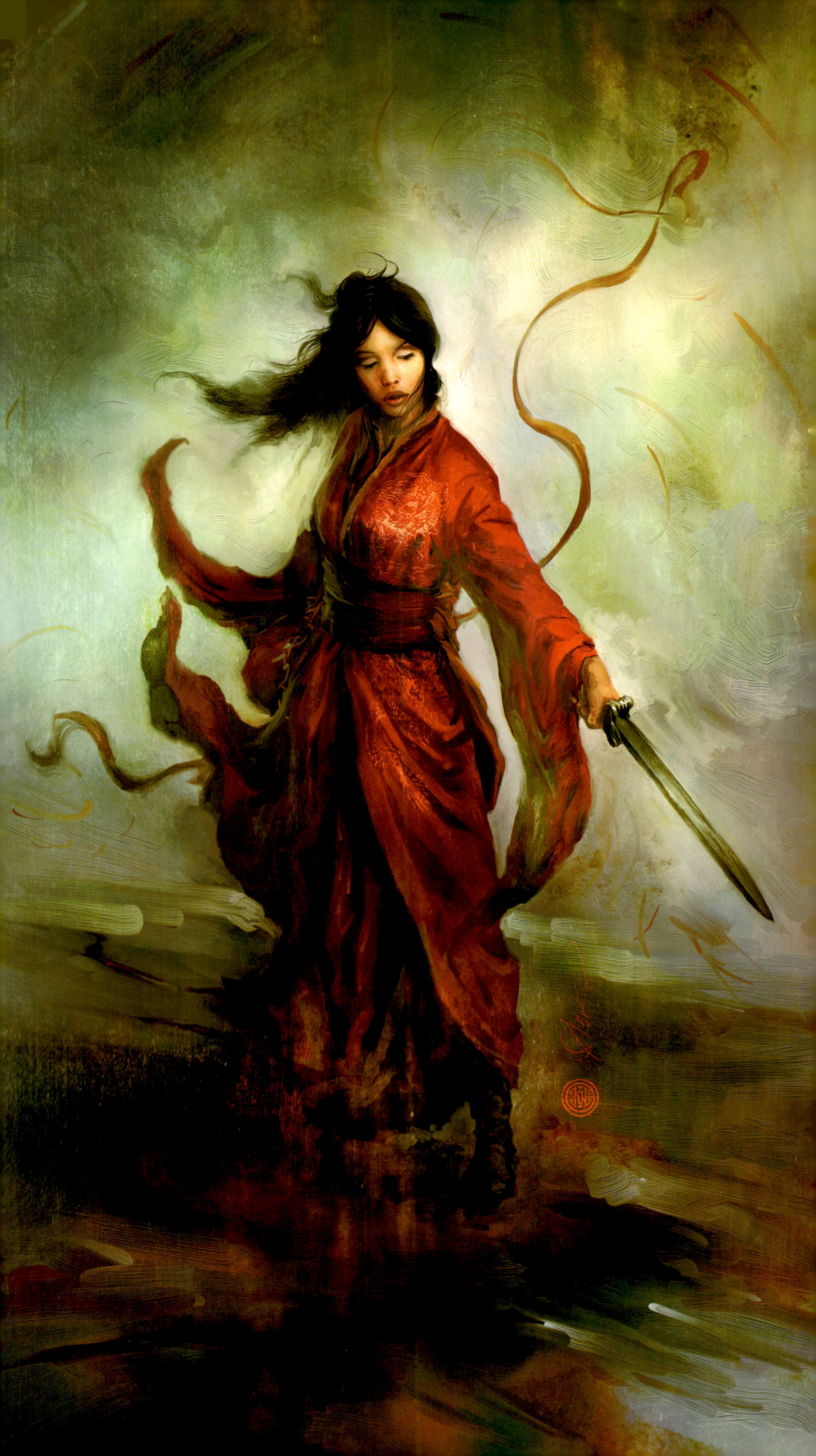

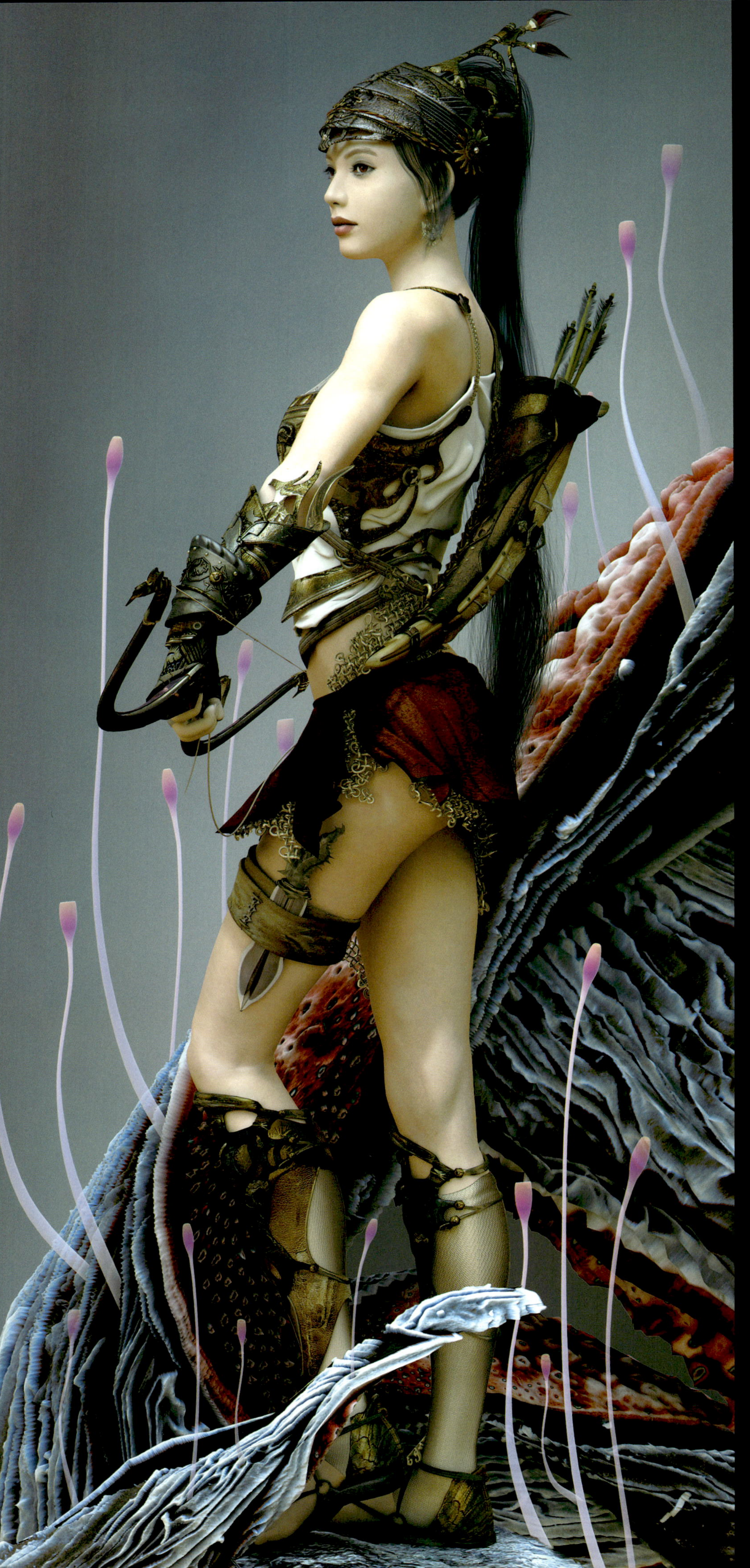

Divine Protection
3ds Max, Photoshop
Hyung-Jun Kim, KOREA
[left]

Dragon and Phoenix of Ancient Chinese
Photoshop
Camille Kuo, TAIWAN
[right]

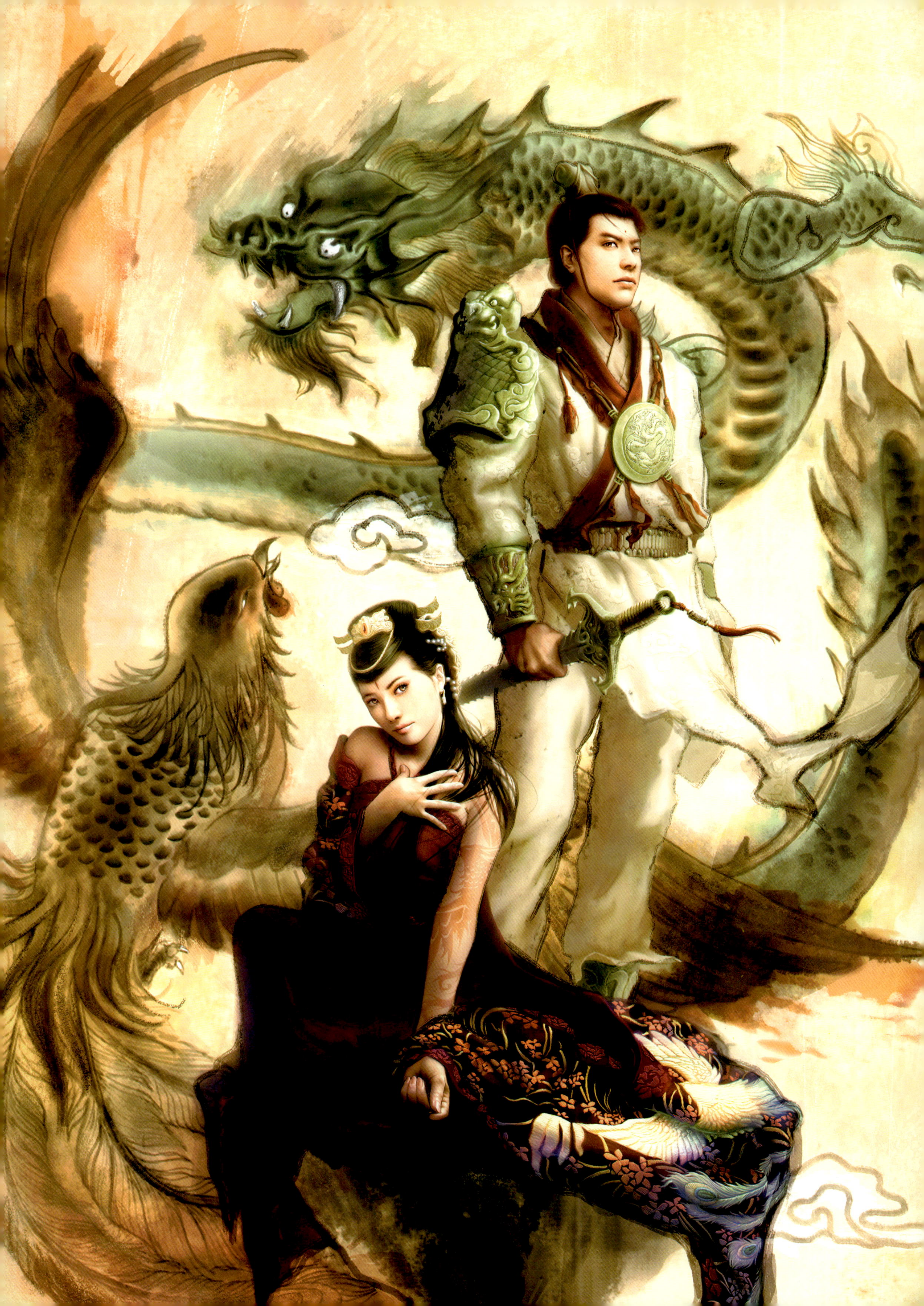

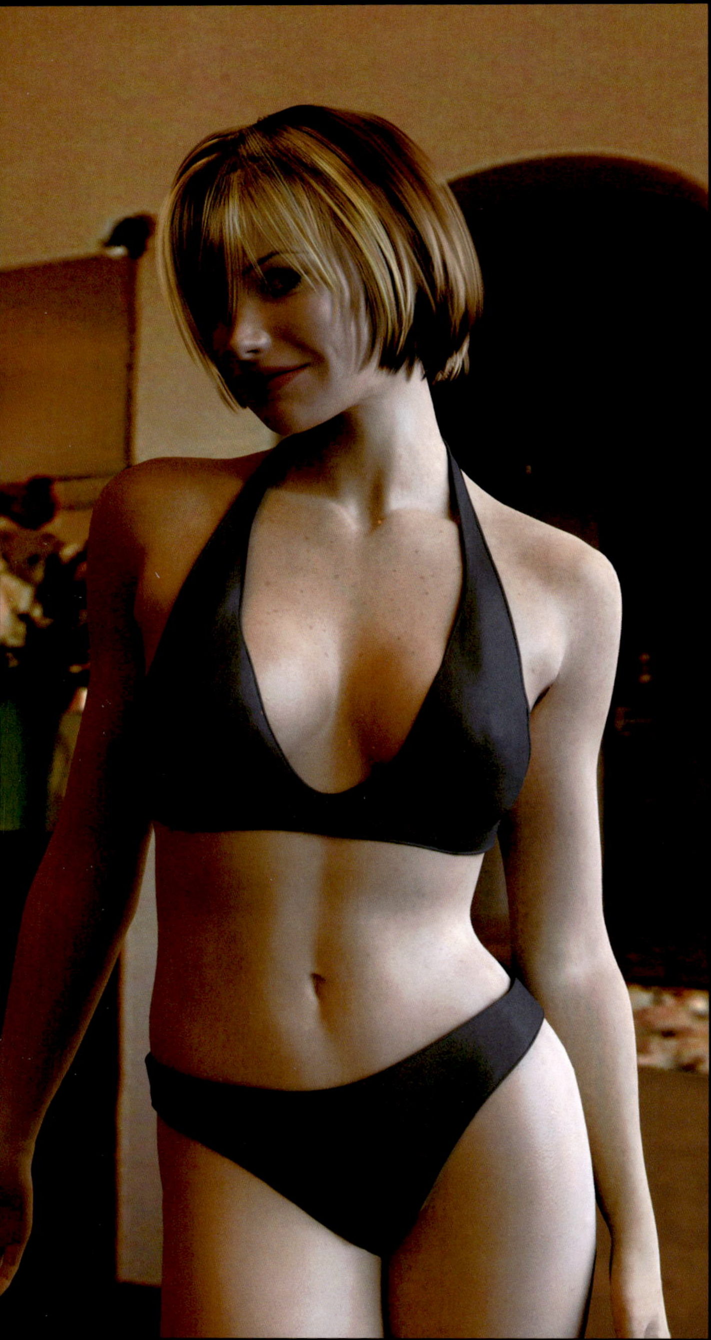

'This Wonderful Life' girl
3ds Max, Brazil r/s
Liam Kemp, GREAT BRITAIN
[above]

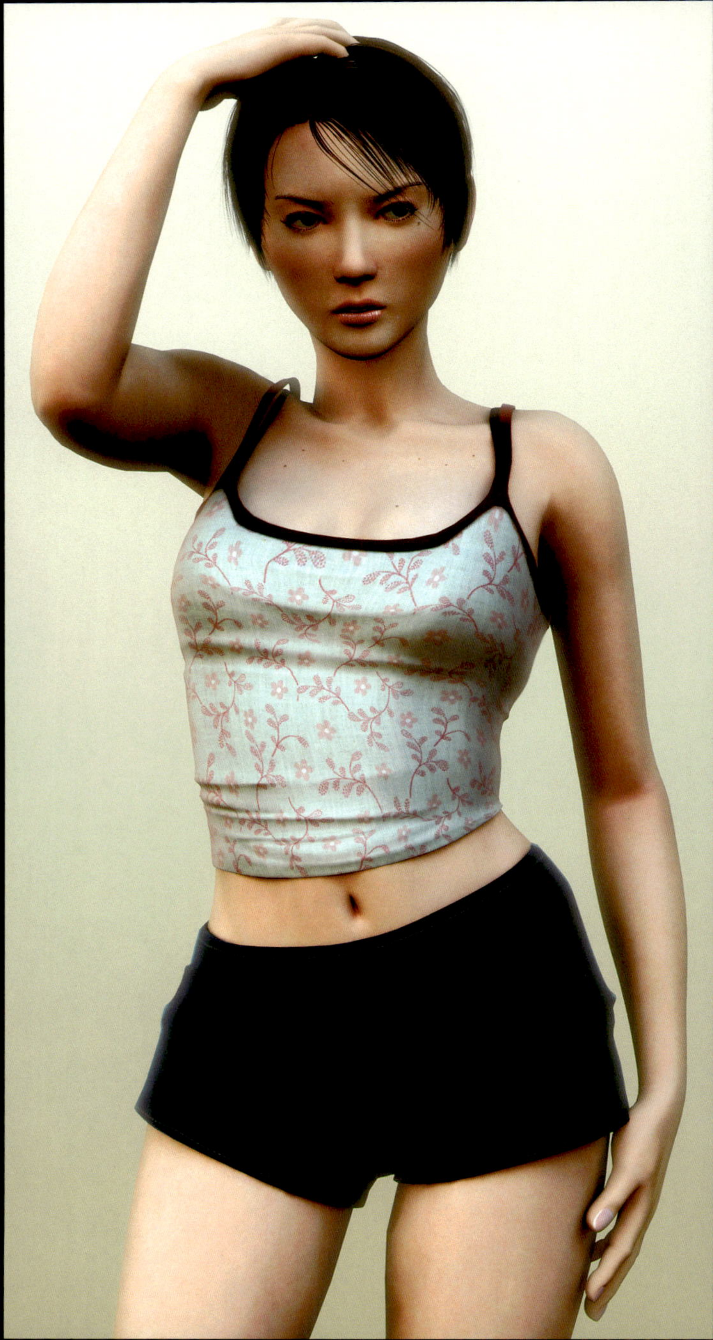

Mei
3ds Max
Mark Tan, Insane Polygons, SINGAPORE
[above]

Character Studio 4
3ds Max, Character Studio, Brazil r/s, Shag Hair
Koji Yamagami, Beans Magic, JAPAN
[right]

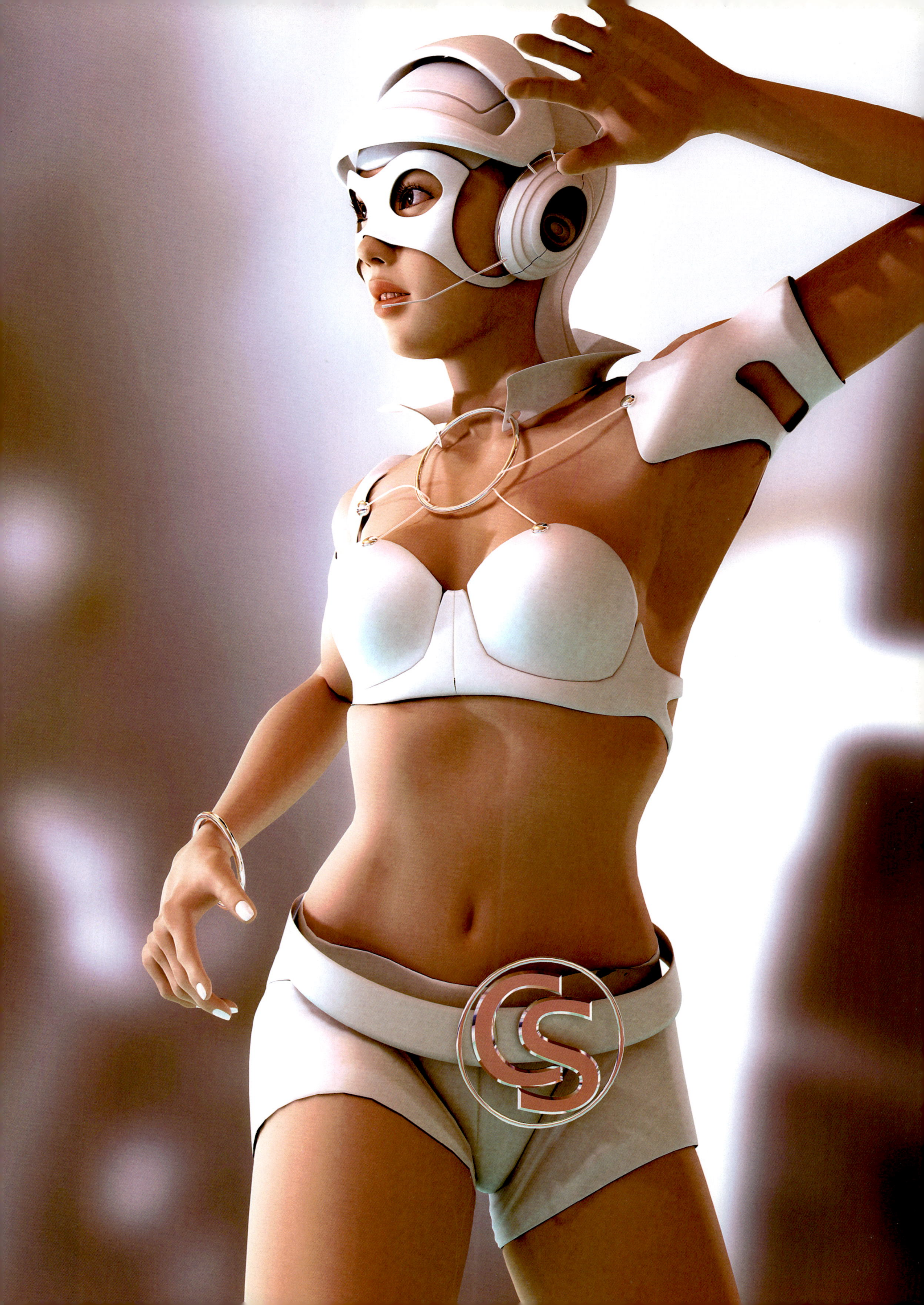
CS

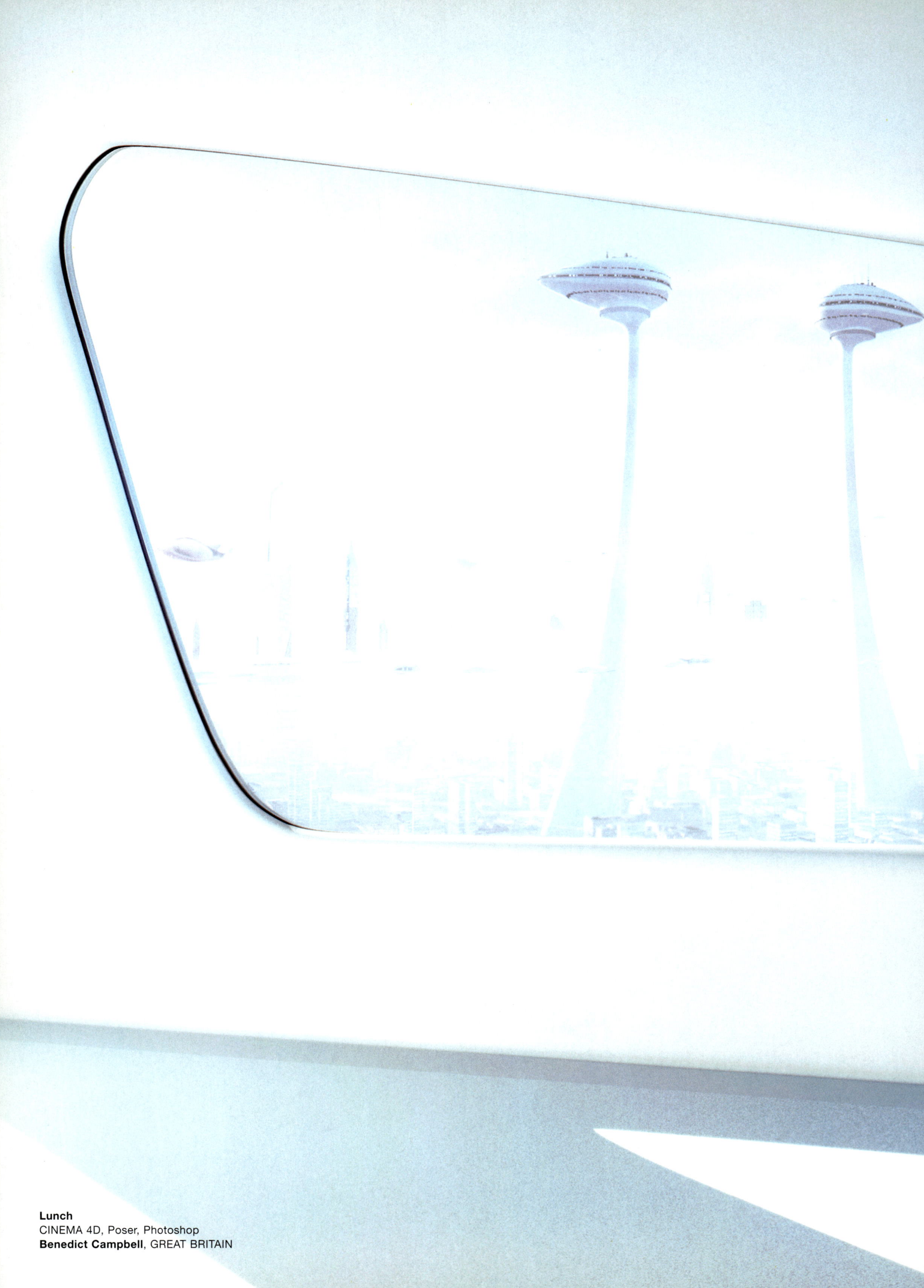

Lunch
CINEMA 4D, Poser, Photoshop
Benedict Campbell, GREAT BRITAIN

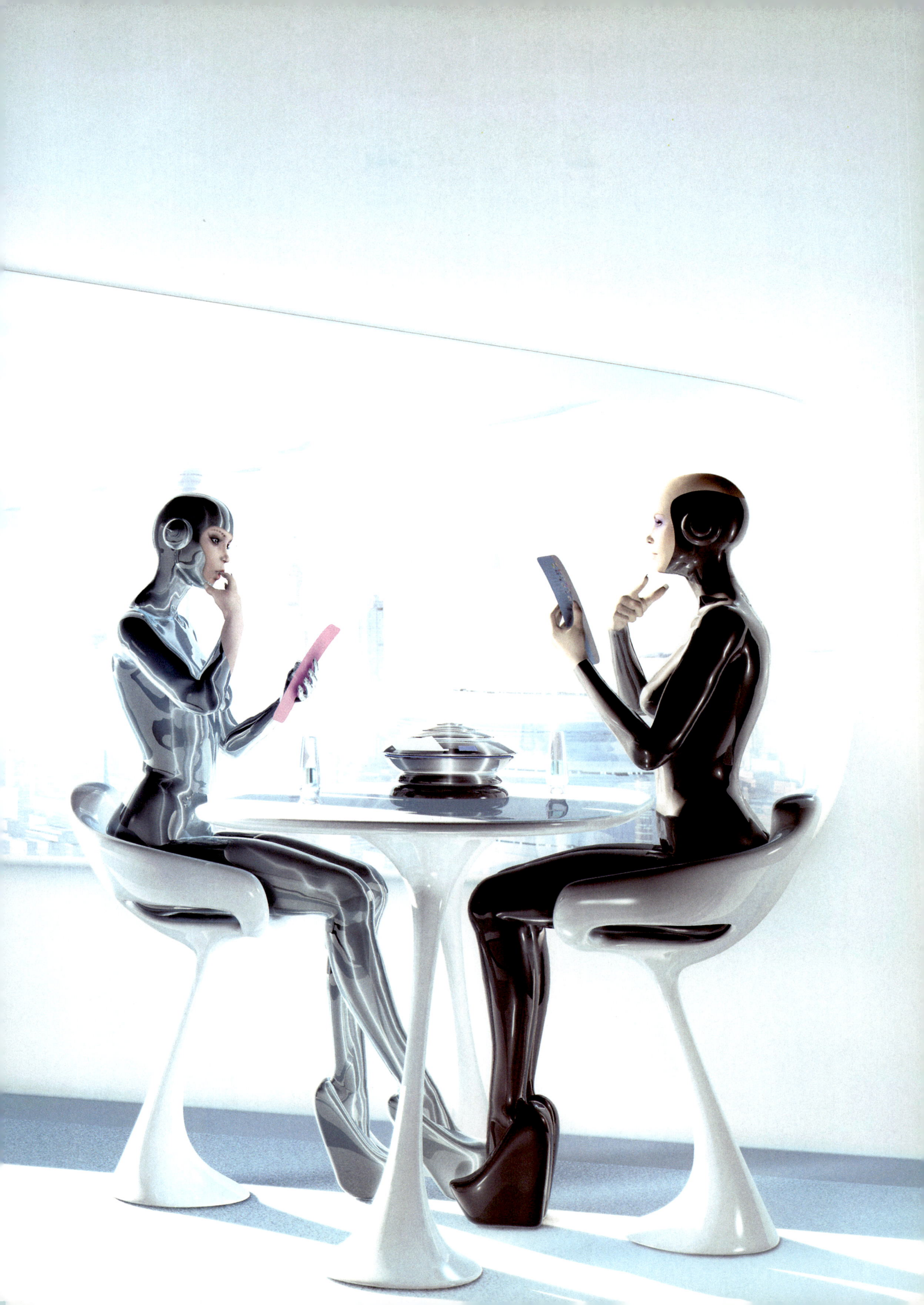

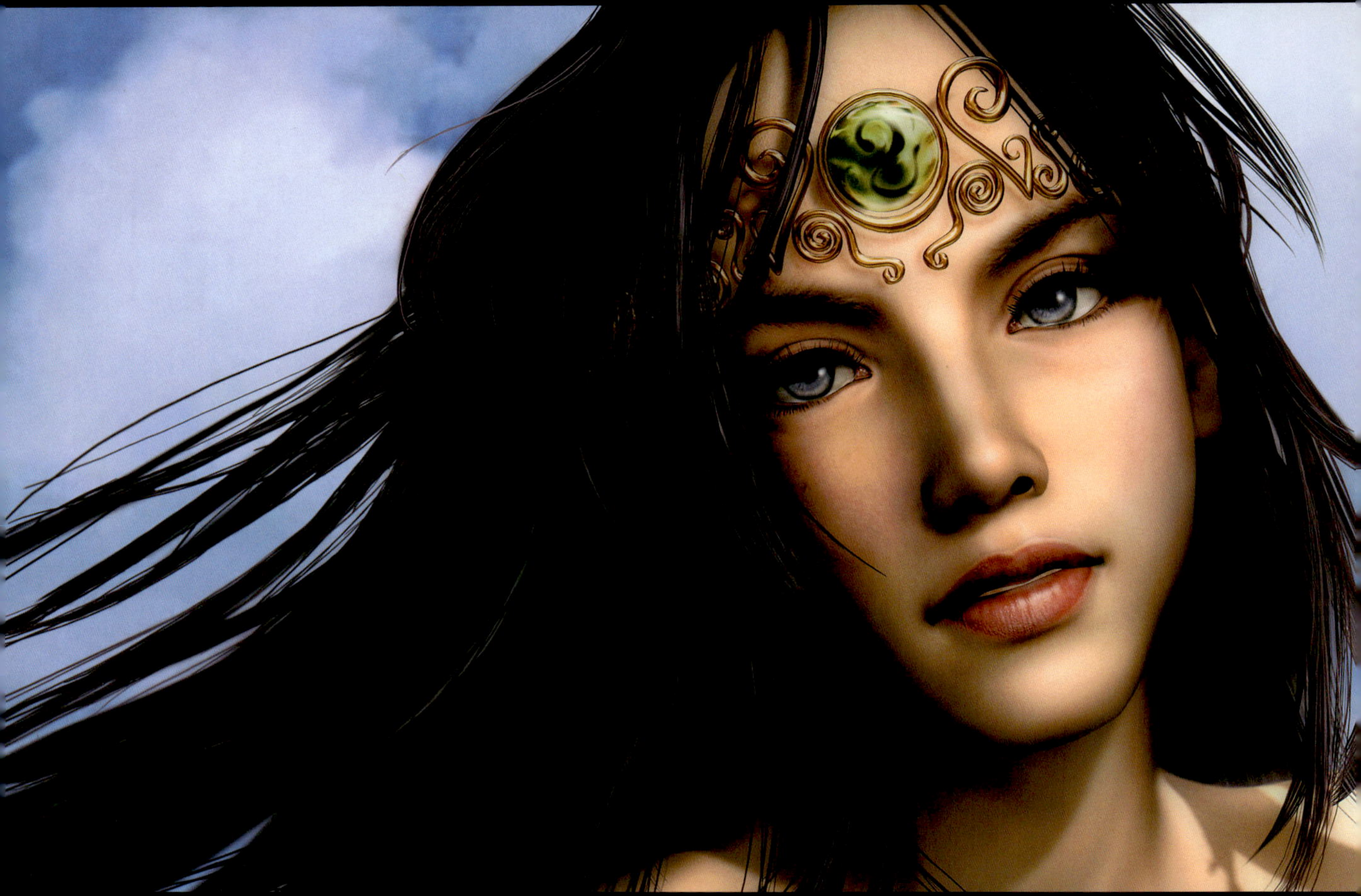

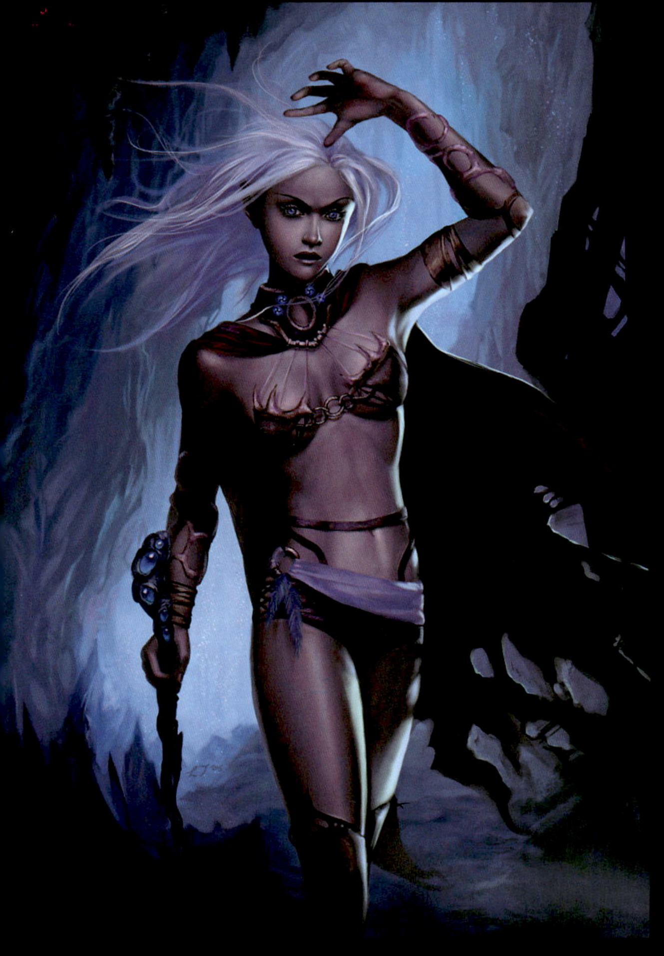

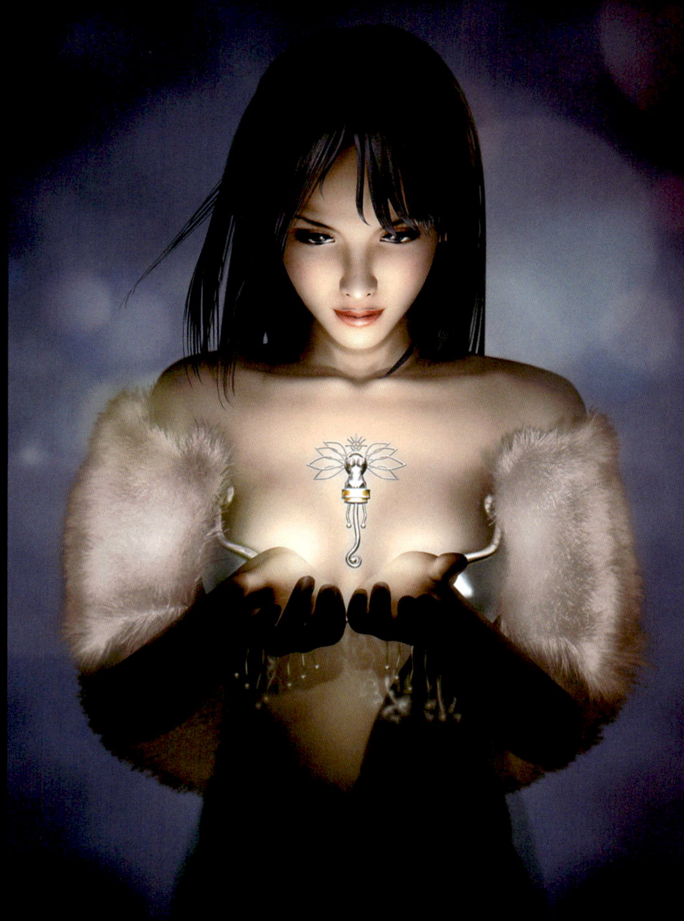

Blue
3ds Max, Photoshop
Soa Lee,
KOREA
[top]

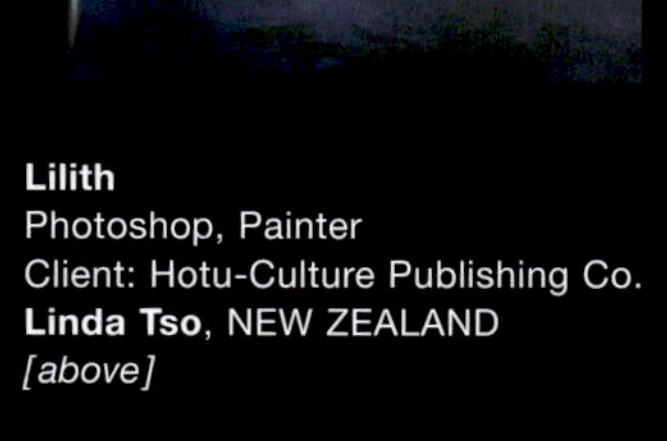

Lilith
Photoshop, Painter
Client: Hotu-Culture Publishing Co.
Linda Tso, NEW ZEALAND
[above]

Christmas
Photoshop, 3ds Max
Client: Actoz soft
Soa Lee, KOREA
[above]

Obsidian Eyes
3ds Max
Olivier Ponsonnet
FRANCE
[right]

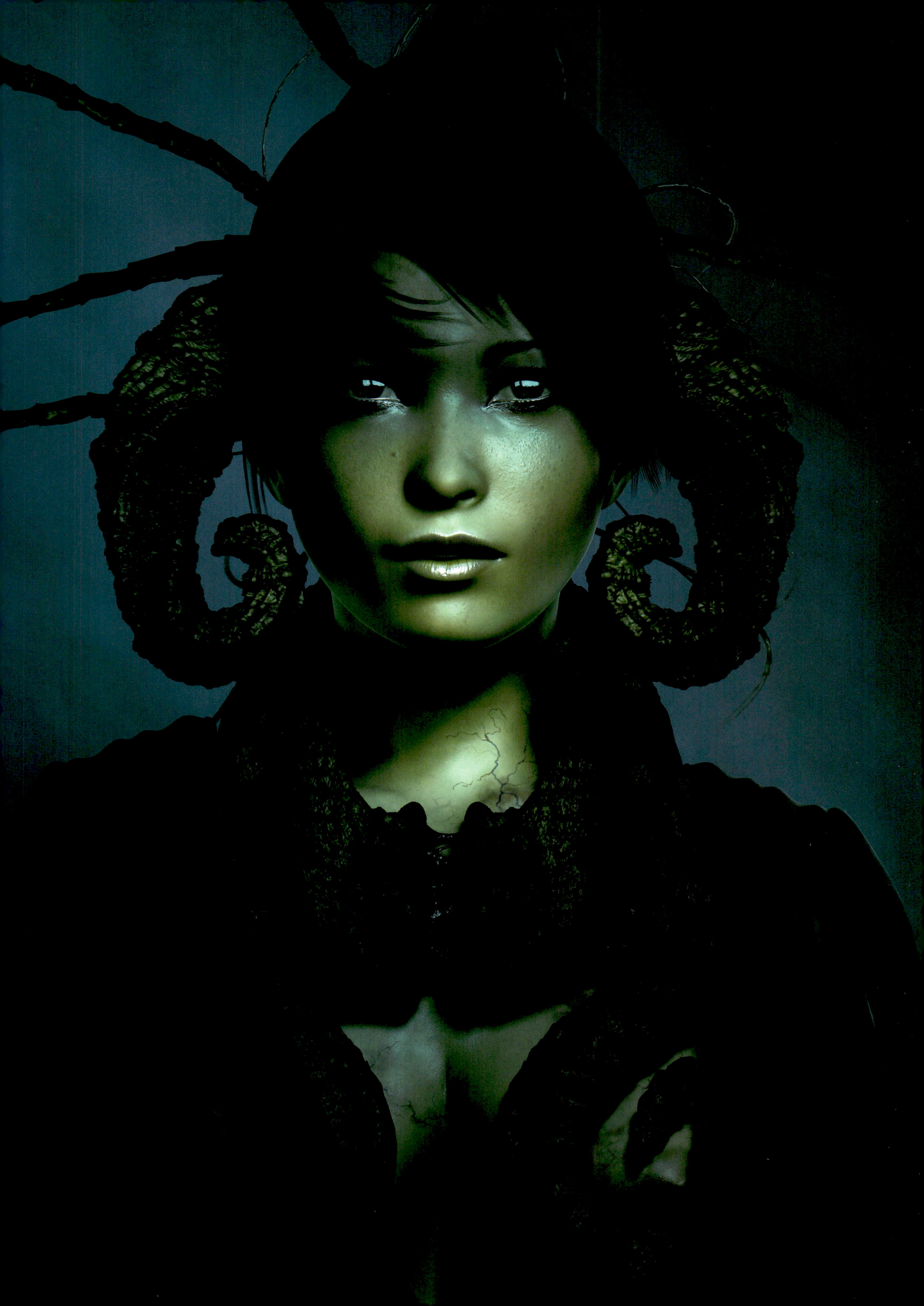

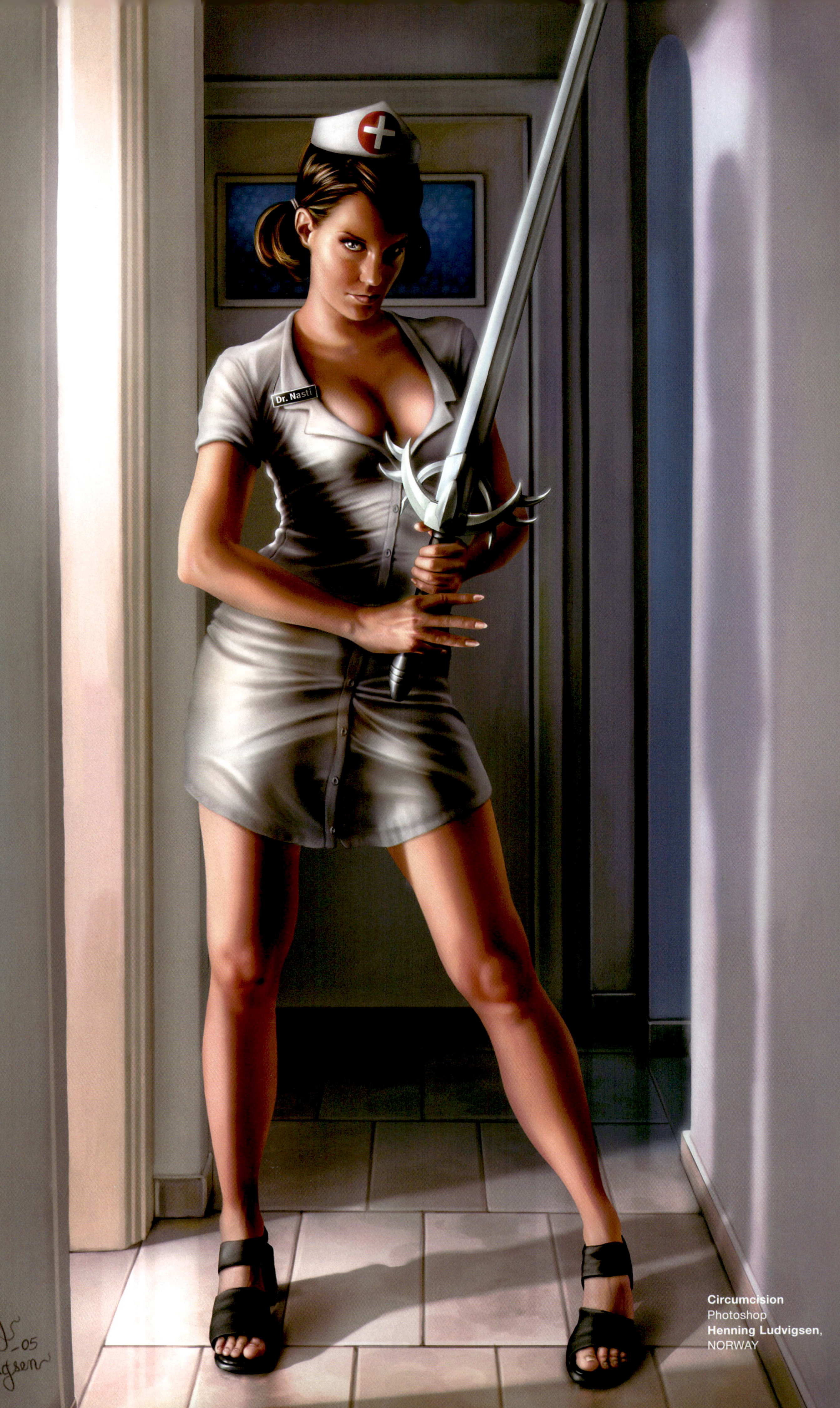

Circumcision
Photoshop
Henning Ludvigsen,
NORWAY

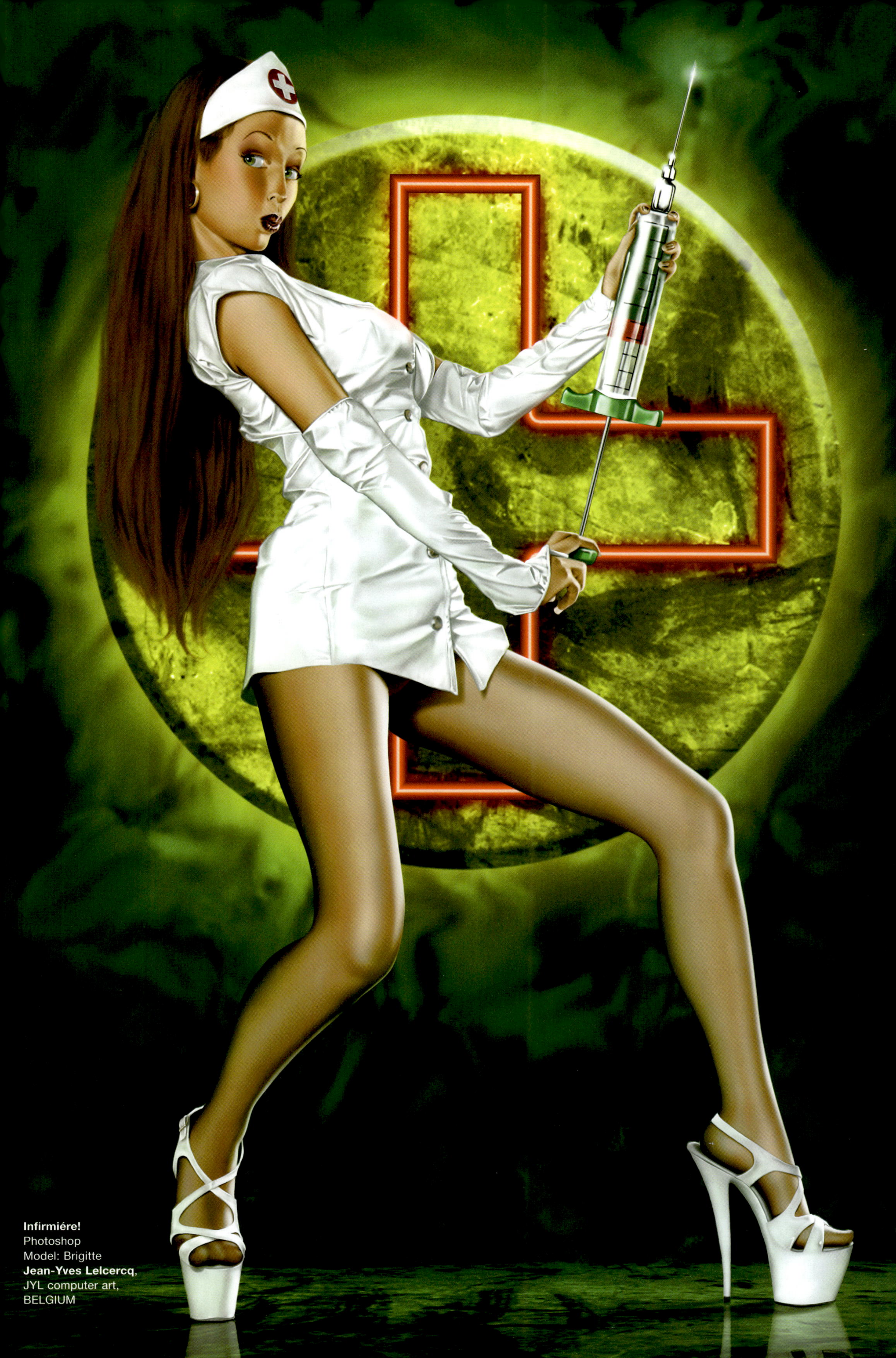

Infirmiére!
Photoshop
Model: Brigitte
Jean-Yves Lelcercq,
JYL computer art,
BELGIUM

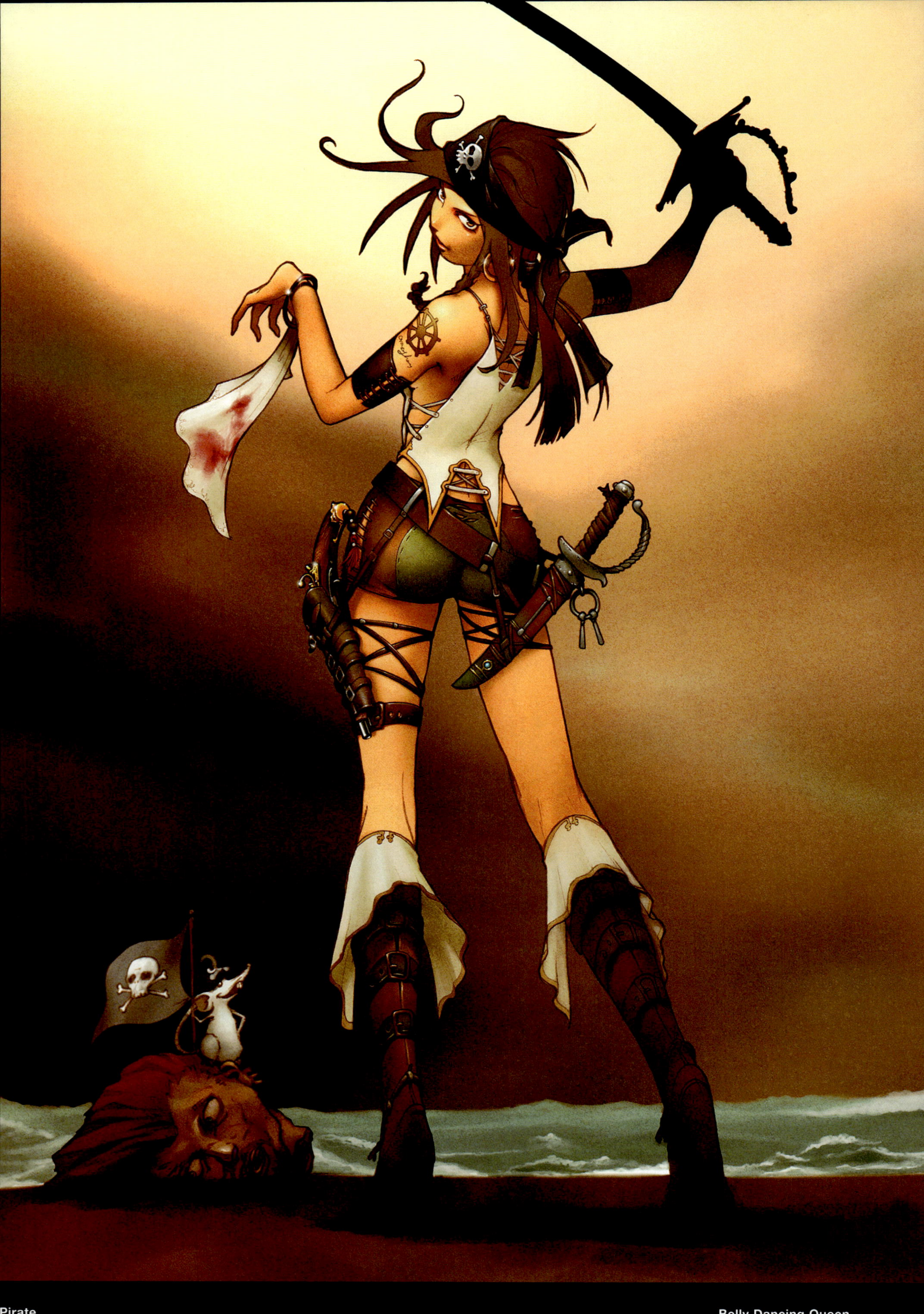

Pirate
Photoshop
Ho Sung Chung, KOREA
[above]

Belly Dancing Queen
Illustrator, Photoshop
Banyen Hongphakdy, AUSTRALIA
[right]

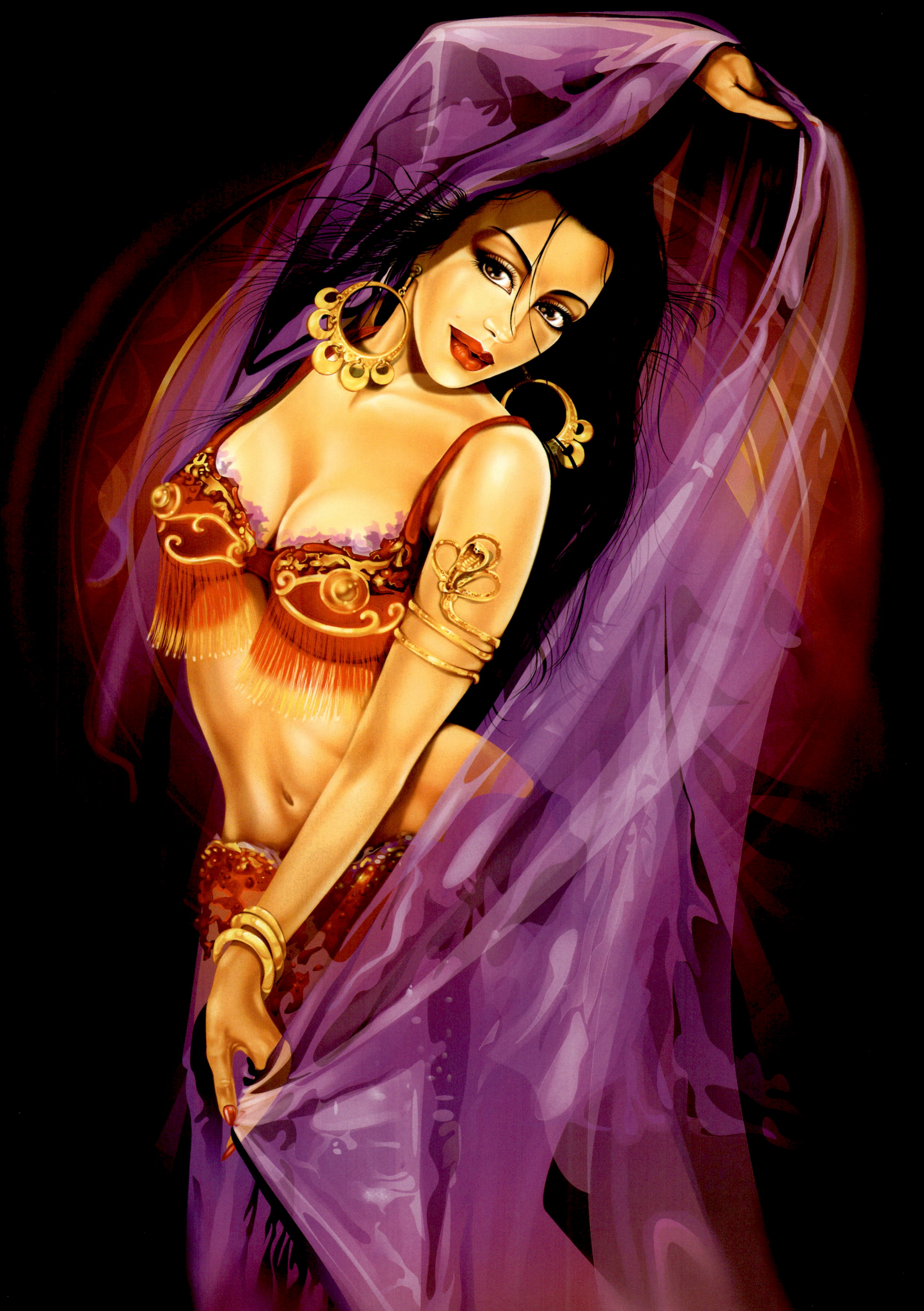

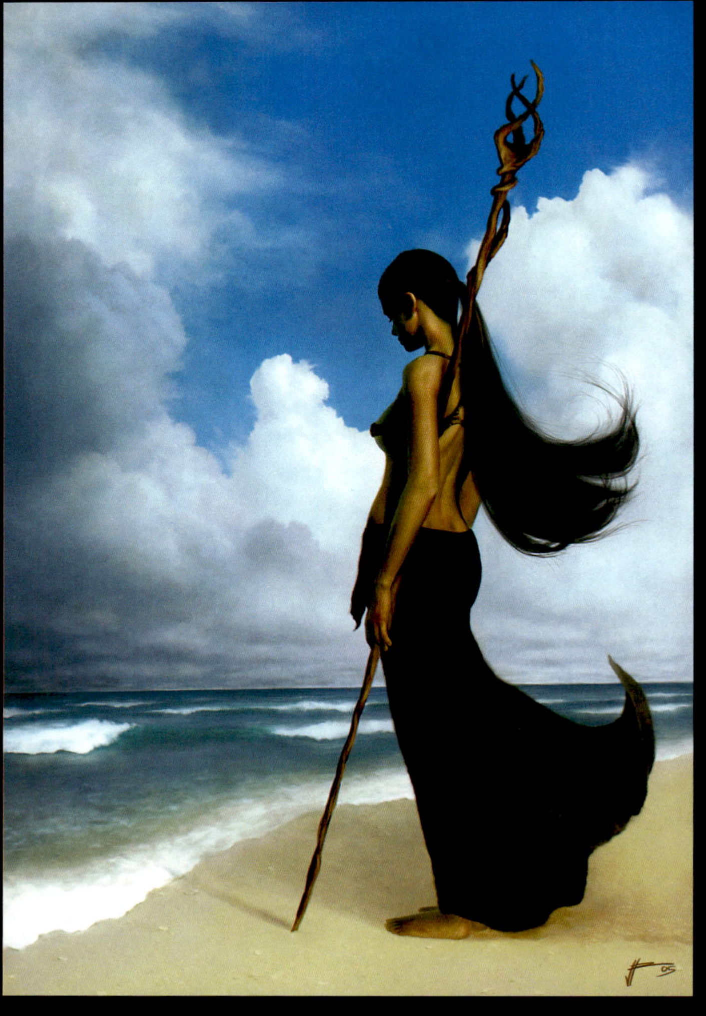

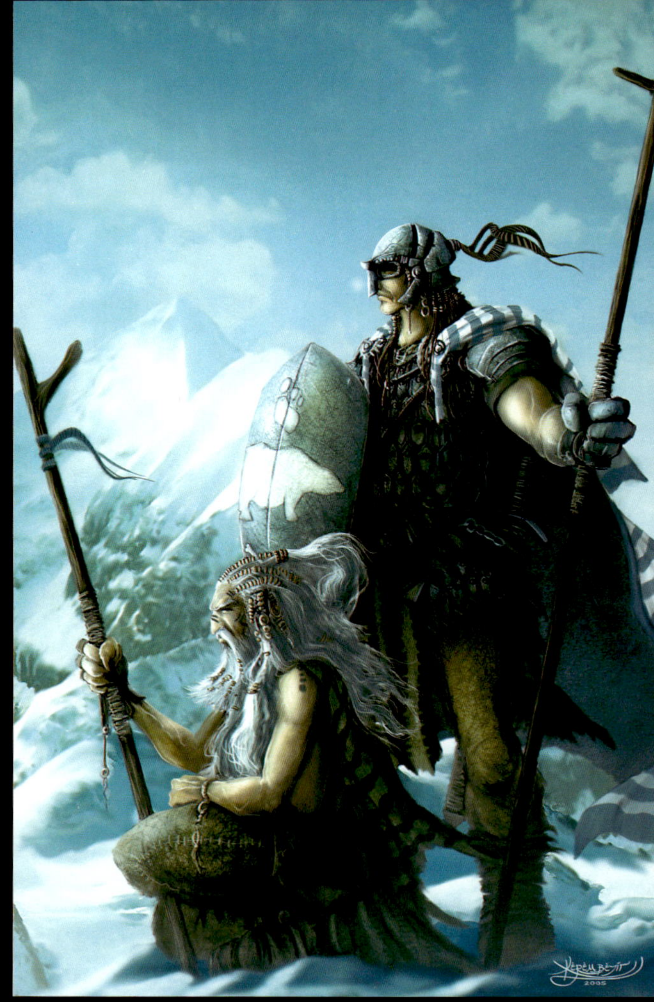

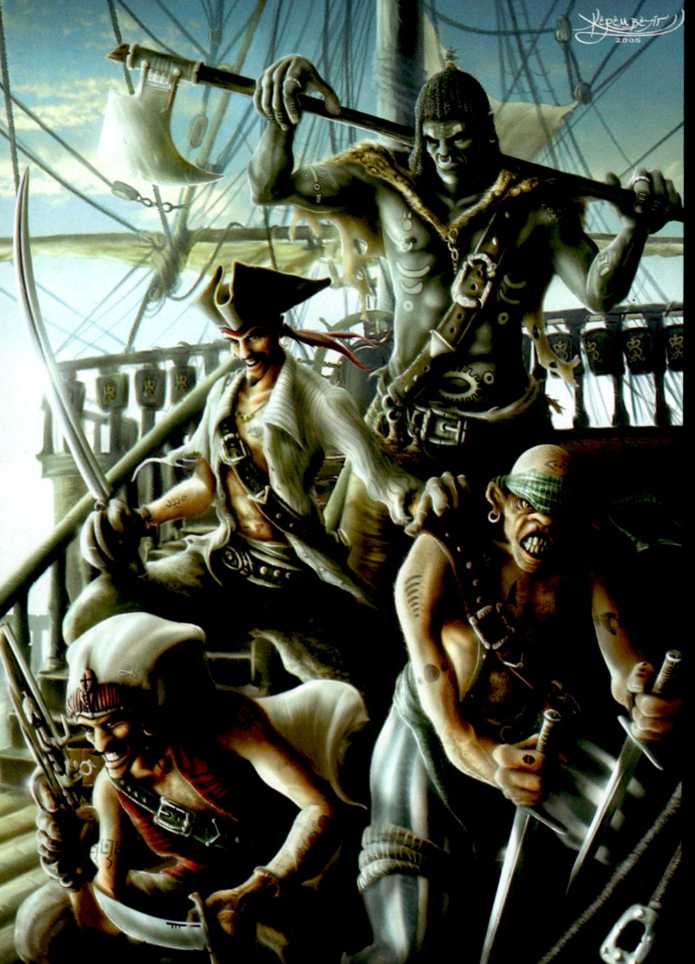

Memories of Lost Happiness
Photoshop
Valentin Fischer, GERMANY
[above left]

Excalibur cover art
Photoshop
Kerem Beyit, Céidot Studios, TURKEY
[top]

William Blood
Photoshop
Kerem Beyit, Céidot Studios, TURKEY
[left]

Dance of Blades
Painter, Photoshop
Jason Chan, USA
[right]

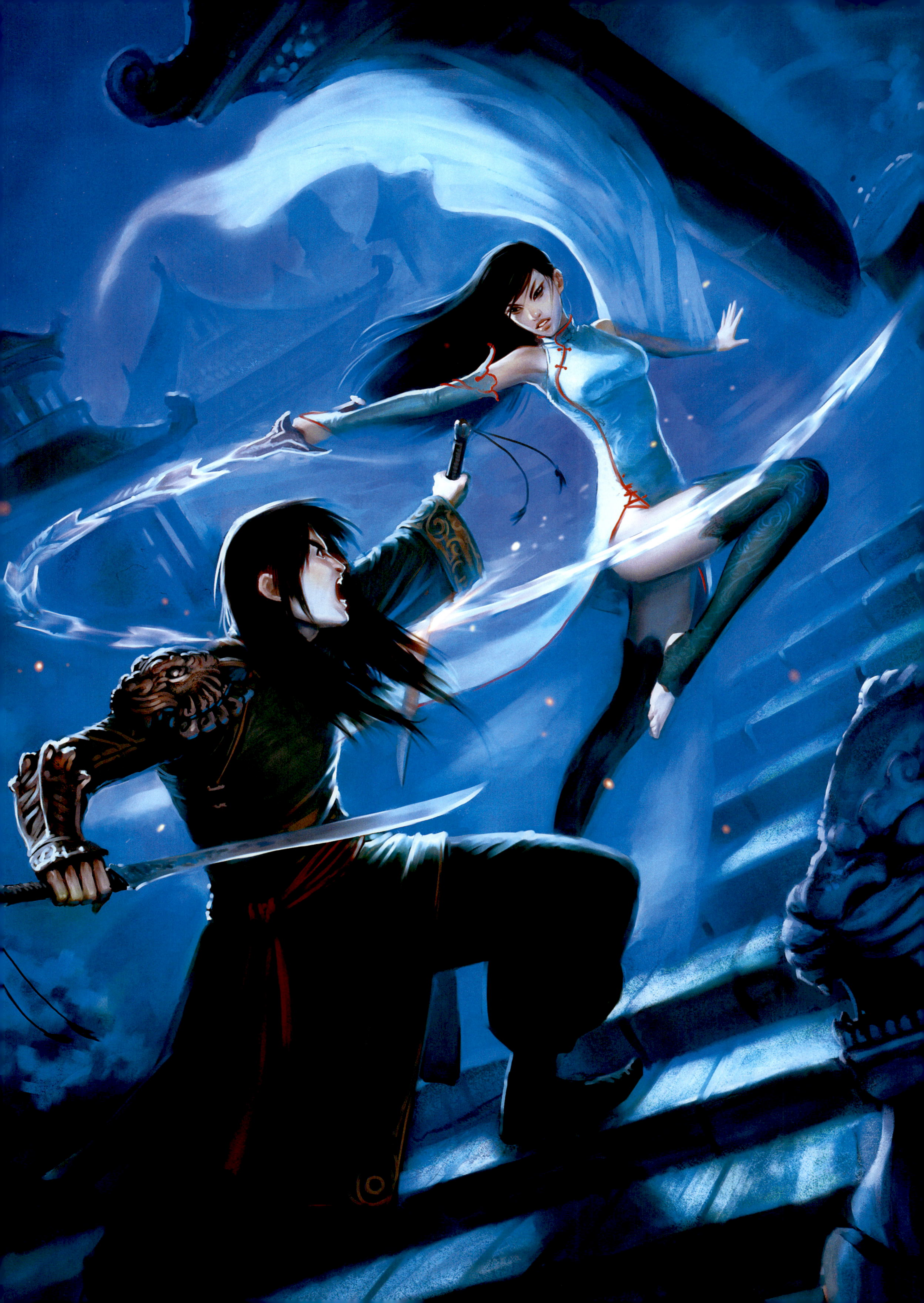

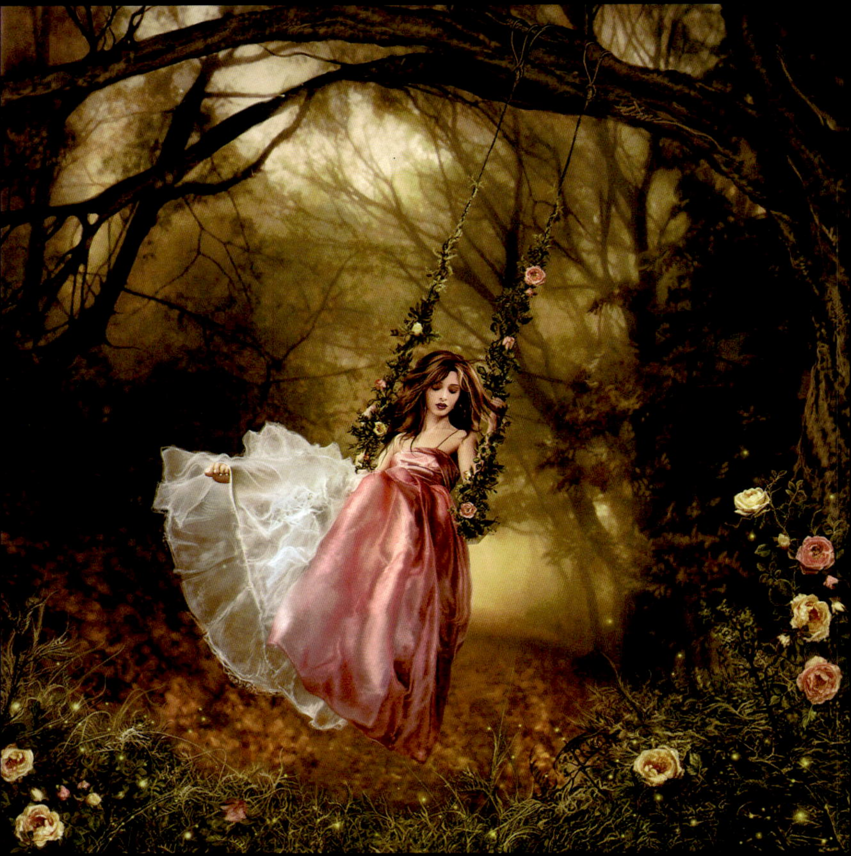

Elanie
Painte
Katari
[left]

Thus r
Photos
Linda
[right]

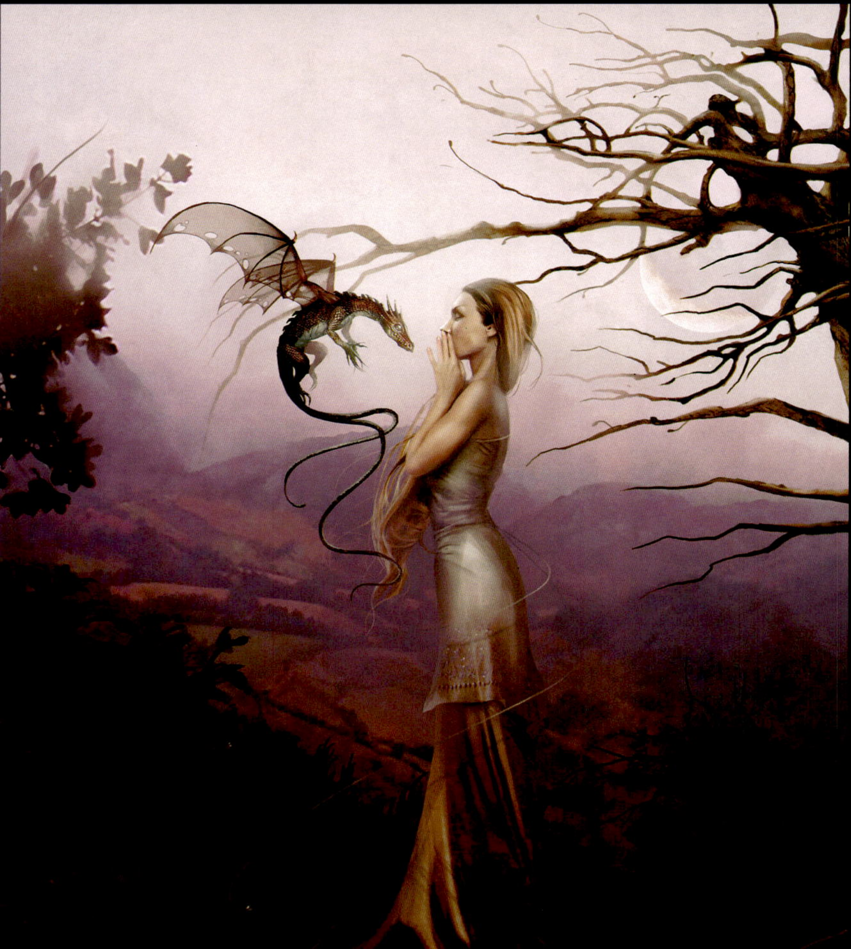

Don't
Photos
Linda
[left]

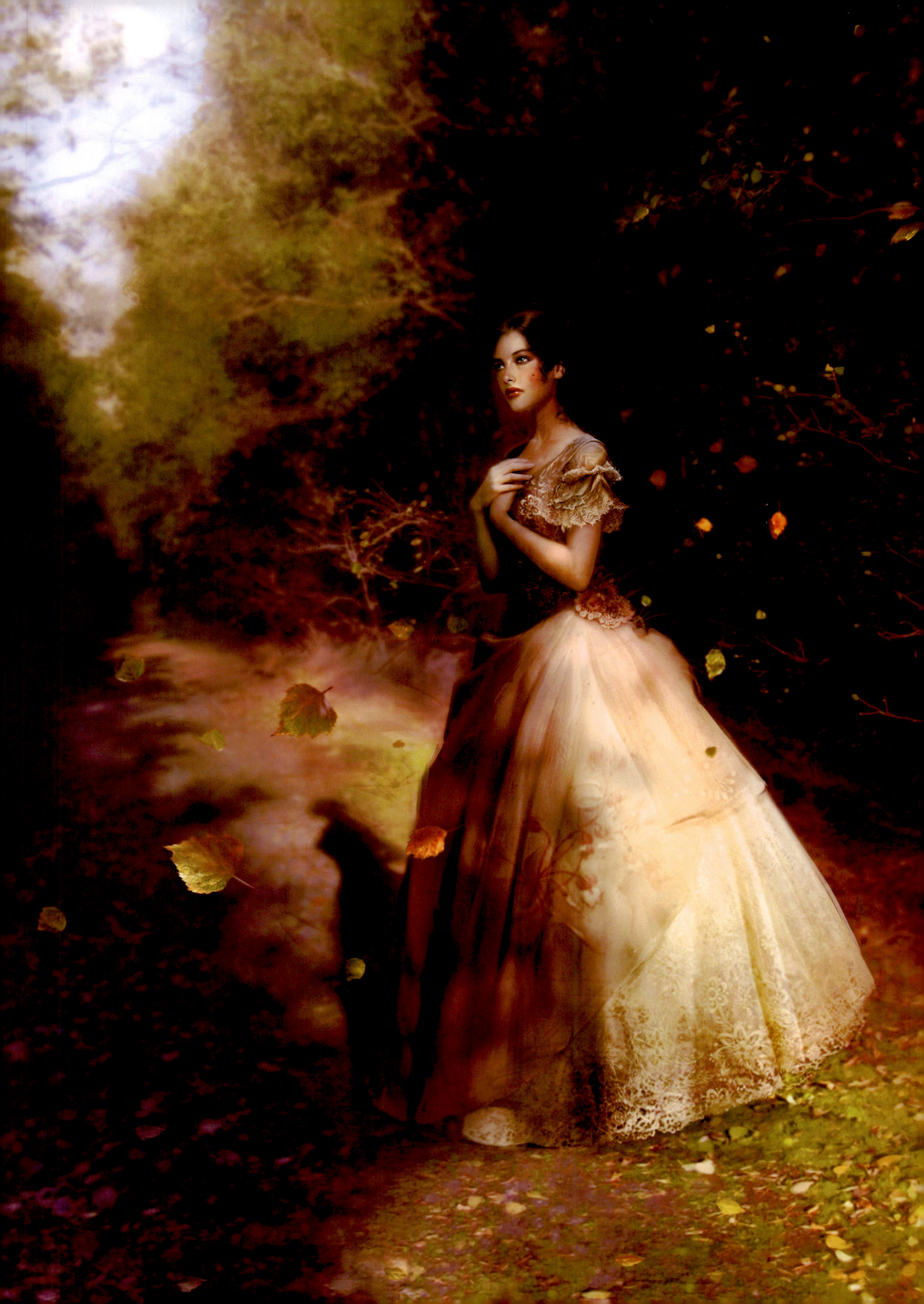

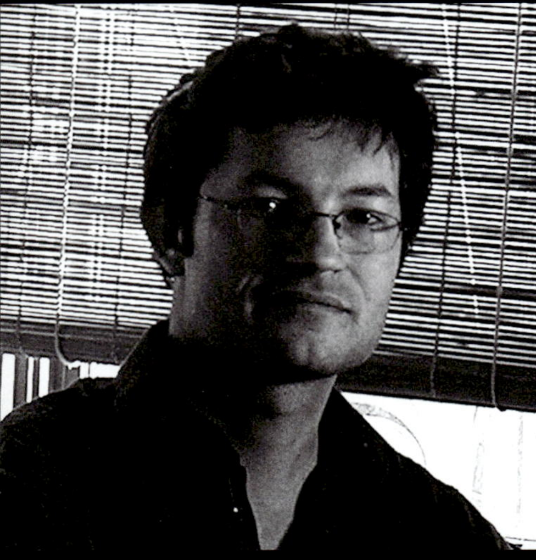

PASCAL BLANCHÉ

www.3dluvr.com/pascalb/
lobo971@yahoo.com

"I've worked in the game field for eleven years, and I still smile in the morning when I go to work."

Pascal Blanché is Art Director at one of the world's biggest gaming companies, Ubisoft Canada based in Montreal. His most recent game project was 'Myst IV: Revelation', the fourth in the cult adventure game series. Pascal started on the path towards a career in art/design for games at the Art School of Luminy, Marseille. Following art school, he freelanced for TILT magazine, an early video games magazine and then worked in modeling, concept art, texturing, lighting and animation for various French gaming companies. Pascal worked for one year as an animator, then lead animator on the first French/Canadian full-CG movie—Kaena: The Prophecy (distributed by Sony). Pascal is an influential artist in the CGTalk community and was a central figure in the first CG challenge concept where artists came up with a collective brief, then created a piece according to those restrictions. CGTalk's CG Challenges now run regularly with thousands of entrants and major prizes on offer.

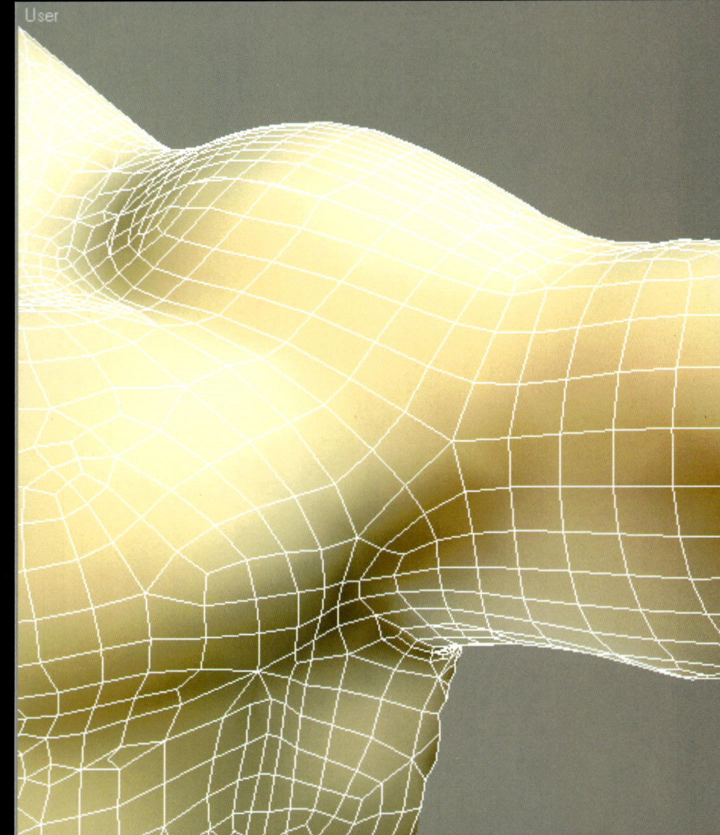

MODELING

This picture was at first a pure anatomy study. I'm inspired by artists such as Corben, Bisley, Frazetta and Brom. I've always been frustrated by the limitations of 3D when it comes to anatomy subtleties. Using the box modeling technique, I created a basic structure, at a very low level of details, to break down the main shape of the model. At this point, the most common tools I use are the Turn Edge option of the editable mesh and the Relax tool. I tend to exaggerate the shape of a muscle then I use a Relax to smooth all of the odd angles and I go back into extreme shapes, then repeat the process again. The Relax tool has to be used with caution as it always flattens your structure. When I feel I've gone far enough with the low poly cage, I add a subdivision or MeshSmooth on it and start to build up the details again.

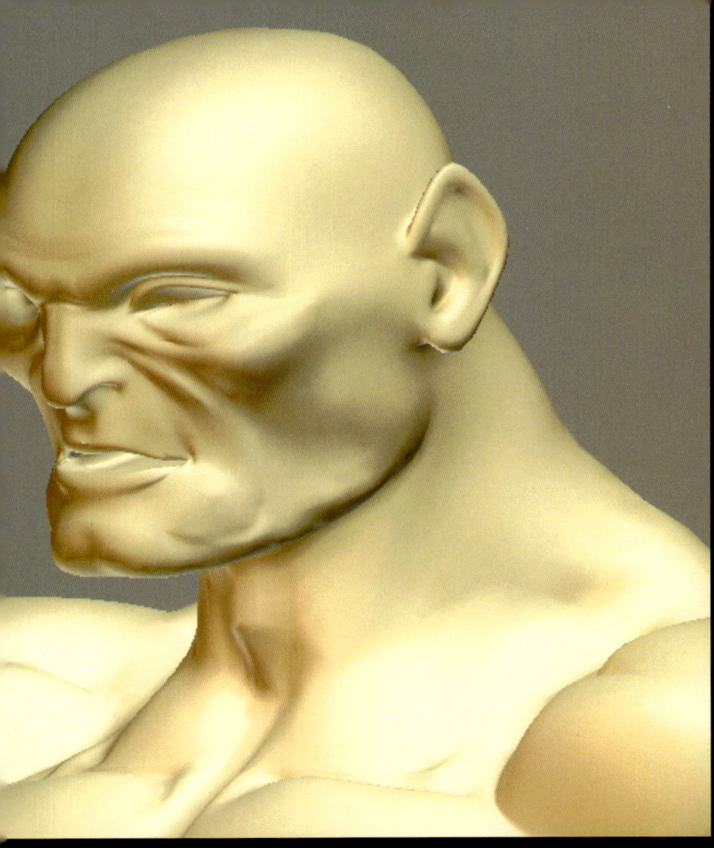

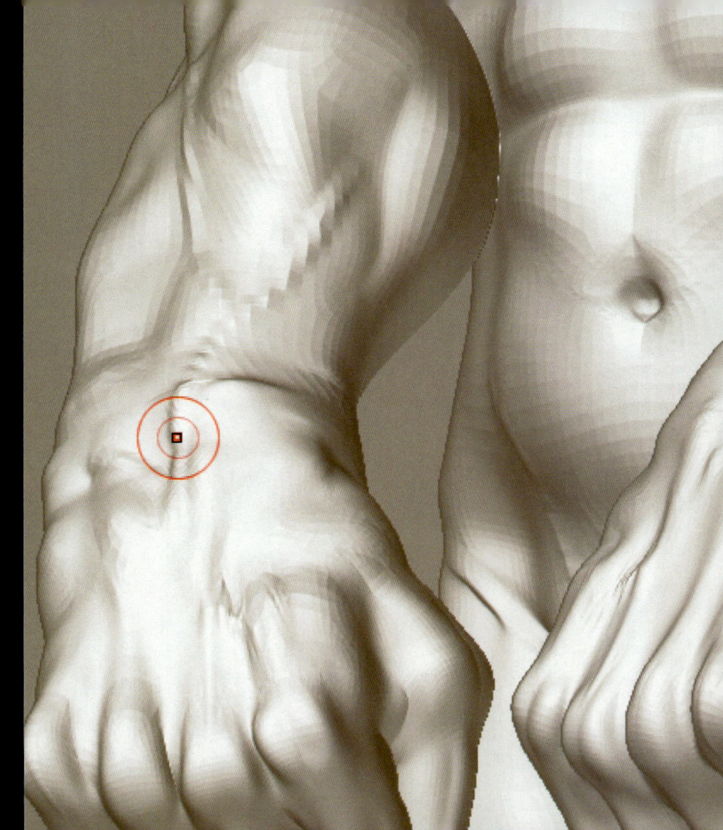

DEFINITION

Now that I have the general proportions I wanted (not fully and totally photorealistic I know), I can start to work on muscle definition and face details using the smooth cage I've just built. It's easy to create nice subtleties following the cage, and it's also where I find the limits of this technique. Before going any further into the details, I did a fast rigging and skinning of the mesh, using the built-in Character Studio Skeleton and Physique modifier. After creating the basic influences of the bones deformation, I set my character into its final pose, and then I refined the deformation assignation so it fit with the new pose, correcting little errors here and there. Finally, I created a snapshot of the model and exported it in .obj for ZBrush.

ZBRUSH

I have to admit that I've been impressed by the ZBrush experience. I've been following the package since its beginnings, and was not quite sure how it could help me in my work process. When I saw the demos of ZBrush 2, I knew I would have to give it a try. I was also able to refine the overall shape using the Move tool and push a little more of the general shape of the character to give him a nicer silhouette. By using the Drawing tool in Standard mode, Inflate or Pinch mode (transform options) and by using a large variety of brush sizes and brush z intensity, I started to literally sculpt the model without bothering with the cage. The best technique I found was to start with a low resolution cage refining general shapes, and the more I work on details, the more I work on high resolution cage. By going back and forth from time to time into those different levels of details I was able to totally control my model, from reshaping muscles, to adding flesh wrinkles and veins. After exporting the model back from 3ds Max I played around with different lighting and renderings to put more emphasis on the body definition. I added the steel bar and bent it into the final picture shape to add a little more story to the picture

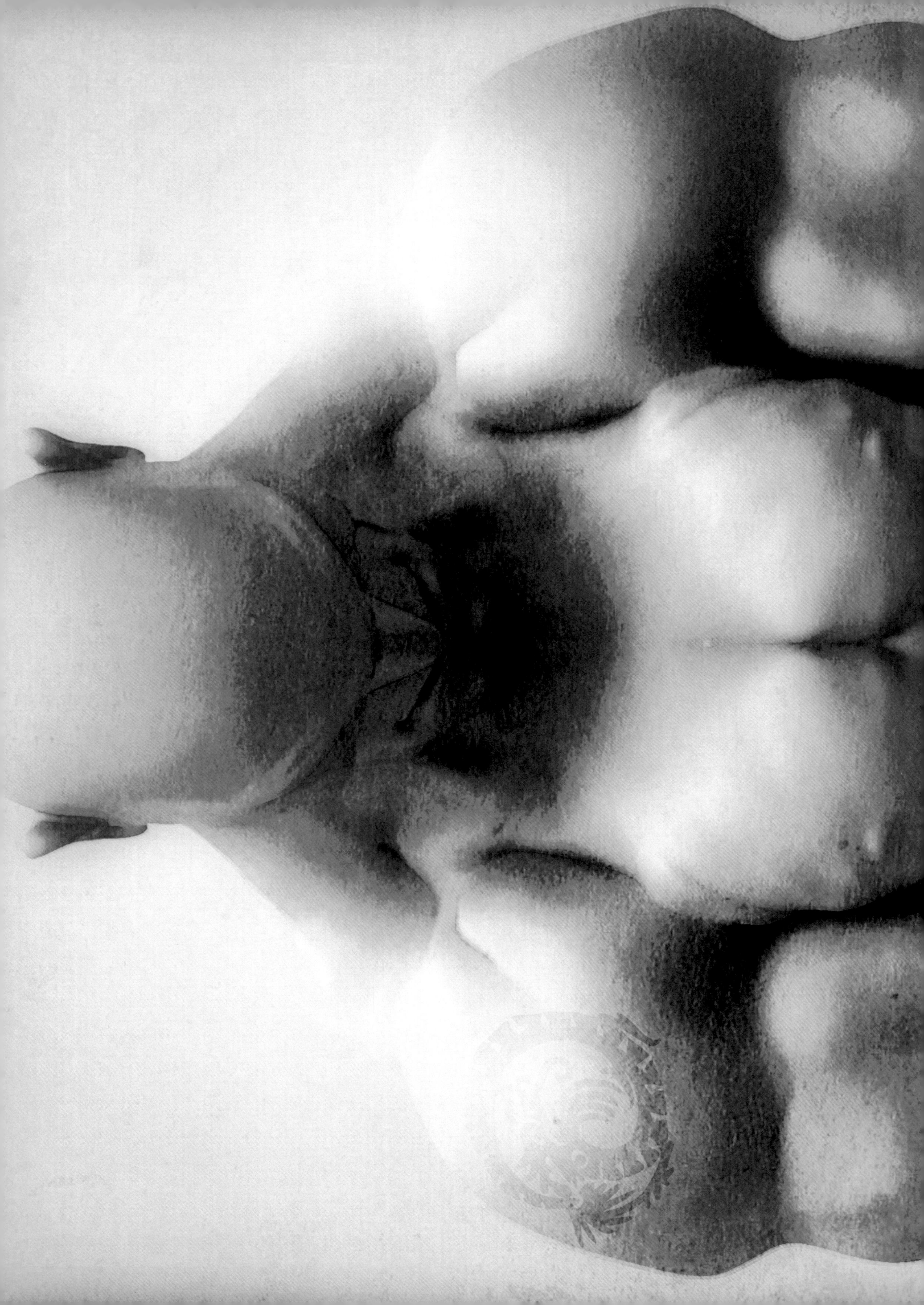

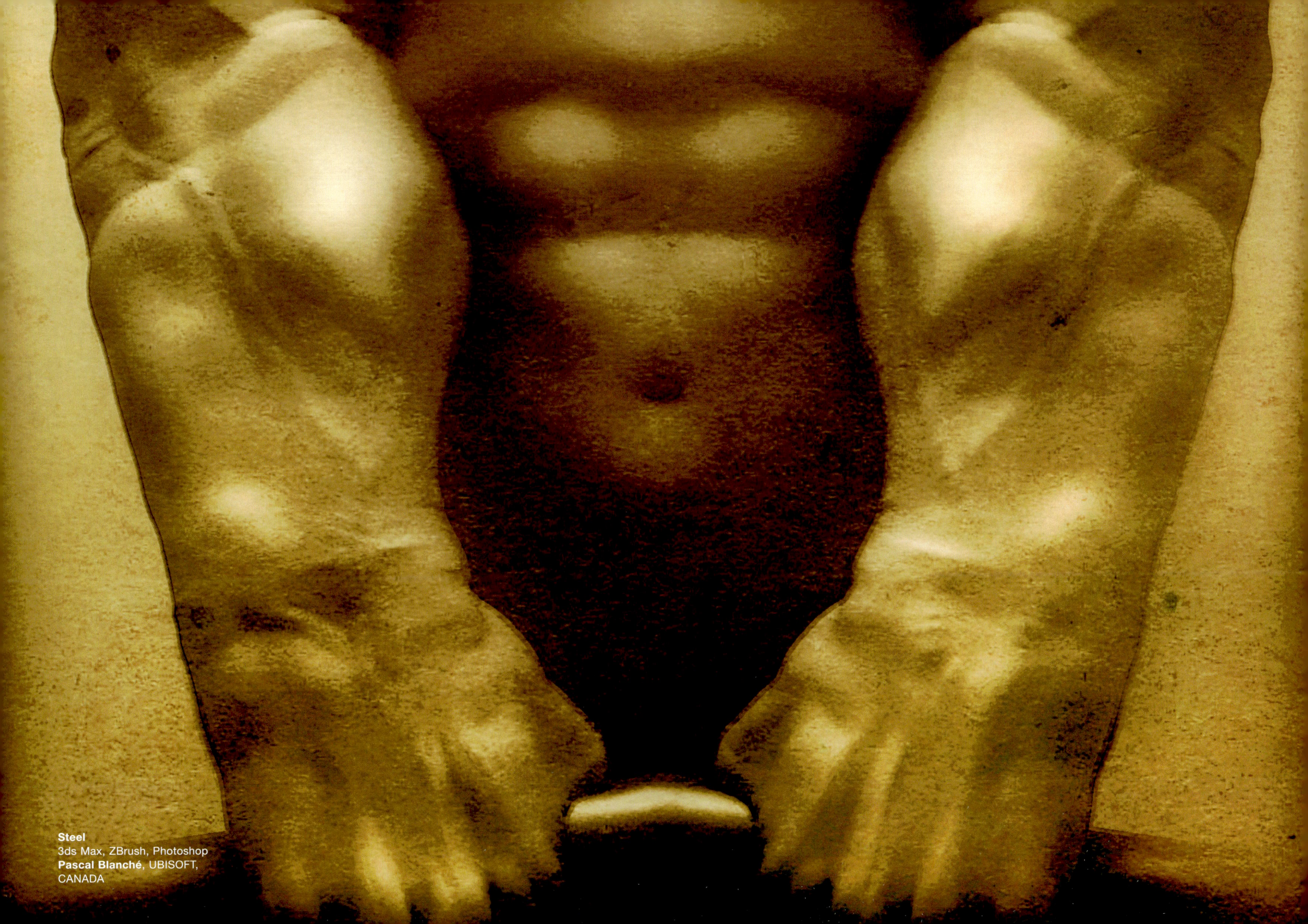

Steel
3ds Max, ZBrush, Photoshop
Pascal Blanché, UBISOFT,
CANADA

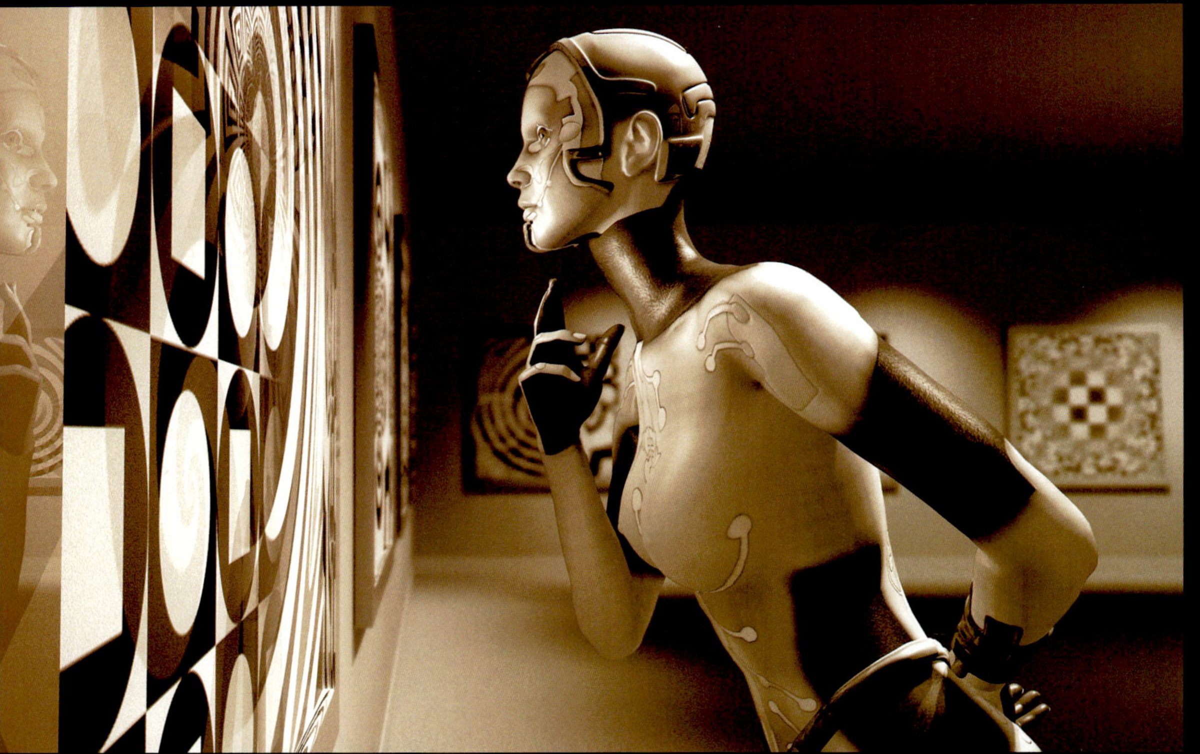

Andromeda - The AI Critic
Bryce, Poser, CINEMA 4D,
Photoshop
Adam Benton,
GREAT BRITAIN
[left]

Bio Bot 1
Photoshop, CINEMA 4D
Benedict Campbell,
GREAT BRITAIN
[right]

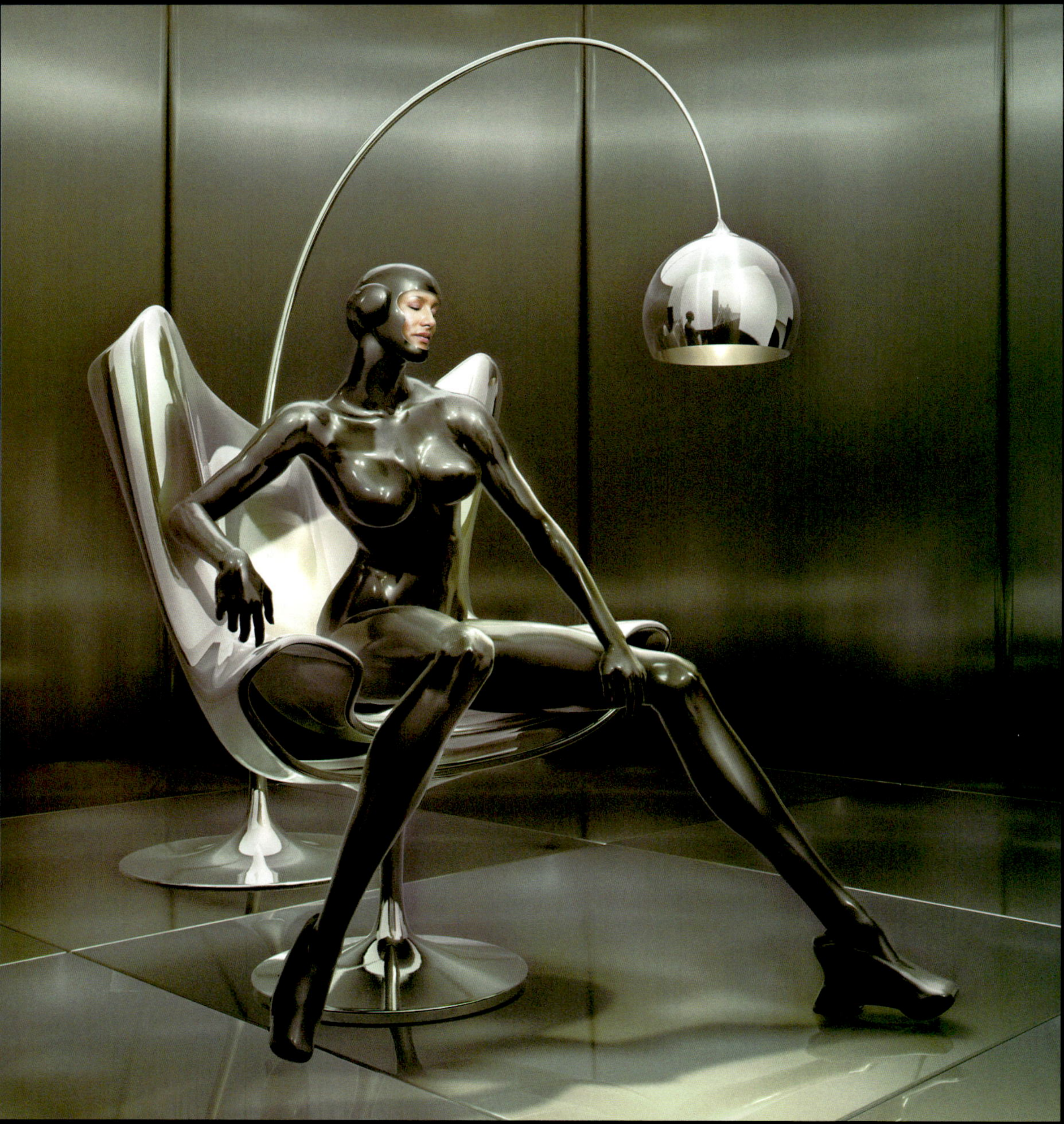

2sid
Photoshop, Poser,
BodyPaint, CINEMA 4D
Benedict Campbell,
GREAT BRITAIN
[left]

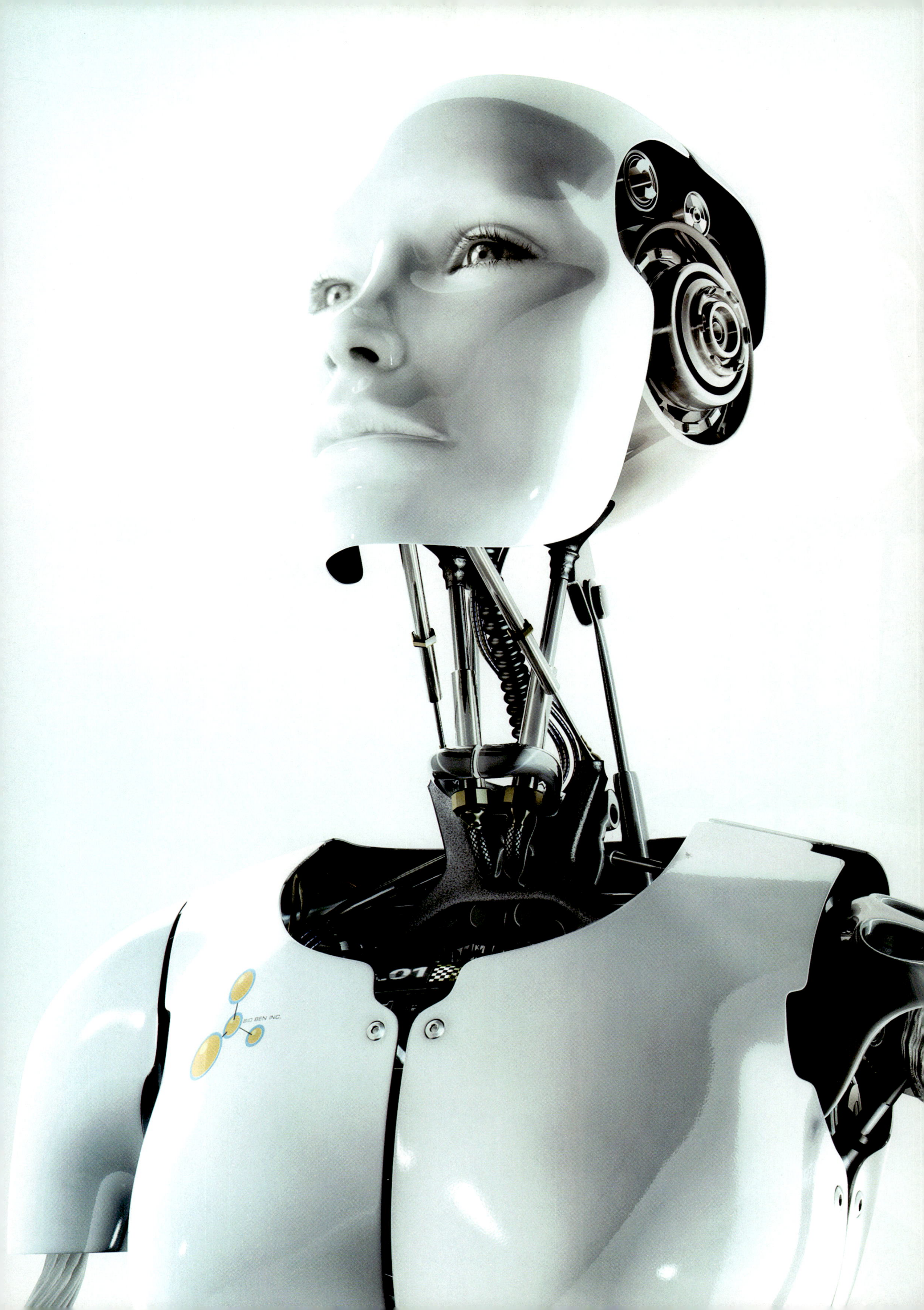
BIO BEN INC.

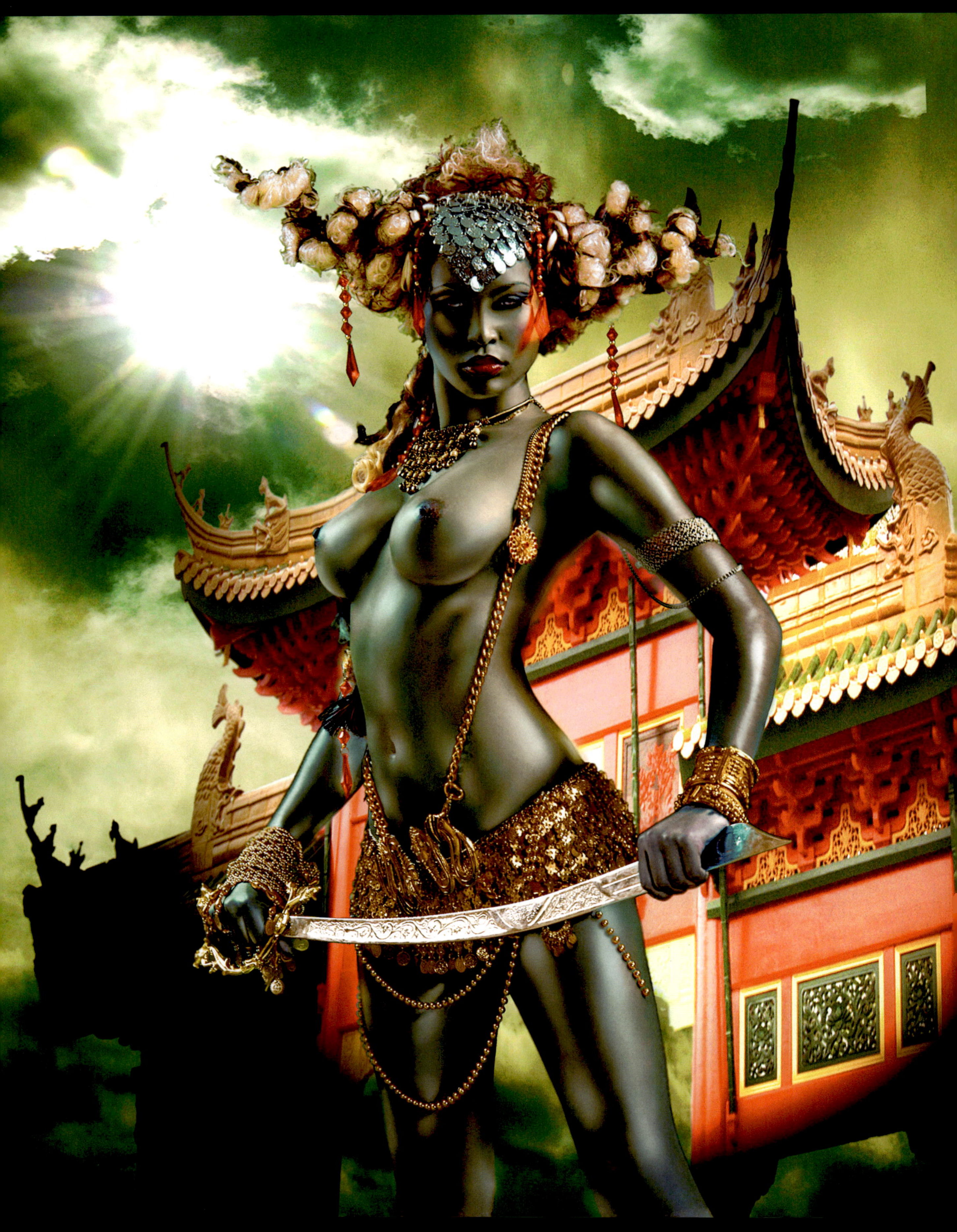

Temple Guard Priestess
Photoshop
Oz Spiniello, AUSTRALIA
[above]

Bride of Lucifer
Painter
Hong Kuang, SINGAPORE
[right]

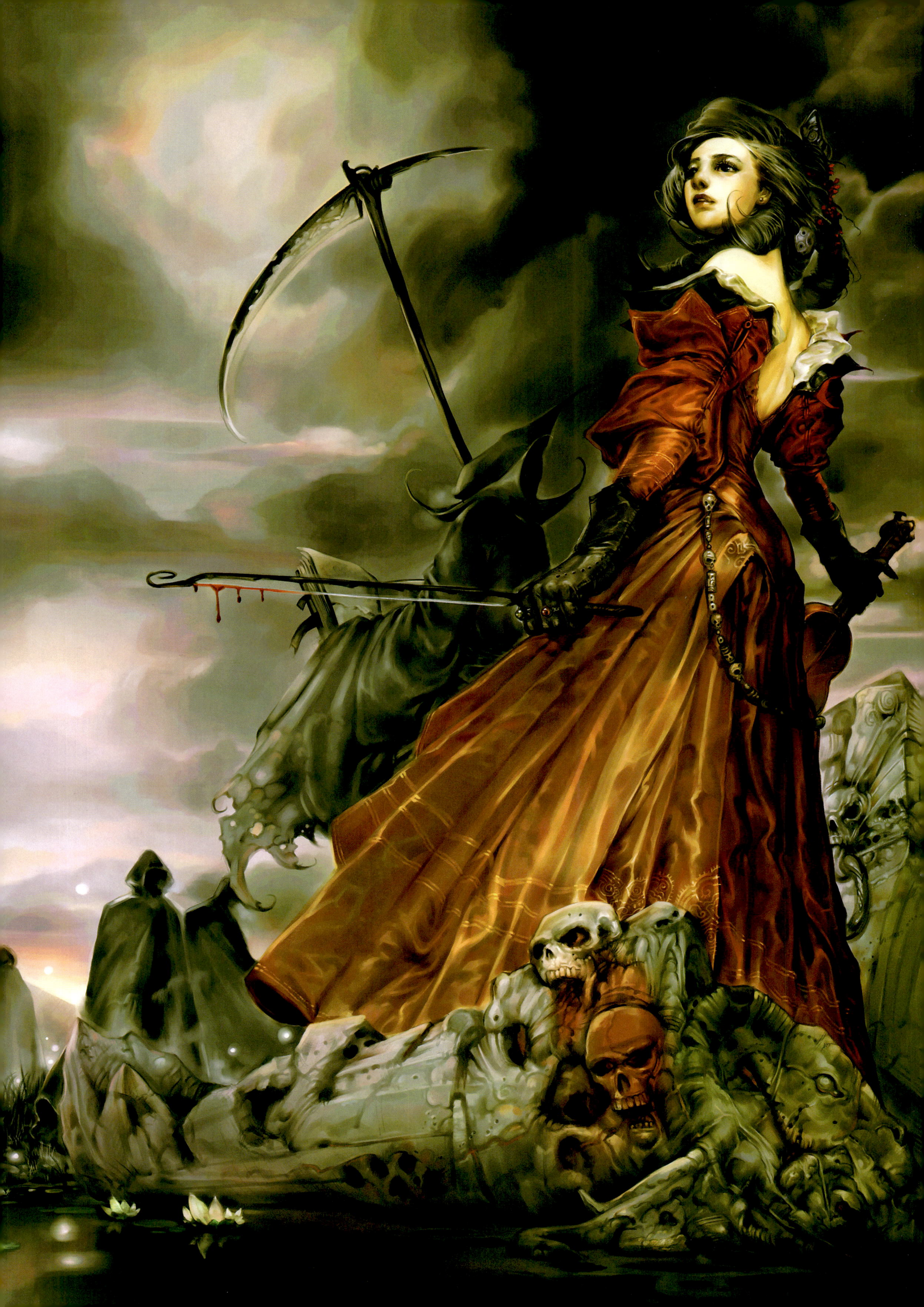

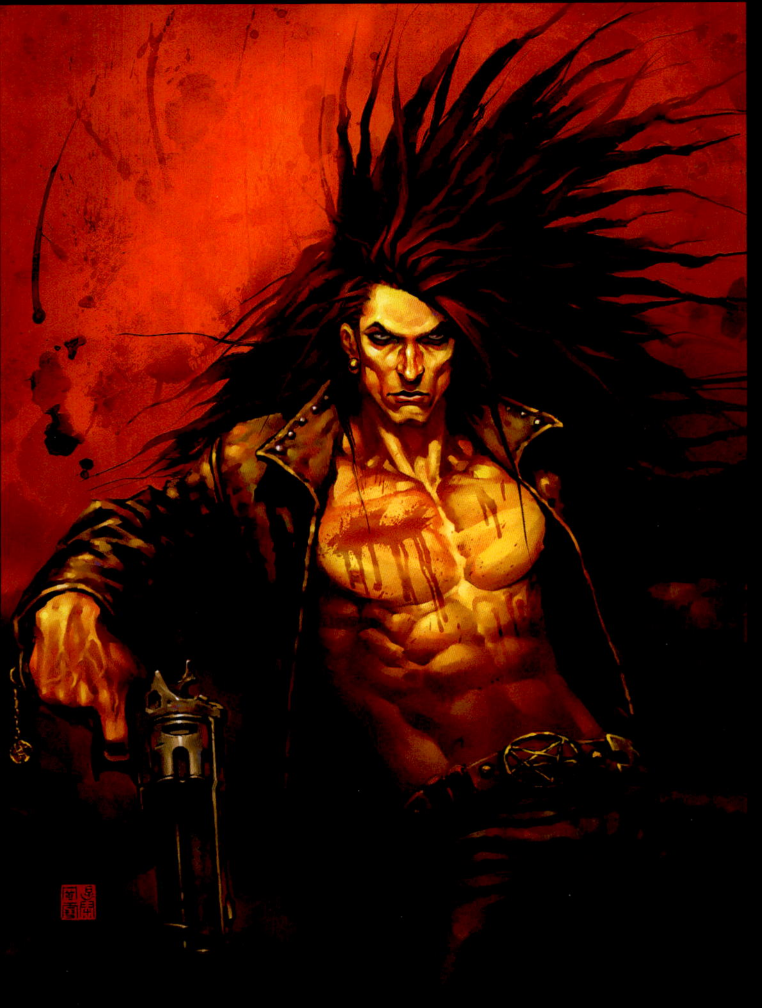

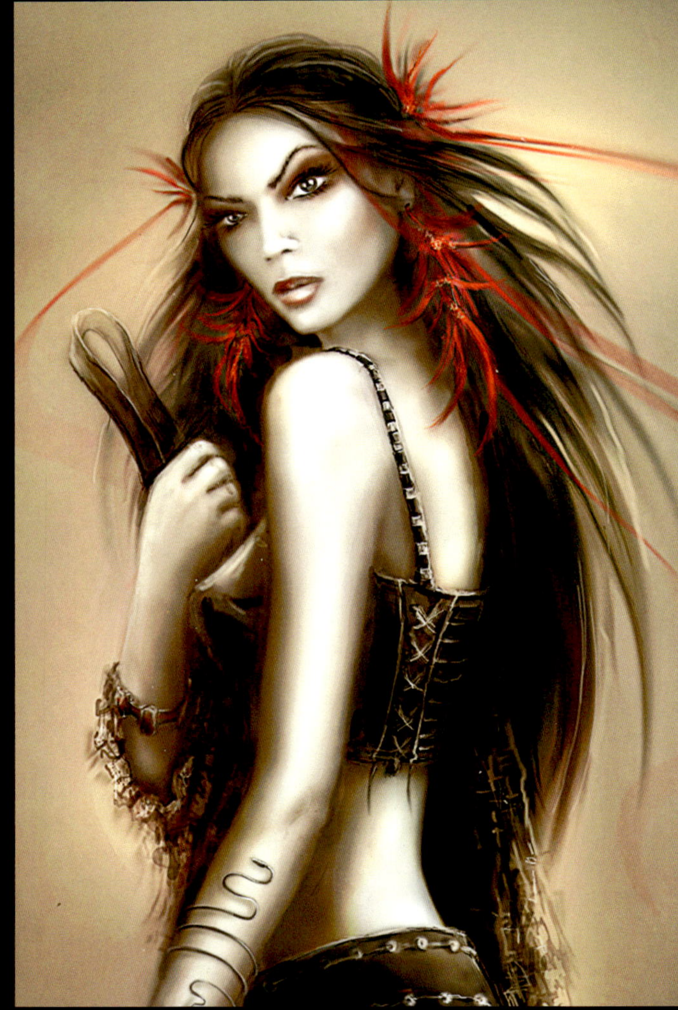

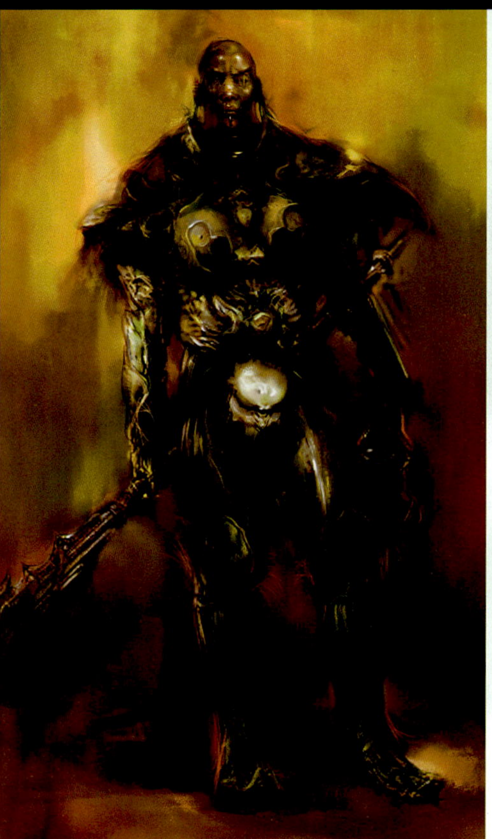

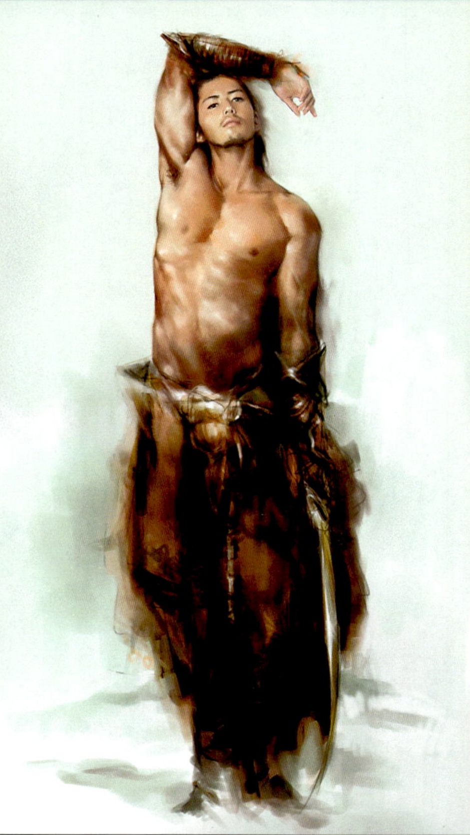

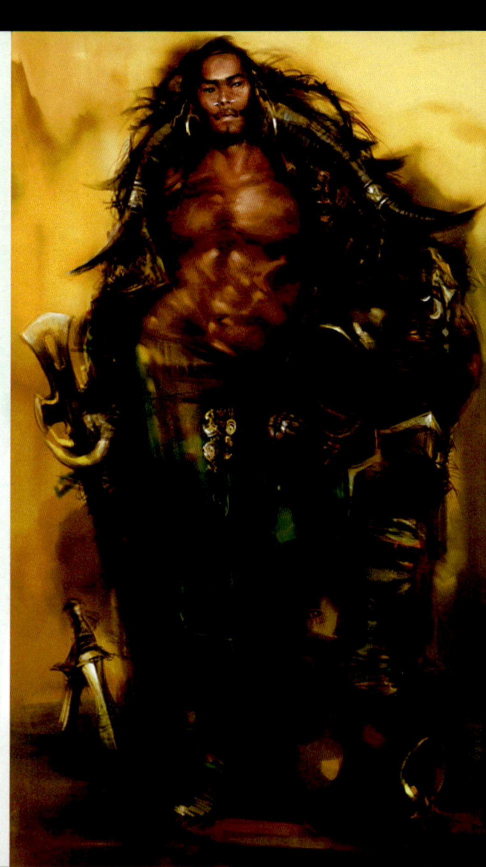

Metal
Painter, Photoshop
Wei Wang,
CHINA
[top left]

Chinese Persons of Ancient Times
Photoshop, Painter
Weng Ziyang,
Chinese Fantasy Magazine, CHINA
[above series]

In the Fear Slavery
Photoshop
Olga Barkhatova,
CANADA
[top right]

Portrait of an Asian Vampire
Photoshop
Christine Griffin,
USA
[right]

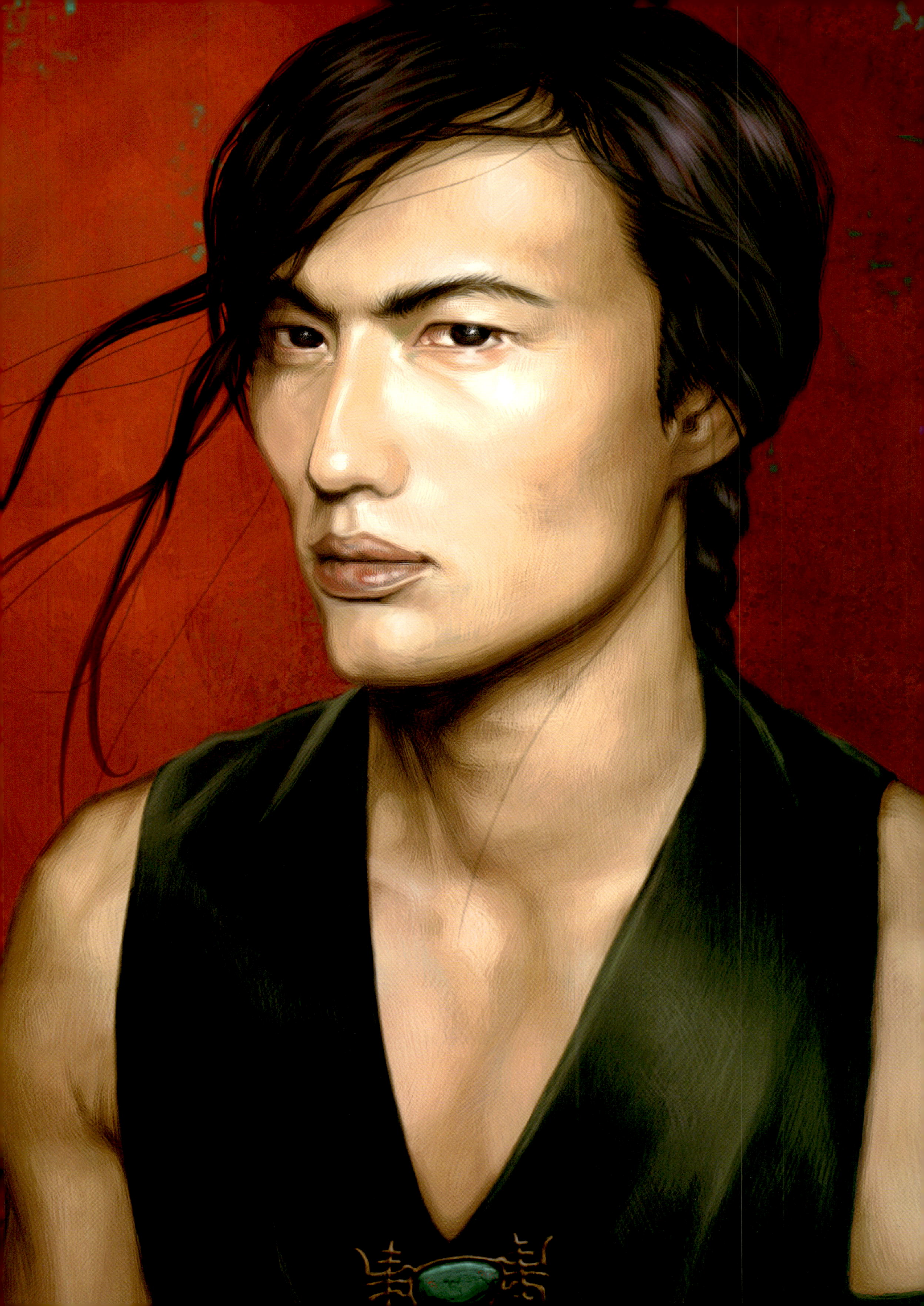

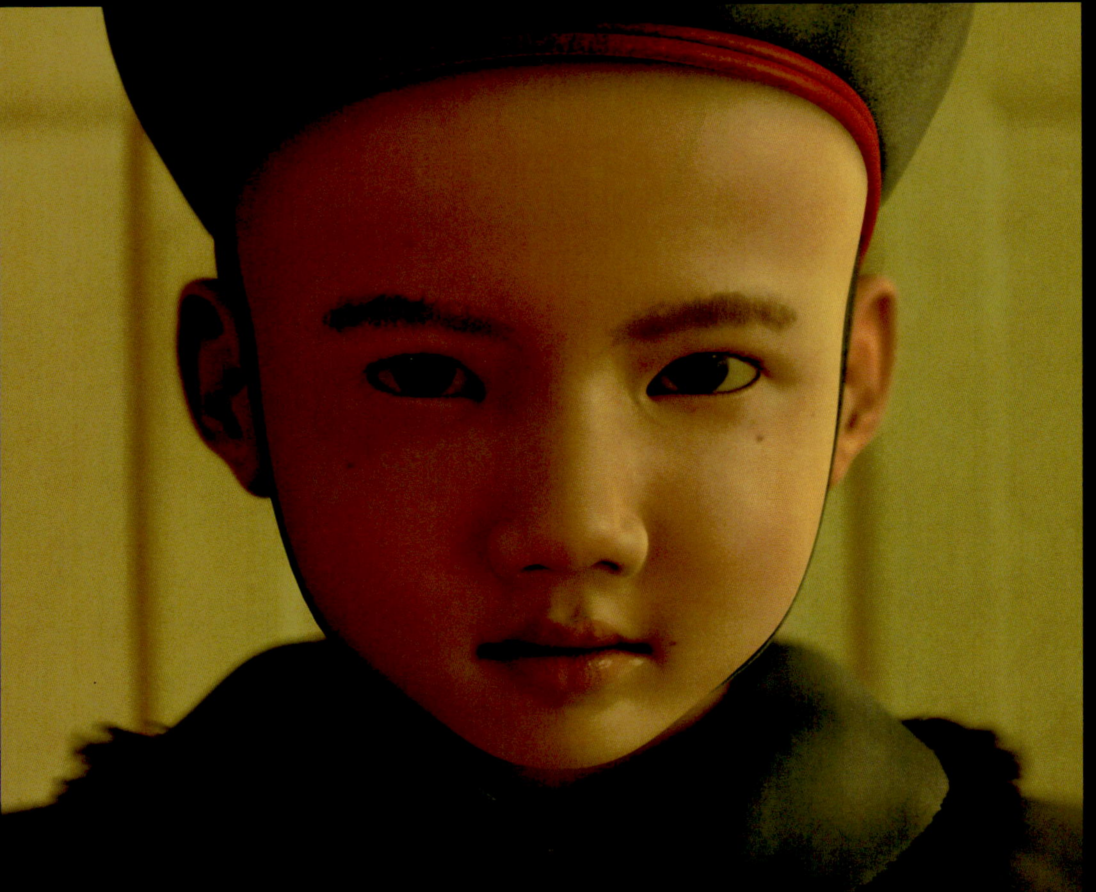

Pu Yi
CINEMA 4D, BodyPaint
Alberto Blasi, ITALY
[left]

The Messenger
Photoshop, Painter
Oliver Wetter, Fantasio Fine Arts
GERMANY
[right]

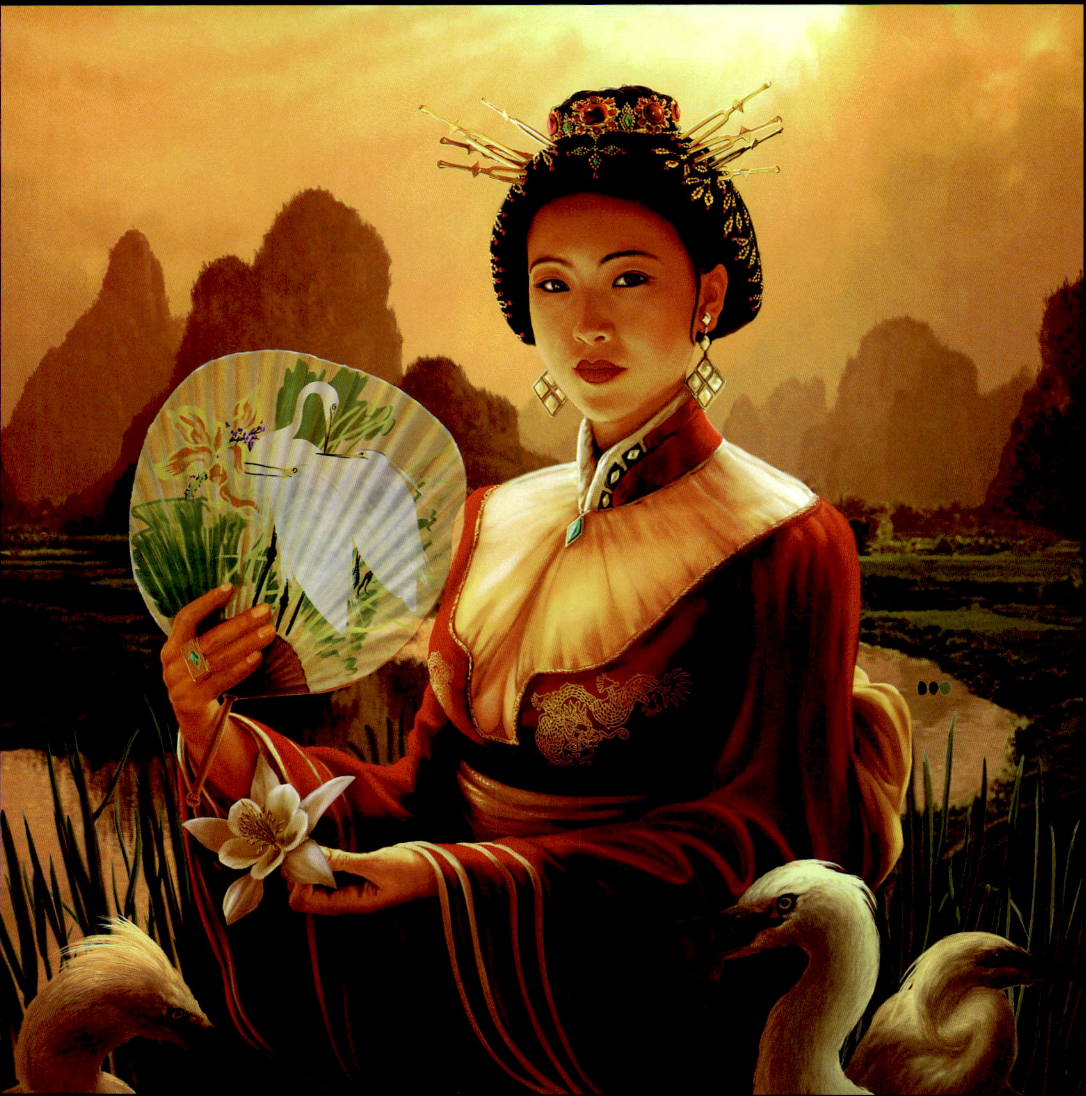

Chinese Princess
Painter, Photoshop, 3ds Max
Kornél Ravadits, HUNGARY
[left]

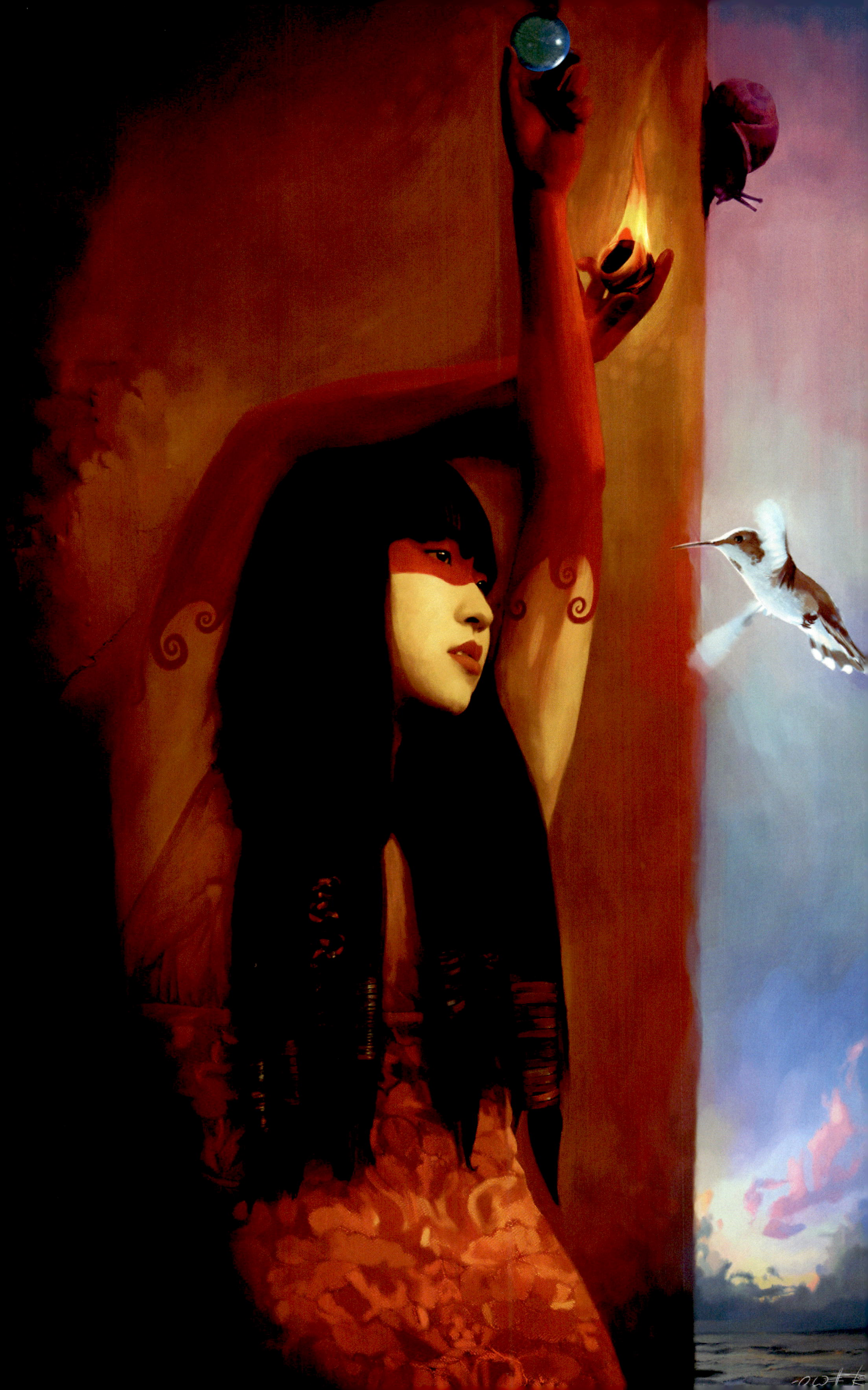

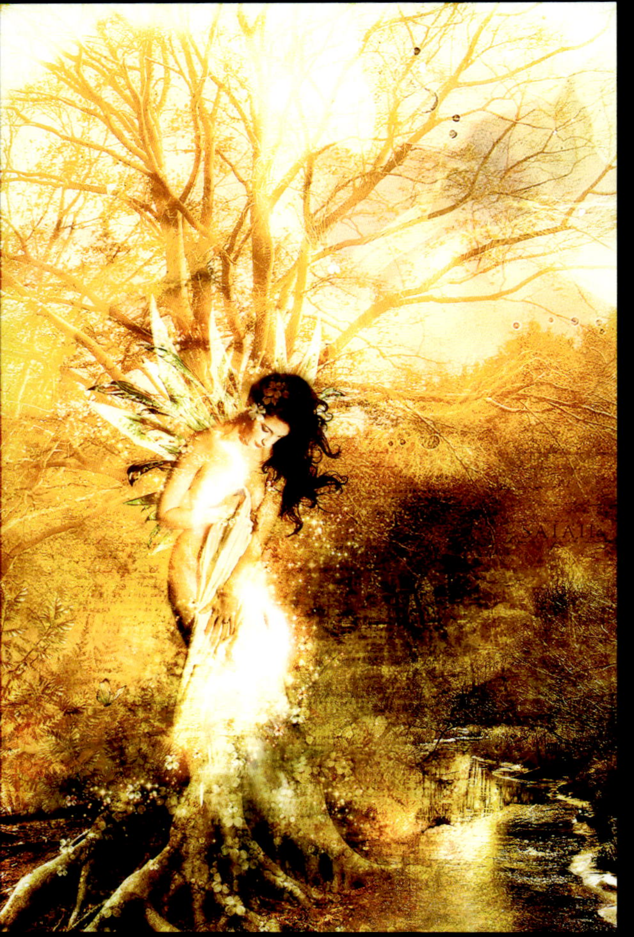

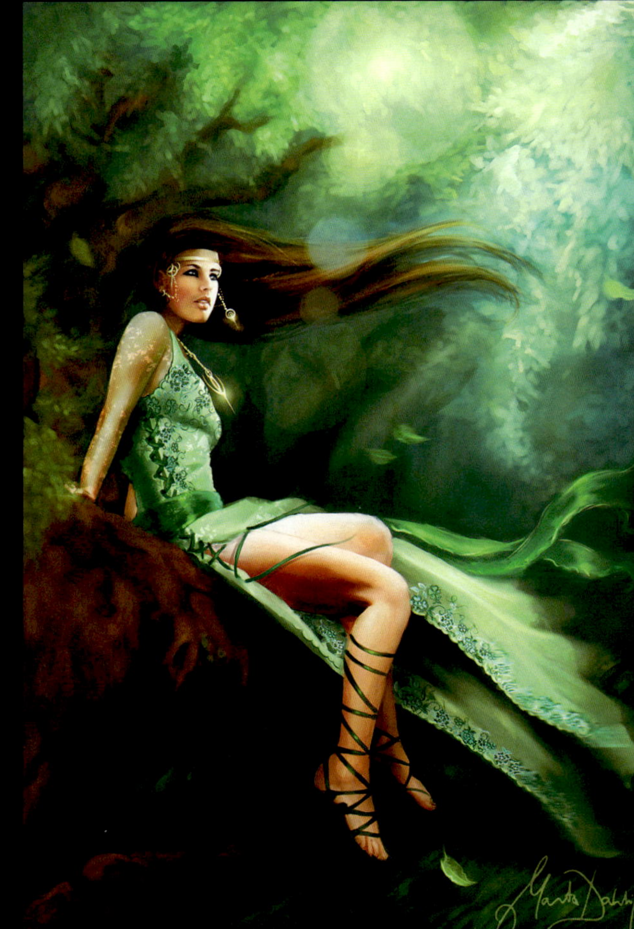

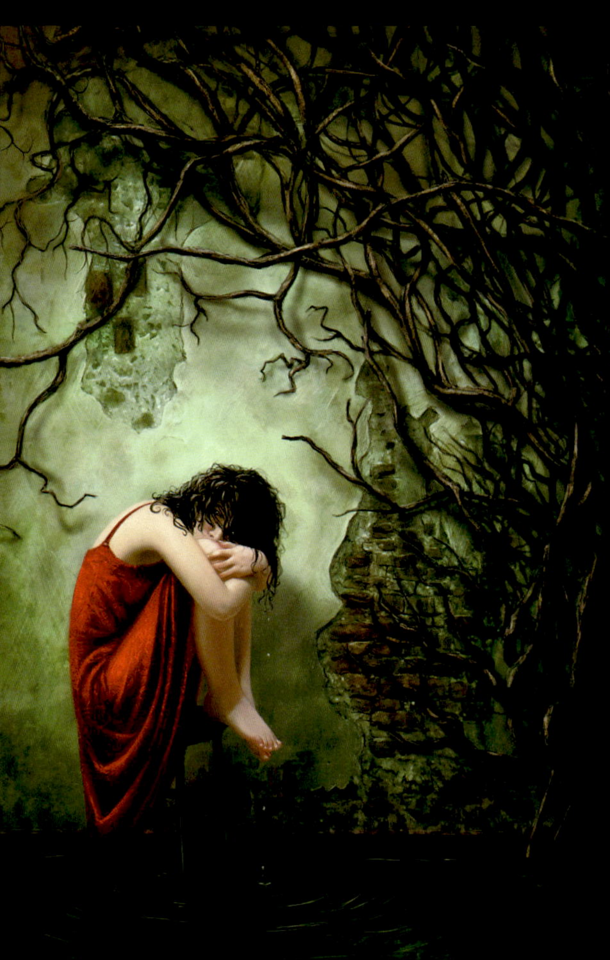

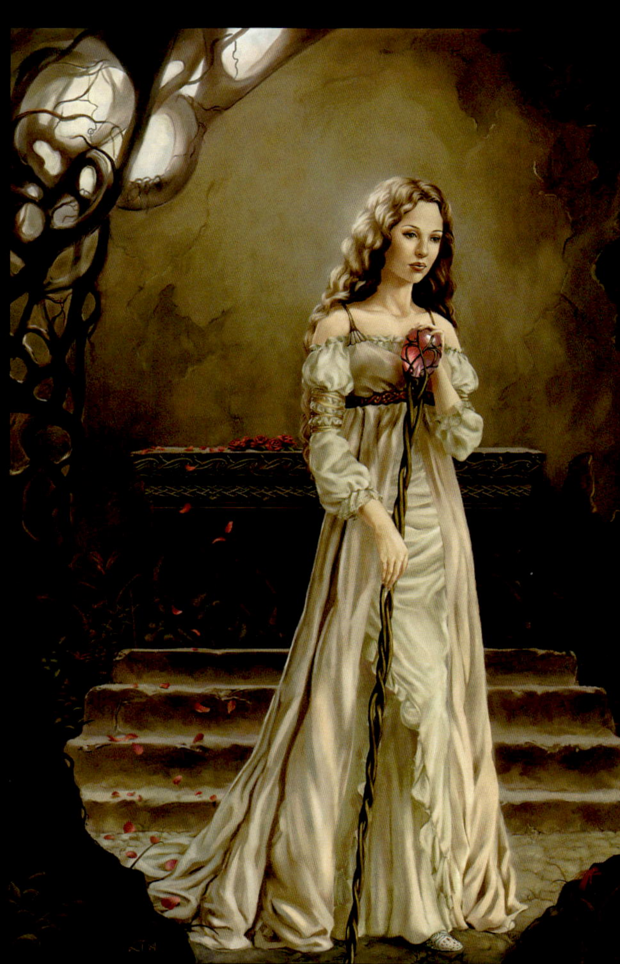

Xaea
Photoshop, Painter
Jennifer Reagles, Saiaii, USA
[top]

The Red Dress
Photoshop
Yulia Startsev, CANADA
[above]

Andromeda
Painter
Marta Dahlig, POLAND
[top]

The Passing
Photoshop, Painter
Linda Tso, NEW ZEALAND
[above]

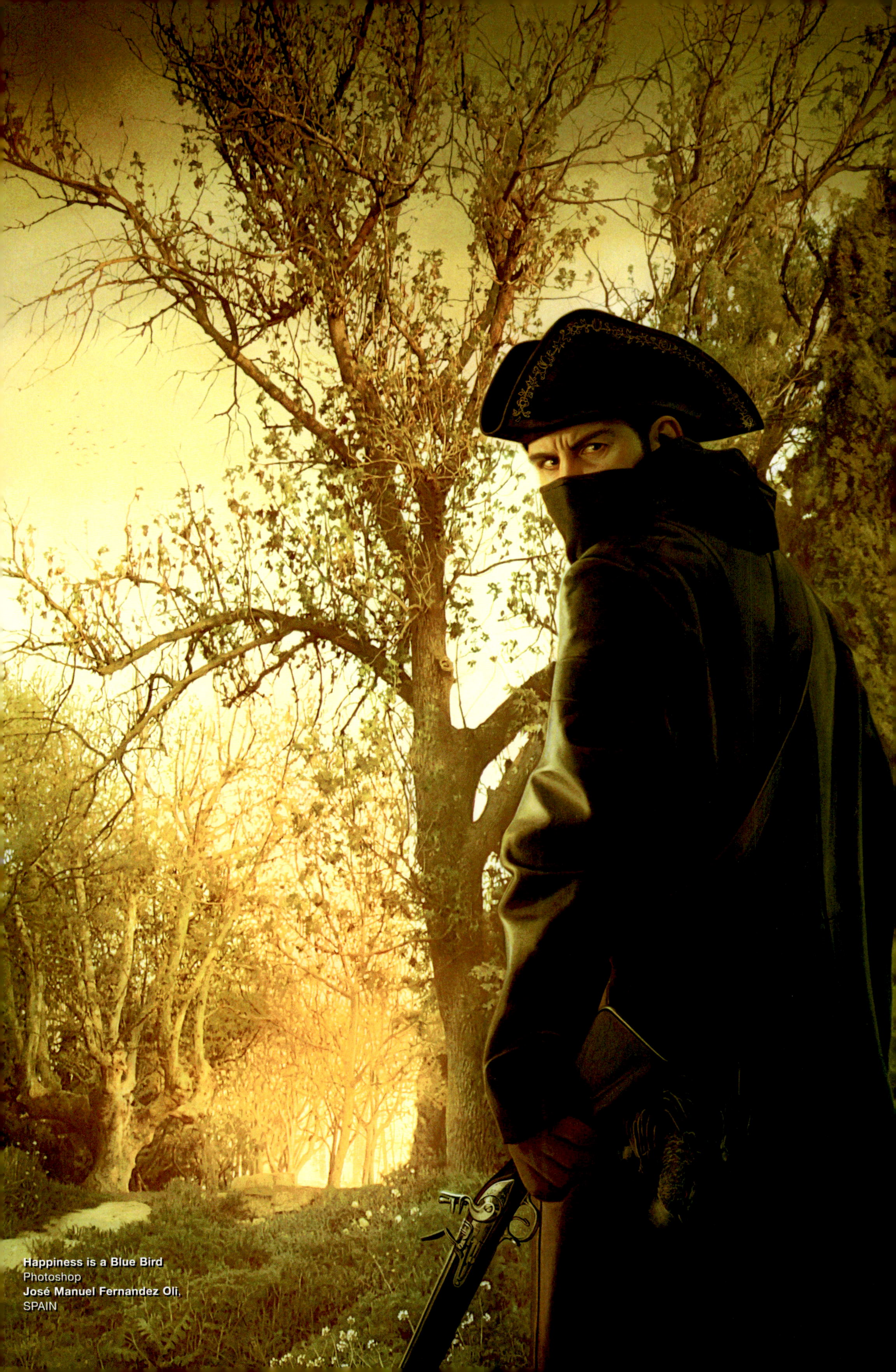

Happiness is a Blue Bird
Photoshop
José Manuel Fernandez Oli,
SPAIN

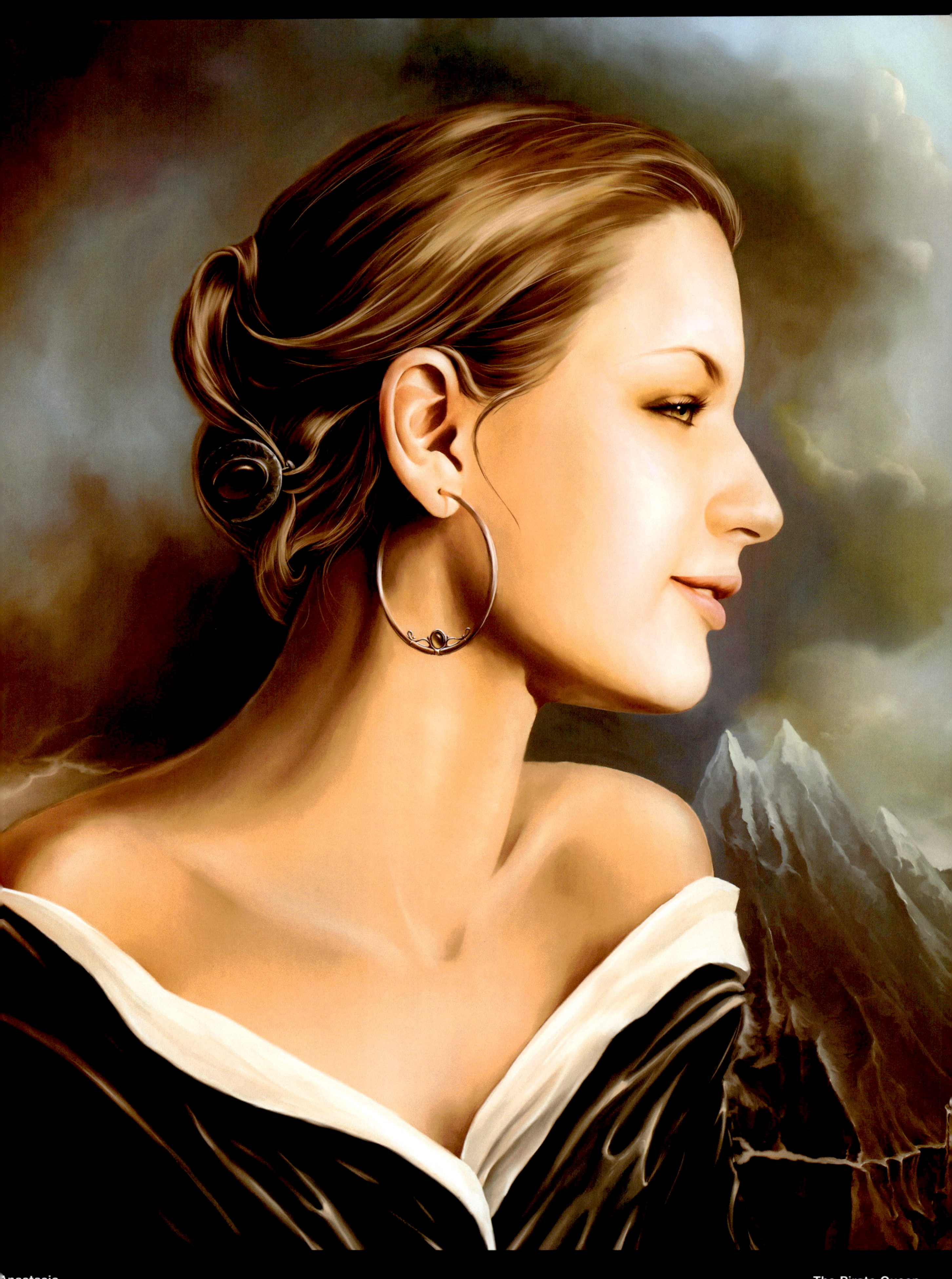

Anastasia
Painter
Client: Anastasia
Vadim-Leon Strelkov, LATVIA
[above]

The Pirate Queen
Photoshop
Client: Elizabeth Weimer
Christine Griffin, USA
[right]

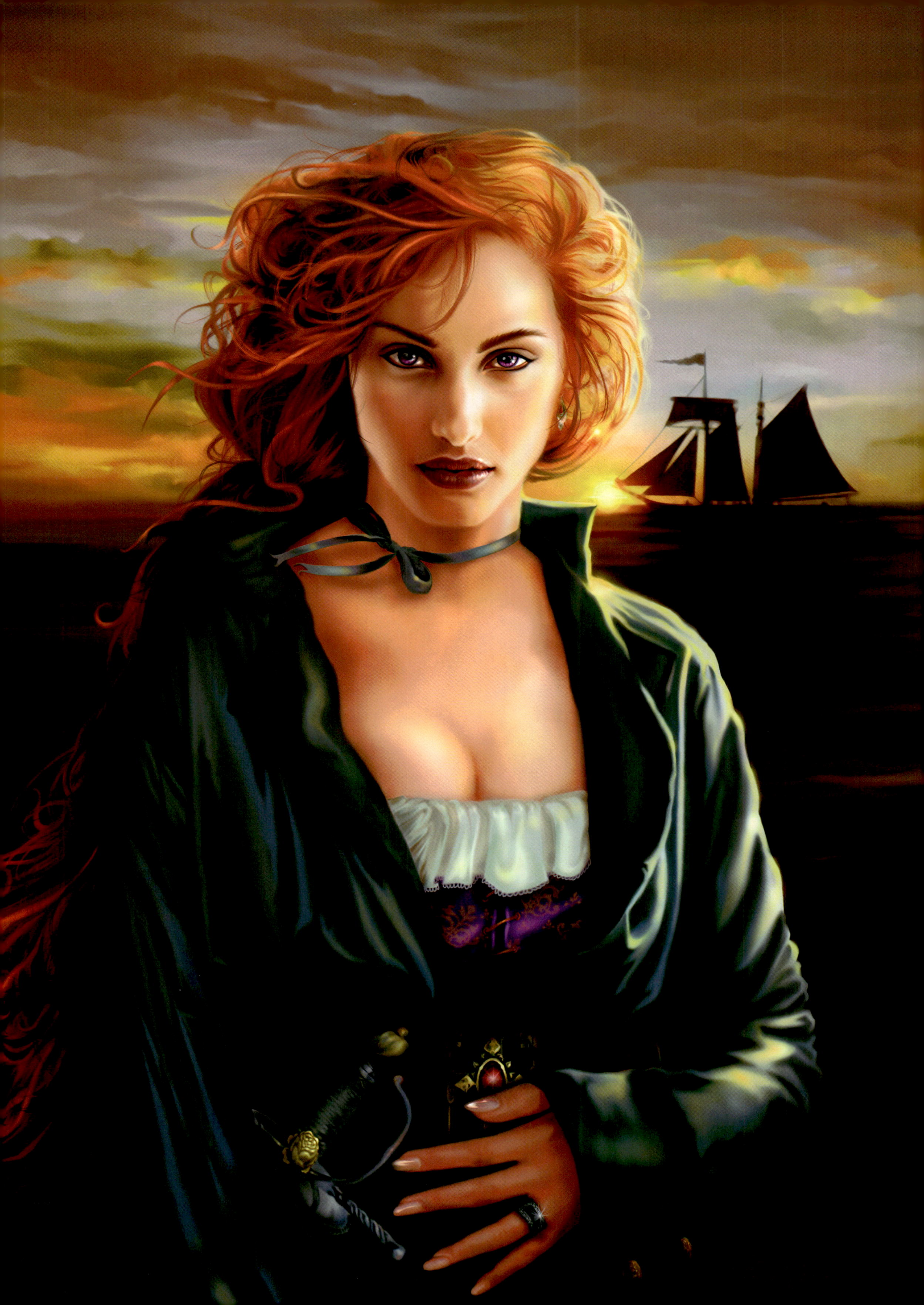

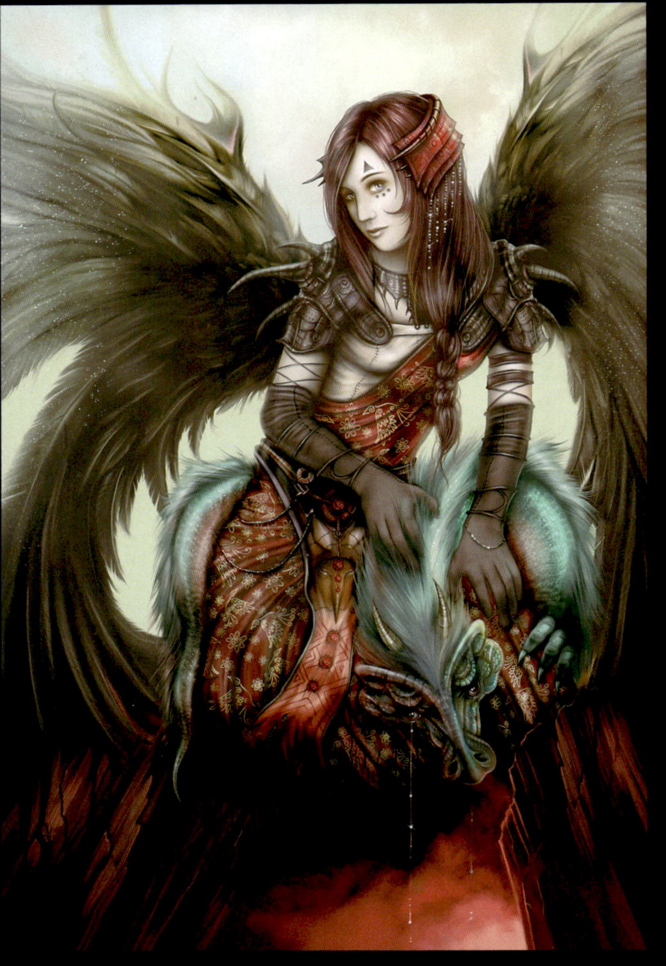

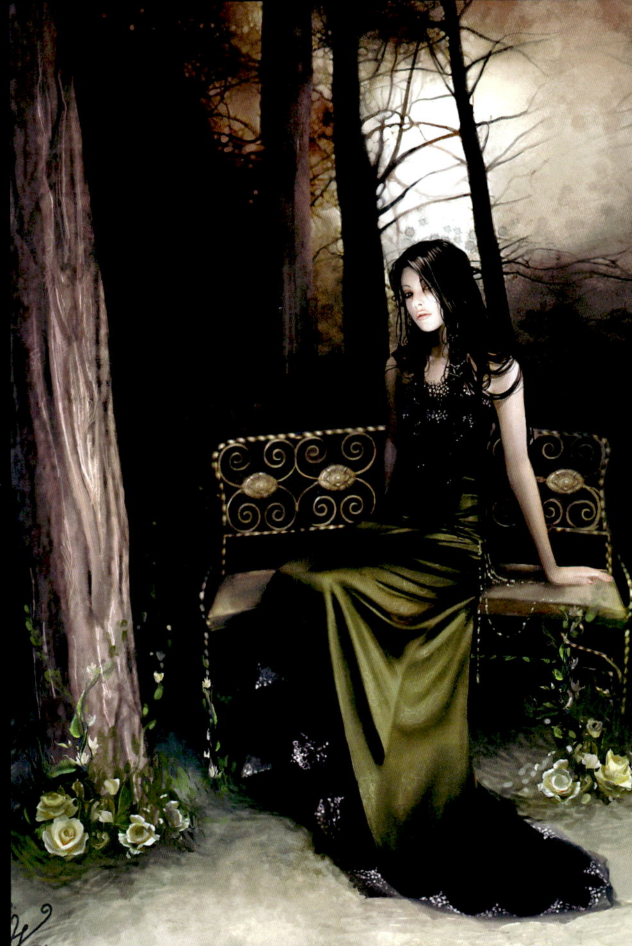

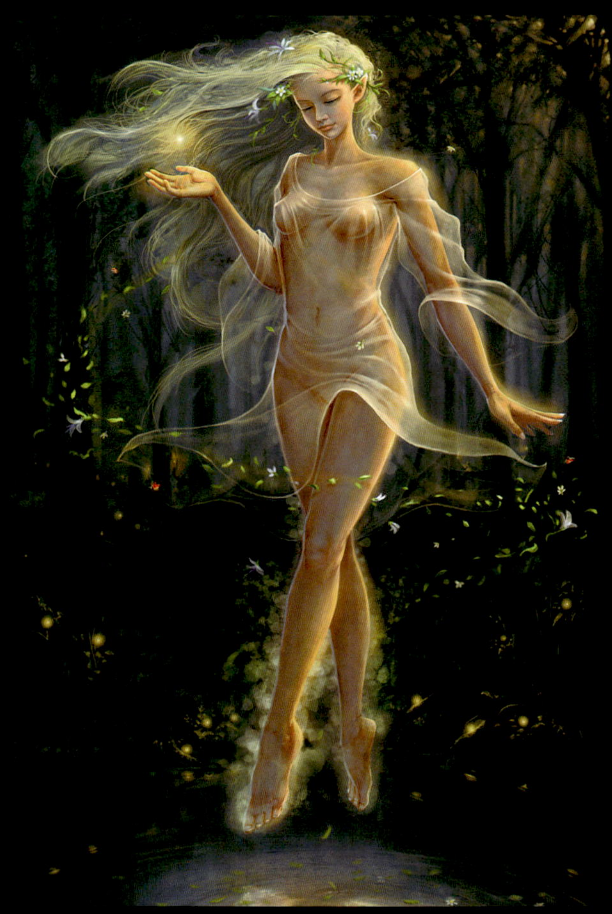

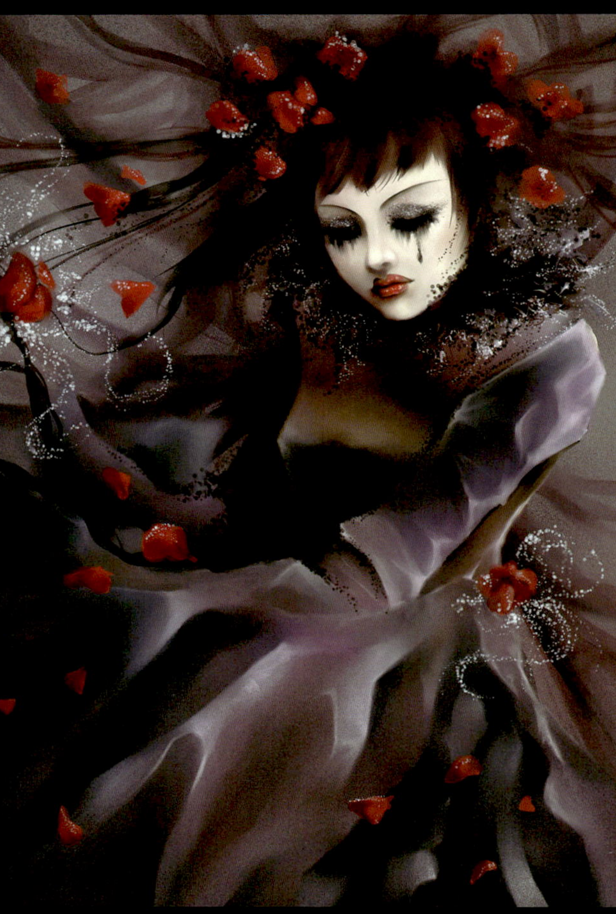

The Well of Tears
Photoshop
Annah Hutchings,
GREAT BRITAIN
[top]

Elf of Forest
Photoshop
Client: Suvist
Kwang Sub Shin, KOREA
[above]

Nelicquele
Photoshop
Linda Bergkvist,
SWEDEN
[top]

Red Weed Brocade.
Painter
Gracjana Zielinska,
POLAND
[above]

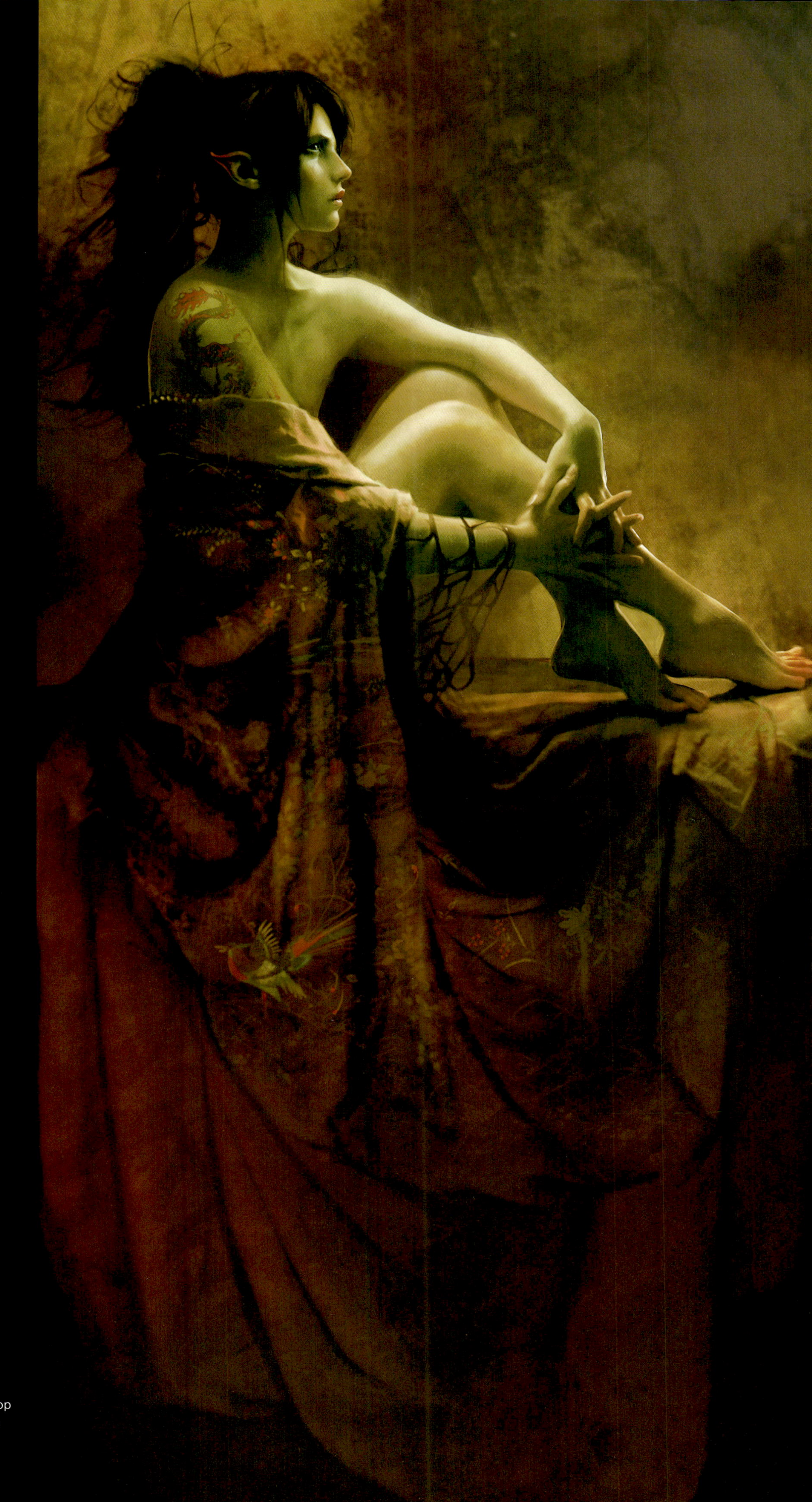

Hajieelkhe
Painter, Photoshop
Linda Bergkvist,
SWEDEN

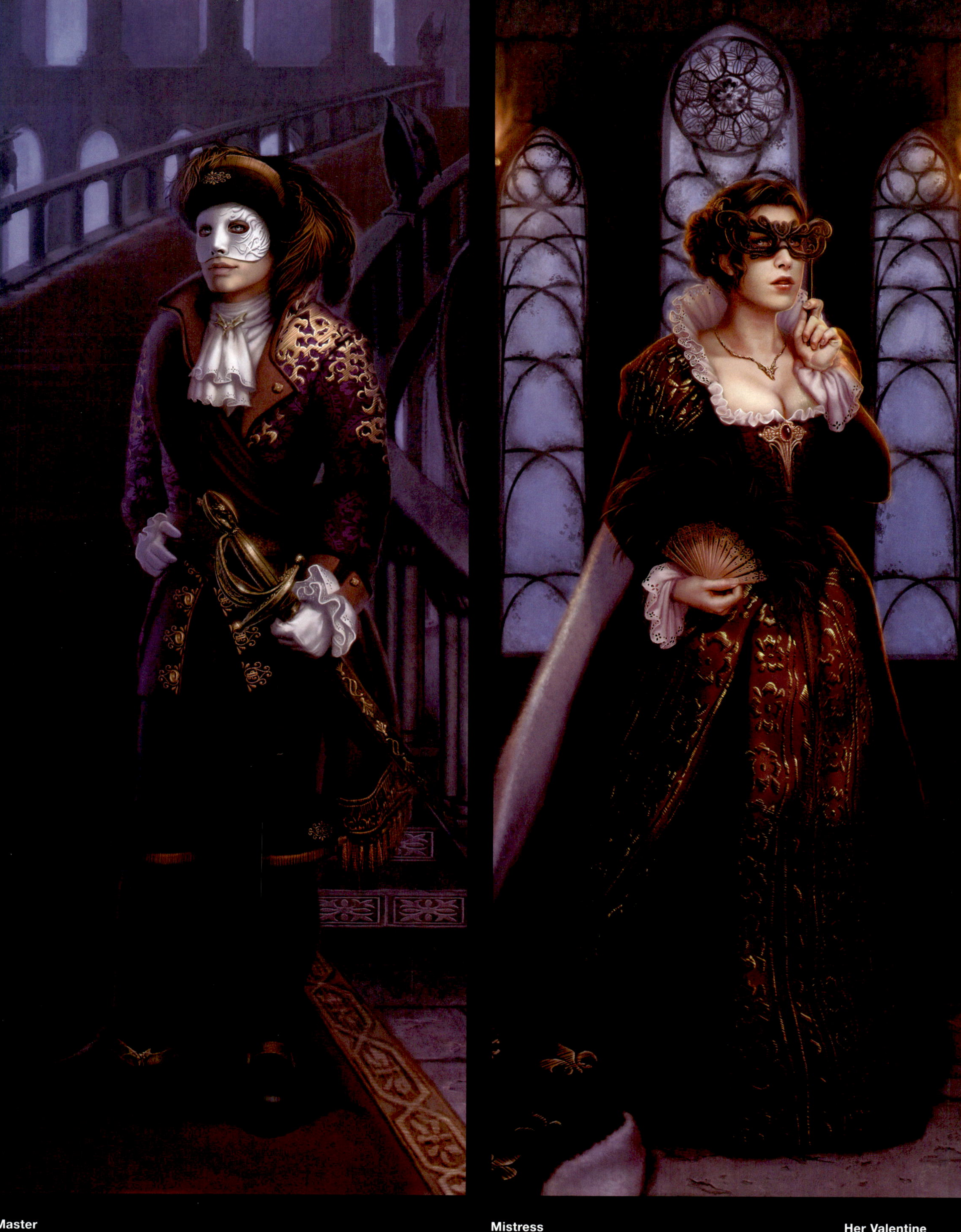

Master
Photoshop
Client: Aesthetic Compounds, LLC
Camille Kuo, TAIWAN
[above]

Mistress
Photoshop
Client: Aesthetic Compounds, LLC
Camille Kuo, TAIWAN
[above]

Her Valentine
Photoshop
Ian Field-Richards,
GREAT BRITAIN
[right]

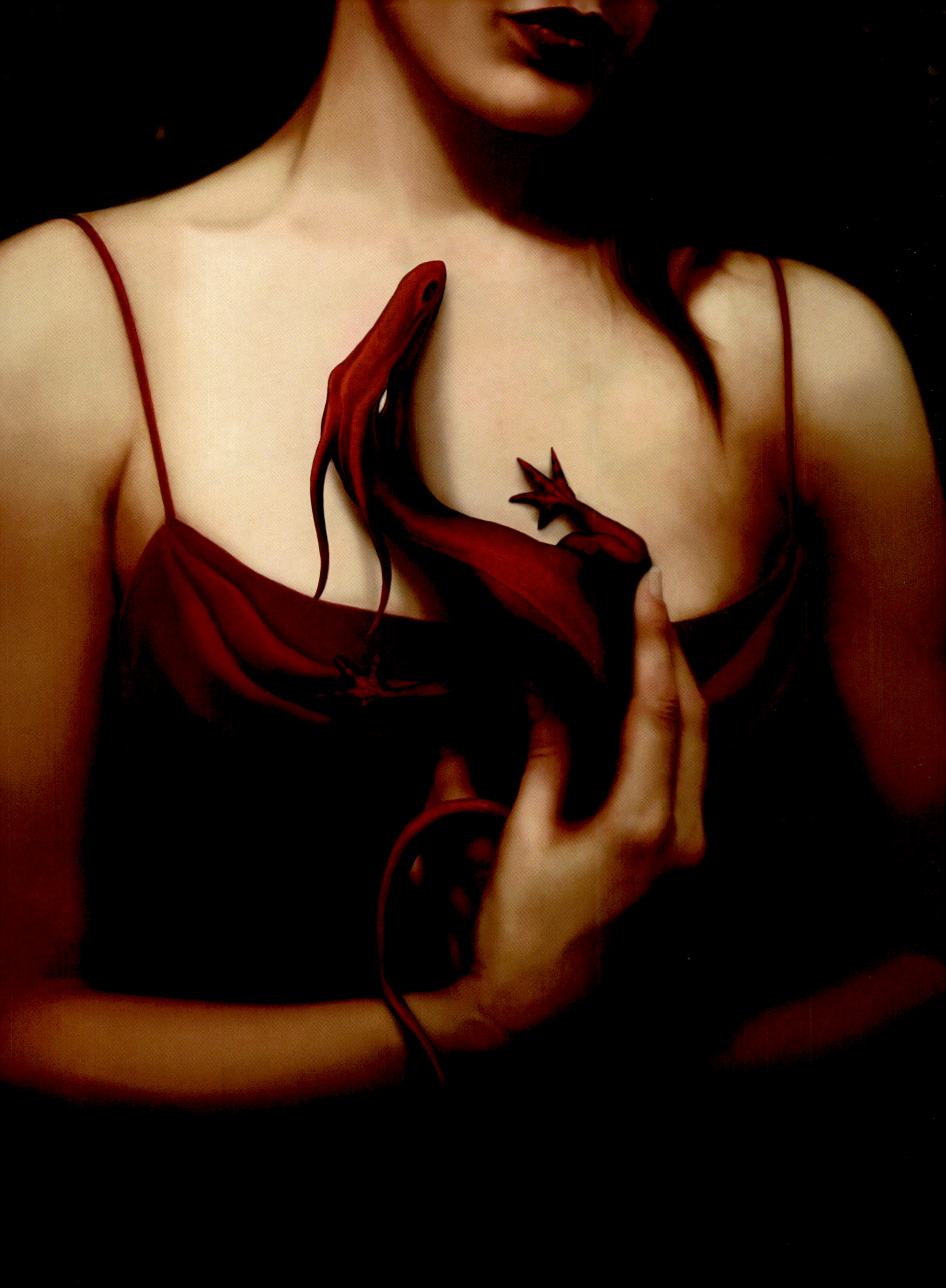

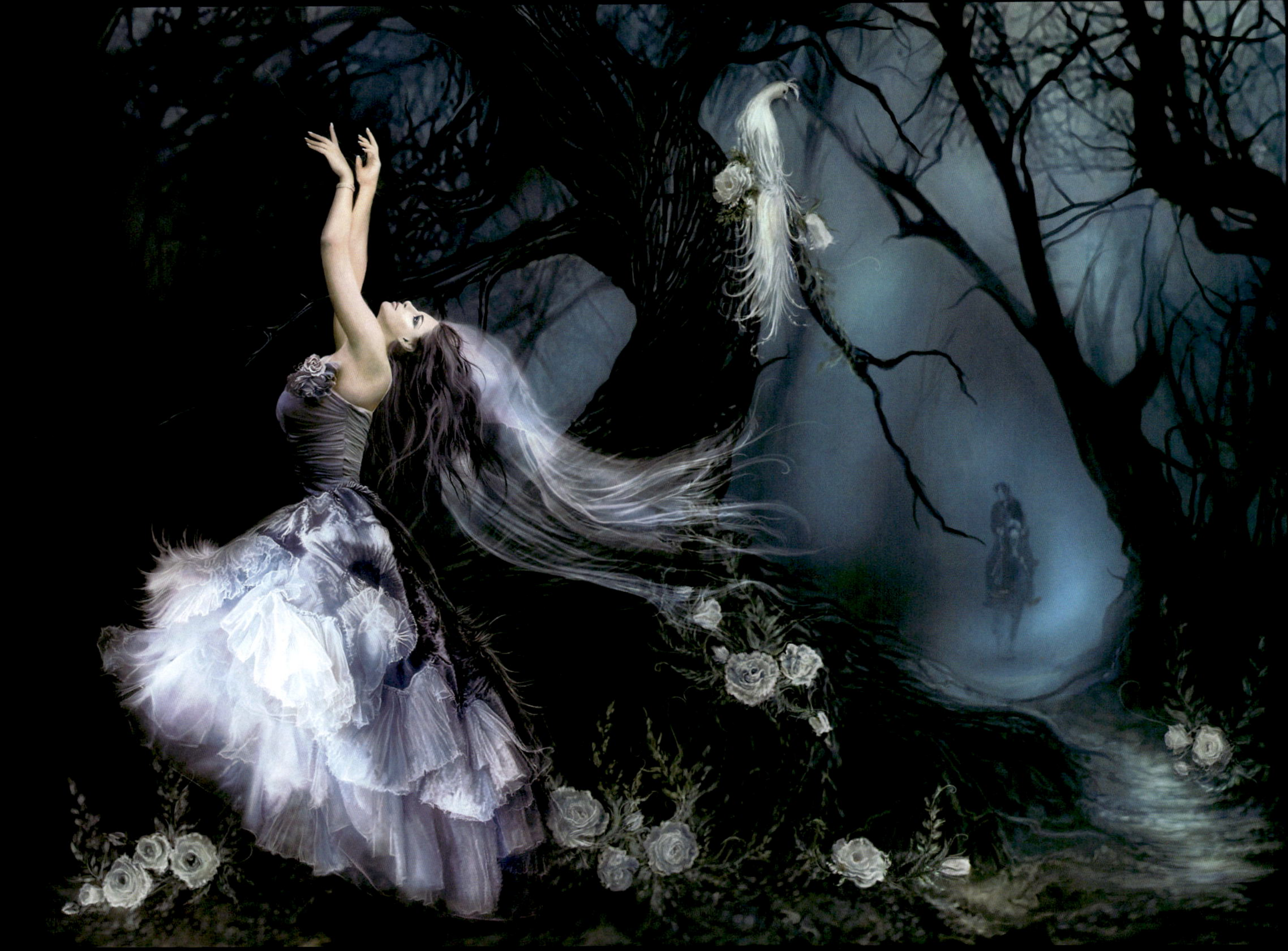

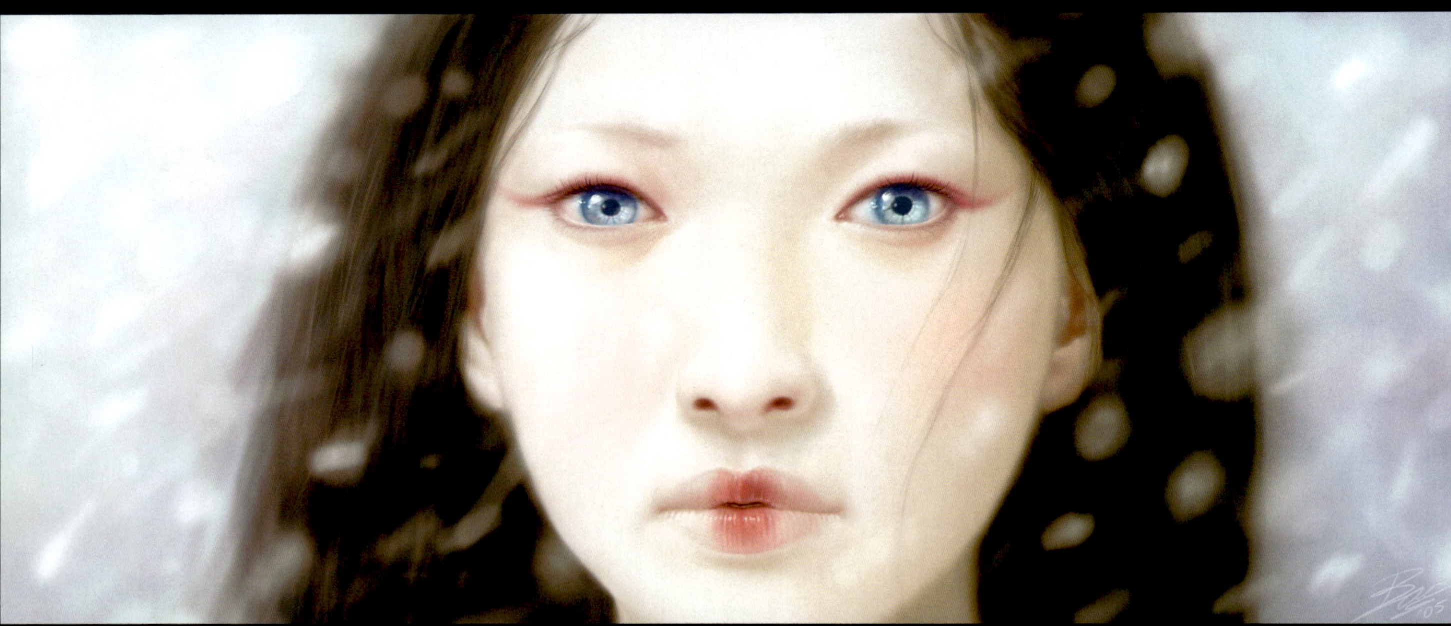

Face to Face with the Guardian Angel
Painter, Photoshop
Katarina Sokolova, UKRAINE
[top]

Her Eyes...
Photoshop
Bao Pham, USA
[above]

Winterfall
Painter
Hong Kuang, SINGAPORE
[right]

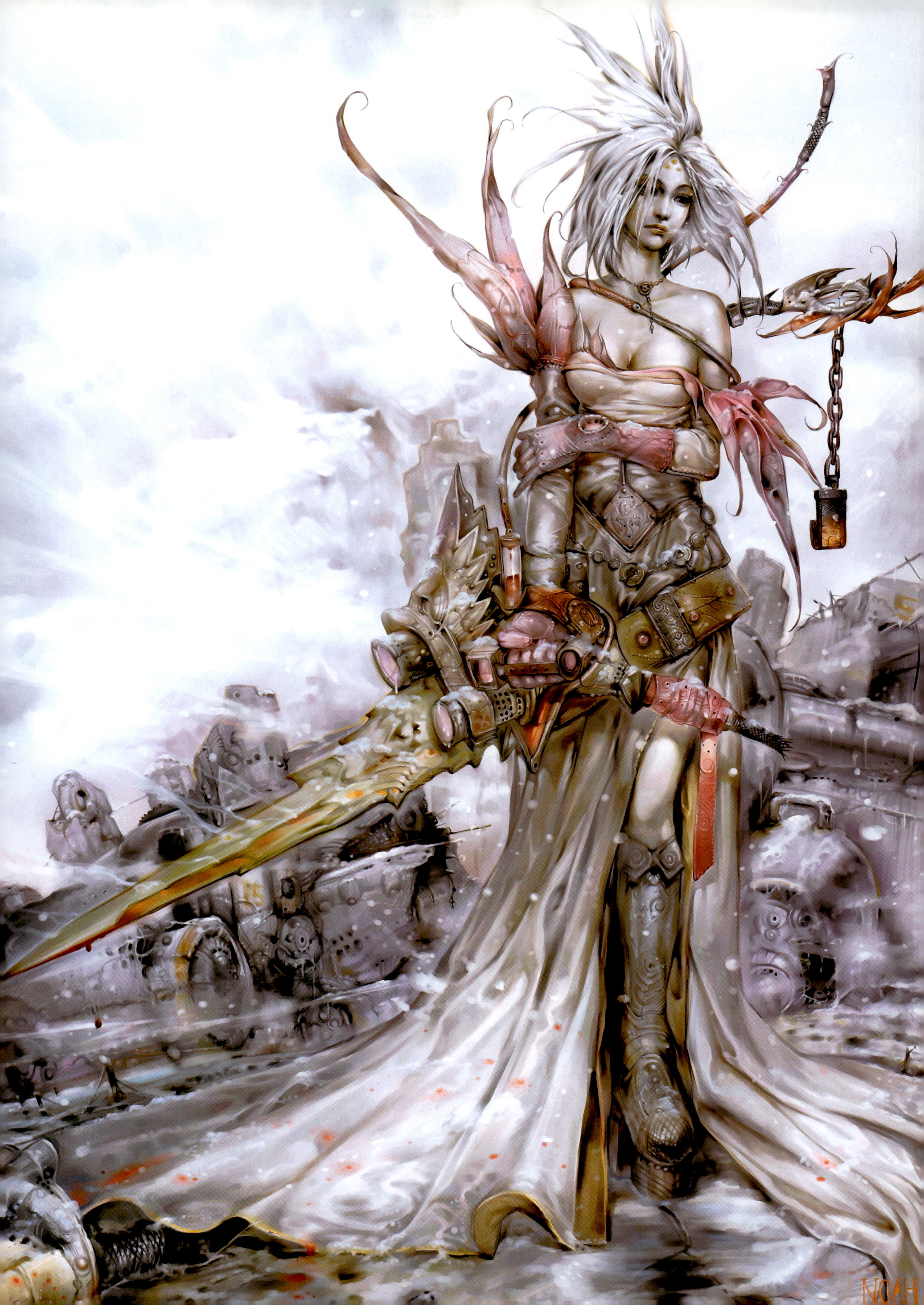
NOAH

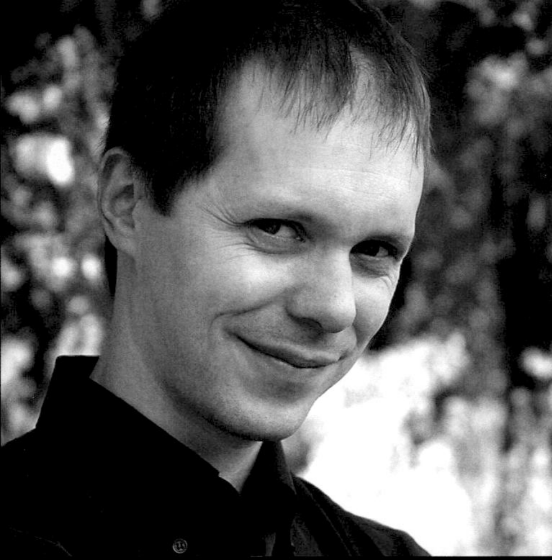

JEAN-YVES LELCERCQ

www.jyl.be
jyl@swing.be

"I mainly work in Photoshop, sometimes adding a little bit of 3D. I show my art in exhibitions, and also demonstrate how I use Photoshop to paint my pin-ups"

Jean-Yves Lelcercq is best known for his stylized pin-ups of beautiful female characters. He has always drawn, as far back as he can remember: "I followed courses here and there, but I don't have an art degree. The main reason is that when I decided to become a freelance artist, computers had invaded the professional art world, but not yet the Belgian art schools. So I learned computer graphics by myself. I've been working as a freelance illustrator for an image bank, producing two pin-ups per month, and for several other clients. My activities are now diversified: illustrations (for magazines, mobile phones images, card games), digital photography and post-treatments, advertising, posters and flyers. I mainly work in Photoshop, sometimes adding a little bit of 3D. I show my

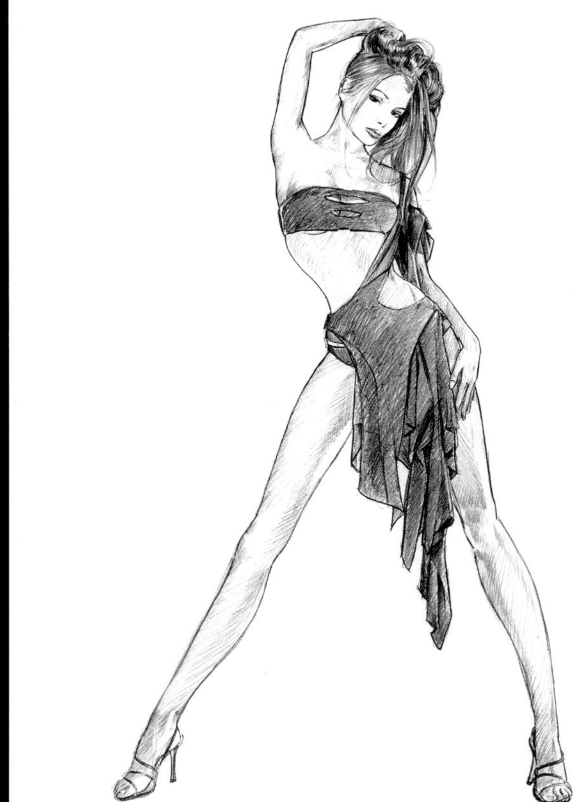

SKETCH

This drawing was made for a client who designs dresses and swimsuits in Paris (Feel Good). They wanted an image in the style of my pin-ups, with a discrete background with 'so good' written twice. The purpose was to publish it as an ad on the back cover of a magazine. I received the black skirt via mail, and did a photo shoot with my girlfriend as the model. I used a Nikon D70 with two studio flashes: one main light in front of the model, and one back light to give volume on the right side of the character. The six megapixel image from the D70 provides more details than an illustrator needs, but with a black dress like this one, or with black latex, the levels need to be pushed up a little bit to make all the details visible. I drew on an A3 sheet of paper, transforming the normal proportions of my model into a kind of stretched fashion model. It's a drawing—exaggeration is normality. I then scanned the pencil sketch and my work on the computer started using Photoshop and a Wacom A4+ tablet.

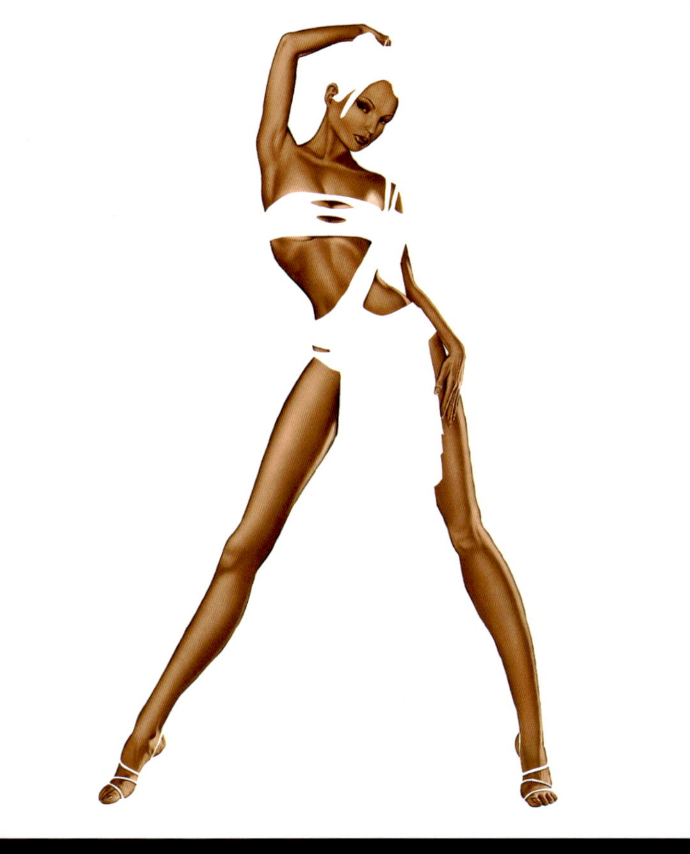

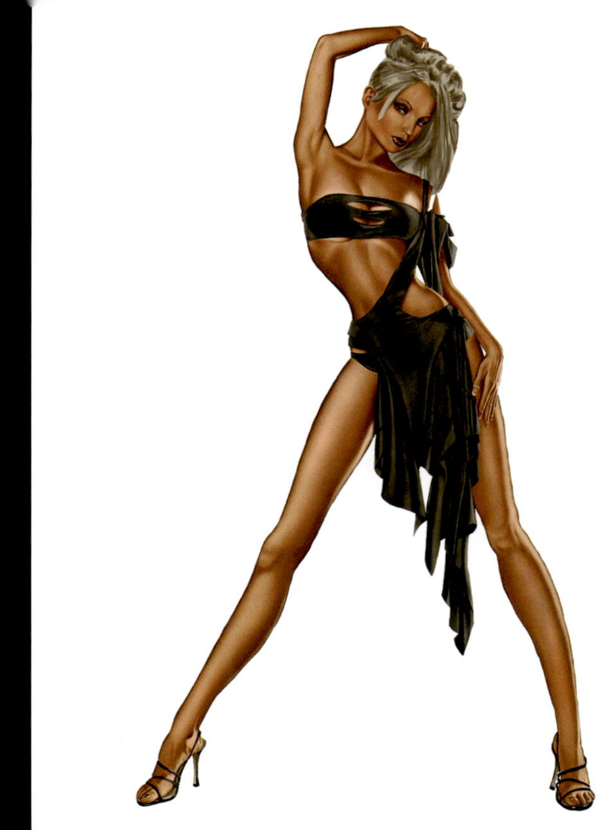

PAINTING IN SELECTIONS

The first thing I do with the scan is to separate all the different parts of the body into selections, stored as alpha channels. This drawing had only four selections: hair, skin, skirt and shoes. When that was done, I added a white background, keeping the scan on top of the layers in a 'Multiply' mode, to see only the pencil lines. On top of the background, on a new layer, I made the 'skin' selection active, and filled it with a medium skin tone. I then created a new layer again and painted darker and lighter to define all the volumes. I used a brush with a hardness of 50%, and progressively made it softer and softer. This simulated the feeling that I had used a classical brush and smoothed the painting with an airbrush. Opacity was about 10%, though never more than 15%. When all the volumes were visible, with all the details, in a sepia color, I added a bit of red and pink to give 'life' to the skin. When the background was defined, I also painted the reflected lights that would integrate the character into the image. With a grey background, the reflected lights are not colorful. I used a little bit of yellow to suggest a light source on the left side of the image.

REFINING SKIN TONES

All the other parts of the character followed the same process. I defined the volumes with two values of the same color, added the colors that would give life and realism, then added the reflected lights. I used a hard brush to start and a soft one to finish, to copy an airbrush technique that I used before working with a computer. I usually spend a day on the skin of a pin-up, which is the most difficult part of the job. When all the areas are colorized, the connections between them need to be 'cleaned' with the Smudge tool with all the selections being inactive. The ground was made with a texture, modified with a perspective effect. The rest was a combination of text and gradients. Some gradients were applied on the background layer, and some layer effects for the text.

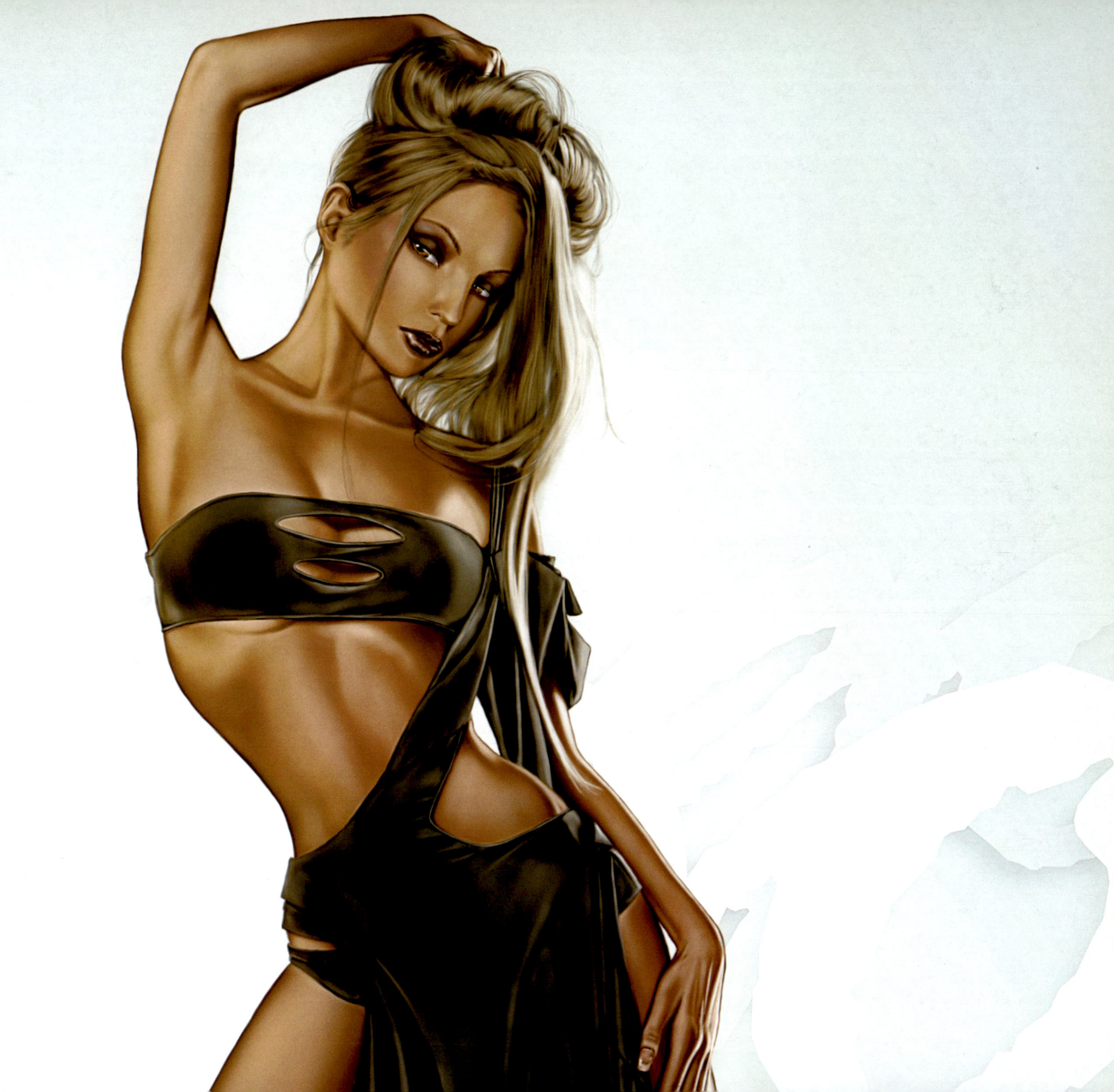

So Good
Photoshop
Model: Brigitte
Client: Feel Good, Daniel Wertel
Jean-Yves Lelcercq,
JYL computer art,
BELGIUM

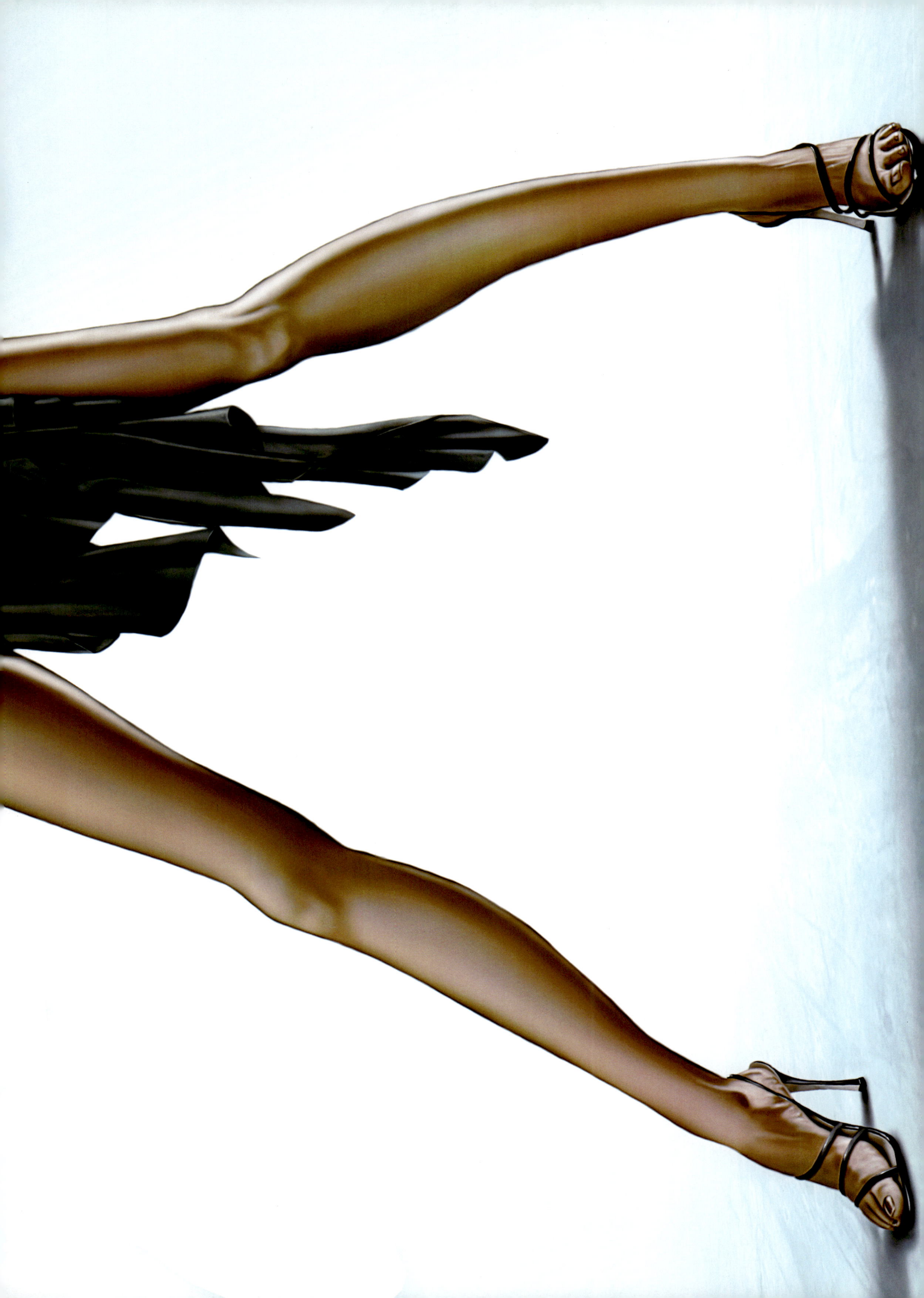

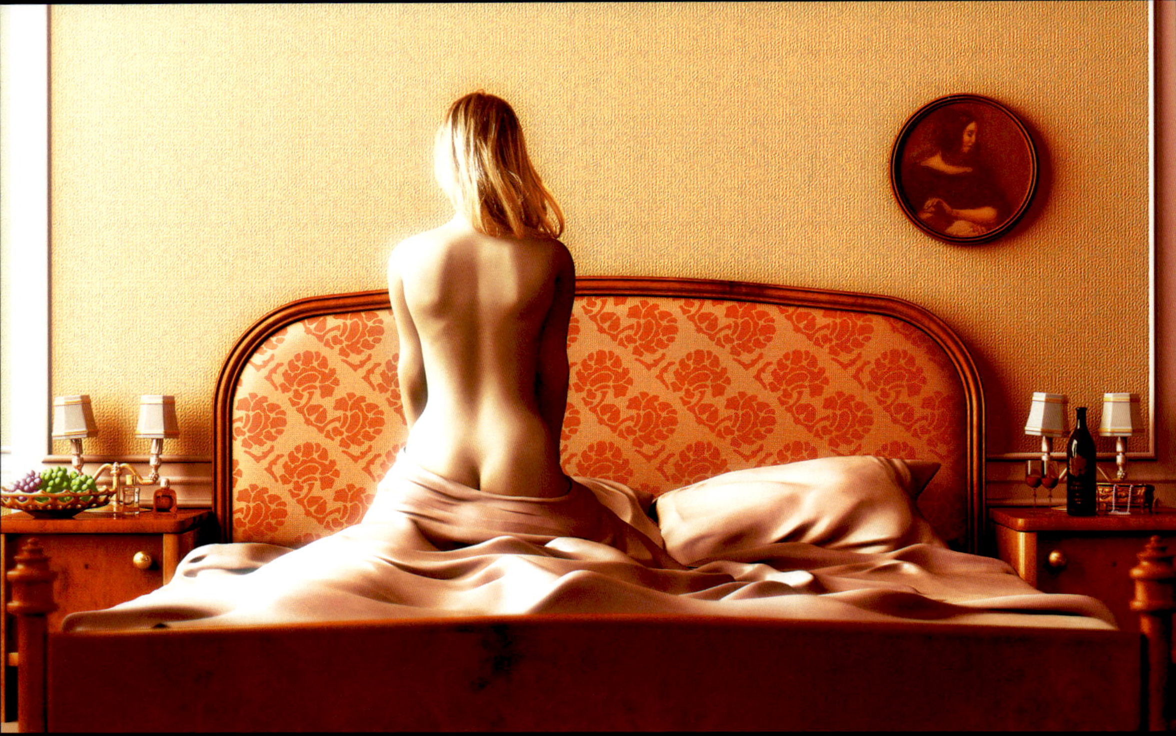

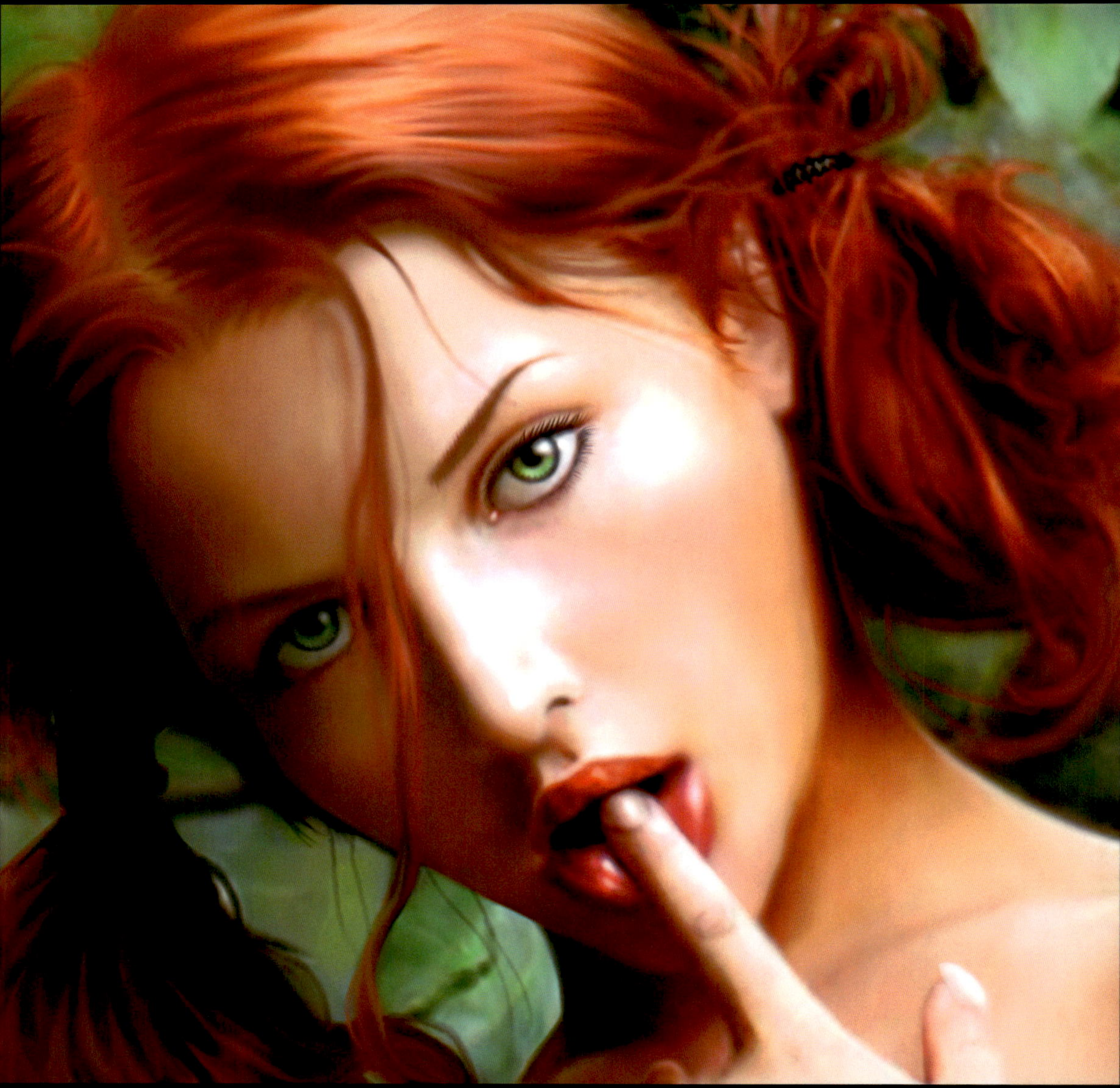

My Love in Bed
3ds Max, finalRender
Marek Denko, SLOVAKIA
[top]

A Pure Coincidence
Photoshop
Raffaele Marinetti, ITALY
[above]

I was made to love you
Photoshop
Raffaele Marinetti, ITALY
[right]

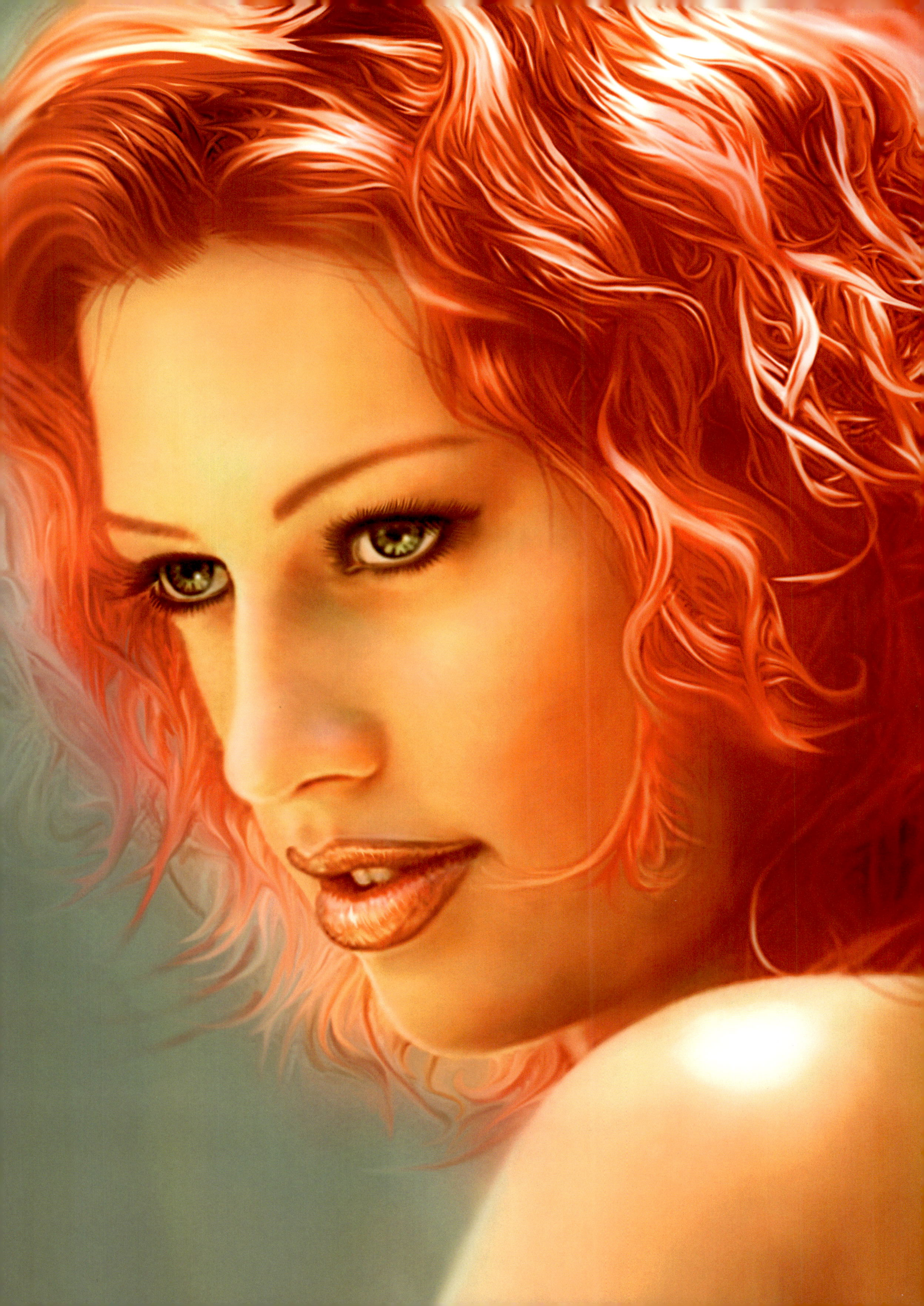

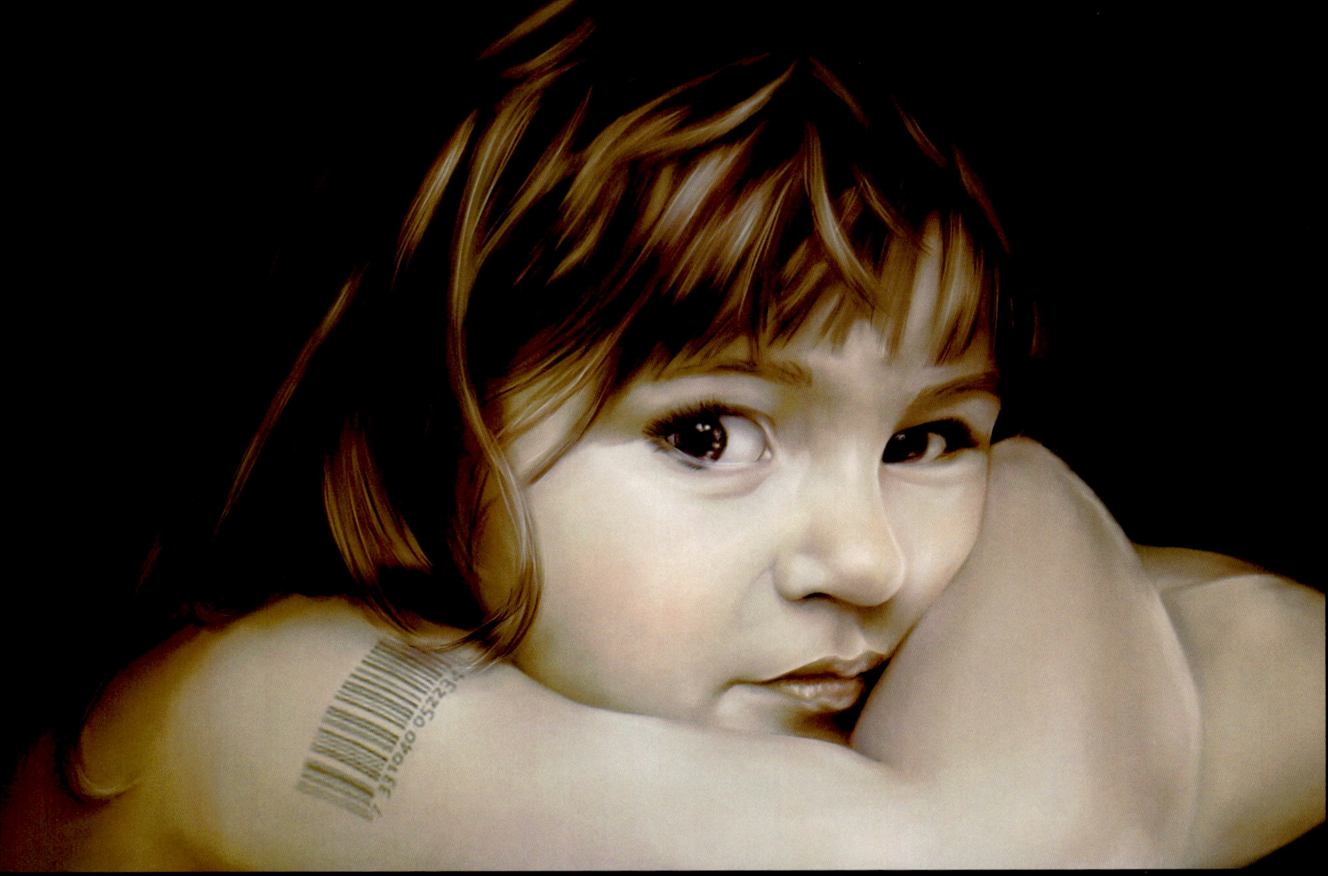

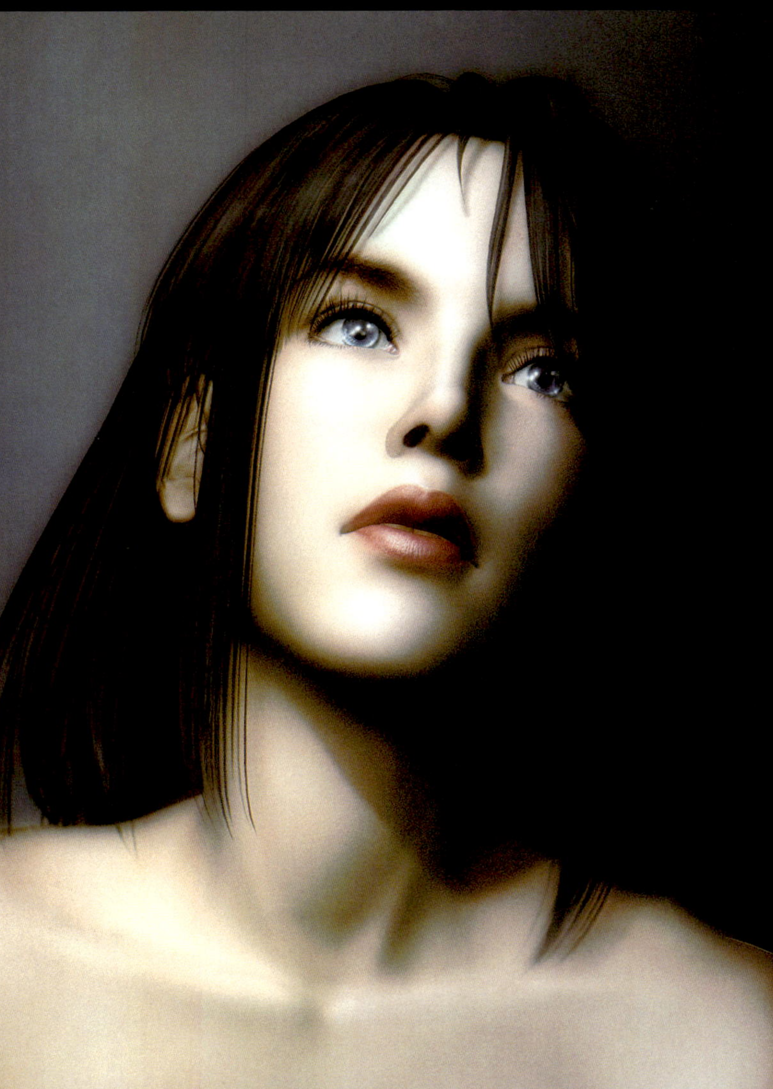

Tina
Painter, Photoshop
René Blom, SWEDEN
[above]

Redyan
Photoshop, 3ds Max
Client: Actoz soft
Soa Lee, KOREA
[left]

Ilana
Maya, Photoshop
Alceu Baptistao, Vetor Zero,
BRAZIL
[right]

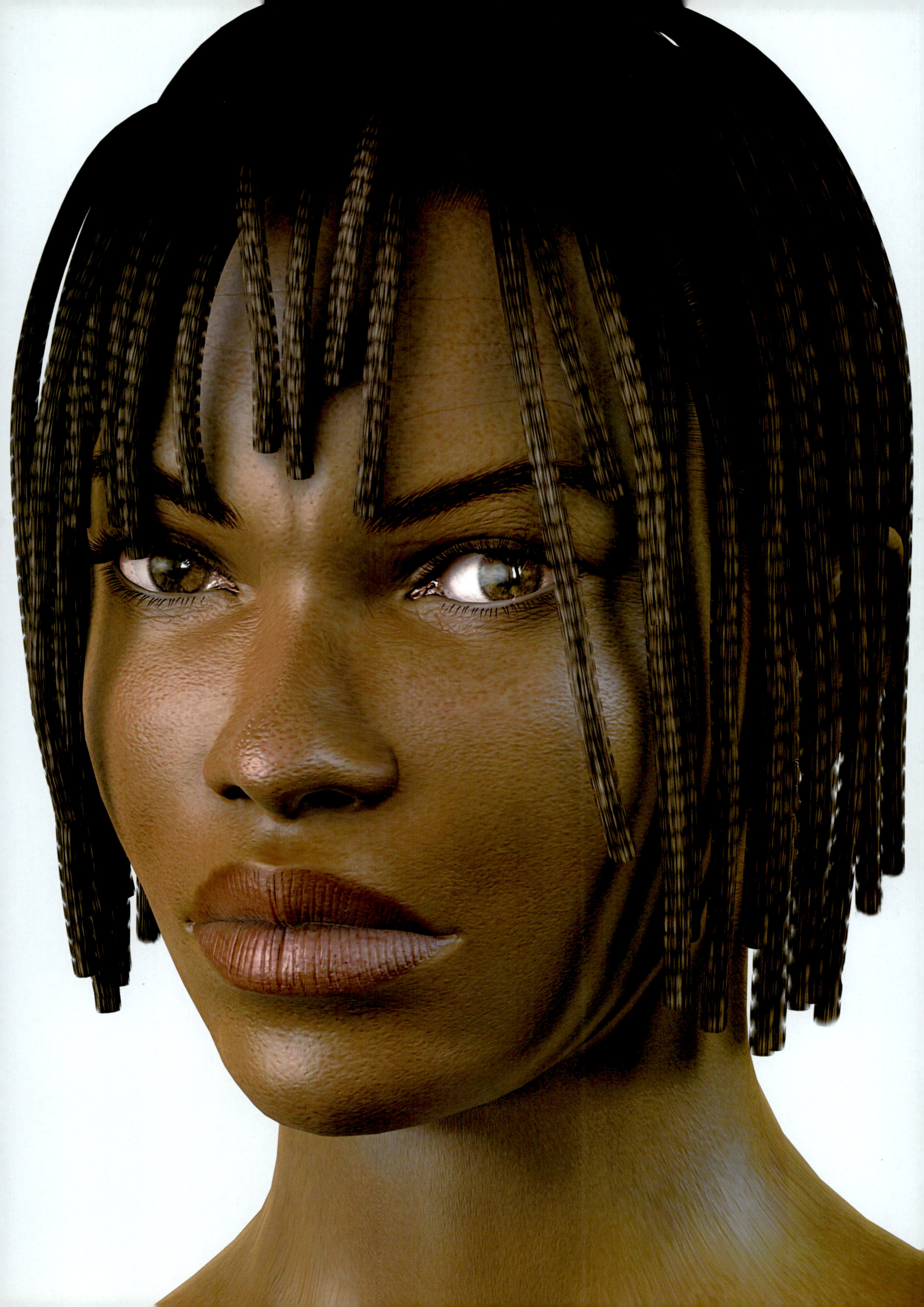

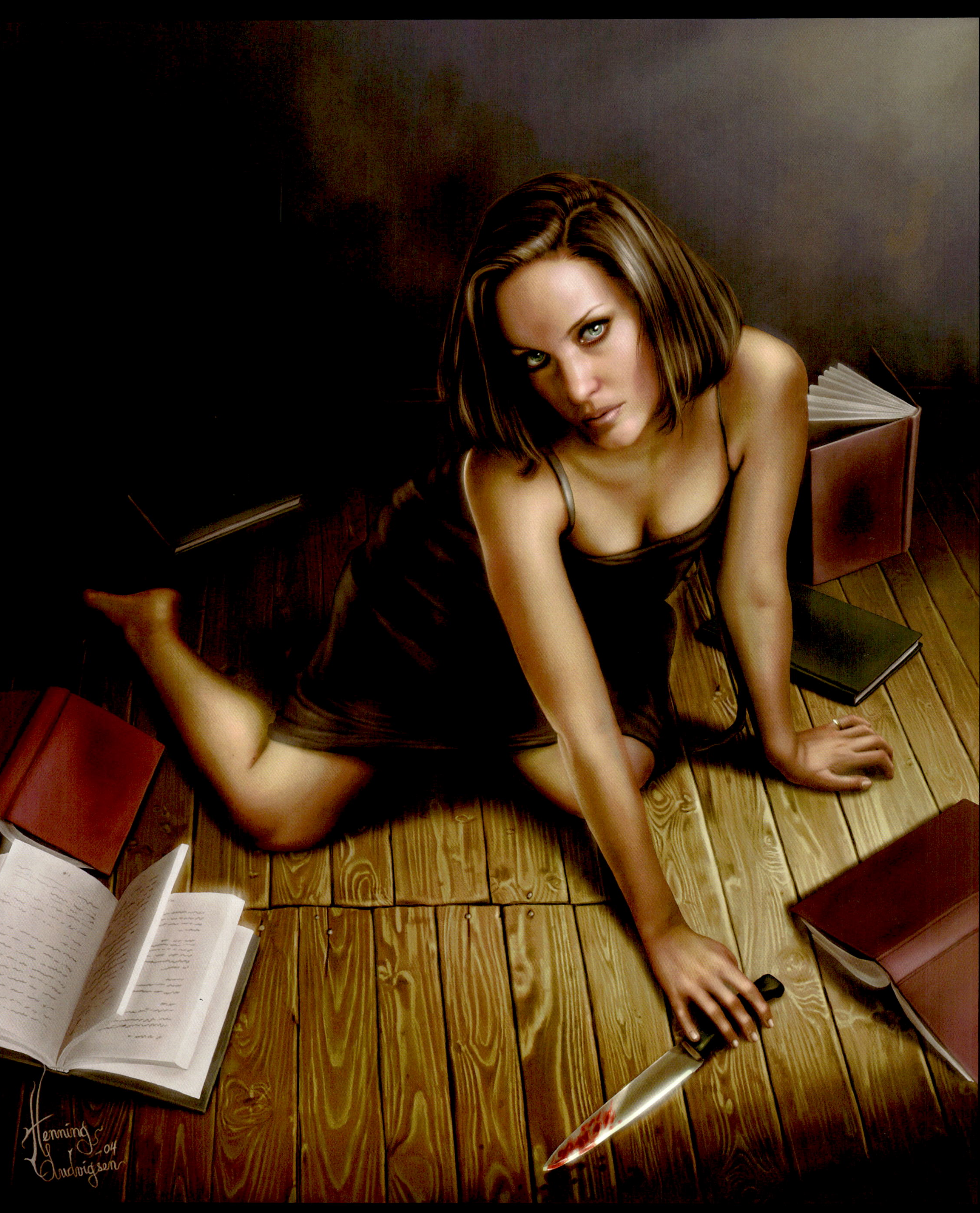

The Wrapture
Photoshop
Henning Ludvigsen, NORWAY
[above]

Belle
Photoshop, 3ds Max
Derek Herring, USA
[right]

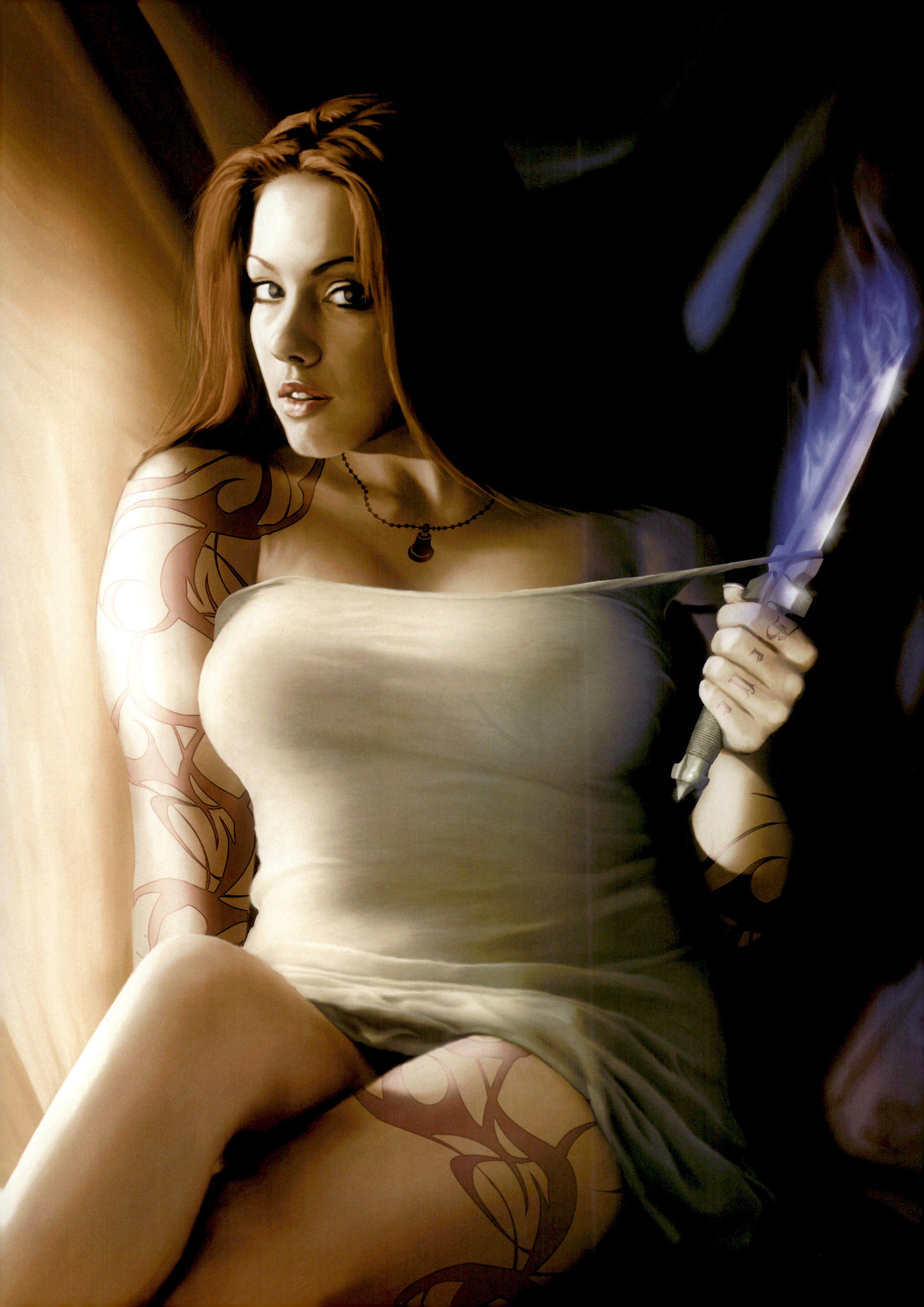

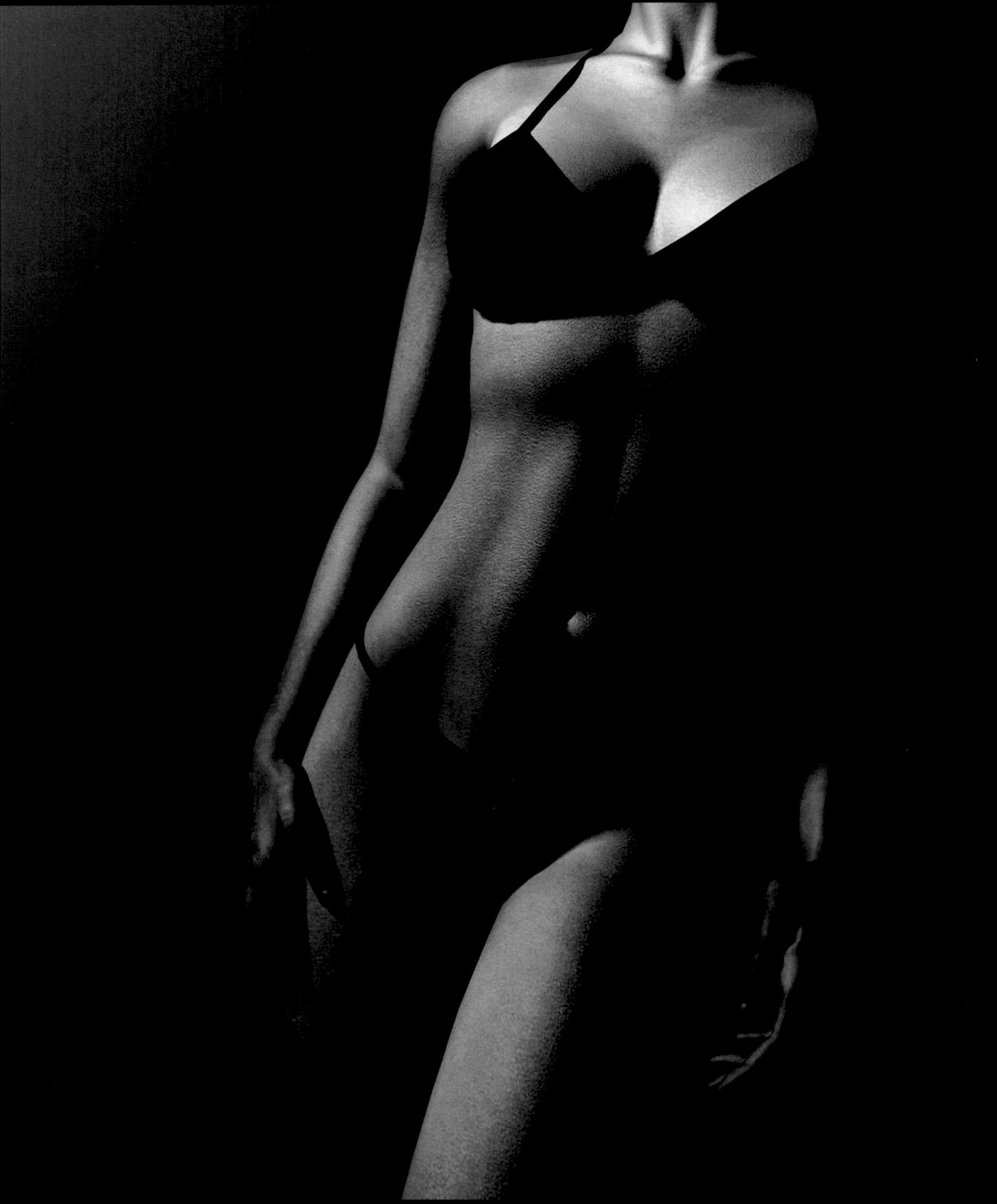

Exotic Beauty
3ds Max, Photoshop
Shoaib Zaheer Malik, Image Dynamics, PAKISTAN
[left]

Gray Mag
Maya, Renderman
Francisco A. Cortina and Steven Giesler, USA
[right]

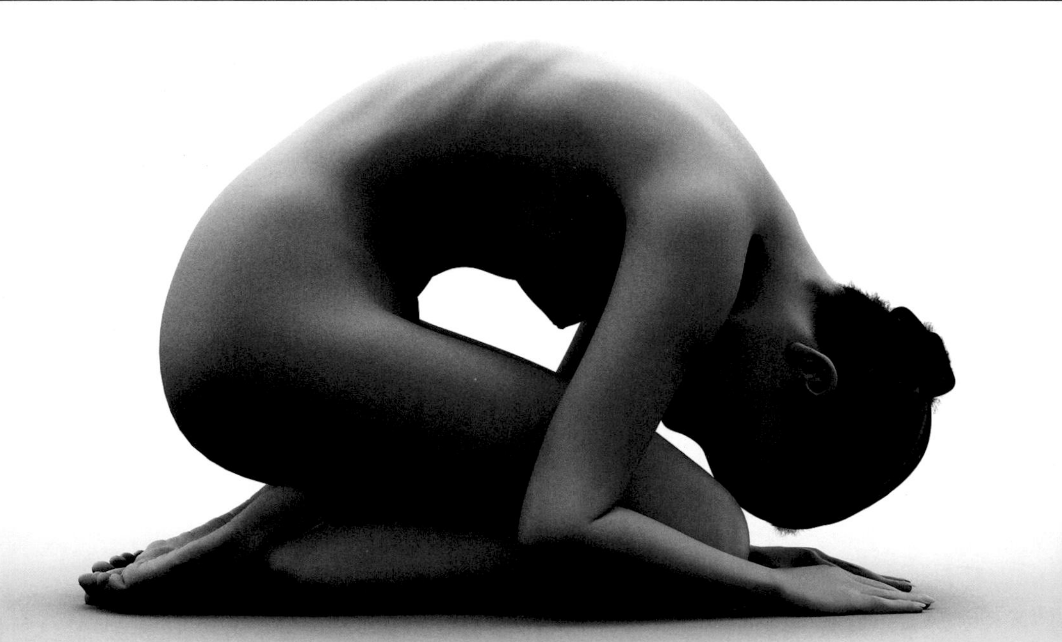

Female anatomy study
3ds Max, finalRender
Marek Denko, SLOVAKIA
[left]

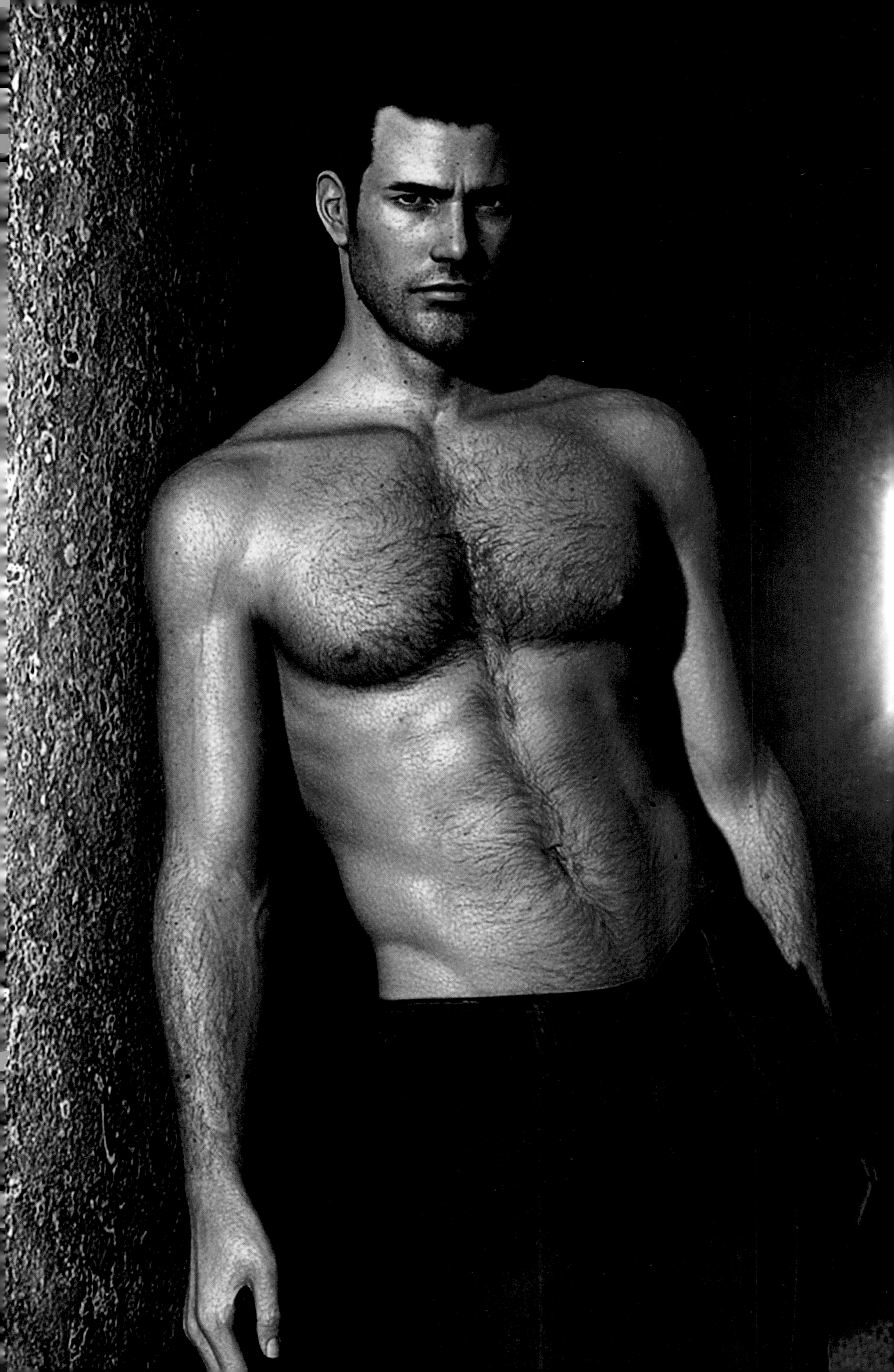

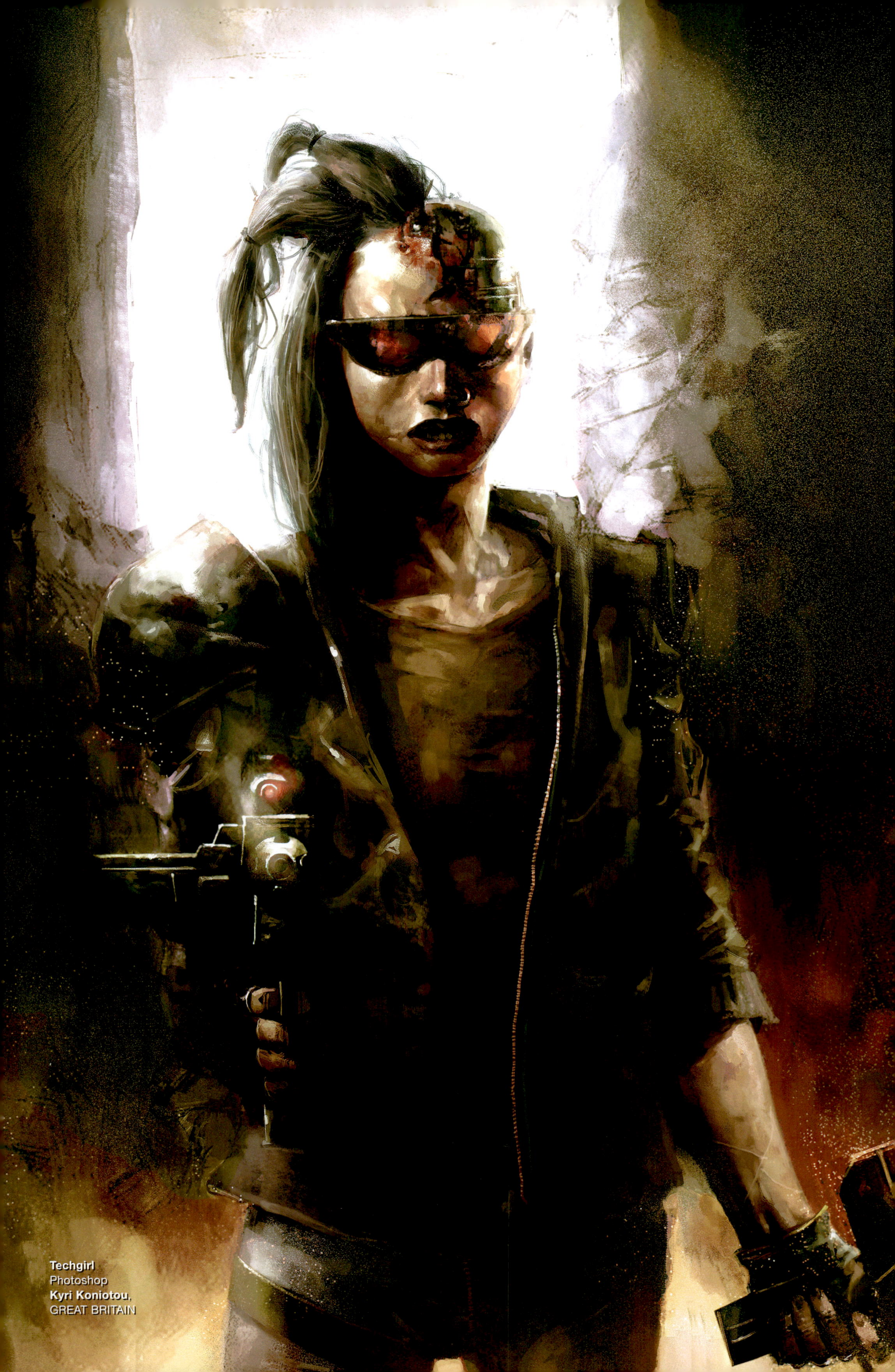

Techgirl
Photoshop
Kyri Koniotou,
GREAT BRITAIN

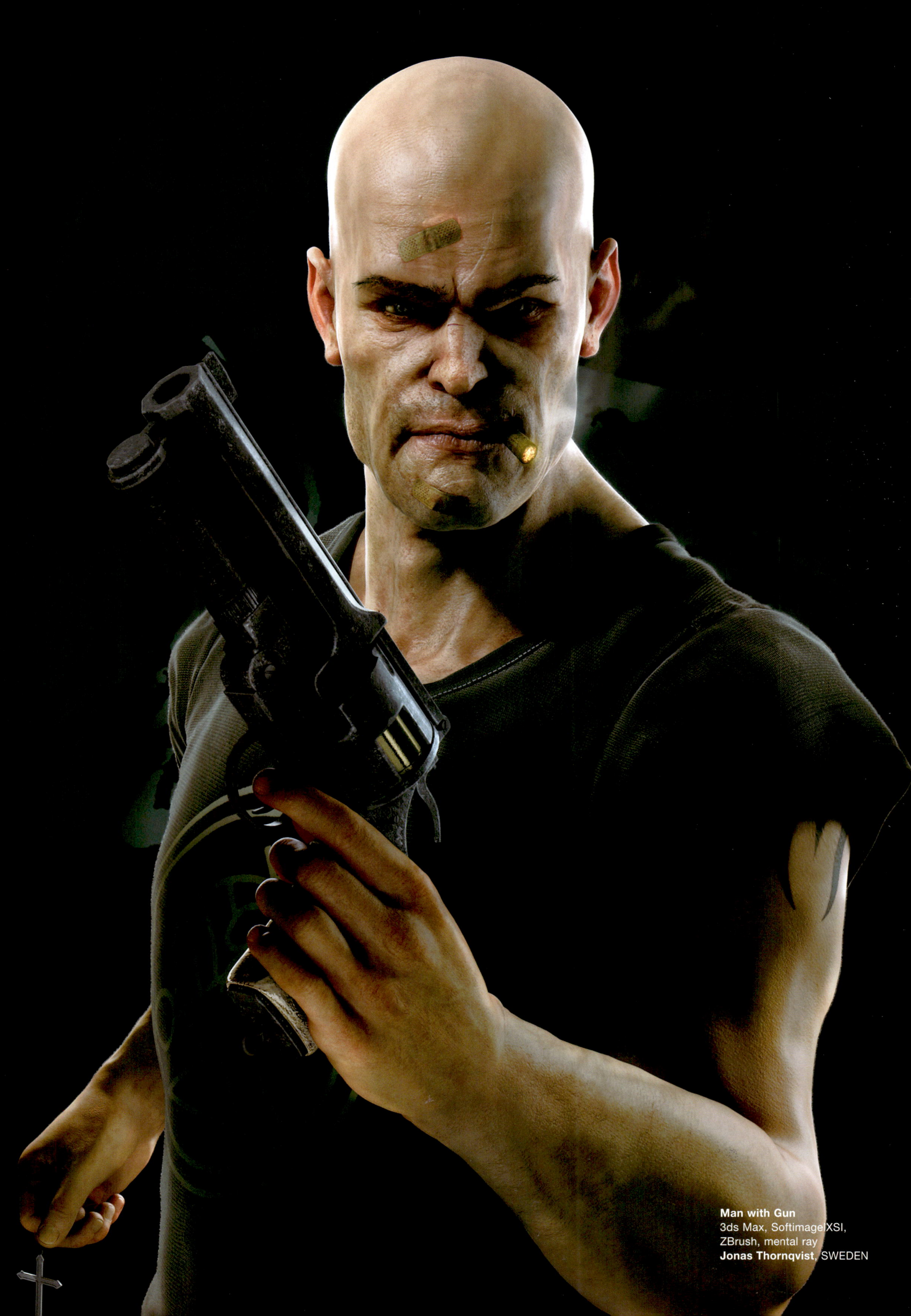

Man with Gun
3ds Max, Softimage|XSI, ZBrush, mental ray
Jonas Thornqvist, SWEDEN

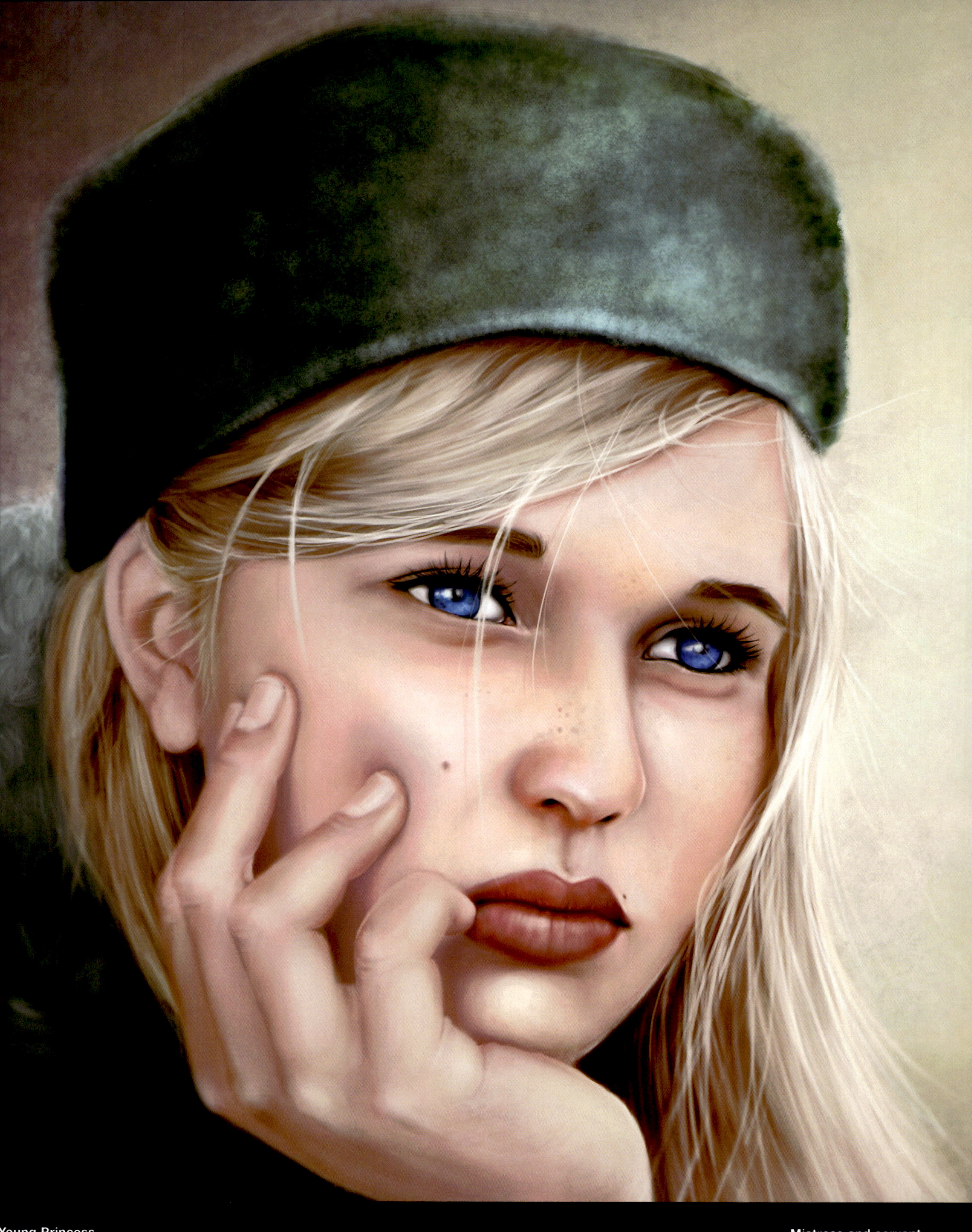

Young Princess
Photoshop
Valentin Fischer, GERMANY
[above]

Mistress and servant
Photoshop
Henning Ludvigsen, NORWAY
[right]

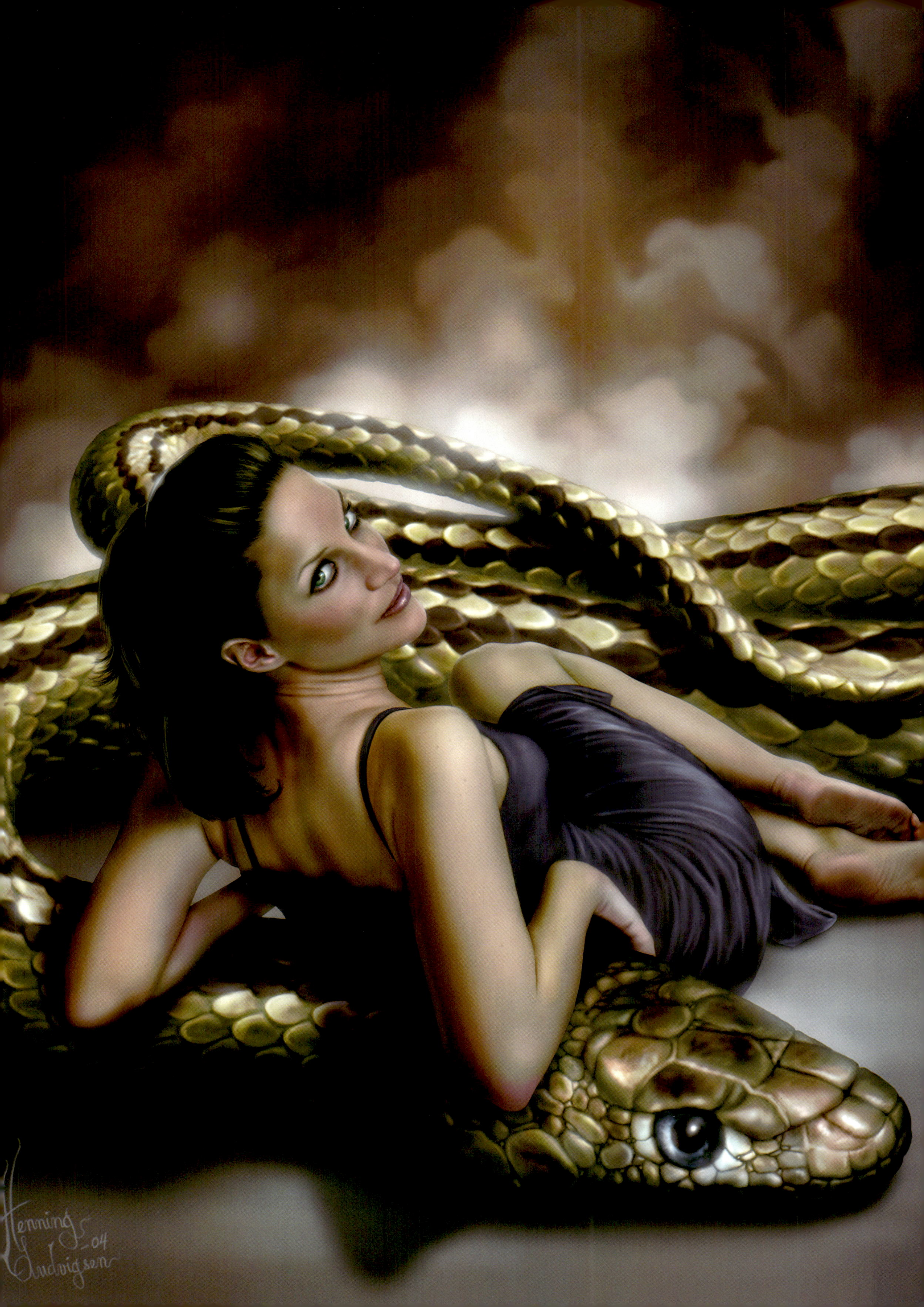
Henning -04
Ludvigsen

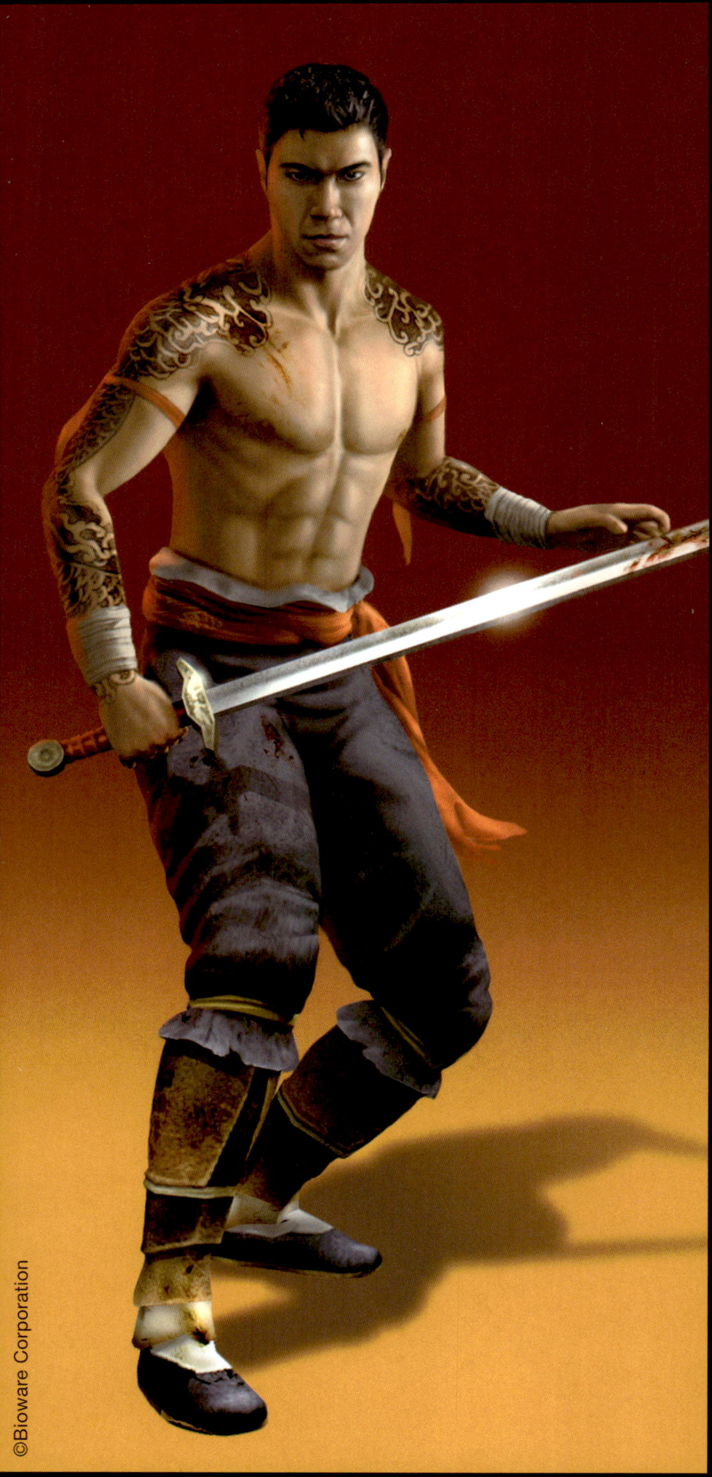

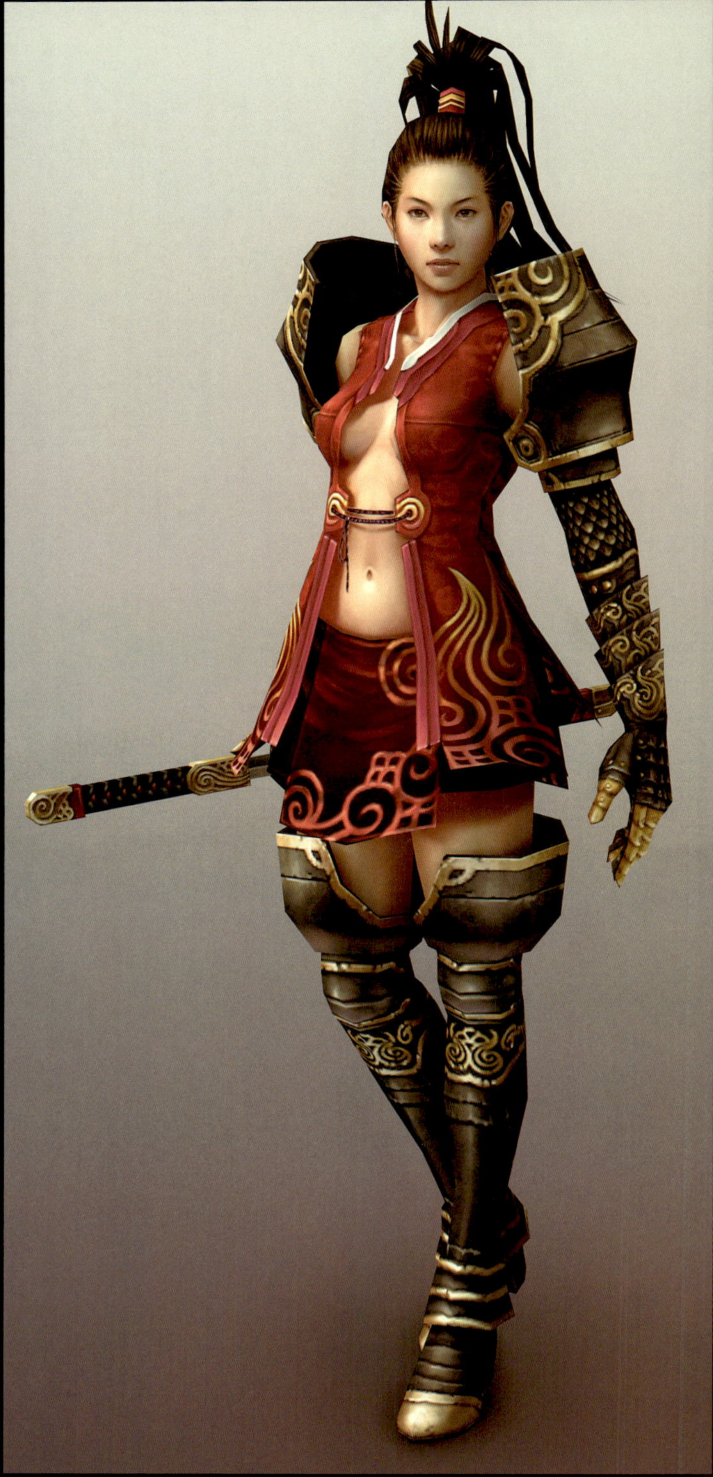

Furious Ming
3ds Max, Photoshop
Copyright: Bioware Corporation
Mike Sass, CANADA
[above]

Red Cloud
3ds Max
Seong-Wha Jeong,
KOREA
[above]

Redyan
3ds Max, Photoshop
Client: Actoz soft
Soa Lee, KOREA
[right]

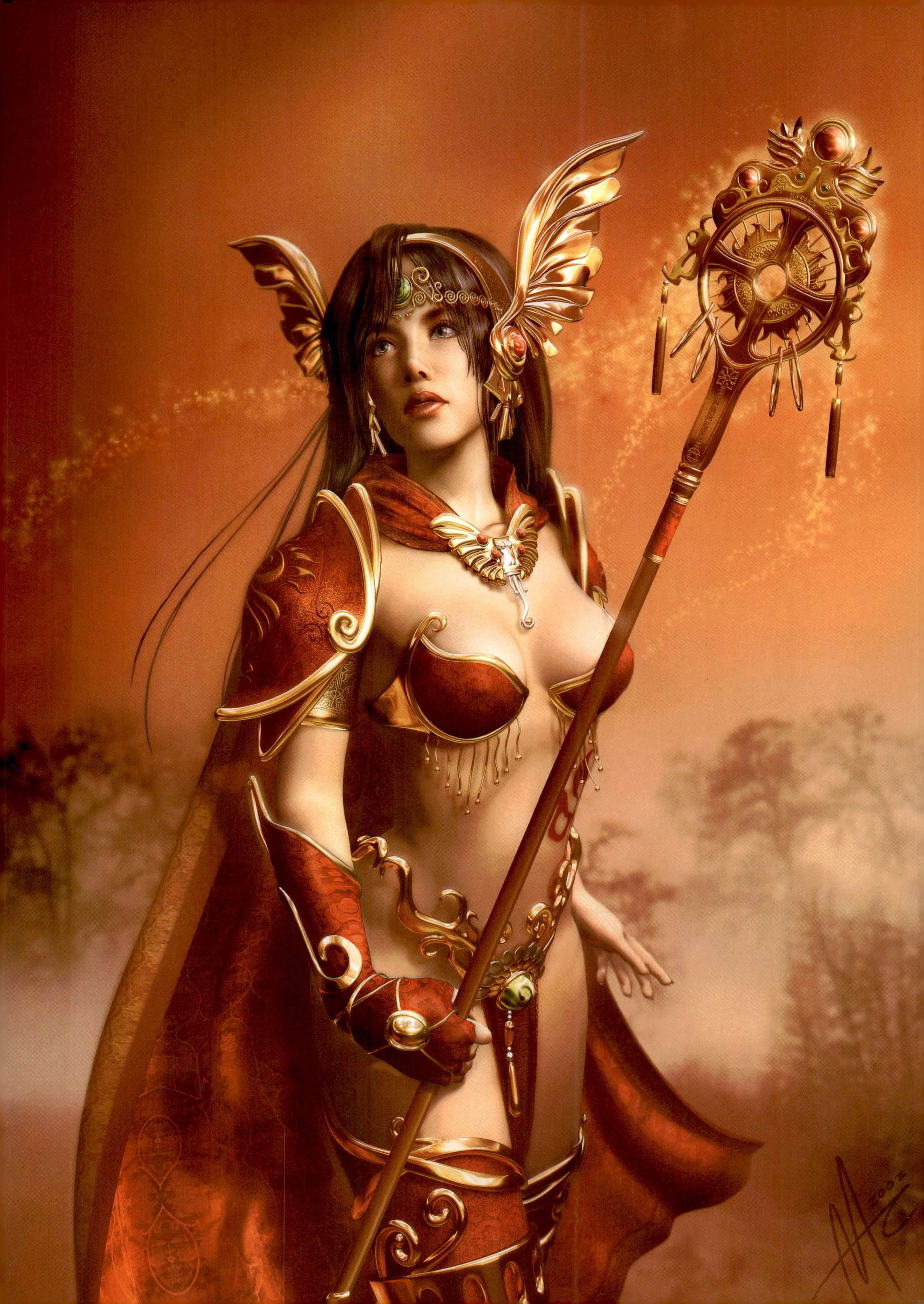

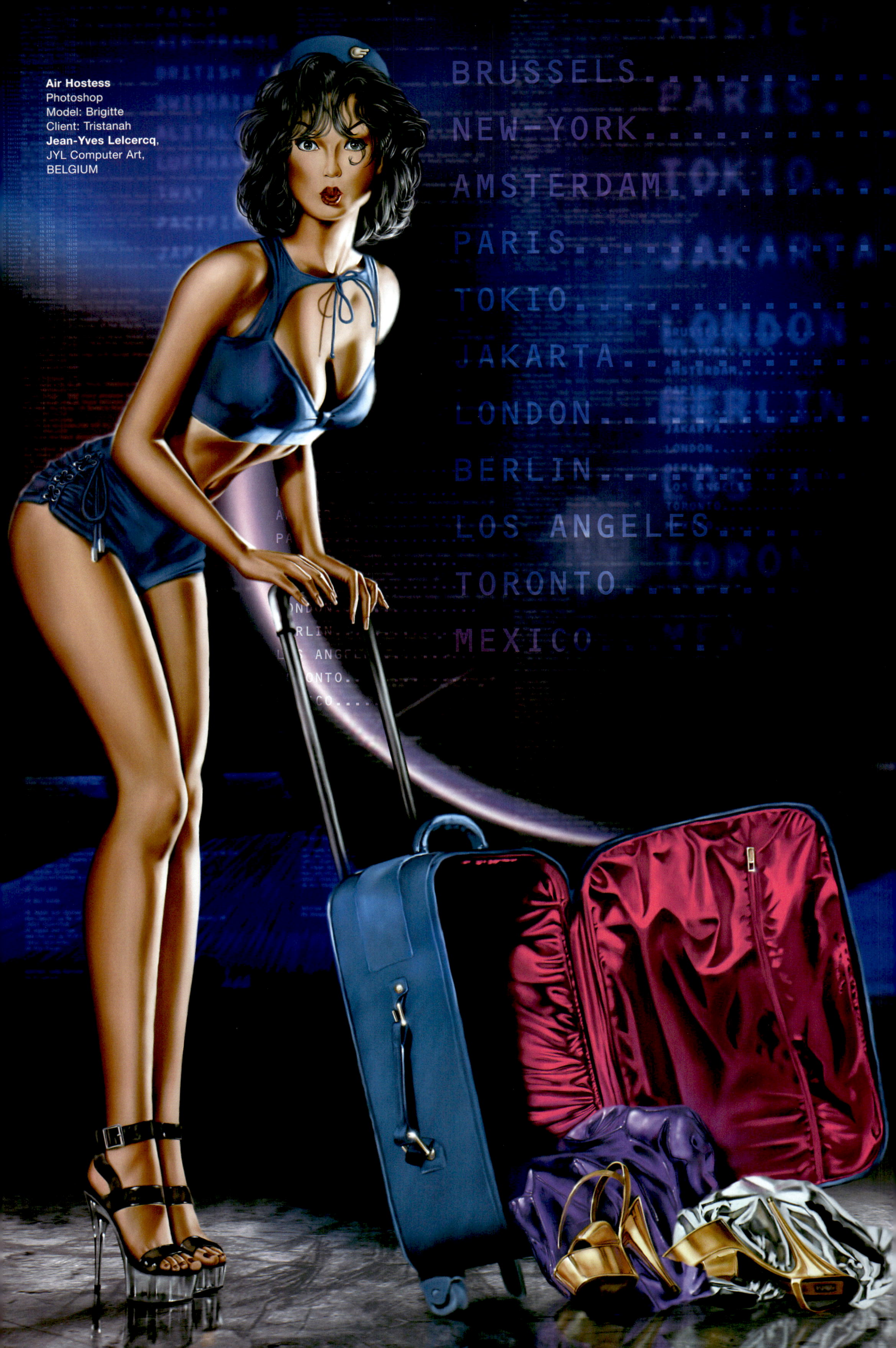

Air Hostess
Photoshop
Model: Brigitte
Client: Tristanah
Jean-Yves Lelcercq,
JYL Computer Art,
BELGIUM

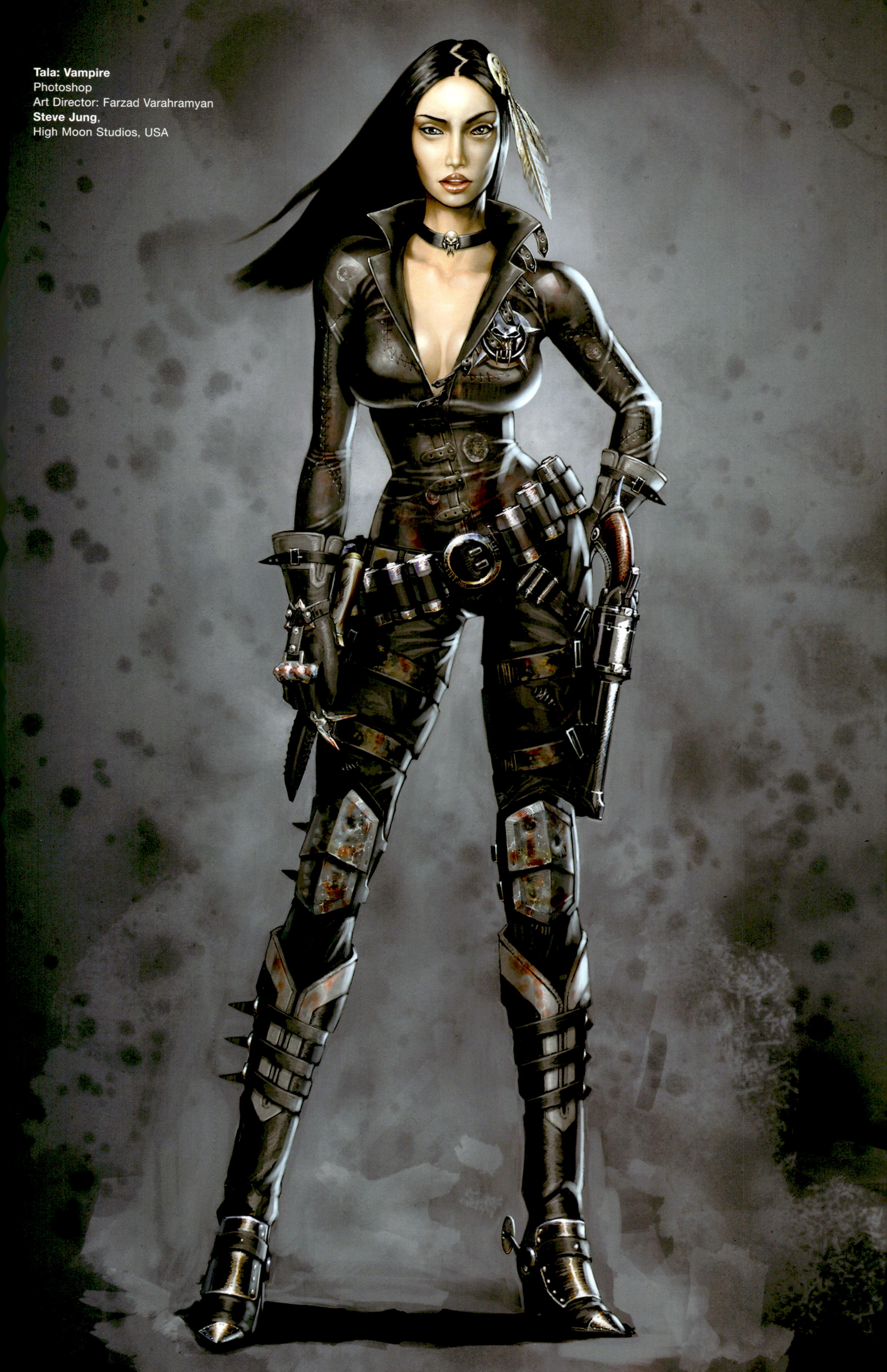

Tala: Vampire
Photoshop
Art Director: Farzad Varahramyan
Steve Jung,
High Moon Studios, USA

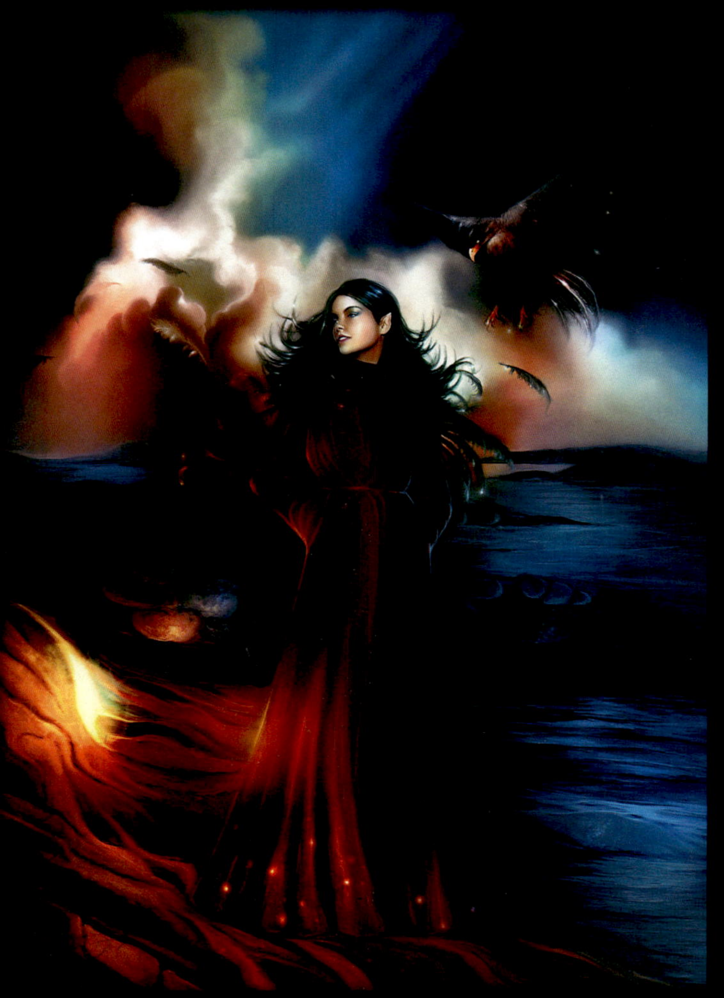

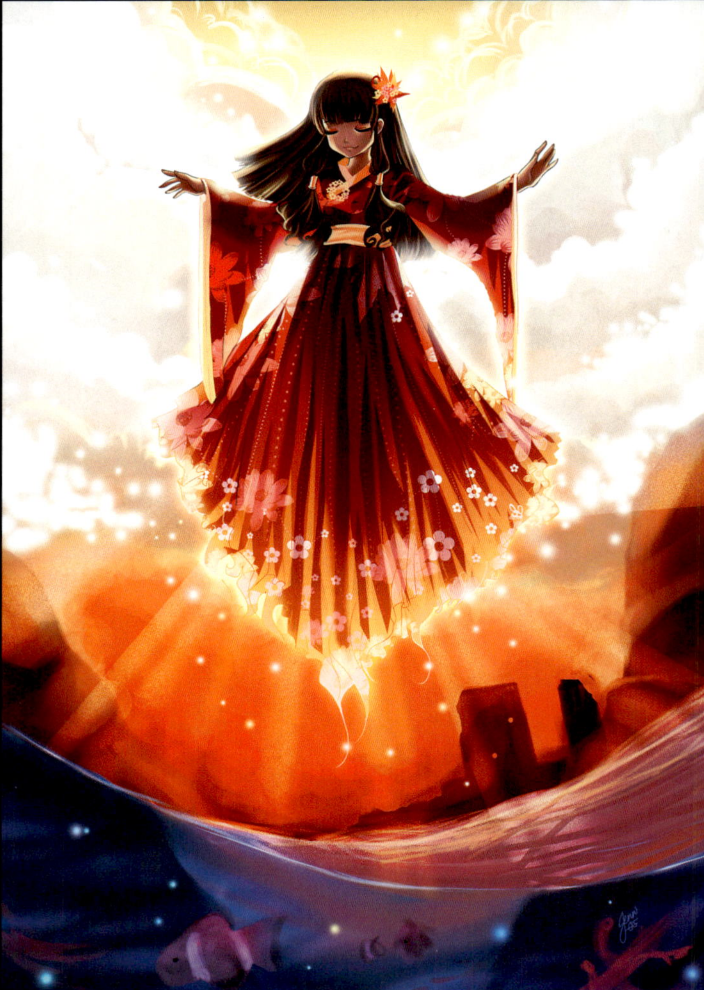

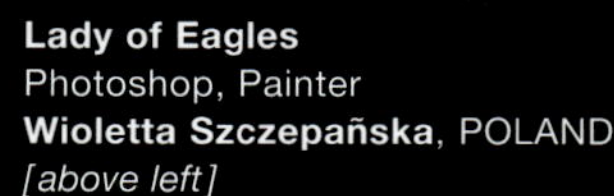

Lady of Eagles
Photoshop, Painter
Wioletta Szczepańska, POLAND
[above left]

Sunshine After the Rain
Painter, Photoshop
Jennifer Duong, CANADA
[above]

Dark Stalker
Painter
Howard Lyon, USA
[left]

Spellforce Cover
3ds Max
Virgin Lands Animated Pictures GmbH, GERMANY
[right]

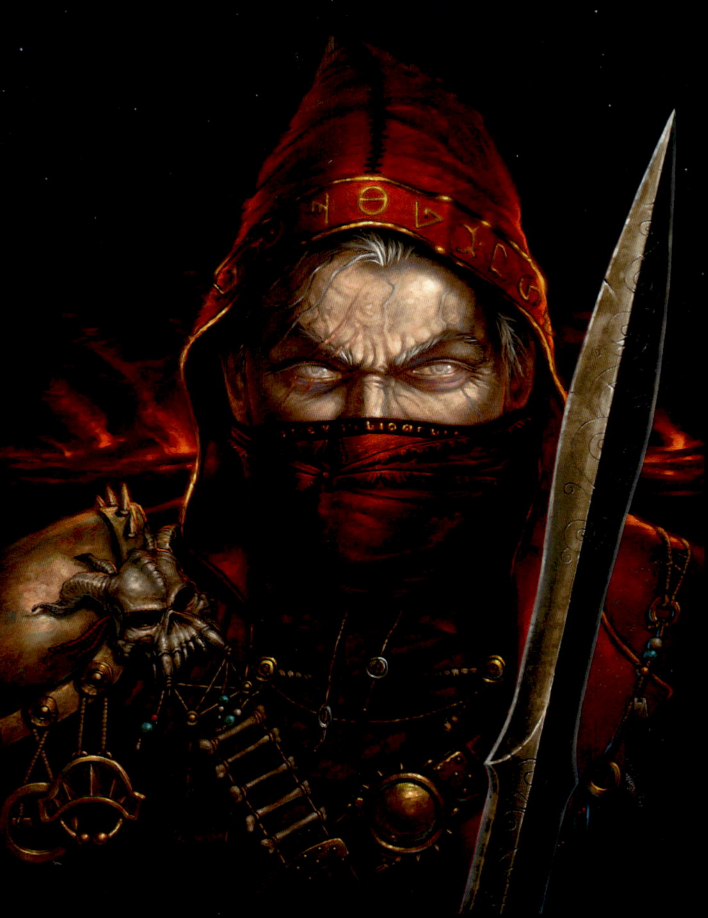

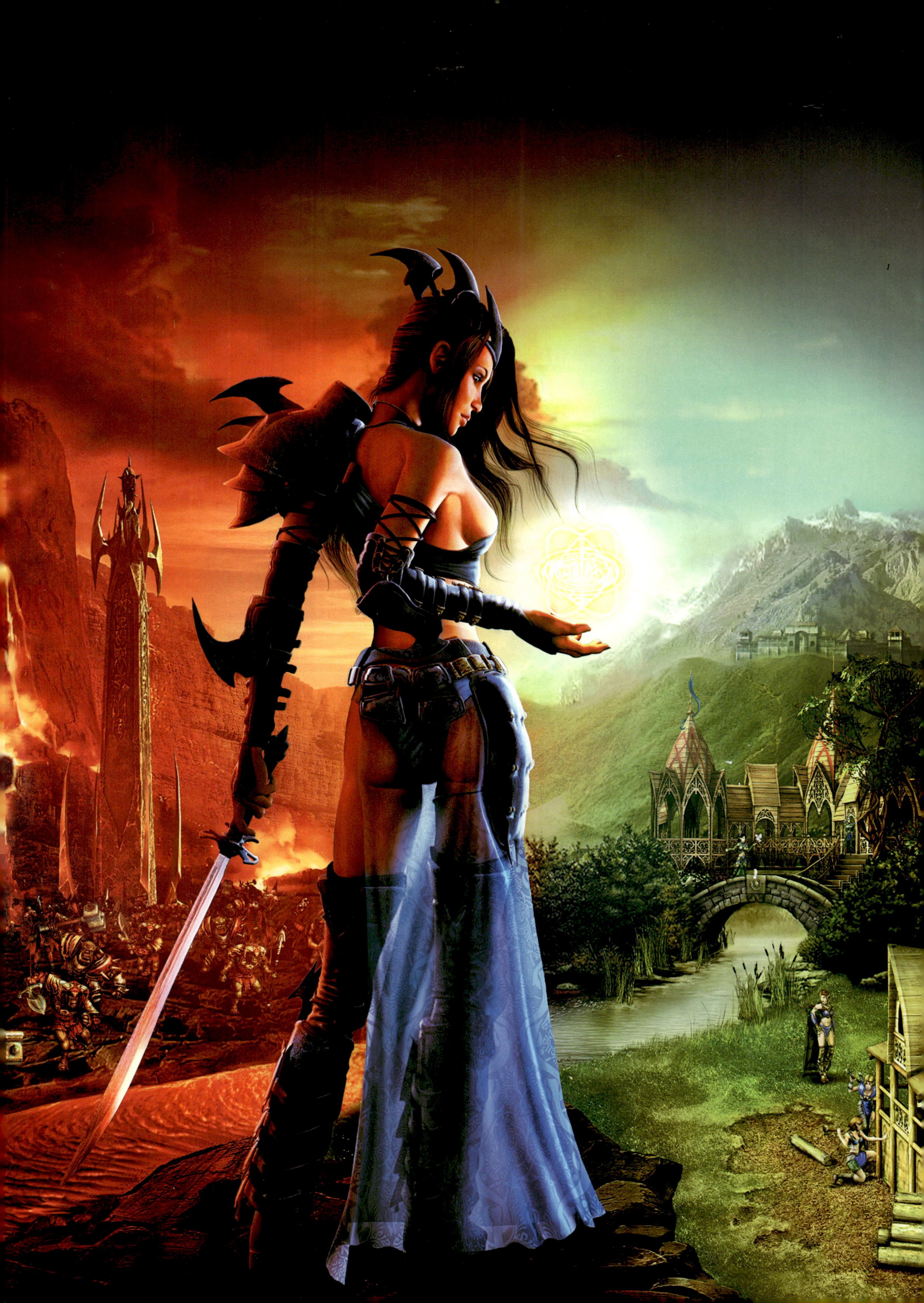

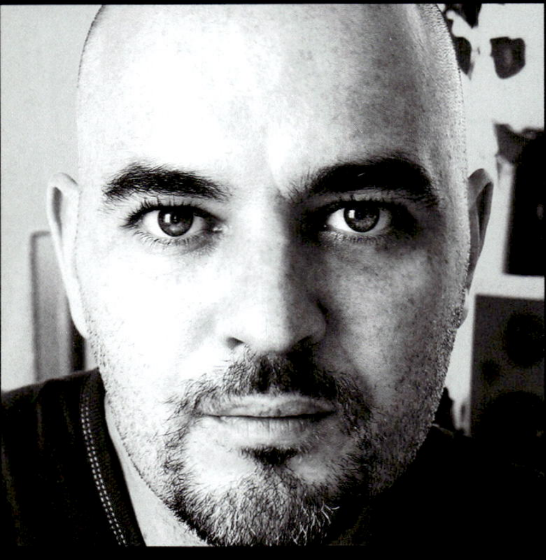

FRED BASTIDE

www.texwelt.net
tex@texwelt.net

"When I work on human characters, I like to express a monstrous nature. When creating non-human characters, I try to accentuate human characteristics."

Fred Bastide had a classical art education. At 34, he is a graduate of the 'Ecole des arts appliqués de Vevey', and 'Ecole supérieure d'arts décoratifs de Genève'. While he was there, he learned the many aspects of drawing, painting, sculpture and photography, but as an autodidact with CG, he had the most fun sitting at home with the very first version of 3ds Max. He began tinkering with the artistic boundaries of computer-generated art about eight years ago. Although curious, he admits he wasn't completely convinced of the creative potential of CG, so the first few years of studying the phenomenon were not very intensive. "It was more like a kind of videogame for me," explains Fred. "Just a bit of fun." Fred lives and works in Montreux, the French-speaking part of Switzerland. He is presently working in an unrelated field of

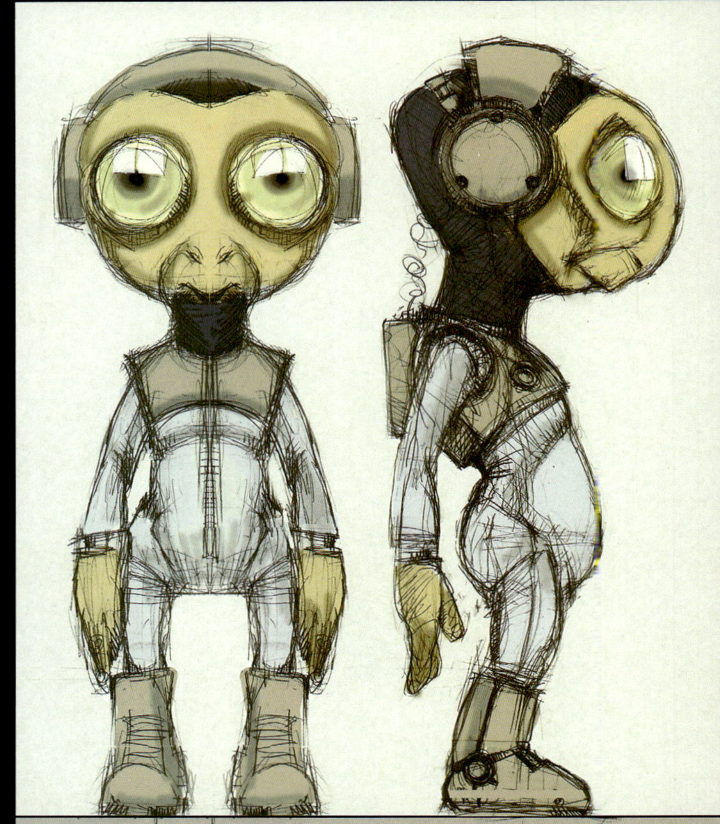

SKETCHING

This small alien came from a picture more ambitious than a simple "character in repose" image named "the most boring planet of the universe". For technical reasons, I scheduled it for a later endeavor, but chose to exploit this little guy in a "portrait like" feature. I really don't know how much time I've spent on it, and I've made drastic changes during the process. Usually, I make better preparations for my images, but this one was more experimental and clearly disorganized. As I usually do, I made some quick sketches to define the color scheme, proportions and principal characteristics of the small invader. I chose very neutral colors to give an annoying feel to the space suit, and I avoided decals or decorative elements on the armour elements for the same reasons. My goal was to give him the most inoffensive appearance possible. I gave him human baby proportions, chubby fingers and very big eyes, inspired by those of a Loris, a kind of monkey-lemurian like creature.

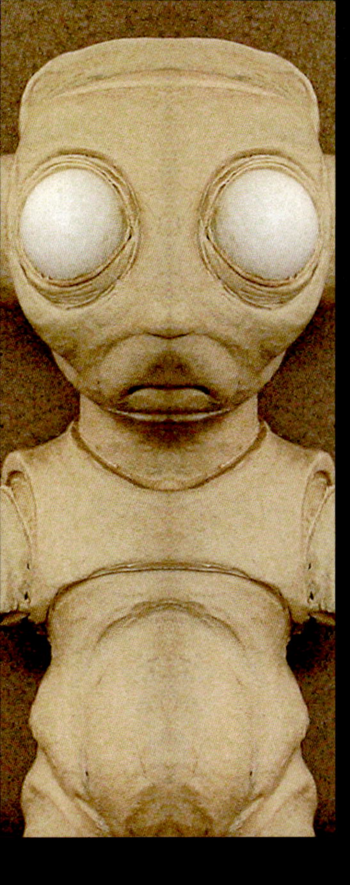

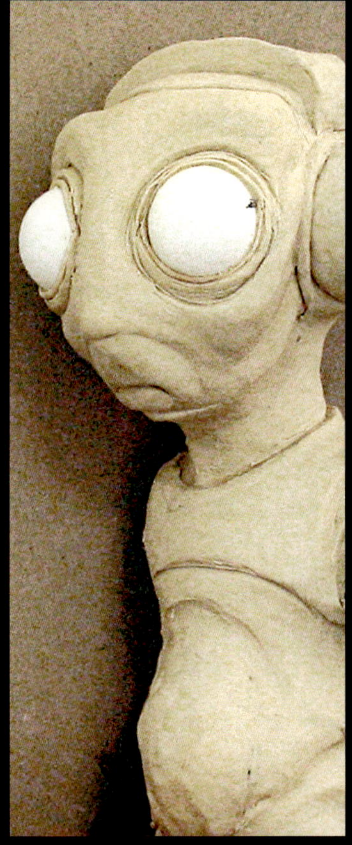

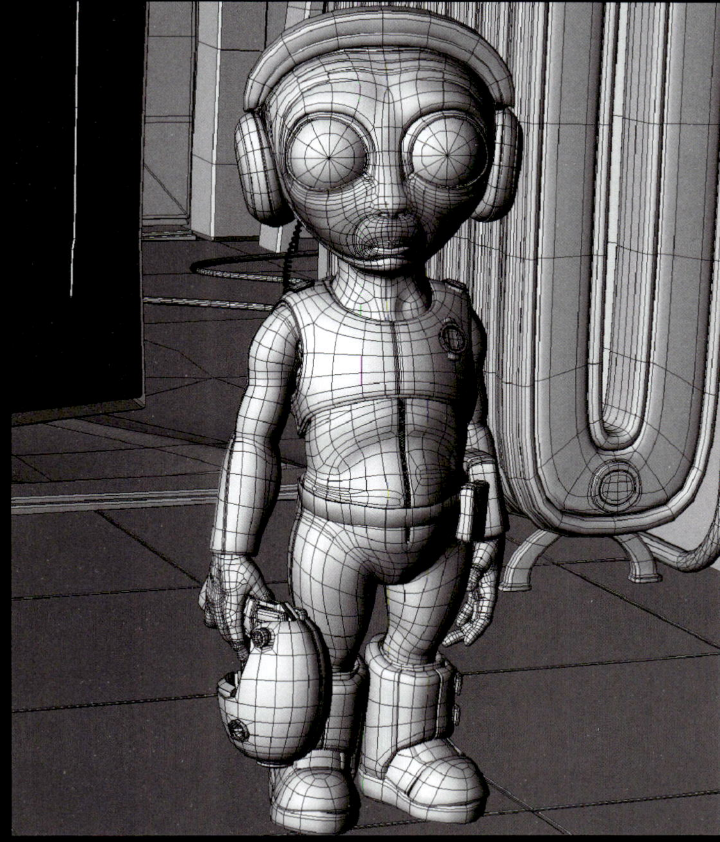

CLAY MODELING

I made a very quick plasticine model to have a better idea of proportions. Where possible, I prefer to have a conceptual approach with a physical material, which is more sensitive and moldable than a set of vertex. Of course, the small sculpture didn't need to be precise or beautiful, but just be sufficient to be used as a reference. I originally planned to make the little guy 15 centimeters small, and to place him on a desk covered with typical pre-1990s (computerless) office materials like a stapler, paperclips, a paper punch and highlighters. I completely modeled, unwarped and textured these boring office objects, only to decide that they didn't work in the scene.

SETTING THE SCENE

Once the small alien was placed in the environment, a problem with proportions became evident: a very small creature like this would certainly have very thin limbs like a tiny monkey or an insect. I decided to re-scale the character and re-think the entire scene. I settled on a small corner of my own apartment. The floor was very important in the image, so I reproduced a kind of early 20th century tile of my corridor with textures found on www.mayang.com. They were not exactly the same as those in my corridor, but gave the same feeling of old time elegance and coldness that I was searching for in my image. I chose an old and heavy 1950s radiator (from my own apartment too), to contrast the fragile and shy invader. I used 3ds Max for modelling, VRay for the render (chosen principally for the efficiency of the GI illumination) and Photoshop to paint the textures.

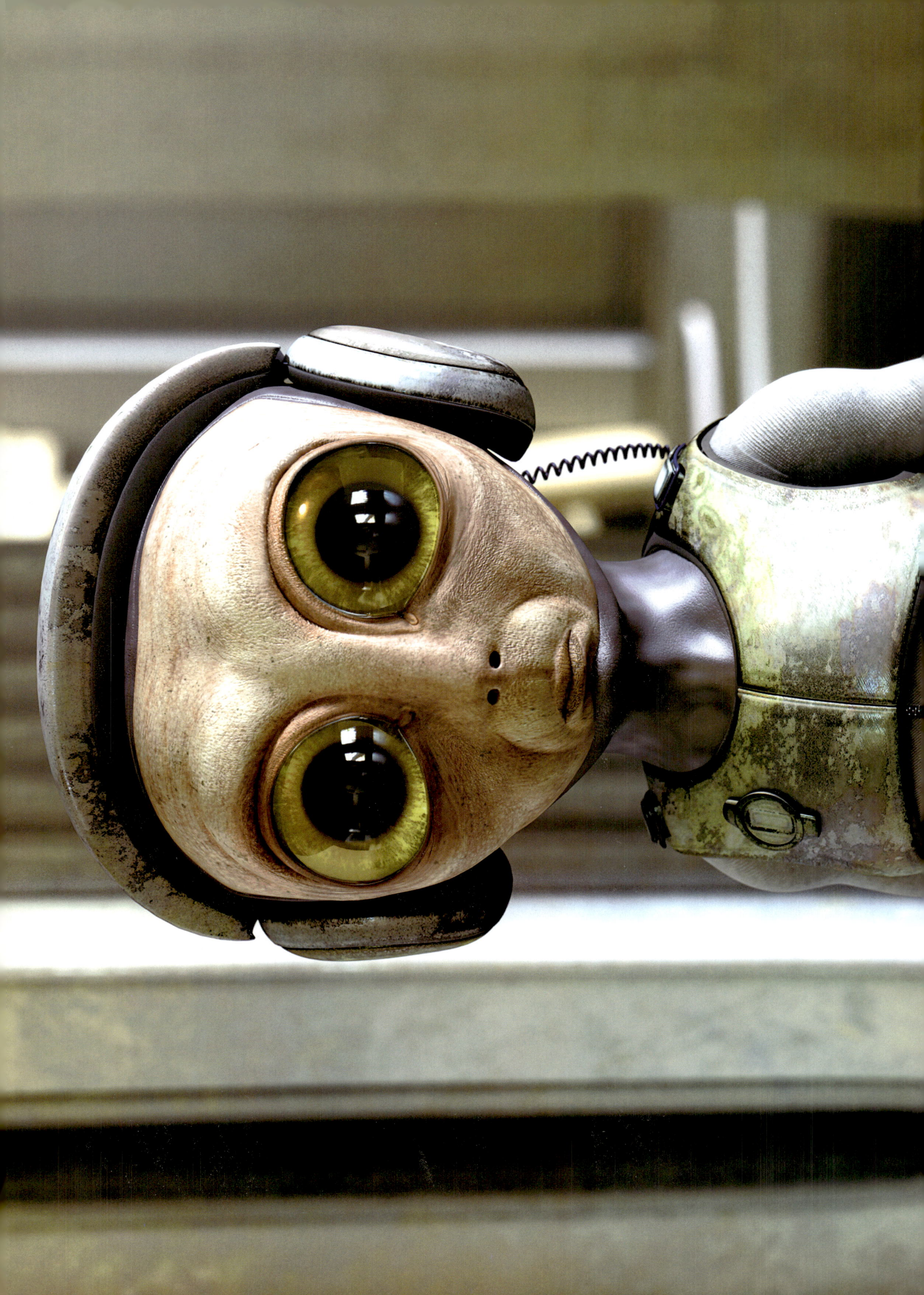

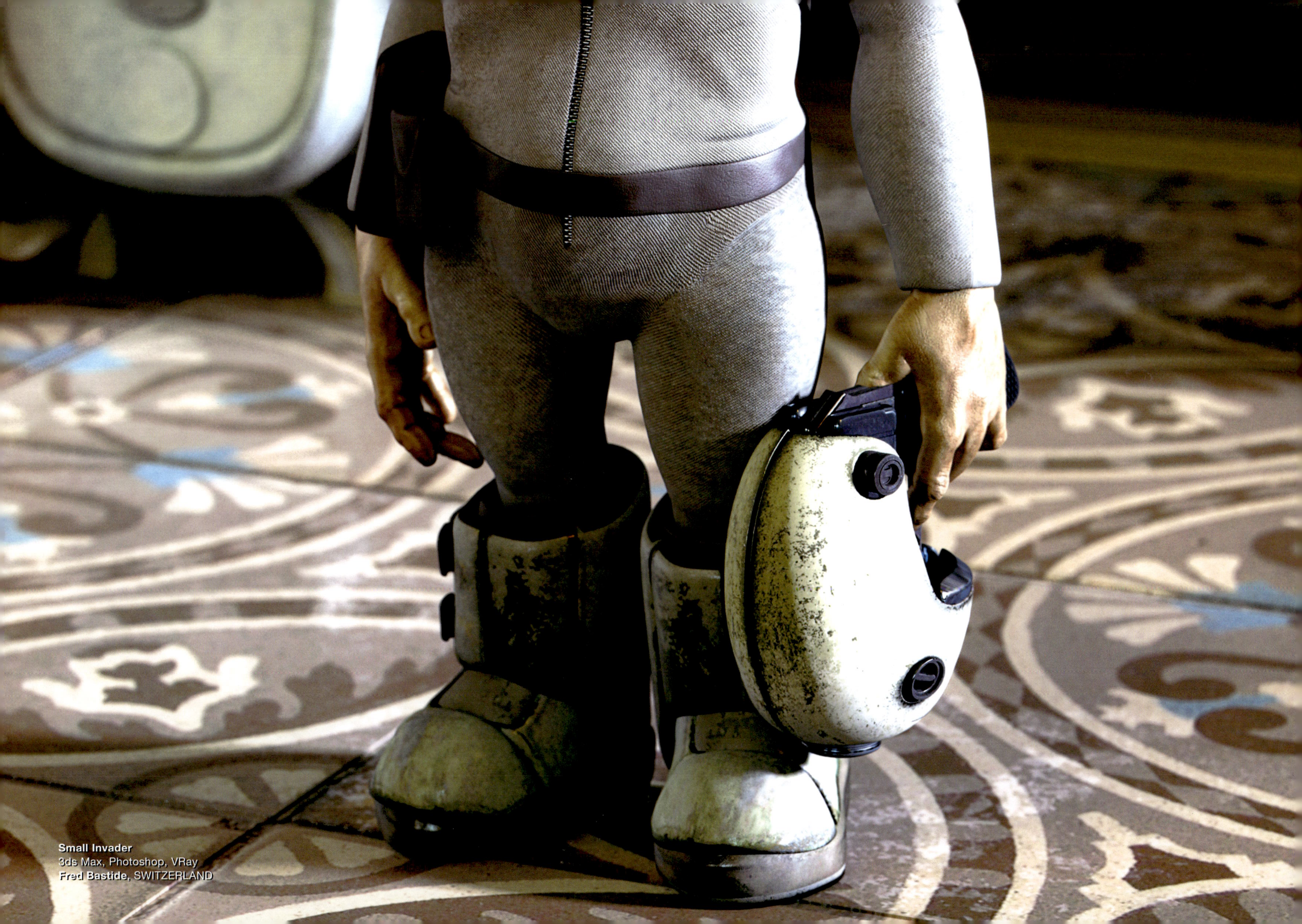

Small Invader
3ds Max, Photoshop, VRay
Fred Bastide, SWITZERLAND

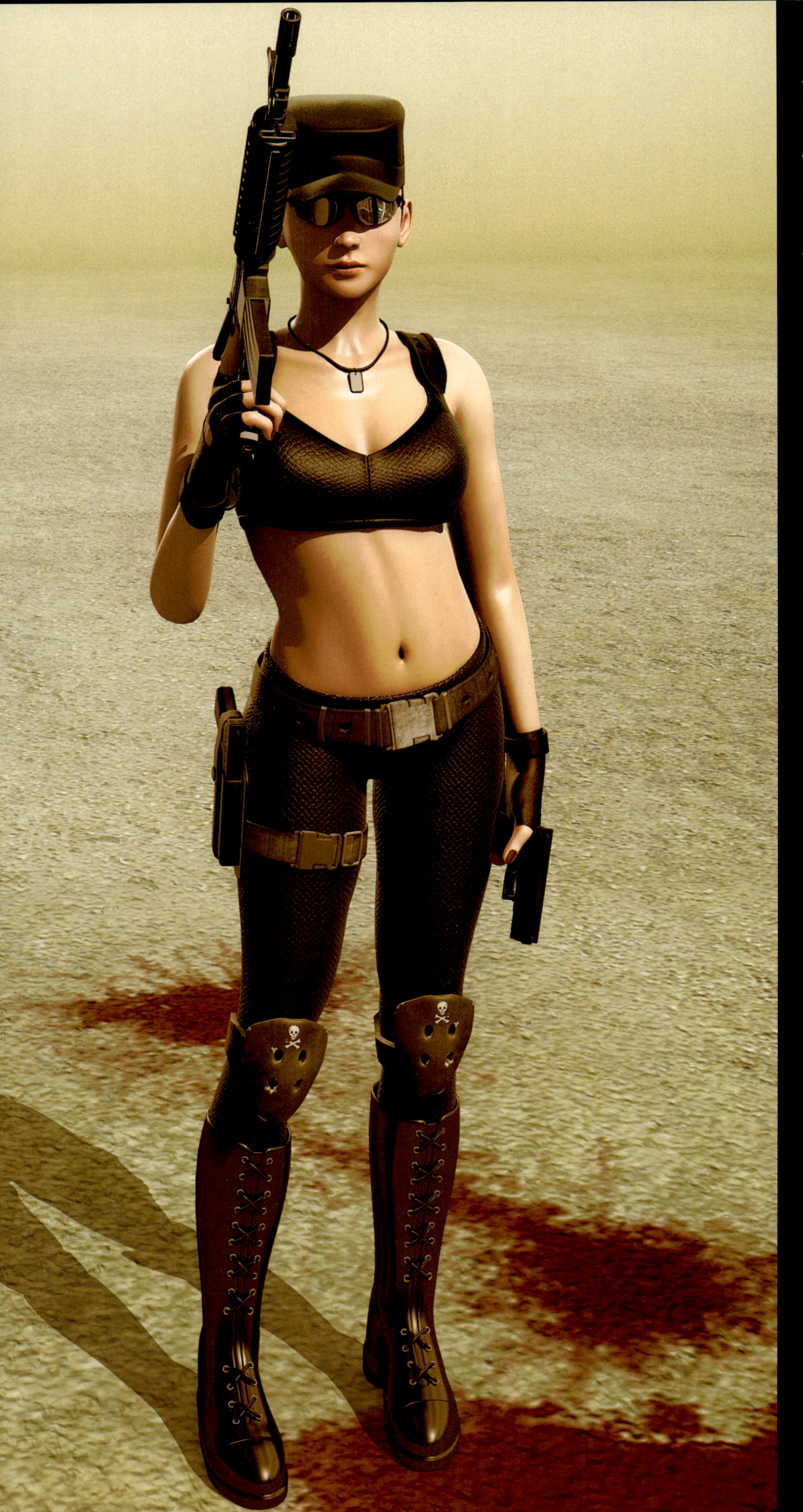

The Mercenary
3ds Max, Photoshop
Marc Tan, Insane Polygons, SINGAPORE
[left]

Blackman
Maya, ZBrush
Francois Rimasson, FRANCE
[right]

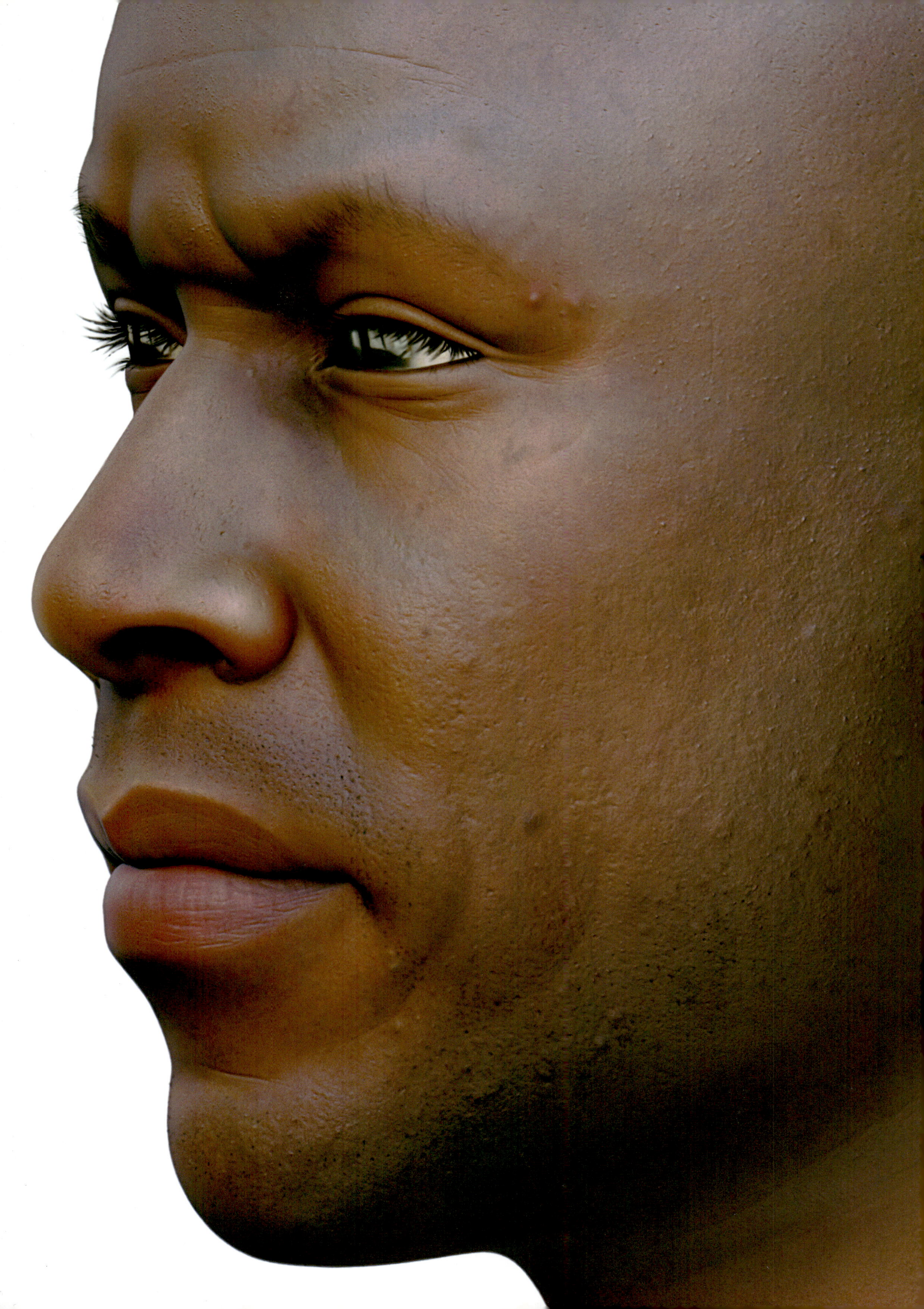

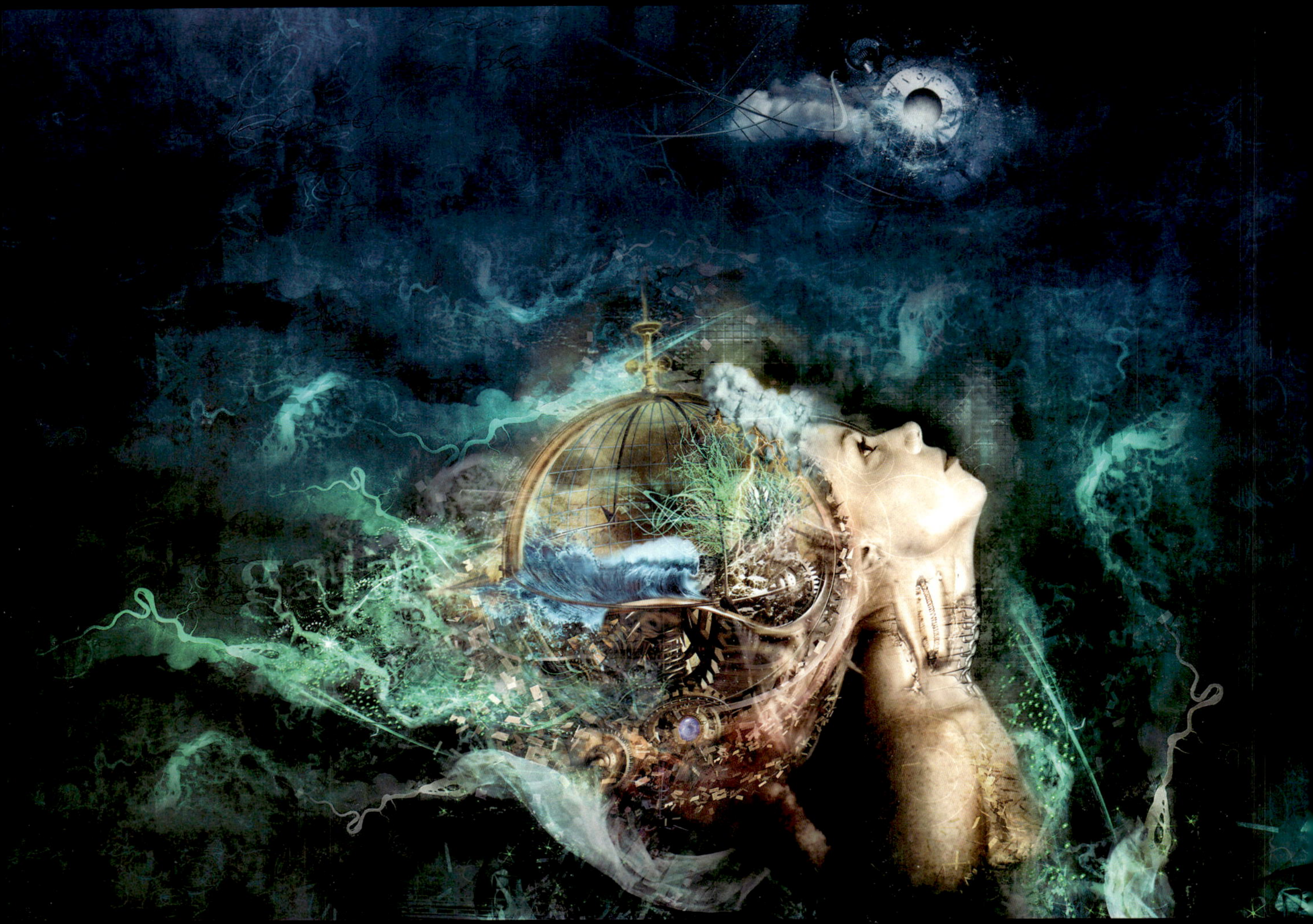

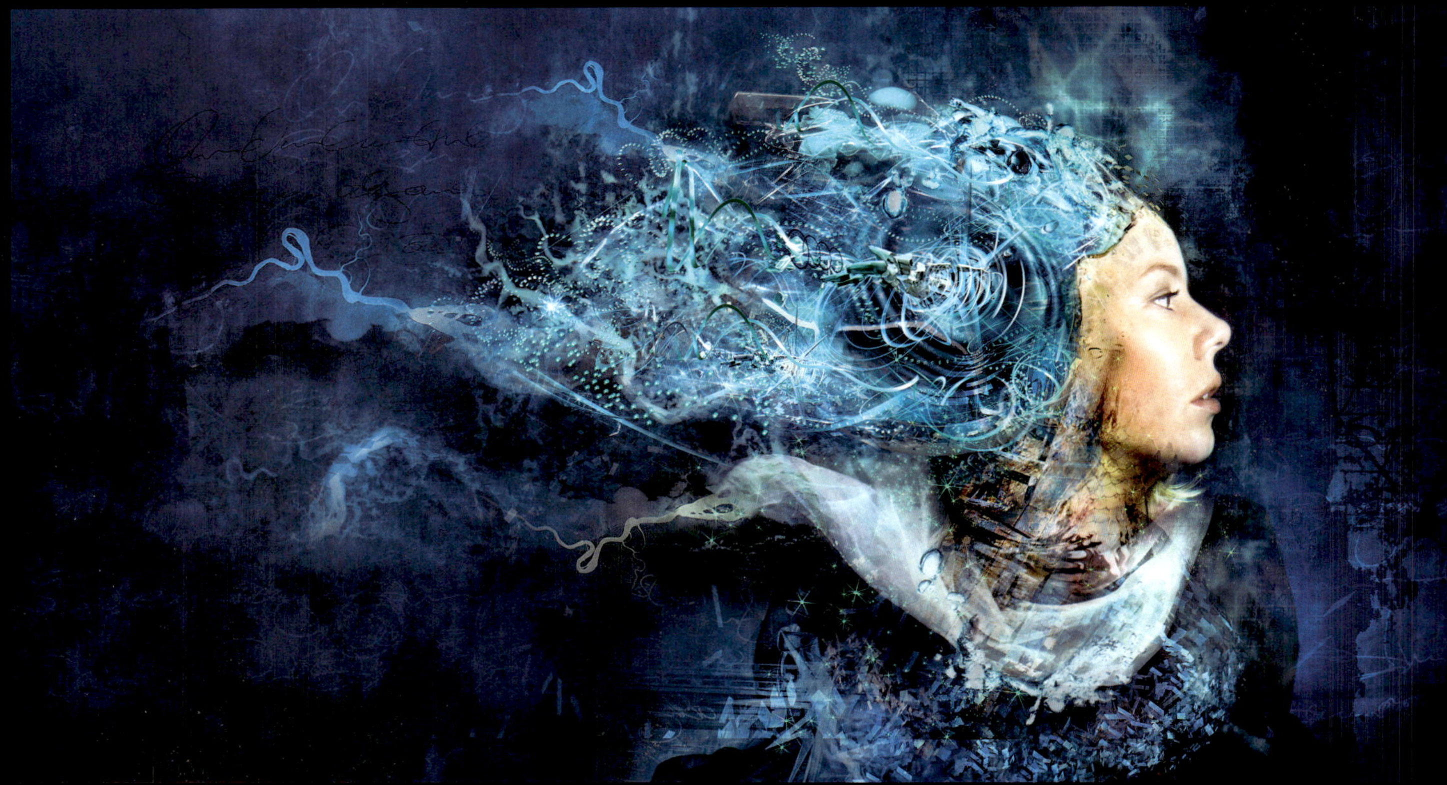

Gaia (Earth)
Photoshop, 3ds Max
Client: Cyber Mythologia
Christos Magganas, GREECE
[top]

Thallasa (Sea)
Photoshop, 3ds Max
Client: Cyber Mythologia
Christos Magganas, GREECE
[above]

Lilith
Photoshop
Thitipon Dicruen, THAILAND
[right]

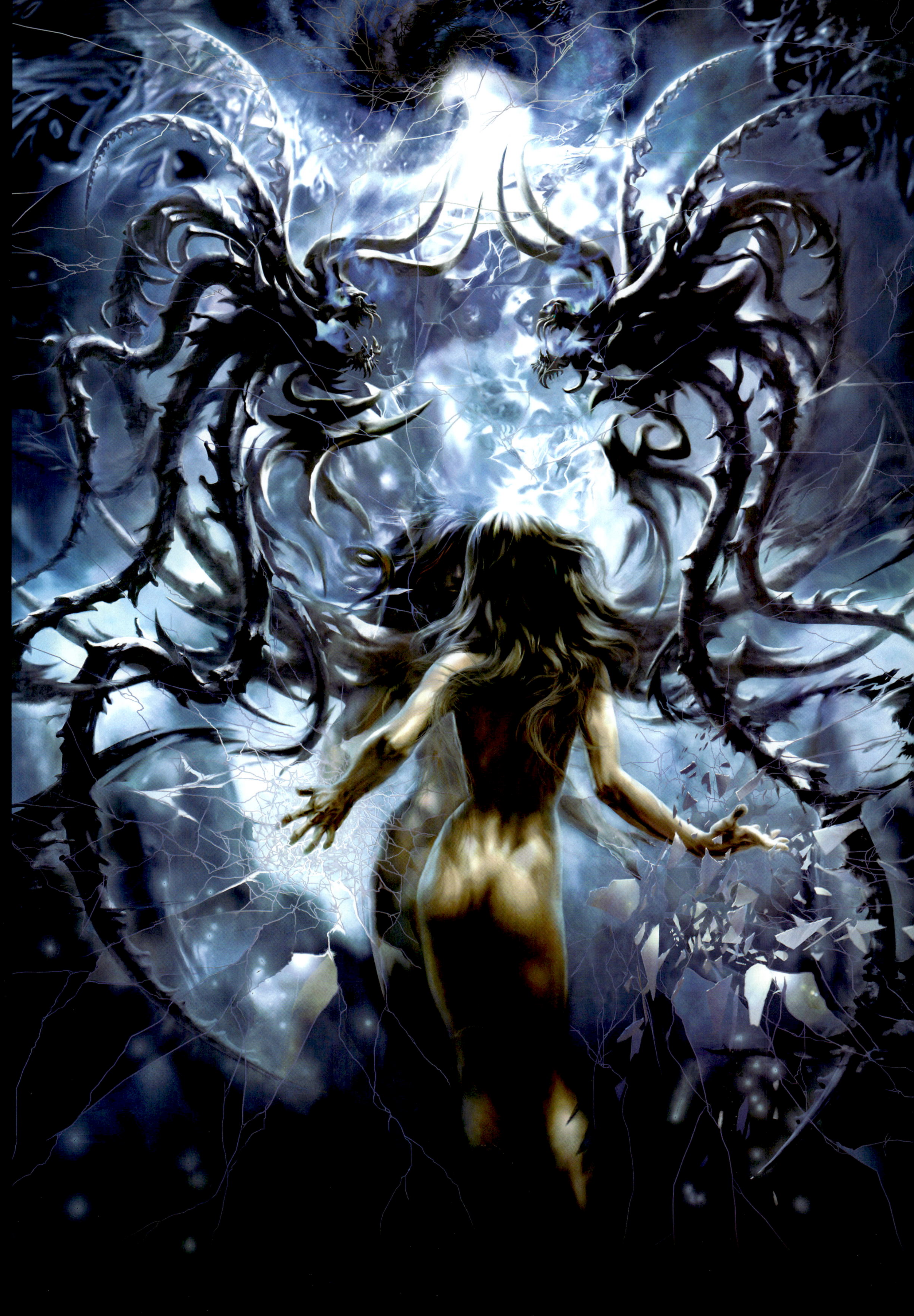

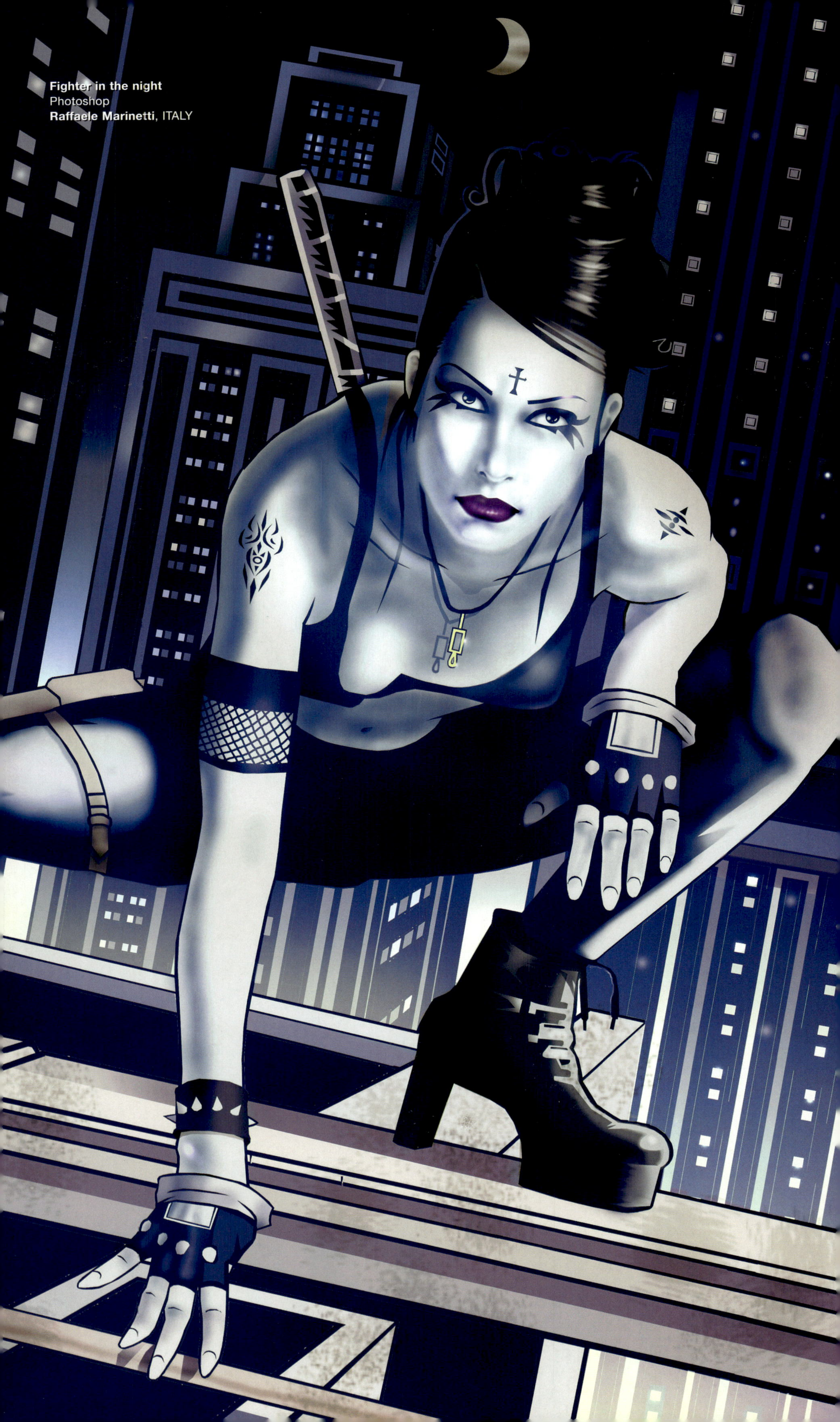

Fighter in the night
Photoshop
Raffaele Marinetti, ITALY

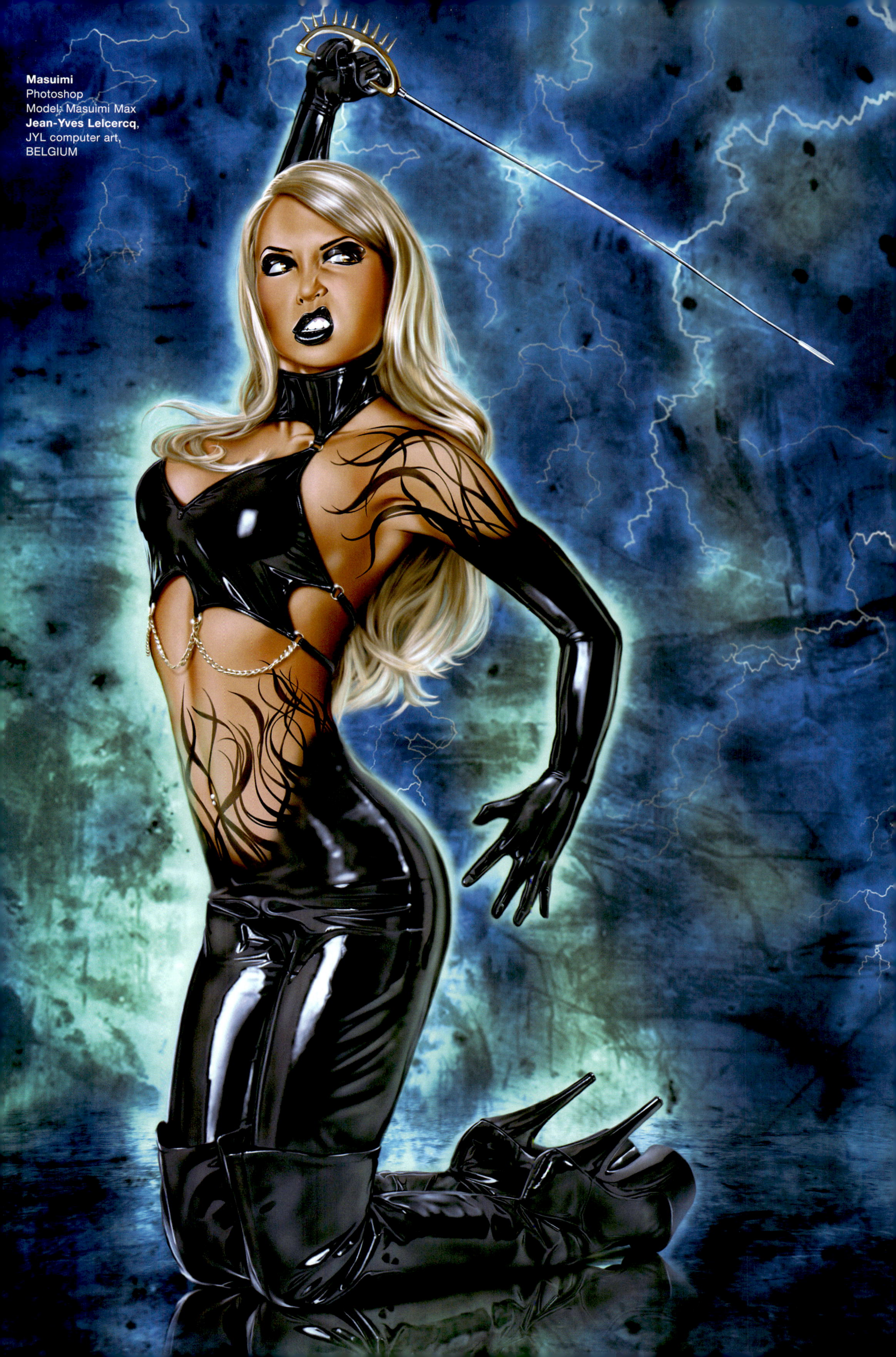

Masuimi
Photoshop
Model: Masuimi Max
Jean-Yves Lelcercq,
JYL computer art,
BELGIUM

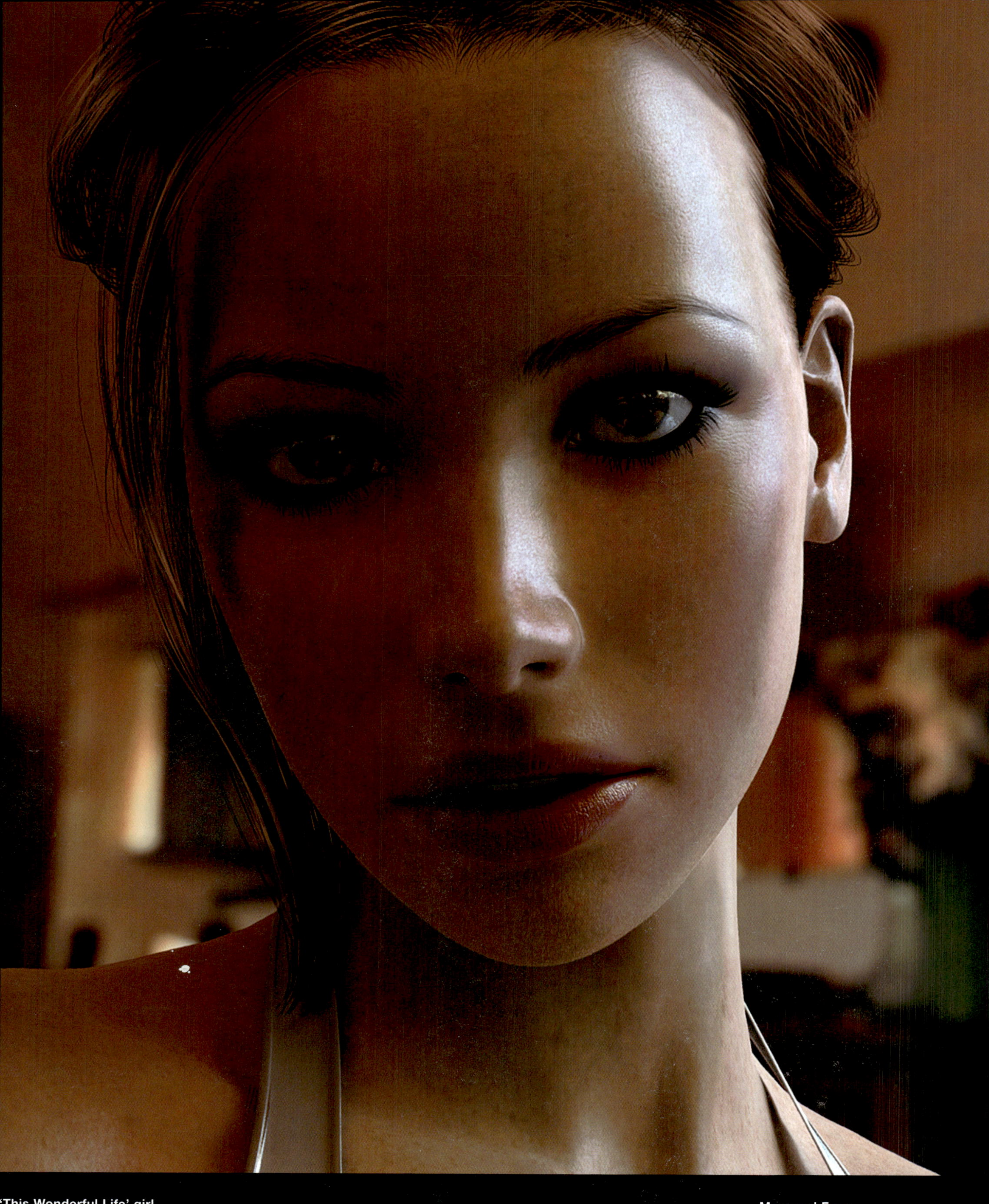

'This Wonderful Life' girl
3ds Max, Brazil r/s
Liam Kemp, GREAT BRITAIN
[above]

Mamegal Face
3ds Max, Character Studio,
Brazil r/s, Shag Hair
Koji Yamagami, Beans Magic, JAPAN

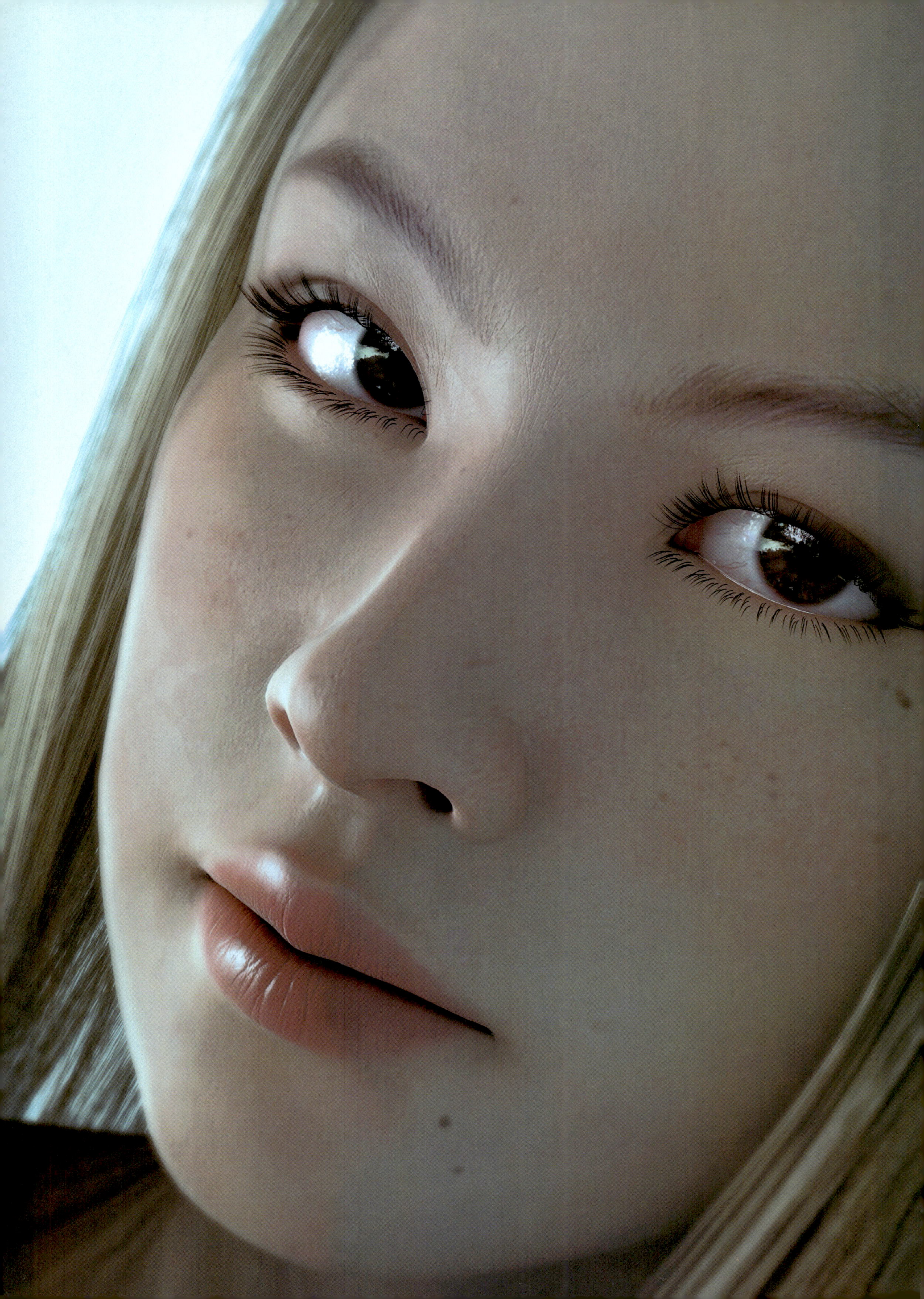

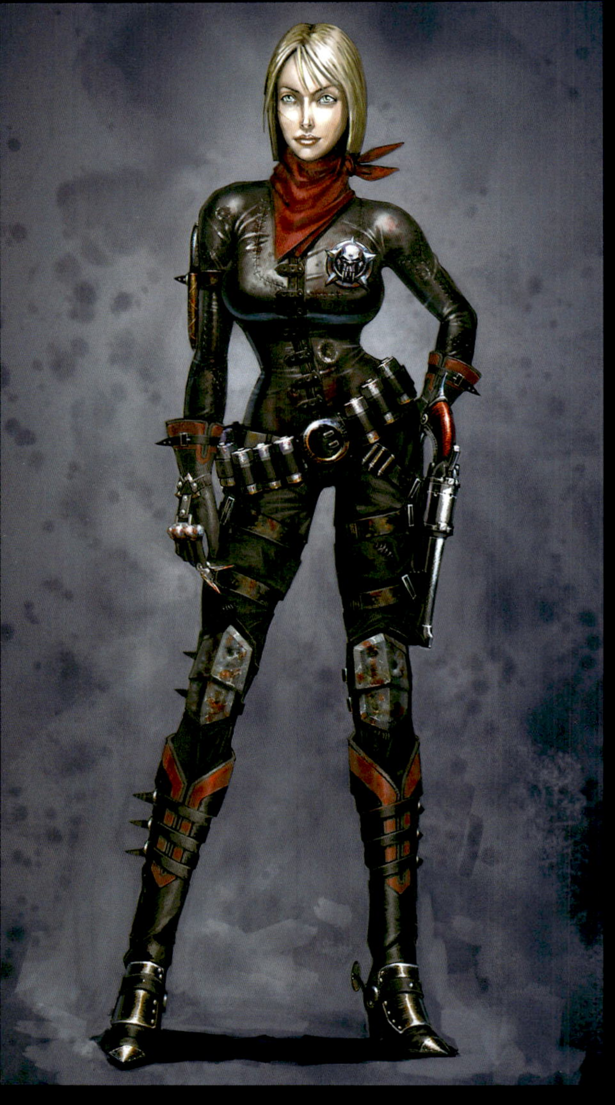

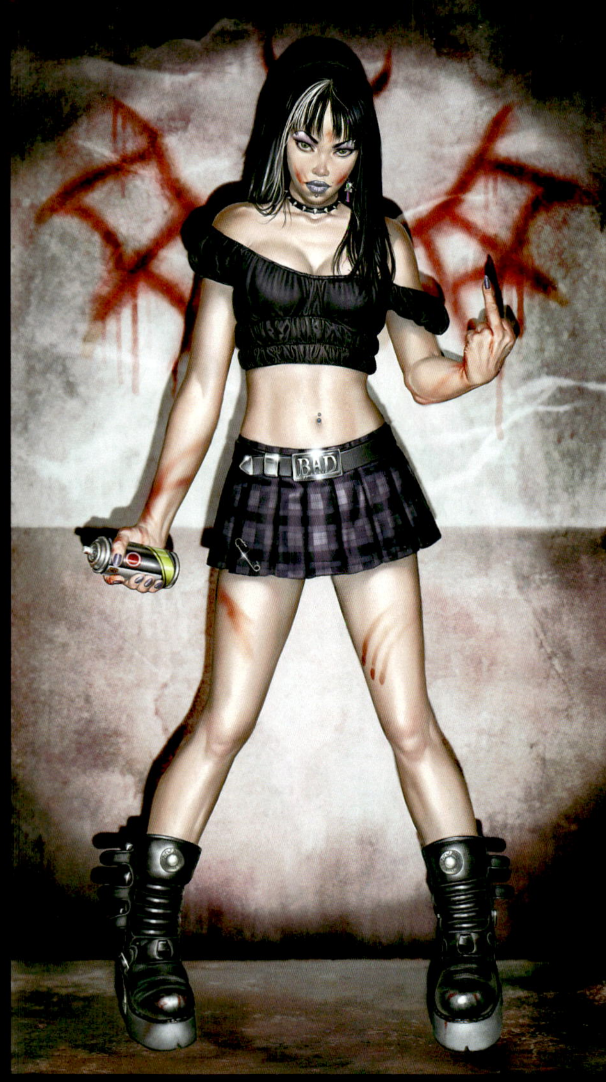

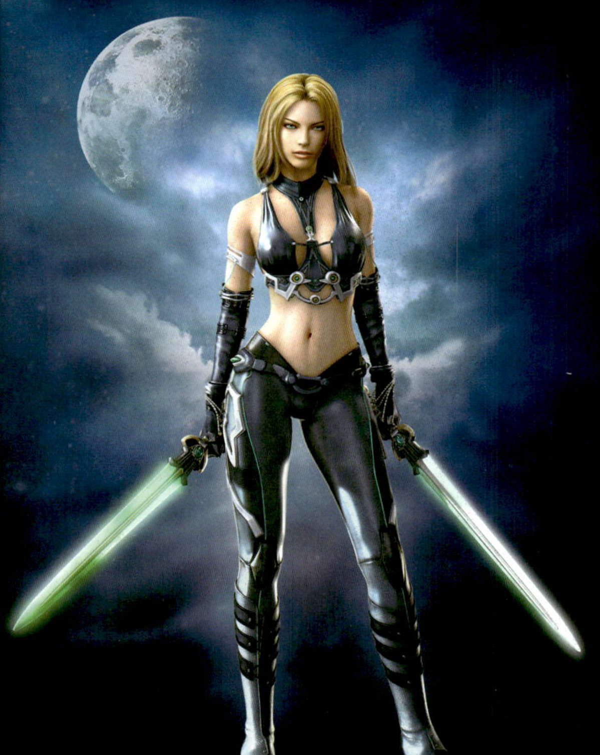

Cassidy Sharp
Photoshop
Art Director: Farzad Varahramyan
Steve Jung,
High Moon Studios, USA
[above left]

Lil' Devil
Photoshop
Alistair Fell, GREAT BRITAIN
[above]

S-girl
Photoshop
Client: NAKO Interactive
Seok Chan-yoo, KOREA
[left]

Lady Frances Drake
Photoshop
Alistair Fell, GREAT BRITAIN
[right]

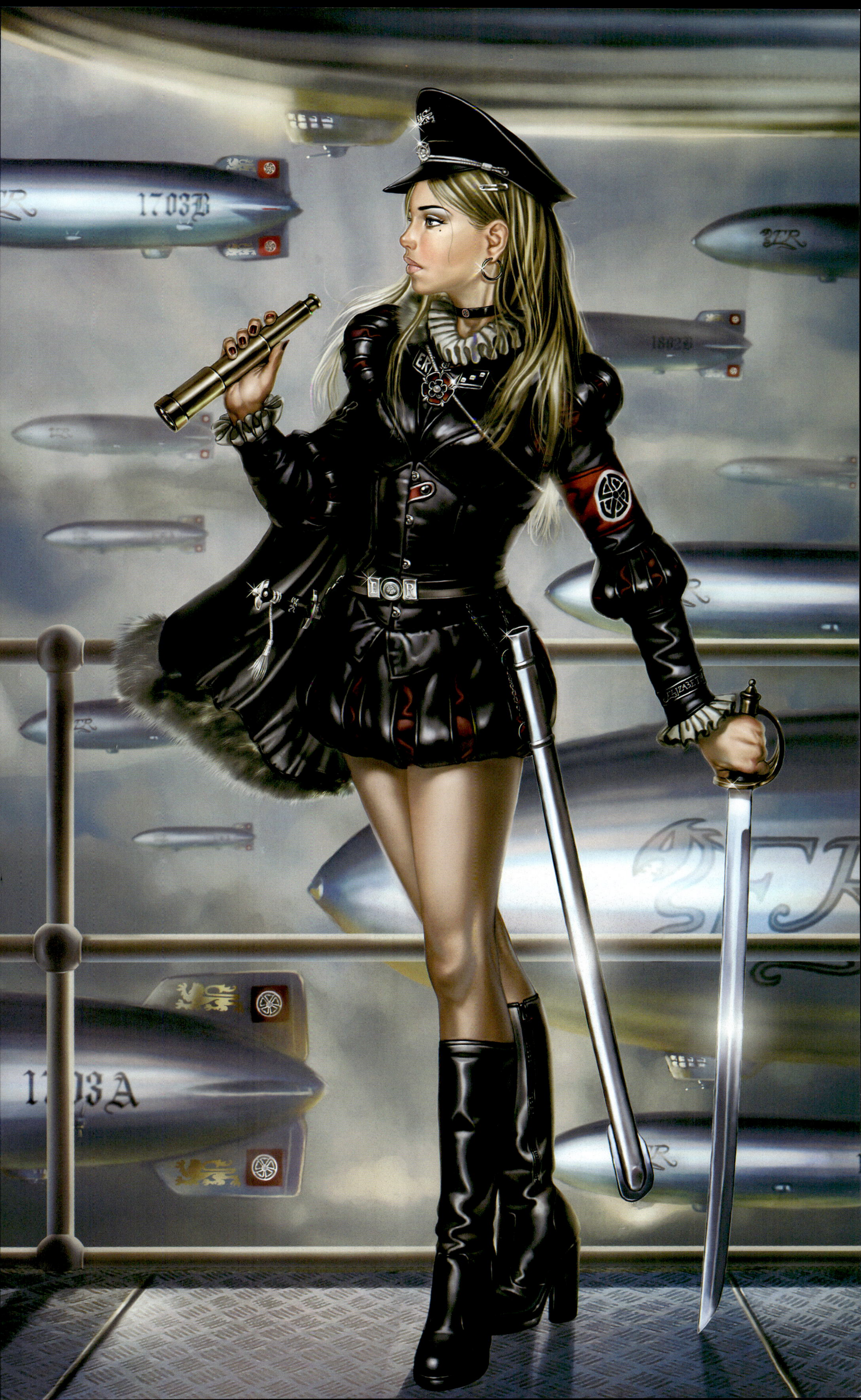
1703B

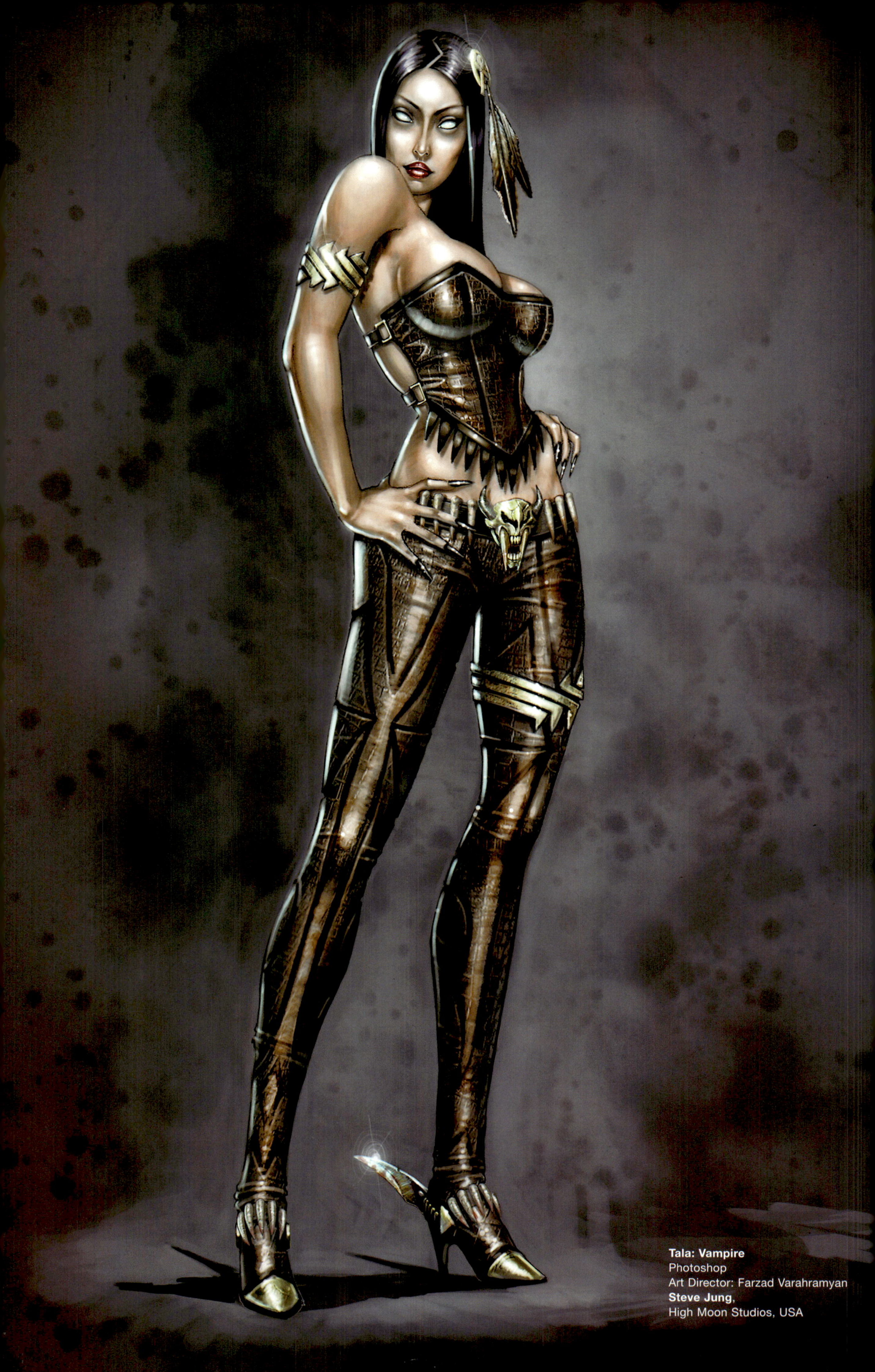

Tala: Vampire
Photoshop
Art Director: Farzad Varahramyan
Steve Jung,
High Moon Studios, USA

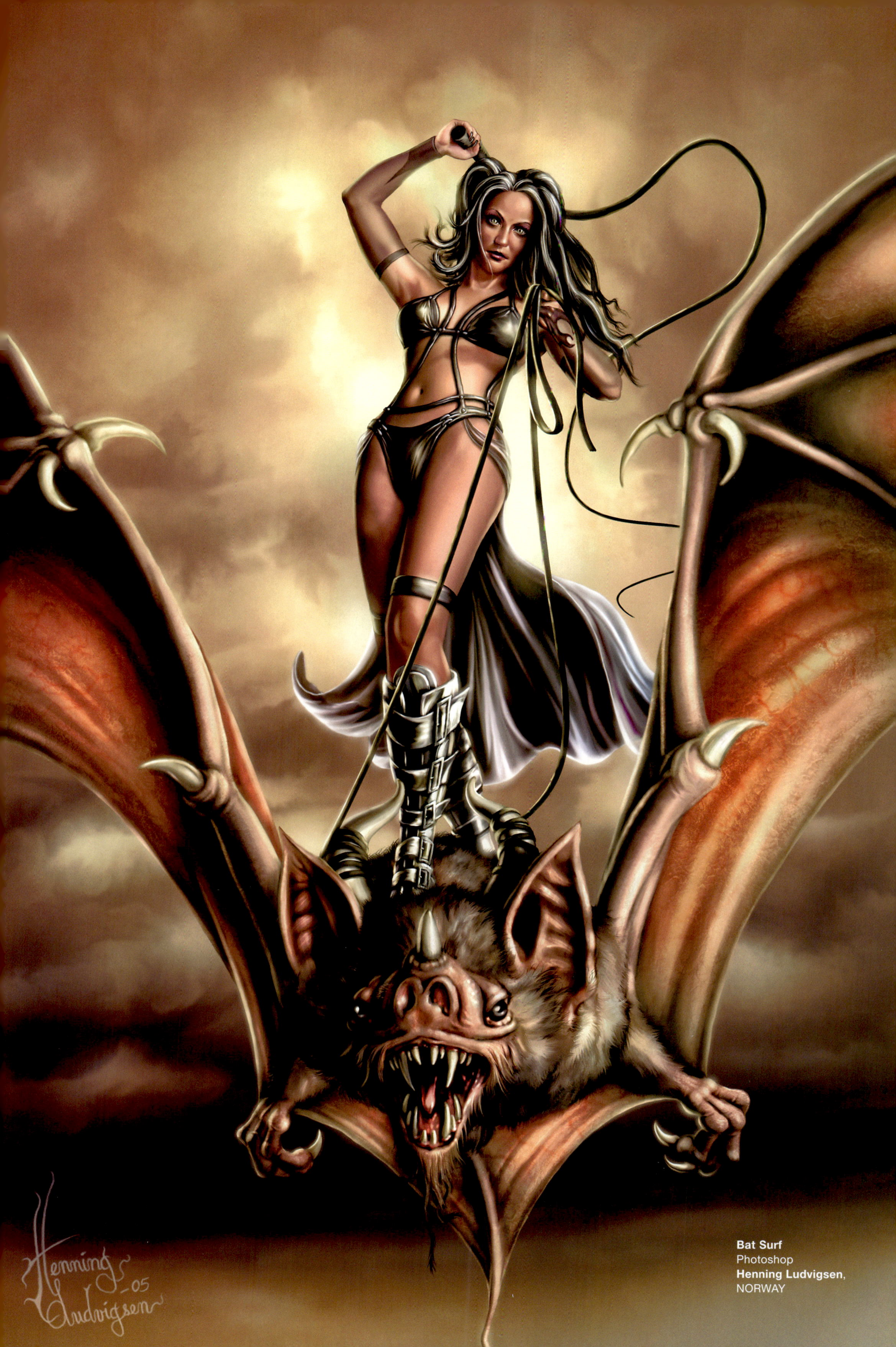

Bat Surf
Photoshop
Henning Ludvigsen, NORWAY

Face
Maya, mental ray
Francisco A. Cortina,
[left]

Luscious
Maya, Photoshop
Rene Morel, CANADA
[right]

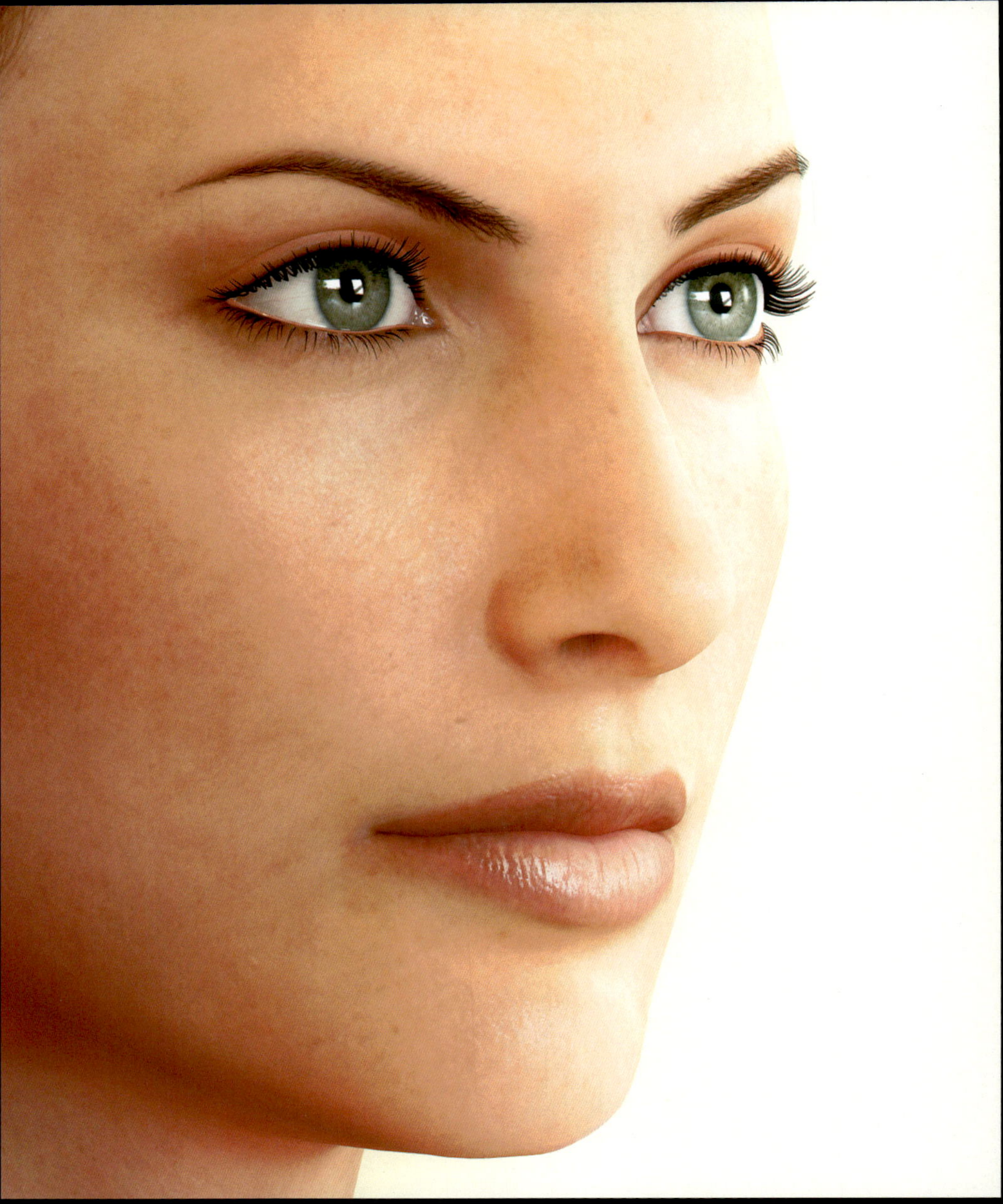

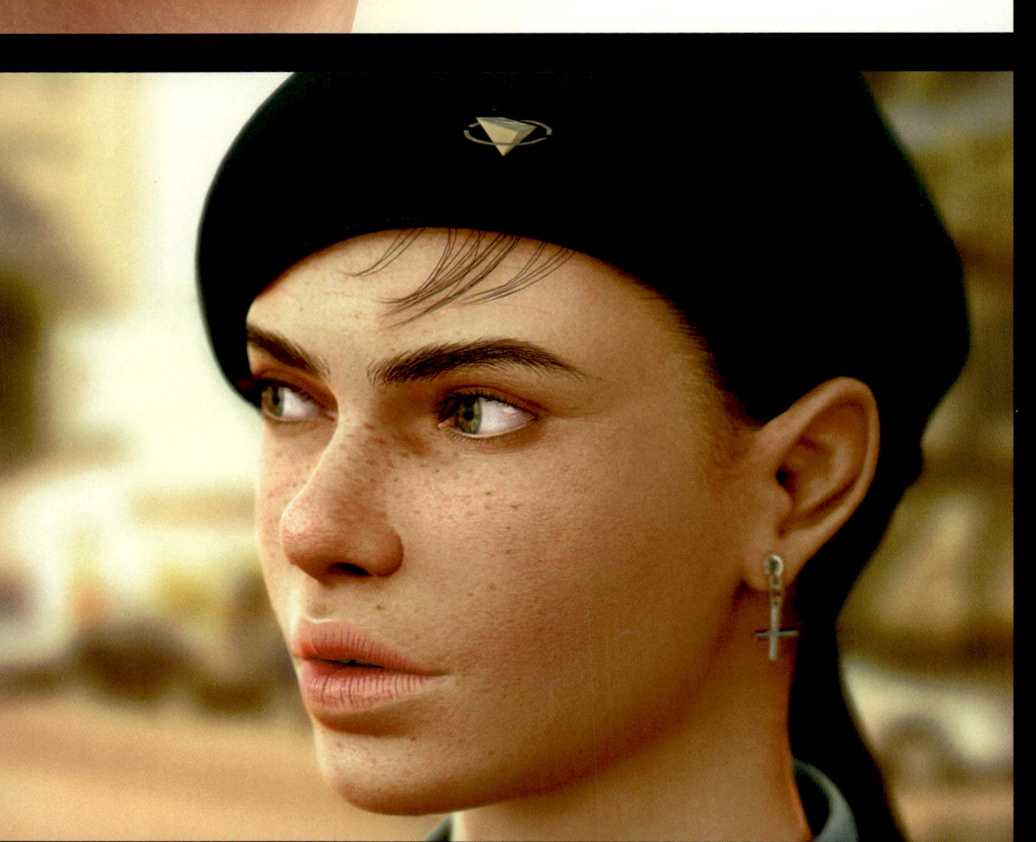

Kaya Pose
Maya, Photoshop
Alceu Baptistao, Veto
BRAZIL
[left]

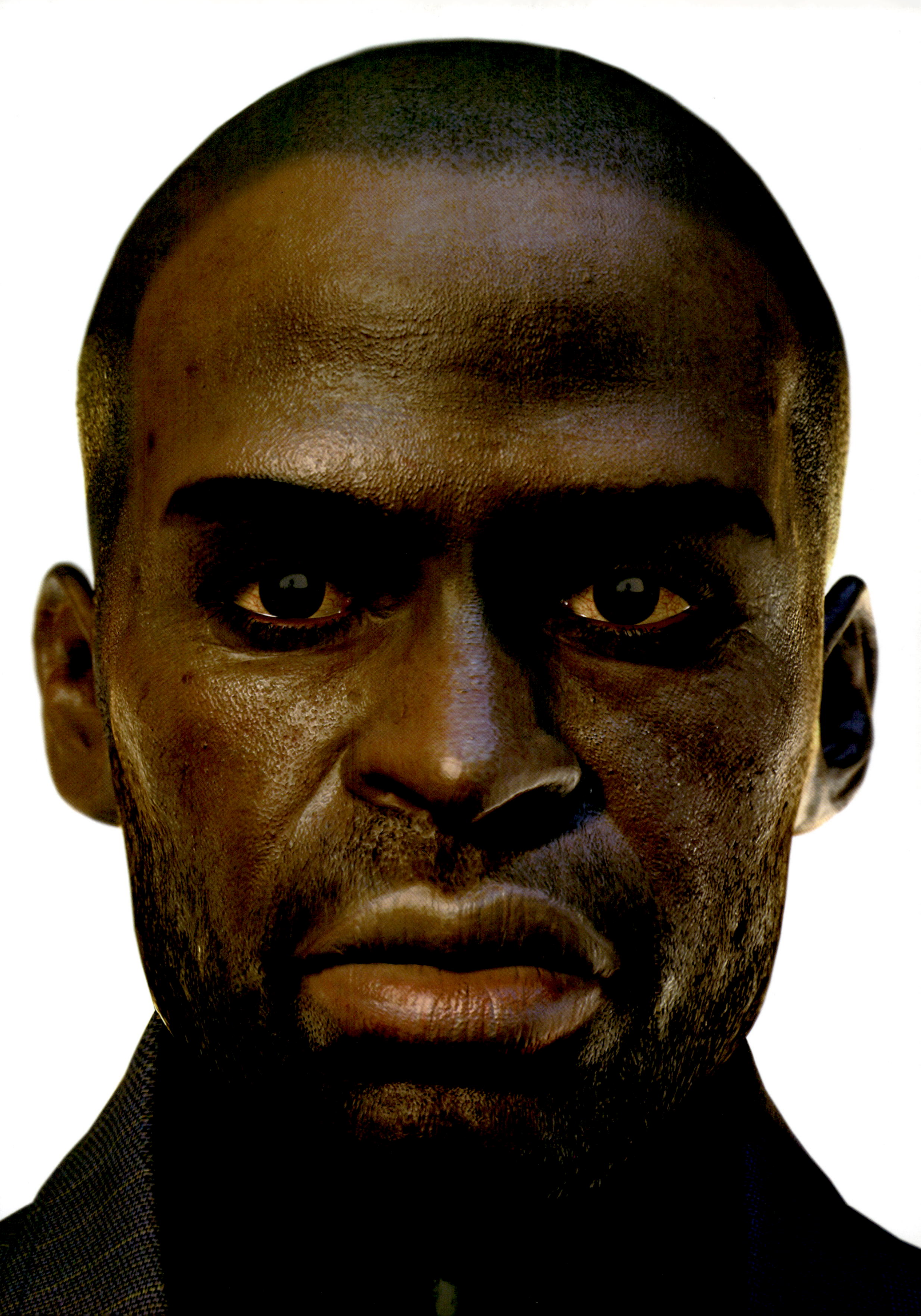

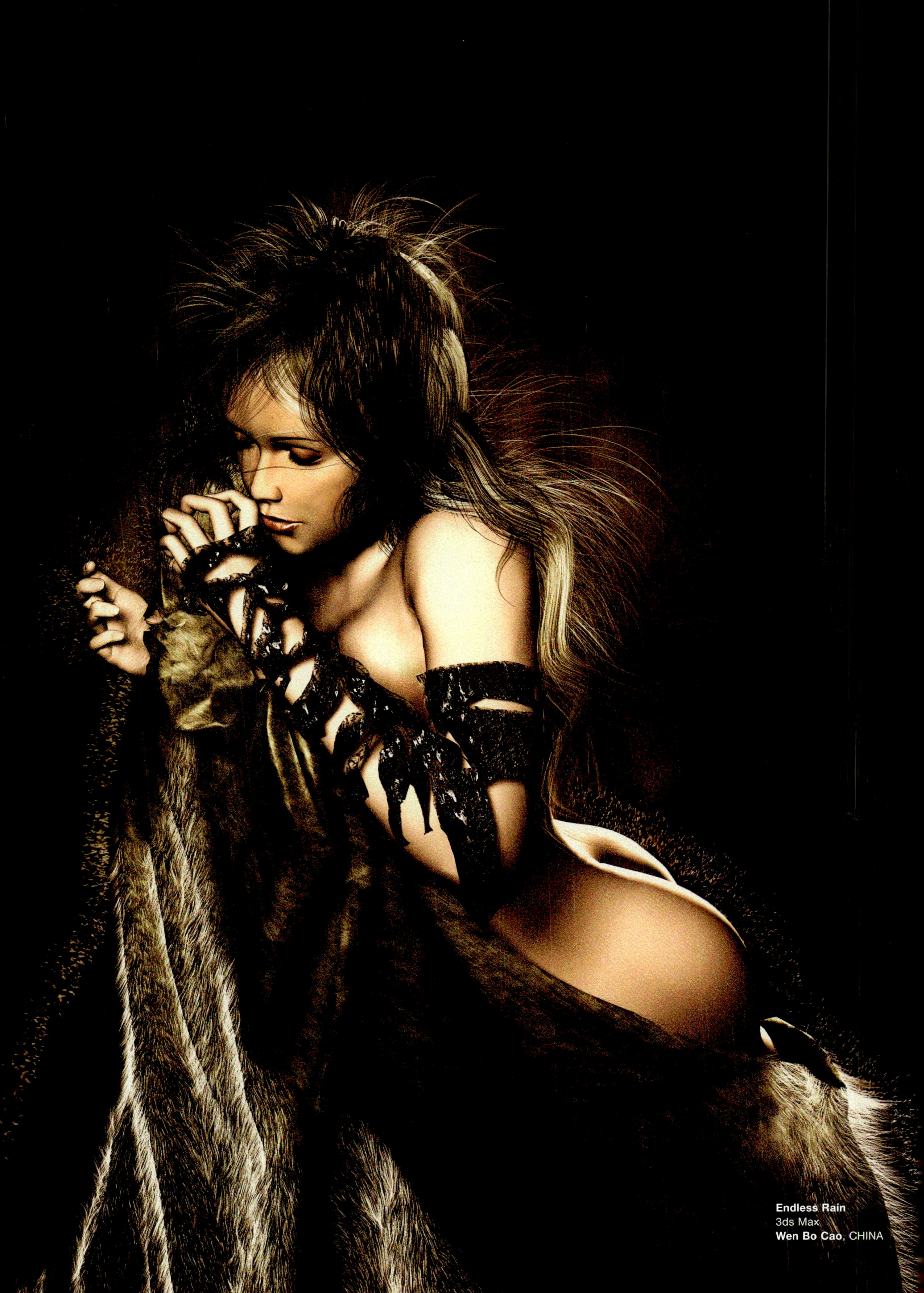

Endless Rain
3ds Max
Wen Bo Cao, CHINA

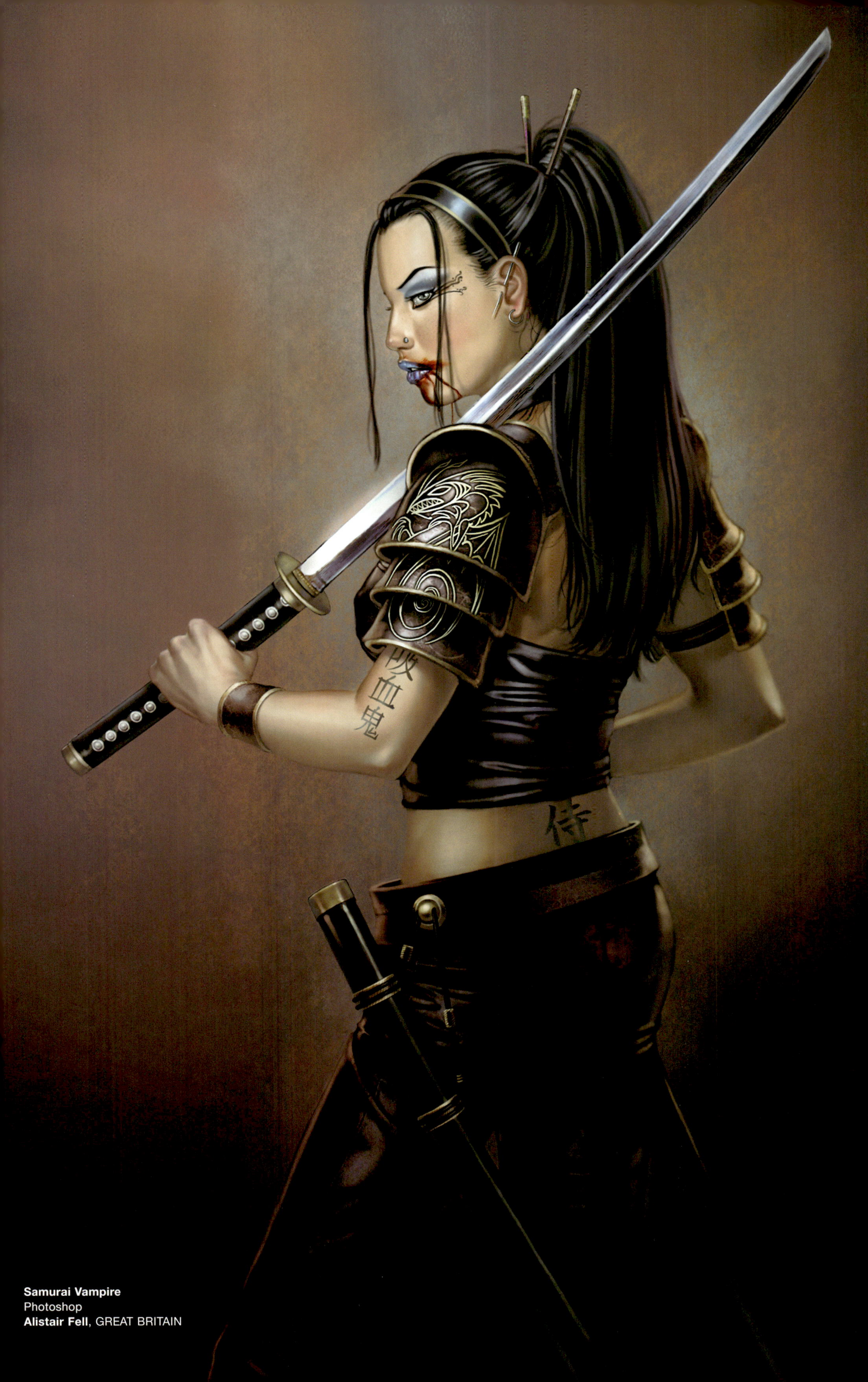

Samurai Vampire
Photoshop
Alistair Fell, GREAT BRITAIN

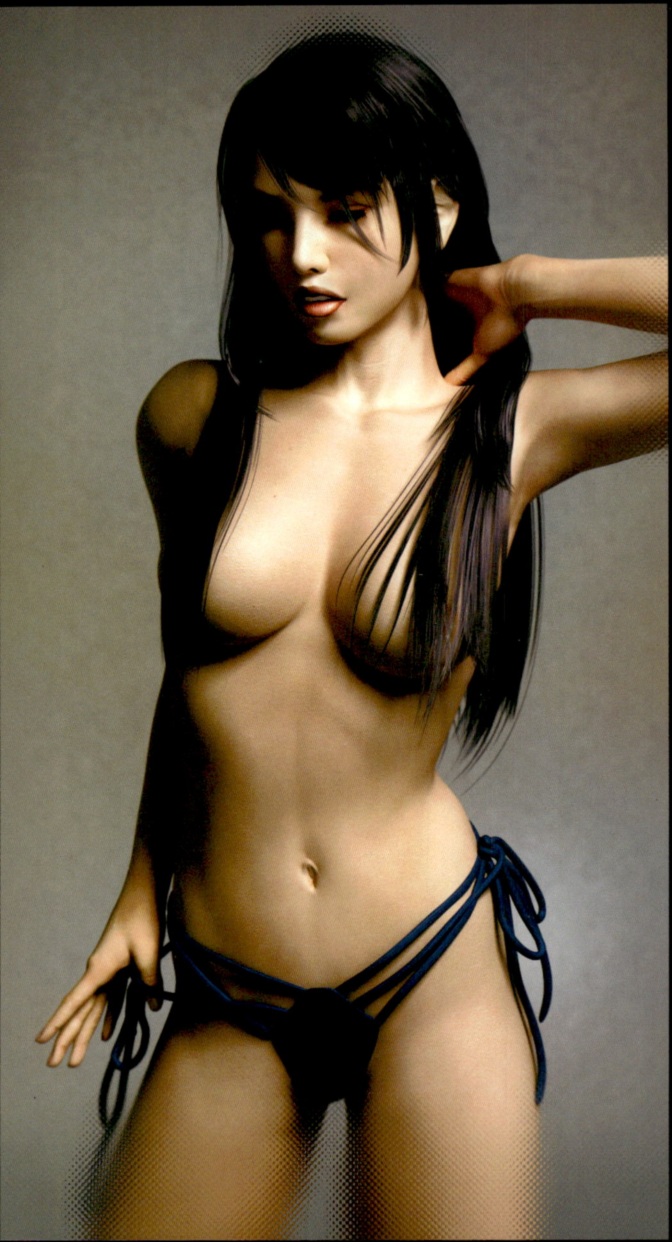

Pants
Photoshop, 3ds Max
Client: Actoz soft
Soa Lee, KOREA

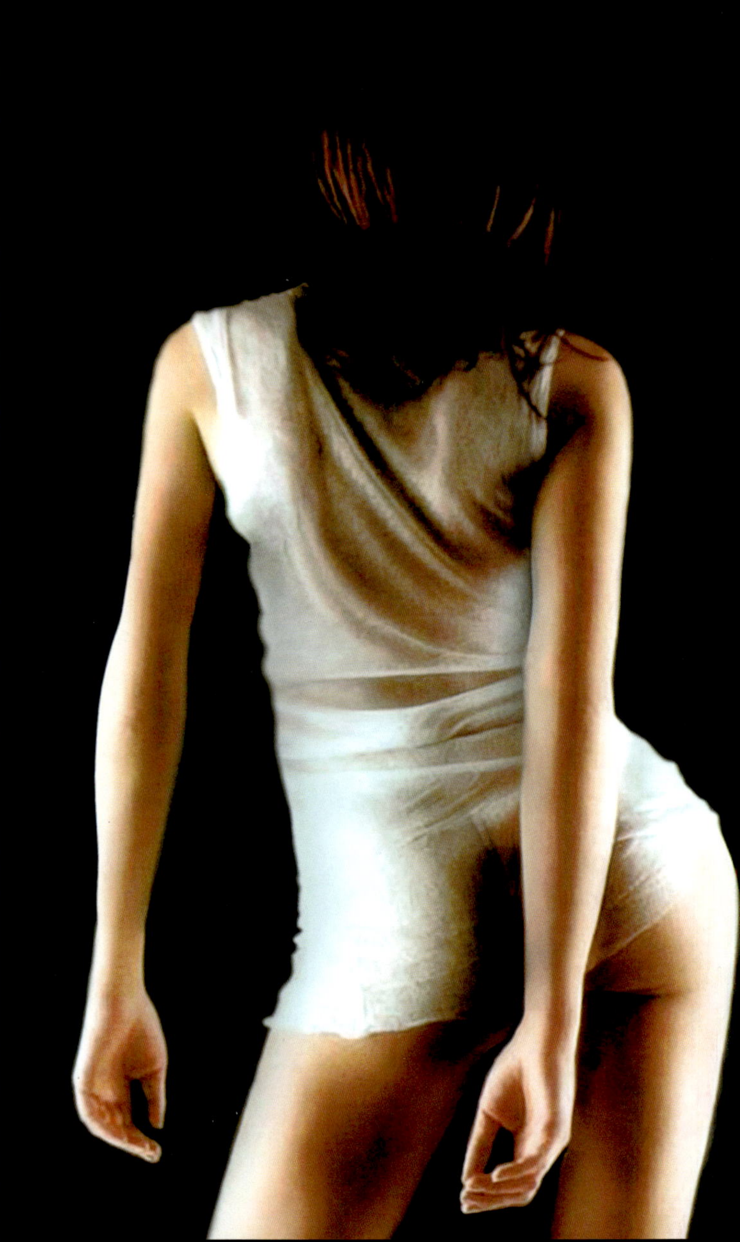

Curves
Maya, Photoshop
Dustin Davis, EA Chicago,
USA

Figure study
Maya, mental ray
Francisco A. Cor
USA

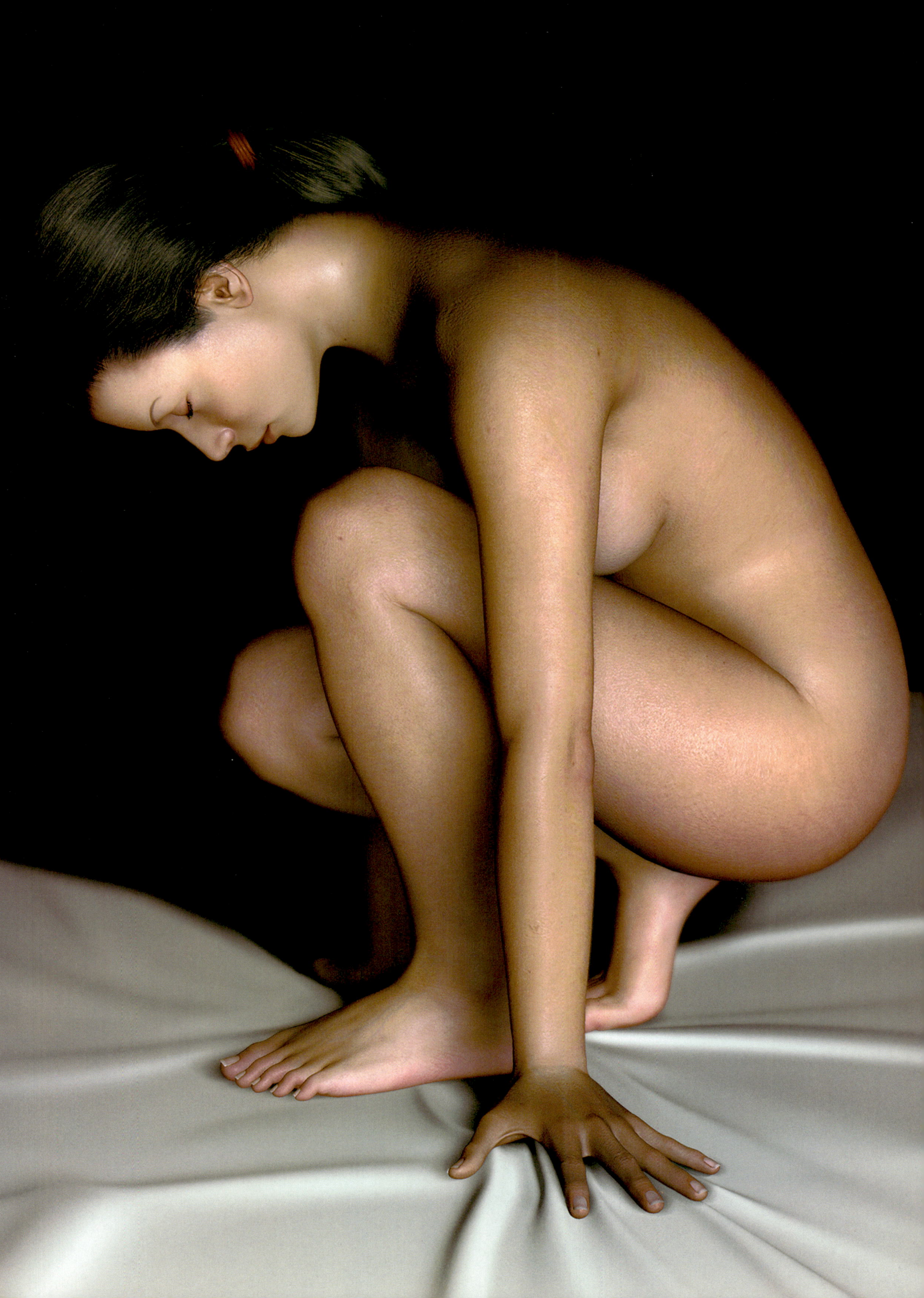

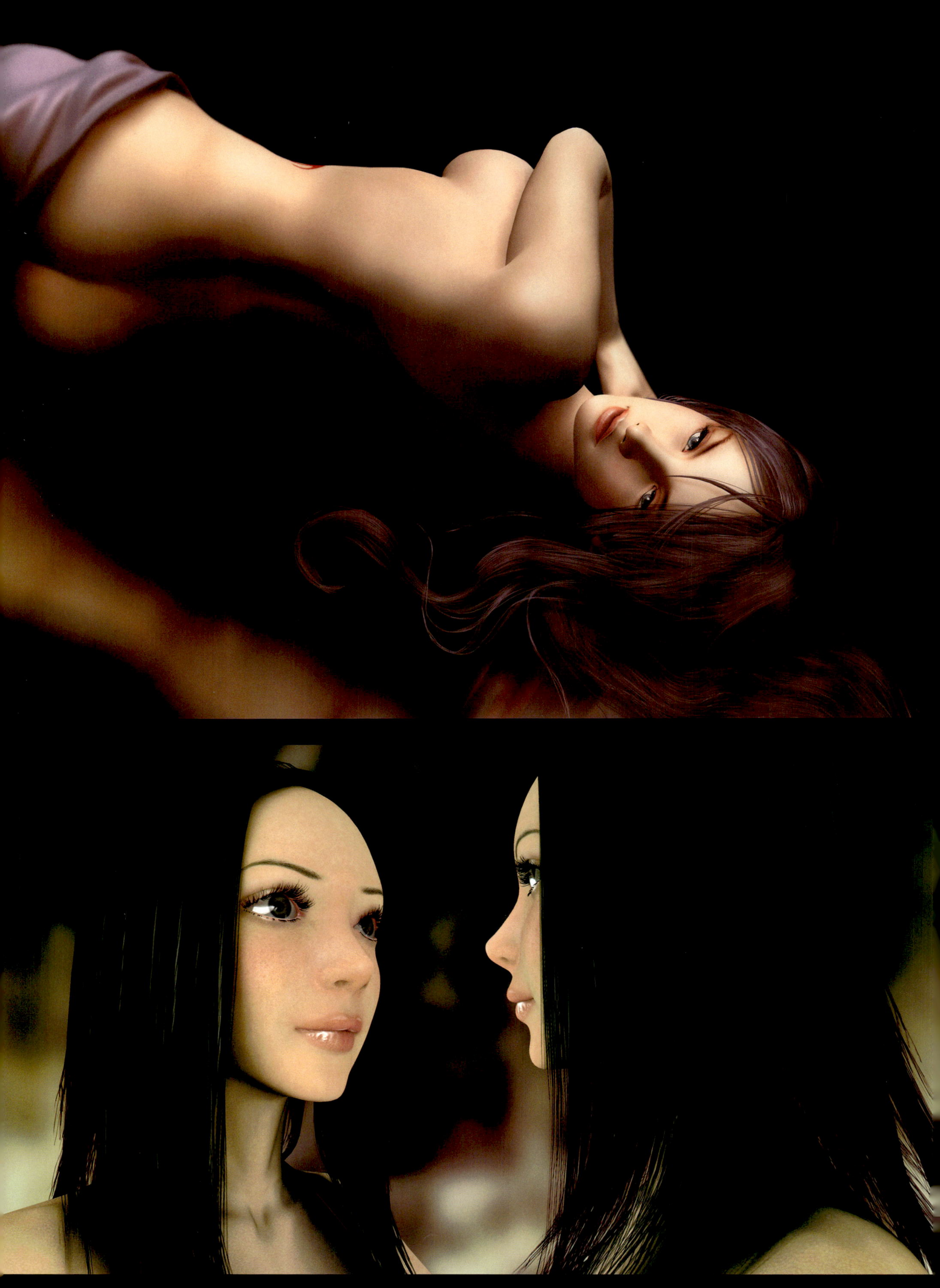

Redyan
Photoshop, 3ds Max
Client: Actoz soft
Soa Lee, KOREA
[top]

Twin
3ds Max, Photoshop
Liu Chun-Nan,
TAIWAN
[above]

Aki Maxim
Maya, Renderman
Francisco A. Cortina and Steven Giesler, USA
[right]

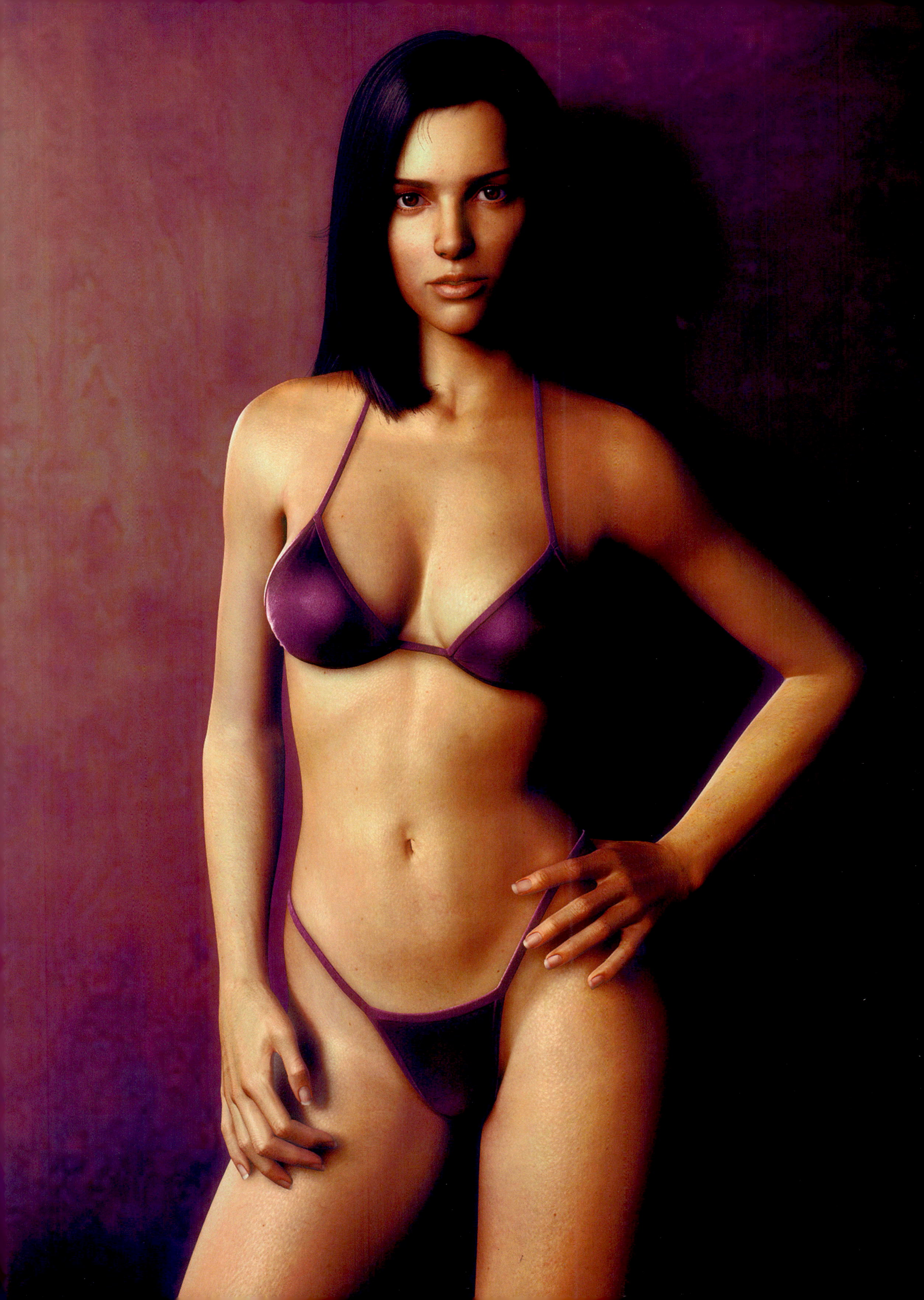

INDEX

INDEX

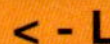

T

Marc Tan
Insane Polygons,
Block 29, #12-645,
Havelock Road,
Singapore, S160029
SINGAPORE
nospam@insanepoly.com
www.insanepoly.com
106, 168

Jonas Thornqvist
Østgøtagatan 32,
Stockhom, 116 25
SWEDEN
jonas@subdivme.com
155

Linda Tso
NEW ZEALAND
www.stickydoodle.com
38, 110, 132

V

Farzad Varahramyan
High Moon Studios,
6197 El Camino Real,
Carlsbad, CA, 92009
USA
farzad@highmoonstudios.com
www.highmoonstudios.com
48, 94

Svetlin Velinov
Evksinograd, 20 Str. No. 23,
Varna, 1000
BULGARIA
svetlin@velinov.com
www.velinov.com
80

Virgin Lands Animated Pictures GmbH,
Hauptstrasse 5,
Volkach, Bavaria, 97332
GERMANY
info@virgin-lands.com
www.virgin-lands.com
163

W

Wei Wang
Room 1901 Plaza,1266
Nanjing(w),
Shanghai, 200040
CHINA
blizzard-art@126.com
www.blizzard-art.com
52, 128

Oliver Wetter
Fantasio Fine Arts,
Obermenniger Str. 20,
Konz, 54329
GERMANY
finearts@fantasio.info
www.fantasio.info
131, 70, 80

Y

Koji Yamagami
Beans Magic,
Hutong103, 6-1-21 Nakano,
Nakano-ku,
Tokyo, 136-0074
JAPAN
beans@beans-magic.com
www.beans-magic.com
29, 107, 175

Fan Yang
14715 Bel-Red Road, Suite #100,
Bellevue, WA, 98007
USA
jiugefan@126.com
20

Chris Young
16 Ormonde Court, Upper Richmond Road, Putney,
London, SW1 56TW
GREAT BRITAIN
chrisyoung20@yahoo.co.uk
38, 68

SOFTWARE INDEX

Products credited by popular name in this book are listed alphabetically here by company.

Company	Product	Website
Adobe	Illustrator	www.adobe.com
Adobe	Photoshop	www.adobe.com
Alias	Maya	www.alias.com
Ambient Design	ArtRage	www.ambientdesign.com
Autodesk	3ds Max	www.autodesk.com
Autodesk	Character Studio	www.autodesk.com
AVID	Softimage|XSI	www.softimage.com
cebas	finalRender	www.finalrender.com
Chaos Group	VRay	www.chaosgroup.com
Corel	Painter	www.corel.com
Corel	Paintshop Pro	www.corel.com
DAZ Productions	Bryce	www.daz3d.com
Digimation	Shag Hair	www.digimation.com
e frontier	Poser	www.e-frontier.com
MAXON	BodyPaint	www.maxoncomputer.com
MAXON	CINEMA 4D	www.maxoncomputer.com
Mental Images	mental ray	www.mentalimages.com
NewTek	LightWave 3D	www.newtek.com
Pixar	RenderMan	www.pixar.com
Pixologic	ZBrush	www.pixologic.com
Splutterfish	Brazil r/s	www.splutterfish.com

Z

Gracjana Zielinska
Warsaw,
POLAND
vinegar@vp.pl
vinegaria.com
136

Weng Ziyang
Chinese Fantasy Magazine,
Mailbox 33, Nangang Post Office,
Harbin, Heilongjiang, 150001
CHINA
contact@fantasymagazine.com
www.fantasy-studio.com
128